MENTAL HEALTH IN LATER LIFE

Taking a Life Course Approach

Alisoun Milne

Foreword by
Judith Phillips

P

First published in Great Britain in 2020 by

Policy Press
University of Bristol
1-9 Old Park Hill
Bristol
BS2 8BB
UK
t: +44 (0)117 954 5940
pp-info@bristol.ac.uk
www.policypress.co.uk

North America office:
Policy Press
c/o The University of Chicago Press
1427 East 60th Street
Chicago, IL 60637, USA
t: +1 773 702 7700
f: +1 773-702-9756
sales@press.uchicago.edu
www.press.uchicago.edu

British Library Cataloguing in Publication Data
A catalogue record for this book is available from the British Library

Library of Congress Cataloging-in-Publication Data
A catalog record for this book has been requested

978-1-4473-0572-9 hardback
978-1-4473-0571-2 paperback
978-1-4473-2339-6 ePub
978-1-4473-0573-6 ePDF

Cover design by Clifford Hayes
Front cover image: Alamy/JSMimages
Printed and bound in Great Britain by CMP, Poole
Policy Press uses environmentally responsible print partners

Contents

List of figures and boxes

Figures

Boxes

Acknowledgements

Without the generous and consistent contributions of two wonderful people this book would simply not have happened. I cannot thank Denise Tanner and Rasa Mikelyte enough for their kindness and support.

I want to acknowledge the influence of the following people on my career and my thinking: Mary Larkin, Toby Williamson, Tom Dening, Liz Jewell, Reinhard Guss, Hilary Brighton, Alison Culverwell, Jennie Williams, Sarah Vickerstaff, Peter McGill and the late Jim Mansell.

Also, the intellectual, professional and personal commitment to older people and to social work: Liz Lloyd, Sally Richards, Mary Pat Sullivan, Mo Ray, Emma Parry, Paul Willis, Holly Nelson-Becker, Denise Tanner (again!) and Mark Silver.

For their specific help, advice and encouragement: Anna Conochie, Kate Hamilton-West, Jo Warner, Scott Huggins and Gabrielle McNaughton. For his kindness and patience – and his willingness to read the whole draft book – my husband Simon.

I also want to acknowledge the support of my dear friends Pe, Linda, Trudie, Steph, Jayne, Vicky, Frank, Paul and Kim over the many years it has taken me to write this book.

Special thanks go to the staff of Policy Press for their endless patience with me and for their superb advice, particularly Isobel Bainton and Laura Vickers-Rendall. Thanks also to Judith Phillips for her early help and encouragement and for writing the book's foreword.

Foreword

Judith Phillips

Mental Health in Later Life is a significant and timely book. It will be welcomed by those concerned with issues around mental health and well-being not only in later life but throughout the life course. Given growing life expectancy and the potential for complex mental and physical health problems the issues raised in this book are of increasing relevance to academics, policy makers, health and social care professionals and students in a range of disciplines.

What readers will find particularly interesting is the lens through which issues are viewed and analysed – not a medical or clinical perspective but one informed by a fusion of critical social gerontology, the life course and inequalities perspectives. A commitment to social justice and to engaging with the lived experiences and voices of older people are also prominent dimensions of the discourse. These are themes that resonate with an earlier Policy Press series, Ageing and the Life Course.

Milne takes us on a journey starting with her own interest in the topic as a social worker in the 1990s. These experiences alongside those of a long-standing gerontological researcher and social work lecturer offer a particularly rich critical optic on the multiplicity of issues that impact on mental health in later life.

A book which influenced my own thinking on mental health in later life as a social worker was *Past Trauma in Late Life European Perspectives on Therapeutic Work with Older People* edited by Hunt, Marshall and Rowlings. It analysed the lives of older people who had experienced trauma in early life, including individual experiences of the Holocaust as well as the resurfacing of psychic pain in dementia. This was published in 1977 and many of the themes are picked up in Milne's book. We have come a considerable distance since 1977 but much remains to be done to understand the causes of, and prevent, mental ill health in later life. Key challenges include highlighting the influence of issues that are life course embedded such as gender, socio-economic status and childhood adversity; also to reframe factors such as 'resilience' as a feature of a socio-cultural context rather than a feature of an individual. Establishing connections between what has gone before in a person's life and mental health in later life is also key to appreciating what needs to change to improve outcomes and promote mental health and well-being.

By exploring the location and nature of risks to mental health (social inequality, policy, practice, community and individual) and where responsibilities for their resolution may lie (medical, socio-political, policy, services) Milne offers a fresh approach to understanding mental health in later life and to exploring ways that causes and threats can be differently understood and addressed. She pays particular attention to less explored issues including the life course consequences of childhood stress, abuse and neglect; the role that exposure to long-term socio-economic disadvantage can play; the bi-directional relationship between physical and mental health problems; how older people themselves define mental health and well-being; and how different conceptual models of dementia influence the ways people living with dementia are treated and supported and their well-being promoted. Milne proposes a paradigm shift in thinking, research, policy and practice incorporating the principles of human rights and social justice.

This book raises the profile of mental health in later life in a powerful and imaginative way. Milne brings together a wide range of material from a number of hitherto largely separate sources offering the reader a clear and coherent narrative that both captures and explores the myriad issues that damage and/or promote mental health in later life. She provides us with a refreshing and positive approach to reframing and addressing (many of) the key issues that undermine mental health and well-being in later life and challenges the current narrow, reductionist and rather nihilistic, model that tends to dominate thinking, investment and action in this underdeveloped field of enquiry. In many ways it represents a call to arms and one we should all heed!

Introduction

Mental health in later life is an important issue for us all. Most of us have elderly relatives, are older ourselves or will be older in the future. Despite this, it is an issue that has attracted limited academic attention. The attention that it has been given focuses primarily on mental illness: dementia in particular, and increasingly functional mental health problems such as depression (Westerhof and Keyes, 2010; Segal et al, 2017). Even books which have the term 'mental health' in the title tend to be dominated by a focus on mental illness. An underlying message that pervades much of the literature is that mental ill health is not only an inevitable – and linear – consequence of 'old age' but also that risks are linked to age-related issues themselves, for example physical health problems, rather than life course factors or social inequalities (Age Concern and Mental Health Foundation, 2006). There is very little discourse about mental health in later life and its location inside, and links with, life course analysis and inequalities. Limited engagement with theory, including that relating to ageing, is also a weakness of the field.

The book is timely for a number of reasons. The older population in the UK is growing: it is also increasingly complex, heterogeneous and diverse. That British society is also shifting, and traditional models, for example 'the family' and assumed patterning, for example the definition of a 'generation', are being unsettled is also relevant. Ageing and older populations are paramount concerns for UK and European governments; they are also the focus of a wide range of public and policy initiatives, some of which include mental (ill) health. Dementia-related policies abound and there has been a recent drive to place mental health services on the same footing as services for people with physical health problems (Department of Health, 2009b; 2009d; 2012b; 2015b; HM Government, 2011; NHS England, 2016). There is also a growing recognition of the need to include older people in policies that are for all 'people with mental health problems' (Mental Health Foundation, 2009; 2016a) and to ensure that they are not discriminated against in terms of accessing treatments (Ghosh, 2009). Some policies targeting older people may also incorporate a mental health dimension. Public health initiatives to address both physical and mental health issues are beginning to include older people, and there are examples of specific interventions targeted at older people who may be vulnerable to developing mental ill health. *Fulfilling Lives*, a National Lottery Community-funded initiative to tackle loneliness among older people, is one such example: it explicitly recognises the link between isolation, loneliness and depression (Moreton et al, 2018).

Mental ill health among older people has also been identified as expensive in terms of spending on health and social care, older workers' (and carers') lost earnings, and as profoundly damaging of older people's quality of life (Knapp et al, 2011). While it is important to focus on raising the profile of people with lifelong mental health problems as they move into later life, it is equally, if not more important, to explore the much larger proportion of older people who remain obscured from view. Mental health in later life remains firmly conceptualised *inside* later life – or at a stretch late midlife – and its causes as narrowly constructed inside a medical model dominated by biological determinism associated with 'universal decline' (Weinstein, 2014). The fact that abuse earlier in life may be a risk factor for late life depression or that 'daily acts of ageism' undermine older people's sense of well-being finds limited purchase inside this discourse (Age Concern and University of Kent, 2005).

Once one starts to explore how far back in life the roots of mental health risk may go or begins to take account of social inequalities such as poverty, a different story unfolds and one that requires an alternative, and more complex, framework of understanding (Cattan, 2009; Ray et al, 2009). Re-focusing the conceptual lens introduces the potential for developing new ways of understanding cause and causal mechanisms, including accommodating social and structural inequalities and recognising the role played by life course *and* age-related issues. In addition, such an approach engages with the possibility of understanding more positive stories: how do older people maintain or promote their mental health, survive the assaults that old age often brings and overcome, or at least deal effectively with, late life challenges?

From another source, and in parallel to these developments, there has been a growth in work focusing on 'active' and 'successful' ageing and on older people's quality of life, well-being and 'health' as a broad concept (Tanner, 2010). The latter body of work (in particular) incorporates the perspectives of older people, including their views on the meaning of 'mental health' and its importance as a key component of overall well-being (Bowling, 2005). Work relating to the influence of life course disadvantage on health-related outcomes for younger adults and, to a more limited extent, older people is also noteworthy, specifically the role played by inequalities in contributing to chronic illness and shorter life expectancy (Marmot, 2015).

These areas of work have much to offer thinking about mental health in later life. To date no authors have systematically attempted to explore the role of life course and age-related influences, particularly inequalities, on mental health in later life or adopted a multi-dimensional lens through which to view risks and protective factors. Mental health in later life sits on the intersection of a range of interrelated concepts: quality of life, well-being, health and mental health, theories of ageing, health inequalities, social determinants of health and life course analysis (Dow and Gaffy, 2015). Extending understanding requires drawing on work from a number of different sources: gerontology, psychology, social work, sociology, health studies and public health. This is a complex task and one that needs to reflect older people's lives, experiences and perspectives if it is to be credible and meaningful.

While the tone of this book is academic – in its broadest sense – it is intended to be accessible. It is not targeted at a single audience but will be of interest to undergraduate and postgraduate students in the social sciences – including sociology, social policy and psychology – and gerontology, those training to be health professionals or social workers, public health staff, health and care professionals undertaking continuing professional development, researchers and lecturers. It may also be of interest to older people and their families, (some) third sector organisations and policy makers. While the book does not face towards practitioners as its primary audience, much of its content is directly relevant to practice and to health and social care services. Those working in the mental health field with older people are likely to find it especially useful. The ground it occupies sits on the intersection of mental health, gerontology, ageing studies, life course analysis and inequalities.

The book aims to both explore and explain mental health outcomes in later life through the lens of critical gerontology and via the conduit of life course analysis. It adopts an approach underpinned by a commitment to understanding, and making visible, the role of life course and age-related inequalities in creating or amplifying mental health vulnerabilities – or conversely – affording protection. Both the upstream and downstream, and both the micro and macro social determinants of mental health outcomes are identified (Karban, 2017). Specific effort has been made to incorporate evidence that draws on the perspectives and lived experiences of older people.

This approach allows for the development of thinking, and interventions, that reduce risk and/or prevent mental ill health during the life course *and* in later life itself (Livingstone et al, 2008). One of the key issues that I wish to challenge is the increasingly atomised and individualised notions of 'health', 'need' and 'resolution' which dominate contemporary welfare discourse (Bolam et al, 2004). The current narrow purview on the concept of 'recovery' in the mental health arena is one such example. The recovery model is grounded in a discourse of choice and responsibility and located within an individualised neo-liberal agenda. It does not engage with causative mechanisms that lie in the life course, such as abuse experienced in childhood or with structural issues related to gender, race or socio-economic disadvantage.

Mental health in later life is complex, multi-factorial and an issue that cuts across time, place, cohort, social categories and individual differences and experiences. It is of policy, familial, social and societal concern. It is of particular interest to me for three reasons. As a social worker in London in the early 1990s I worked with older people with mental health problems and their families. I was struck powerfully by how poorly resourced services for this group were, how little attention was paid to their experiences and voices and how easily dismissed, marginalised and labelled older people were. One of the main foci of my academic career (since 1995) has been mental health in later life. In academia I have attempted to retain links with practice – mainly social work – as well as teach and do research, resisting situating myself in only one of these domains. It is the synergy that will create change and generate new knowledge and it is in the meeting spaces between these arenas that new understandings evolve. A third driver relates to social justice. Increasing numbers of older people in UK society are exposed to life course and age-related inequalities that profoundly damage their mental health. These inequalities are socially and/or structurally produced and are, in the main, preventable. As a society we could address them and by so doing reduce harm; it is a political choice that we do not and a matter of social justice.

In the book I draw on material from across the UK; relevant literature from Europe, North American and Australia is also included. The book's reach is extensive; it is especially applicable to the developed world context. The book does not review evidence relating to people with severe and enduring mental health problems or people with learning disabilities nor does it address issues relating to the end of life. These populations have particular needs; it is beyond the scope of my book to include them. This is not to suggest that a number of the key arguments around inequalities and the life course are not relevant to these groups, but exploration of the particular nature of intersections and causal connections requires academic attention in its own right.

Structure of the book

The book is made up of ten chapters and a conclusion. Relevant policy themes are discussed at the end of each chapter, or where they link, at the end of a pair or group of chapters.

Chapter 1: Demography, topography and mental health problems in later life. By way of situating the book's broader discourse on mental health in later life, Chapter 1 offers an overview of the UK's socio-demographic and policy context. It also offers key data on the prevalence and nature of primary mental health problems associated with later life and discussion of those issues that are situated on the boundary of mental ill health, such as loneliness.

Chapter 2: Mental health, psychological well-being, successful ageing and quality of life. This chapter focuses on 'what we know' about mental health in later life as opposed to mental illness. It addresses two key areas. The definitions, dimensions, theoretical foundation, and links between four intersecting concepts: mental health, psychological well-being, quality of life and successful or active ageing. It also reviews older peoples' perspectives on well-being and quality of life, what 'good mental health' means to them and evidence about quality of life in the older population.

Chapter 3: The life course, inequalities and mental health in later life. This chapter explores three key issues. It foregrounds the importance of taking a life course approach to understanding health outcomes and the contribution of social gerontology to extending this perspective; explores the nature of life course inequalities and their influence on health; and discusses the specific impact of inequalities on mental health, especially as they pertain to later life. The role and relevance of chronic psychosocial stress, abuse and/or neglect in childhood and other adversities experienced earlier in the life course are specifically highlighted. The rationale for introducing the life course approach in Chapter 3 and not earlier is that Chapters 1 and 2 set the scene for the rest of the book and provide a foundation upon which to develop a wider, more sociologically informed and critical lens of analysis.

Chapter 4: The impact of age-related risks and inequalities on mental health in later life. The influence of more prevalent age-related risks and inequalities on psychological well-being and mental health is the focus of Chapter 4. It explores the role and impact of two sets of risks: those arising directly from experiences common to old age including physical ill health, bereavement and loss, and exposure to the structural inequalities of ageism and age discrimination.

Chapters 5 to 7 explore the nature and impact of three specific groups – or sets – of risks and inequalities that affect the mental health and well-being of particular subpopulations of older people. Chapter 5 reviews the evidence relating to older people exposed to Socio-economic disadvantage and poverty, Chapter 6 focuses on Abuse, mistreatment and neglect, and Chapter 7 on The fourth age, frailty and transitions. As these are risks that have powerful implications for mental health they warrant distinctive exploration.

Chapter 8: The mental health and well-being of people living with dementia. This chapter is the first of two focusing on dementia. It reviews four sets of intersecting material: inequality-related risks relating to dementia that are a product of the life course and later life itself; mental health problems among people living with dementia; what we know about the mental health, well-being and quality of life of people living with dementia; and evidence relating to how we understand and measure quality of life and well-being in this growing population.

Chapter 9: Conceptualising dementia. This chapter reviews links between the ways we conceptualise and construct dementia and treat people living with dementia, and explores the extent to which existing frameworks and models take account of life course issues and social and structural inequalities. The implications of adopting a broader lens for the mental health and well-being of people living with dementia, and for understanding and responding to their needs, is also explored. Links with policy and the role of policy in the dementia field is discussed too.

Chapter 10: Promotion and prevention. This chapter reviews what is known about the prevention of mental ill health in later life and the protection and promotion of mental health across the life course and in later life itself. This includes research evidence about the issues that offer protection and, importantly, incorporates the perspectives, lived experiences and knowledge of older people. The relevance of conceptual issues, of models of ageing, and frameworks for understanding mental health promotion and prevention are also explored, as is the role played by policy.

The Conclusion offers a way forward in relationship to conceptualising and thinking about different ways to respond to, and do research on, mental health in later life and with older people. A paradigmatic shift is suggested focused around five cross-cutting domains: public mental health; policy and services for people living with dementia and their families; care services and care practice; research lenses, approaches and methods; and values and principles.

1

Demography, topography and mental health problems in later life

Introduction

By way of situating the book's broader discourse on mental health in later life, Chapter 1 offers an overview of the UK's socio-demographic and policy context. It also offers key data on the prevalence and nature of primary mental health problems associated with later life and discussion of those issues that are situated on its boundary, such as loneliness and social exclusion.

First, a word about terminology. The term 'later life' will be used throughout the book in preference to the more commonly used terms 'old age' or 'the elderly'. This is in part to make the link between the reader's current life (assuming some readers will be younger) and their own later life and partly to challenge existing stereotypes and prejudices in relationship to 'old age'. 'Old age' positions people inside an age – however ill-defined – which not only obscures the importance of issues unrelated to age but tends to also obscure the complexity and heterogeneity of a large and varied cohort(s) of people. The fact that someone aged 100 is very likely to have a profoundly different life course, lifestyle, health status, and situation than someone aged 65 is a primary challenge to 'age related' evidence. Data around trends in prevalence and incidence of ill health among older people hides important distinctions and encourages a tendency towards simplification and homogenisation (Lloyd, 2012). UK-wide (and European) data may also eclipse country and regional differences. The fact that people in Glasgow die 12 to 14 years earlier than people in a wealthy inner London borough (for example Kensington and Chelsea) is a distinctive example (Moffatt et al, 2012). Another, intra-area, example is that in Stockton-on-Tees (North-East England) the gap in life expectancy between the most and least affluent wards is 17 years for men and 12 years for women (Bambra, 2016).

The World Health Organization (WHO) (2002b) notes that in most (developed) countries a person is considered 'old' at 65 years. This simply reflects the age at which many people retire from paid work although this pattern is not as established as it once was (Phillipson, 2013). It is important to acknowledge that old age is a contested term and a social construct (Vincent, 2006). Chronological age is not synonymous with biological age, and both the situated and historical context of ageing can be masked by the adoption of a universal definition. The length of old age as a life stage is a related definitional challenge; it is the only stage of life without a chronologically defined end point. This is because length of life varies hugely; increasing differential longevity amplifies this variability (Caselli and Luy, 2013).

Mental health is also subject to considerable terminological variation. It is important to acknowledge that the 'language associated with mental health is contentious' and disputed (Karban, 2017, p 886). Terminology tends to reflect a paradigmatic optic. As the underpinning paradigm of this book is a fusion of critical gerontology, life course analysis and an inequalities perspective (see Chapter 3), biomedically infused terms such as mental disorder will not be used (unless in a quote from an original text). The terms mental health problems or mental ill health are used to refer to mental health conditions that are linked to identifiable symptoms and/or are widely recognised. Terminology relating to the broader, more nuanced, terrain of compromised mental health reflects the range of language used by contributors to the field, including older people themselves. An important aim is to challenge the dichotomous thinking that characterises much of the discourse and engage with the shifting and dynamic boundary between mental health and mental ill health *and* their intersection with related constructs, for example psychological well-being (see Chapter 2). Disruption to the binary of physical health and mental health is also relevant especially in later life when links between the two are both significant and complex. A second aim is to recognise how concepts and definitions of mental health and mental ill health vary between cultures, cohorts and generations. A third definitional issue relates to 'mental health outcomes'. This term is used regularly in the book to reflect the fact that mental health is (often) a 'product' of a context and a life course; it encapsulates both positive and negative mental health issues and captures the notion that mental health is affected by temporal, structural, social and personal issues in intersecting and multiple ways. As terminology in this arena is not fixed, and no universal set of terms is acceptable to all, some variation in language is both reflective and justified. At the same time I recognise a need to ensure that the book's narrative, and key arguments, retain coherence.

How 'links' between old age and ill health, including mental health, are presented, especially in the care and health-related literature, is a third issue that needs to be highlighted. Crude calculations of so-called 'dependency ratios' based on a population's age structure are one such example and are the subject of much criticism within gerontology. Not only do they suggest a linear and static relationship between age, health and dependence but they also construct *all* older people as 'dependent' and 'unproductive' (Lloyd, 2012). This not only ignores the significant contribution older people make to family and community life and to the UK economy, but also the fluid, differential, embedded and life course nature of health outcomes and in/dependence (Milne and Larkin, 2015). These are issues to which I return later in the book. However, whatever the limitations of existing data may be it is important to locate any discussion on mental health in later life inside its demographic and policy context. It is to these issues that I now turn.

Profile of the UK's older population

A key feature of the late 20th-century/early 21st-century UK population is its ageing profile (see Figure 1.1). This is a consequence, primarily, of declining fertility rates. There are 11.8 million older people[1] in the UK (19 per cent of the total), a figure estimated to rise to over 16.4 million by 2033. Of this population, 1.6 million are aged 85 years or over and 14,570 are centenarians (Office for National Statistics (ONS), 2011; 2017a). The number of people aged over 85 years is predicted to double

Figure 1.1: Age structure of the UK population, mid-2016 to mid-2041

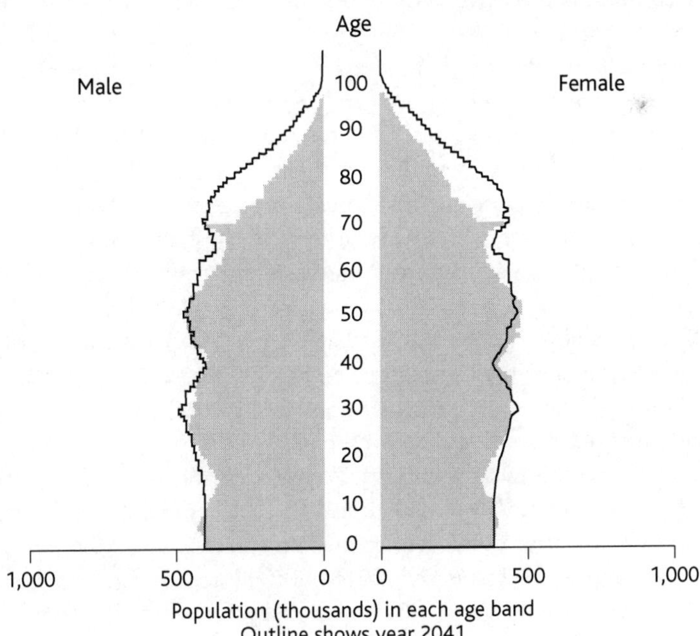

Source: ONS, 2017a

in the next 20 years and nearly treble in the next 30 years (Centre for Ageing Better, 2019).

One of the other main causes of the ageing population is increasing longevity. Average life expectancy in the UK has increased dramatically over the last 100 years. In 1901 this was 45 for males and 49 for females. By 2014 life expectancy was 79 and 83 respectively, and these figures are expected to rise to 93 and 97 by 2056 (Bennett et al, 2015; ONS, 2015a). Recent evidence suggests that improvements in life expectancy may be slowing; in 2015 life expectancy at birth actually fell, picking up again in 2016 and 2017 (King's Fund, 2018). If we consider old age to begin at 65 it is a life stage that could last for 25 or 30 years. It is irrefutable that for many older people life expectancy and quality of life has vastly improved since the introduction of the welfare state in the 1940s. In 2014 'healthy life expectancy' – a concept defined as life spent in 'good' or 'very good' health – was 64.2 years for men and 66.1 years for women. This equates to more than 81 per cent of a man's life being lived in good health and 80 per cent of a woman's (ONS, 2015b). A baby born in 2011 is almost eight times more likely to reach 100 than one born in 1931, and men aged 65 can expect to live only the last 7.5 years of their life with a disability; for women the average is 9.7 years (ONS, 2015b).

However, it is also the case that the prevalence of ill health and long-term conditions increases with advancing age (Age UK, 2016a). The incidence of acute and chronic physical health problems peaks in old age with the sharpest increase in those over 75 years. In 2013, 57 per cent of people aged 65 to 74 and 69 per cent of people aged 75 years and over reported having a long-standing illness or disability (ONS, 2016a). The percentages for those who report that their illness has a 'limiting' impact on their lives are 32 per cent and 47 per cent respectively (ONS, 2015b). In the European Union an estimated two thirds of all those who reach pensionable age have at least two limiting long-standing illnesses (Nolte and McKee, 2008).

Long-term physical conditions that disproportionately affect older people are heart and circulatory diseases, particularly strokes, hypertension and coronary heart disease. Dementia is the leading cause of death for women in England and Wales and the second most common cause for men (Alzheimer's Research UK, 2015). It is noteworthy that deaths from dementia have more than doubled over the last decade. Heart disease is the leading causes of death among men and the second most common among women in the UK (ONS, 2016a). By the age of 75, 1 in 5 women and 1 in 6 men will have had a stroke (Age UK, 2016a). Arthritis is estimated to affect 47 per cent of older people and osteoporosis about 8 per cent. Over a third of all cancers (36 per cent) are diagnosed in those over 75 and older. Death rates from cancer for both males and females rise with increasing age (Larkin, 2013). Sensory impairments and falls are common; among people aged 70 years and over 71.5 per cent have some hearing loss. Those aged over 80 are much more likely to suffer multi-morbidity; frail older people tend to have three or four long-term conditions (British Geriatrics Society, 2014). It is noteworthy that, in general, diseases advance at a slower rate among older people than younger people (Green, 2010).

It is important to recognise that traditional disease patterns are the subject of recent challenge. There is emerging evidence that the 'compression of morbidity' thesis – whereby most older people only become ill near the end of their lives – is beginning to reverse. Gains in life expectancy are starting to outstrip gains in healthy life expectancy, that is, a greater proportion of an older person's life is now being lived in ill health or with a disability (Westendorp and Kirkwood, 2007). In part this is a reflection of the impact of new 'lifestyle related diseases' such as obesity and lack of physical activity but it is also likely that social changes, such as divorce and lower levels of occupational pension, also play a role (Lloyd, 2012).

The differential implications of life course inequalities and widely diverse life experiences are also relevant (Dannefer and Settersten, 2010). Overarching trends and patterns mask these, often profound, differences. There is some evidence, for example, that although life expectancy increased across all social classes in the first decade of the 21st century, improvements were more rapid for those in the higher managerial and professional occupations (Marmot et al, 2010). There is additional evidence of an increasing gap between the life expectancy of rich and poor populations (Bennett et al, 2015). These issues are explored in some depth in Chapter 3.

Difference and diversity

The UK's older population is not only larger but is also becoming increasingly diverse and heterogeneous. How differences are conceptualised underpins how its dimensions are taken account of.

A key issue relates to how we make sense of 'later life' itself. In terms of understanding health outcomes it is helpful to make a distinction between chronological age, historical time, and belonging to a specific generation or cohort. Cohort effects are those that impact on a specific birth cohort, for example the 'baby boomers', and historical effects are events such as a world war that impact all those alive at the time of that event. The fundamental premise is that what may have affected a cohort is located in historical events or circumstances rather than linked to age. In terms of late life 'stages' a recent schism has appeared between the 'third age' and the 'fourth age' (Lloyd, 2012). The third age is conceptualised as a period of growth and development, of travel and enjoyment, consumption, and active engagement while the fourth age – in contrast – is viewed as a 'black hole' about which little is understood but much is feared (Gilleard and Higgs, 2010a). As the 'fourth age' grows in size it will be increasingly important to ensure that the perspectives and experiences of members of this group are captured and understood. Issues relating to the fourth age are explored in Chapter 7.

There are also a number of overarching socio-demographic changes that intersect with cohort and life stage issues and contribute to diversity. A greater number of older people are single, divorced or never married; increasing numbers of people with complex health needs are remaining in the community; and more older people are living in persistent poverty (Larkin, 2013). While the traditional excess of women across the whole of later life remains, gender-based differentials in survival are decreasing. For example, in 1983 there were 155 women aged 65 and over for every 100 men; by 2023 this figure is expected to be 117 women for every 100 men (Ray and Phillips, 2012).

Eight per cent of the UK's older population now belong to black and minority ethnic groups; this proportion is expected to rise dramatically over the next 25 years (Age UK, 2016a). Between 6 per cent and 8 per cent of the older population is estimated to be gay, lesbian, bisexual, transgender or queer (LGBTQ+); this suggests that there are between 800,000 and 1 million LGBTQ+ older people in the UK (Age UK, 2016a). Although approximately 88 per cent of older people report their religious affiliation as Christian, this profile is likely to shift too with the older population becoming more religiously mixed (ONS, 2015b). In terms of household type, nearly half (49 per cent) of all people aged 75 and over live alone; 70 per cent of these are women. While most of those living with others are married, a small number (2 per cent) live in multigenerational households (ONS, 2015b). It is also the case that increasing numbers of older people are ageing without children. By 2030 there will be 2 million people aged 65 or over in this situation (McNeil and Hunter, 2014).

These patterns illustrate a number of key issues that need to be taken account of in exploring later life. Firstly, 'assumed patterning' no longer exists; later life is both dynamic and temporal (Victor, 2010). Secondly, the variation that characterises later life needs to be acknowledged to a much greater degree and in a more nuanced way than has hitherto been the case. The particular importance of socio-structural factors and life course inequalities in shaping mental health outcomes in later life, is an issue to which I return in Chapters 3 and 4. Thirdly, health outcomes, analytical frameworks developed to understand them, and experiences of later life represent an interplay between social, cultural, environmental, socio-economic and individual factors.

Mental health problems

Although some mental health problems increase with age this does not mean – with the possible exception of dementia – that they are linked *to* old age per se (Cattan, 2009). There is growing acceptance that mental health is linked to a person's life course and that the number and frequency of challenges that many older people are required to confront place them at risk of developing functional mental ill health, especially depression. An overview of the key mental health problems experienced by older people is offered here by way of providing context.

It comes with a number of caveats. Research establishing prevalence of mental health conditions is inherently complex: dimensions include the population studied, for example care homes versus community; the accuracy and extent of diagnosed conditions; the nature and applicability of any measures used; the nature of the data itself, for example self-reported or independently assessed; and national or cultural variations in definitions or terminology used. Reluctance to acknowledge symptoms of 'mental illness' by older people themselves is also an issue. A second caveat relates to a tension that underpins this book: a desire to challenge the traditional tendency to discuss mental health *problems* in later life rather than mental *health* alongside recognition that a meaningful exploration of the latter requires some discussion of the former. A third point relates to the temporal and dynamic nature of knowledge generation: how we understand 'mental health' and 'later life' has changed significantly through time, and there is an inevitable challenge in weaving a coherent narrative through shifting terrain.

Dementia

In 2006, at a global level, Ferri and colleagues (2005) estimated that 24 million people had dementia and that this figure would double every 20 years, to 42 million in 2020 and 81 million in 2040. Of all chronic diseases, dementia is one of the most important contributors to death, dependence and disability worldwide. In the UK the number of older people living with dementia is 850,000; this figure is estimated to rise to over 2 million by 2051 (Prince et al, 2014) (see Figure 1.2). One in three people over 65 will die with some form of dementia. Life expectancy from onset to death is on average 4.8 years; median survival ranges from 3.3 years to 11.7 years (Todd et al, 2013).

Figure 1.2: Expected rise in the number of people living with dementia in the UK

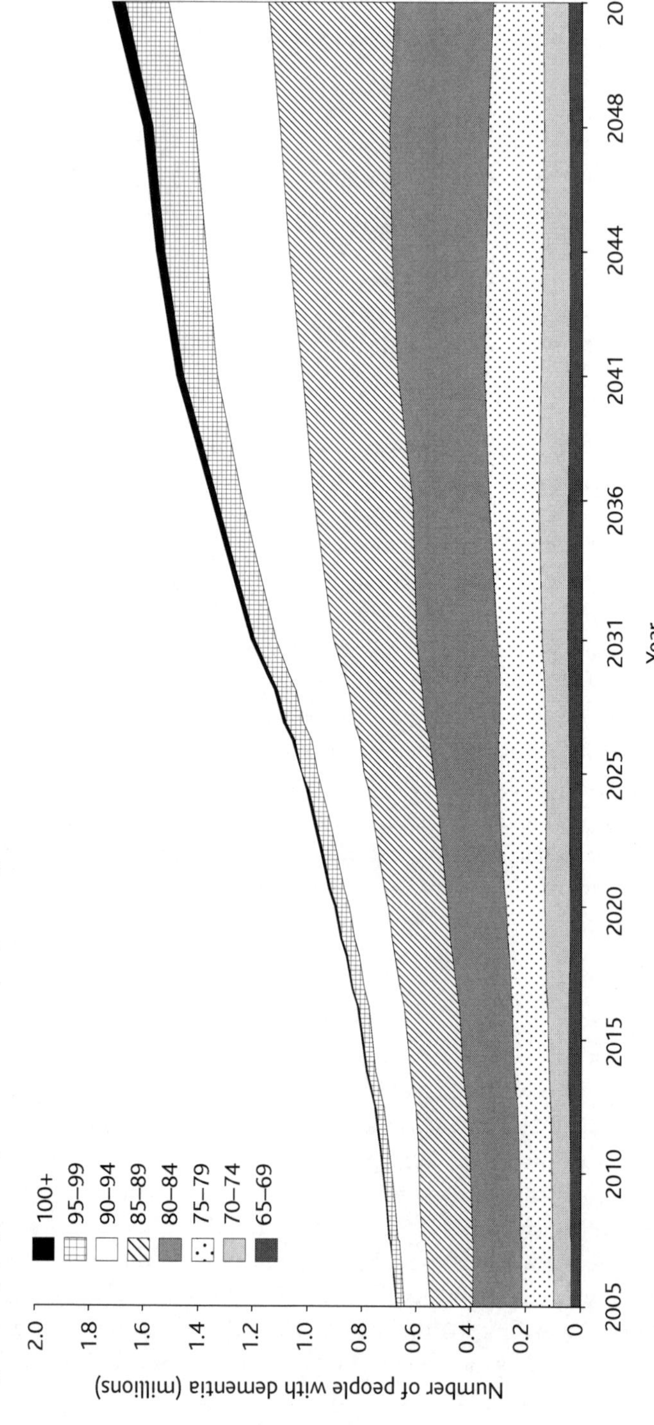

Source: Prince et al, 2014

The most common types of dementia are Alzheimer's disease (62 per cent of all cases), vascular dementia (17 per cent) and mixed dementia, that is, Alzheimer's disease and vascular dementia (10 per cent). Less common types include dementia with Lewy bodies (4 per cent), fronto-temporal dementia (2 per cent), and Parkinson's disease dementia (2 per cent) (Prince et al, 2014). Between two thirds and four fifths of care home residents are estimated to have dementia; it is the biggest single health-related predictor of care home admission (Dening and Milne, 2020). Many people with 'dementia related symptoms' do not have a diagnosis. A 2016 report identifies that at least seven out of ten people living with dementia have one or more additional health conditions; two of the most common being high blood pressure and heart disease (All Party Parliamentary Group on Dementia (APPG), 2016). Cerebrovascular disease (CVD)[2] is a common cause of vascular dementia. High blood pressure and high cholesterol levels in middle age specifically increases the risk of Alzheimer's disease in later life.

Although dementia is not a mental health condition exclusive to old age it is predominantly experienced by older people. The risk of developing dementia, particularly Alzheimer's disease, increases with age, especially very old age. Prevalence rates for dementia in Western Europe approximately double every five years from about 1.3 per cent of those aged 64 to 69, to around 33 per cent of those aged 95 and over (Prince et al, 2015). In the UK only 5 per cent of all those with dementia are aged under 65; a figure of 42,000 in 2016 (APPG, 2016). As a consequence of greater longevity women are at heightened risk of developing dementia (Alzheimer's Research, 2015). There is some evidence of higher rates of dementia among older people from black and minority ethnic groups (Tuerk and Sauer, 2015). This appears to be a consequence of vascular risk factors such as hypertension more commonly found in African-Caribbean and South Asian populations and life course factors such as poor diet (discussed in later chapters) (Scharf et al, 2017). In 2013 there were estimated to be 40,000 people from black and minority ethnic groups with dementia, a figure projected to rise significantly as the number of very elderly people in these populations increases (Botsford and Harrison-Dening, 2015).

Recent evidence suggests that the 'tsunami sized threat' that dementia is often portrayed as being may be inaccurate (Robinson et al, 2015). A UK-wide report published in 2016 identifies that men's chances of getting dementia reduced by two fifths between 1991 and 2011 (Matthews et al, 2016). This is thought to be a result of a change in health-related behaviours: smoking less, eating better and benefiting from drugs such as statins. In particular, this has had a positive impact on the risk of vascular dementia linked to CVD. The most spectacular drop has been among men aged 85 years and over. Women's risk of dementia has barely changed (reduced by 2.5 per cent) because they are more likely to have adopted health-promoting behaviours across their life course. The report's authors conclude that 'staying generally healthy' offers the best chance of protecting the brain, with middle-aged people urged to exercise more and avoid junk food, smoking and excessive drinking. Although the number of new cases of dementia between 1991 and 2015 was much lower than expected – 183,000 instead of the estimated 250,000 – the authors warn that rising numbers of people with diabetes and obesity are likely to undermine efforts to reduce the rate still further (Matthews et al, 2016).

Emerging evidence about two specific populations who have much lower levels of dementia is noteworthy. The first group – the so-called 'super-agers'– are a small number of very elderly people (approximately 5 per cent) who appear resistant to developing dementia-related symptoms despite lifestyles that often include smoking and drinking alcohol (Rogalski et al, 2018). It is especially confounding that their brains (post-mortem) have many of the physiological patterns associated with dementia, including neurofibrillary tangles and deposits of deformed proteins. What the super-agers appear to have in common is a certain personality type: a positive attitude to life, resilience, active lifestyles, social participation and optimism even in the face of adversity. They also share an unusually high proportion of a rare brain cell called a von Economo neuron (Rogalski et al, 2018). It is the combination of the biological and the social-psychological that appear to offer this group protection; it is a more nuanced story than that of biology on its own. The second group are older people who live in one of the world's five geographically delineated Blue Zones.[3] For example, in the Greek Blue Zone (Ikaria), the rate of dementia among people aged 85 years and over is 75 per cent lower than it is in the US (Buettner, 2015). A mix of life course embedded socio-cultural factors including a primarily plant-based diet, daily physical activity, social connectivity, religiosity and regular access to leisure activities appear to explain the reduced risk. It is thought that researchers could learn as much from these groups in terms of understanding dementia as they do from those living with the condition.

Dementia as a condition

Dementia is an organic mental health condition; some would even argue that it is not a mental illness but a degenerative neurological condition that is mistakenly managed and treated under the umbrella of psychiatry rather than neurology. Lines are blurred; for example, older people with Parkinson's disease are at heightened risk of experiencing dementia. Typical symptoms of dementia include: memory loss, poor concentration, disorientation, behavioural changes, problems with motor skills and executive planning and organisation, and sequencing skills. Lack of insight and confabulation are also common. Dementia is generally progressive; symptoms tend to get worse over time. The speed and pattern of deterioration differs markedly, and because each individual is unique, her/his experience of the symptoms will also differ (Alzheimer's Society, 2019b). While by no means a static process dementia is commonly regarded as occurring in a number of stages: mild, moderate, and severe or advanced. Current estimates suggest that among the community-based population of older people living with dementia in the UK 55.4 per cent have mild dementia, 32.1 per cent have moderate dementia and 12.5 per cent have severe dementia (Prince et al, 2014).

In about half of all cases of fronto-temporal dementia there is a family history of it, and there is a specific risk of dementia to a subgroup of all those who suffer from Parkinson's disease (Dening and Thomas, 2013). First-degree relatives of people with Alzheimer's disease have a higher lifetime risk of developing it than relatives of those without the condition. Delirium – acute confusion – is a relatively common disorder among older people; people with dementia are especially vulnerable. It is marked by sudden onset of (greater levels of) confusion, disorientation and memory problems (Anderson, 2005). Vascular dementia predisposes people to Alzheimer's disease. There is recent evidence that 'frailty' significantly increases the risk of developing dementia, a link that is ill understood (Rogers et al, 2018).

The Lancet Commission (Livingstone et al, 2017) on dementia prevention, intervention and care suggests that 35 per cent of all dementia cases could be prevented if the following nine modifiable risk factors were fully eliminated: low levels of education, hearing loss, hypertension, obesity, smoking, depression, physical inactivity, social isolation and diabetes. It is notable that these are a mixture of structural issues related to the life course such as poor education; mental health issues such as depression; and physical risk factors such as diabetes that are part about 'lifestyle' and part about life course. A number of these risk factors are explored in more detail in Chapters 3 and 8.

It is important to acknowledge a number of challenges to the current 'dementia discourse' (Manthorpe and Iliffe, 2016a). One is to celebrate the number of older people, including those aged 90 years and over, who do *not* have dementia; two thirds at least. The second point is a reworking of the nihilistic construction of dementia as a condition, which eclipses personality, identity and selfhood (Milne, 2010a). The social model of dementia, extension of the rights of citizenship, and evidence that people living with dementia, even in its advanced stages, can experience positive mental well-being are distinctive dimensions of the counter discourse (Bartlett and O'Connor, 2010). These are issues to which I return in Chapters 8 and 9.

Cognitive function and mild cognitive impairment

Cognition broadly refers to the mental ability to function as a 'competent' adult. This ranges from fully competent at one end of the continuum to advanced dementia at the other: mild cognitive impairment is somewhere in the middle. It describes a condition where a person has a recognisable degree of objective cognitive impairment but falls short of existing definitions of dementia (O'Brien and Grayson, 2013). For some, mild cognitive impairment (MCI) is an early precursor of dementia.

As definitions vary it is difficult to assess the prevalence of MCI. Estimates range from 5 per cent to 20 per cent of community-based older people (Gauthier et al, 2006). Interestingly, between 20 per cent and 50 per cent of those identified as having MCI at baseline appear to return to normal cognitive function a year later. This suggests that MCI is affected by a wide range of factors including depression and anxiety, physical illness, medication side effects and hormonal changes (Gauthier et al, 2006). The primary feature of MCI is memory problems; other symptoms include apathy, agitation, irritability and attention issues (Geda et al, 2008). MCI often occurs alongside depression, but the relationship between the two is unclear (Regan, 2016).

Some reduction of cognitive function with age appears to be normal. A distinction between 'fluid' intelligence – basic information processing activities such as reasoning, memory and attention – and 'crystallised' intelligence – knowledge accumulated over a life course as a result of education, employment and life experience – has been made (O'Brien and Grayson, 2013). There is evidence that fluid intelligence starts to decline in early adulthood while crystallised intelligence remains stable until at least 70 years old. There are huge individual and intra and inter group variations in the patterning of cognitive decline; much like the point made in relationship to MCI the influential factors are likely to be very varied. We know little about how factors such as gender, ethnicity and class, or those linked to genetic heritage, life course, educational opportunities, and relationships influence cognitive function in later life. Cognitive variation in an older cohort is likely to be as great as any found in a younger one (Victor, 2010). There is growing evidence that cognitive losses can be improved with training, psycho-educational programmes and stimulating environments (Diehl et al, 2005).

Depression

Depression is an important but under-recognised aspect of the health of older people (Manthorpe and Iliffe, 2005). As with any chronic condition its definition remains a challenge. Mann (2000) – as reported by Victor (2010) – helpfully suggests a tripartite typology of depression in later life. 'Depressive symptomology' describes the most inclusive definition of depression and is characterised by individuals demonstrating one (or more) of a range of depressive symptoms including 'worry' and/or 'sleeplessness'. 'Depressive syndrome' is a more restrictive definition based on the number, intensity and duration of symptoms. It is at this level of intensity that Mann (2000) argues that quality of life and daily activities start to be compromised and is (often) the threshold for treatment. Major or chronic depression is the most extreme form of the condition and is ascertained by clinical diagnosis based on severity and duration of symptoms; treatment is often, partly or wholly, pharmacological. This typology resonates with the experiences of older people.

Acute depression is commonly a response to the losses and negative transitions that often accompany later life (Milne, 2009b). These include the deaths of a spouse/partner, other relatives and friends and the (consequential) loss of opportunities for social engagement; retirement is, for some, associated with a loss of status, role and identity (Djernes, 2006). Chronic depression is a more persistent state. It is important to make a distinction between late onset depression and depression that is a continuation of a condition which began earlier in the life course.

The typology also helps us to make sense of (some) differences in prevalence estimates as well as reflecting the fact that symptoms exist on a continuum. In 2006 a systematic review estimated that 1.6 per cent of all those aged 65 years and over living in the community experience major (clinical) depression, 10 per cent experience minor depression and 30 per cent have depressive symptoms (Djernes, 2006). Longitudinal survey data reports rates of 'depressive symptomology' among 27 per cent of men and 40 per cent of women (English Longitudinal Survey (ELSA); Barnes et al, 2006). Most evidence demonstrates an age-related gradient with more people aged 85 and over being classified as having depressive symptoms, compared with those aged 65 to 85 years. 'Lack of energy' and 'dropping activities' are the two most commonly reported 'symptoms': other symptoms include low mood, sleeplessness, diminished interest in most or all activities, fatigue, weight loss, diminished ability to think or concentrate and feelings of worthlessness (Thomas, 2013). In terms of incidence it is estimated that between 6 per cent and 12 per cent of all those aged 65 years and over living in the community will have new onset depression: pain and worsening disability are the main causal factors (Harris et al, 2006).

Depression is twice as common (or at least identified to be so) among older women, although this is a life course trend rather than one specific to later life. That a high proportion of the very old, that is, those aged 85 years and over, are women and that 40 per cent of this age group suffer from at least one episode of 'case level depression' is noteworthy (Mental Health Foundation, 2016a). Pakistani and Indian women appear to be especially at risk (McCormick et al, 2009). Using data from a community-based cohort study of older people in north-west London, Williams and colleagues (2015) identified a higher prevalence of depression among people from South Asian (15.5 per cent) and Black Caribbean (17.7 per cent) communities than their white counterparts (9.7 per cent). For Black Caribbean elders heightened risk of depression is largely explained by participants' exposure to long-term socio-economic disadvantage (Scharf et al, 2017). Older people living in poverty, those who have never been married or who are divorced or separated, and older carers are more vulnerable to depression (McGuinness, 2018). Women are also at greater risk of mixed depression and anxiety disorder. This affects 8.6 per cent of all women aged 65 to 74 and 7.3 per cent of all women aged 75 years and over; the proportion of men it affects is 4 per cent in both age groups (McManus et al, 2016).

It has been estimated that between 10 per cent and 20 per cent of older people suffer 'complicated grief', most often linked to the death of a spouse: this is defined as grief which lasts for a longer period, is intense, is associated with disrupted functioning in work and social relationships, a sense of meaninglessness, and prolonged yearning for the deceased (Long et al, 2002). It is associated with increased risk of depression, generalised anxiety and panic disorder, alcohol abuse and suicide (Bartlam and Machin, 2016). Depression is estimated to affect about two fifths of all those entering a care home; of these approximately a quarter have major depression and the remainder have depressive symptoms (Fawcett and Reynolds, 2010). It tends to persist as a condition among care home populations (Dening and Milne, 2020). Further, up to half of care home residents with dementia – two thirds of the total – have depression (Dening and Milne, 2013).

The literature on predictors of depression among older people suggests a set of intersecting health-related risks. Disability, pain and chronic ill health are consistently implicated (Williams et al, 2015). Ischemic heart disease (IHD) and stroke are associated with a two or threefold increase in risk, and it has been estimated that depression occurs in 20 to 40 per cent of people with Parkinson's disease (Mezuk et al, 2008; Thomas, 2013). Episodes of depression earlier in the life course is also a risk factor as is dementia (see Chapter 8). As with all age groups prevalence of depression in later life is contingent upon how it is defined and measured. Assessing the presence of depression in people with advanced dementia is particularly challenging.

Evidence about treatment efficacy and recovery patterns is mixed. One estimate suggests that two thirds of older people with diagnosed depression will continue to have the condition over the long term. This may well be associated with deteriorating health and limited social support. Other evidence suggests that if treated appropriately older people recover from depression more quickly than younger people, although not enough is known about what contributes to this (Healthcare Commission, 2009). In terms of treating people living with dementia who have depression the advice is to offer the same treatment options as for a person without dementia. However, there are complications. Talking therapies, for example, may be more challenging due to the person's (likely) shorter concentration span; there is also evidence that antidepressants are less effective in the presence of dementia (Alzheimer's Society, 2017).

What we do know is that only about a quarter of all community-based older people with depression consult their GP and only a sixth receive any treatment (British Medical Association, 2017). Although it remains the case that few care home residents receive any treatment for depression, there has been a dramatic increase in recognition of the condition and prescribing of antidepressants in recent years (Davison et al, 2007; Dening and Milne, 2011). In all settings depression remains a hidden and stigmatised condition; the assumption that depression is a 'normal' part of ageing persists alongside its partner assumption that 'nothing can be done' (Milne, 2009). Ageism plays a reinforcing role in denying older people access to therapies, especially talk therapy (see Chapter 4). The WHO considers that much more needs to be done in terms of recognition, diagnoses and treatment about a condition that, '... vastly diminishes the quality of life' of many older people (WHO, 2002a).

Depression in later life is complex, and we know surprisingly little about its 'natural history'. The number and intersection of risk factors that accumulate in later life evidently play a key role but our understanding of which older people living in which circumstances manage these challenges well and how they do so, is very limited. What we may be able to learn from them about survival strategies and what prevents depression would be of great benefit. That older people are embedded in a life course, a dyad and/or family, a community and a social network(s) are overarching issues that powerfully underpin and inform how they manage health and other losses that tend to accompany older age. Viewing depression as a situated condition helps us think about responses beyond the biomedical; I return to this issue later in the book.

Suicide

Suicidal behaviour is widely considered to be demonstration of mental ill health. Suicide is an important public health issue, and national suicide prevention initiatives identify 'reducing suicides amongst older people' as one of their goals (HM Government, 2012). In 2008 suicide among older people accounted for one in eight of the total number of suicides in the UK (Hodge, 2016). While the rate of suicide among those aged 60 to 80 years is relatively low it is higher for those aged over 80 years (ONS, 2017c). A concerning trend is that the suicide rate is now increasing faster than it is for any other age group (Manthorpe and Iliffe, 2011). One contributor to this relates to the fact that the life course risk of suicide among the baby boom generation is (relatively) higher than previous cohorts; as the baby boomers age this risk extends into later life (Phillips, 2014). In most developed countries higher numbers of men commit suicide at all ages: in later life double the number of men as women complete suicides (Tsoh and Chiu, 2013). It is important to note that among women, the highest suicide rate is among those aged 75 years and over.

Despite epidemiological variations in suicide rates between, and even within, countries, there is universal agreement that the nature of suicide in later life is distinctive. Older people have a higher risk of completed suicide than any other group (Ray et al, 2009). This is in good part a consequence of the violent methods used, including hanging, use of firearms and taking an overdose of prescription drugs (Steele et al, 2018). Other contributory factors are older peoples' higher level of resolve, diminished physical resilience and reluctance to acknowledge suicidal ideation. There are approximately four 'attempts' for every completed suicide in later life; this figure compares with 200:1 for adolescents (Conwell et al, 2010).

Attempted suicide and deliberate self-harm are relatively rare among older people; a review in 2001 reported that 15 to 20 per cent of para-suicides are among those aged 60 and over (Welch, 2001). Although controversial it is suggested that in addition to 'active suicide' or self-harm, older people may accomplish suicide 'sub-intentionally by means of not eating, not taking medicines, drinking too much alcohol, delaying treatments …' (Butler et al, 1998, p 100 from Ray et al, 2009, p 137). Bonnewyn and colleagues (2014) warn that it is important not to be complacent about recognising suicidal ideation, self-harming behaviour and withdrawal of fluids and food among older people including those living in long-term care.

While not everyone who commits suicide is experiencing a mental health problem there is evidence that major depression is implicated in at least two thirds of cases; another 20 per cent show signs of less severe depression (O'Connell et al, 2004). Dementia is associated with an amplified risk of suicide especially in the first few years post-diagnosis (Erlangsen et al, 2008). Risk factors for suicide mirror those for depression but tend to be more extreme or severe: chronic illness, pain and multiple morbidity; loneliness and isolation; poor functioning; and being widowed, single or divorced (Duberstein et al, 2004; O'Connell et al, 2004; Lou et al, 2012). Stressful life events are also implicated; these include bereavement, intensive caregiving, financial difficulties, housing problems and retirement (Harwood et al, 2006). Child sexual abuse, especially among men, is also a lifelong risk and one that is unlikely to be taken account of in suicide prevention strategies or services (O'Leary and Gould, 2008). Some commentators argue that suicide may be an active choice made by an older person in circumstances that cannot be improved.

In terms of support, there is evidence that older people 'at risk' are denied access to the full range of mental health services; this includes crisis services, drug treatments, psychological therapies and alcohol services (Healthcare Commission, 2009).

Anxiety

Most survey-based evidence suggests that anxiety disorders are less common in older, as compared to younger, people. Rates are higher in women than men but, as with depression, this is a life course pattern. It is generally accepted that about four per cent of all community-based older people suffer from an 'anxiety disorder' although prevalence estimates vary considerably ranging from 2 per cent to 19 per cent (Age Concern England, 2007). Some of this variation relates to the range of conditions that are included under the umbrella of 'anxiety related disorders': sleep disorders, phobias and post-traumatic stress disorder may, or may not be, included. People with both depression and anxiety may also be excluded. Anxiety disorders are much more common in particular groups. For example, nearly a quarter of older carers of people living with dementia experience anxiety (Mahoney et al, 2005), and rates are elevated for those with chronic medical conditions. The symptoms of anxiety include ruminative thinking, low mood, fear and worry and non-specific somatic complaints such as dizziness, shakiness and nausea (Segal et al, 2017).

Generalised anxiety disorders (GAD) tend to be more common than phobias and panic: it has been suggested that older people suffering from GAD can be split (more or less) evenly between those with chronic problems commencing earlier in life and those whose symptoms begin later in life (Keady and Watts, 2011). The most consistent finding relating to GAD is, however, its high level of comorbidity with depression. Recent evidence suggests that about six per cent of community-based older people suffer from a 'mixed anxiety depressive state' (Vink et al, 2009). Dementia produces high rates of anxiety symptoms particularly restlessness, agitation and fear. Anxiety-related symptoms are relatively common in care home populations. In a study of over 300 residents it was estimated that 5.7 per cent had anxiety disorders, 4.2 per cent had sub-threshold anxiety disorders, and nearly 30 per cent had anxiety symptoms (Smalbrugge et al, 2005).

Post-traumatic stress disorder (PTSD) is a specific type of anxiety disorder. It is estimated to affect 15 to 20 per cent of older people exposed to life-threatening trauma. Classically, PTSD follows combat exposure, armed holdup, rape and violent assault (Byrne, 2013). In older people PTSD has often developed earlier in life, for example during military service, or symptoms emerge later in life arising from the earlier life trauma(s). Characteristic symptoms of PTSD include re-experiencing of the traumatic event through flashbacks and nightmares. These intrusive phenomena are often accompanied by hyperarousal (symptoms of this include impaired concentration and insomnia), emotional numbness and avoidance behaviour. Emotional numbness leads individuals to feel they can no longer experience emotions normally and that their interpersonal relationships are impaired. They tend to avoid the scene of the traumatic event and/or reminders of the trauma. In older people PTSD has often been present for many years; older refugees are especially at risk (Mölsä et al, 2017). Among older male veterans, the prevalence of lifetime exposure to traumatic events is approximately 85 per cent (Hankin et al, 1999). PTSD in this group is associated with higher rates of additional mental health problems such as substance misuse (Durai et al, 2011).

In terms of treatment options moderate or severe anxiety symptoms are most often managed via a mix of pharmacological and psychological treatments. Expert opinion generally advises psychological intervention, for example cognitive behaviour therapy, or psychosocial intervention, for example a psycho-educational programme for mild to moderate anxiety disorders, and a combination of psychosocial intervention plus psychotropic medication for more severe disorders. These approaches can be very effective (Byrne, 2013).

Despite their prevalence and the considerable distress they cause, anxiety disorders in older people tend to be both under-diagnosed and undertreated. They are often seen alongside other mental health problems, primarily depression or dementia, and often accompany physical ill health. Greater effort is needed to ensure that treatments are routinely accessed by older people, including those with physical frailty or cognitive impairment and those who live in a care home (Dening and Milne, 2013).

Other psychological issues

While not mental health problems per se there are a number of 'psychological issues' that challenge mental health and/or play a contributory role in creating or amplifying mental health problems.

Alcohol misuse

There has been a steady increase in the amount of alcohol consumed by older age groups in recent years (Smith and Foxcroft, 2009). Currently an estimated 1.4 million people aged 65 and over exceed recommended drinking limits; 3 per cent of men and 0.6 per cent of women aged 65 to 74 are alcohol dependent (Wadd et al, 2011). The proportion of older 'problem drinkers' is growing, particularly among women. For some older people excessive alcohol consumption is associated with 'self-medication' of depression, bereavement and loss, anxiety disorders and loneliness (Byrne, 2013). Alcohol problems are more common in areas of socio-economic deprivation and among some minority groups, for example older Irish people (Rao et al, 2011).

Older people are more susceptible to alcohol-related health problems than younger adults and are also more prone to falls (Hallgren et al, 2010). Alcohol-related deaths and admissions to hospital have risen considerably over the last 15 years. Between 1991 and 2006 alcohol-related mortality rose by nearly 90 per cent among men aged 54 to 74 years in the UK. Although alcohol-related problems are significantly under-detected and/or misdiagnosed in older populations there is no evidence that they are any less amenable to treatment than they are among younger populations.

Social isolation and loneliness

Social isolation and loneliness are two distinct but related concepts. Social isolation refers to the quantitative number of social relationships an individual has. Loneliness refers to the subjective evaluation of the gap between an individual's desired and actual quantity and quality of social relations (Victor et al, 2000). Some commentators describe isolation as having little contact with others and loneliness as the subjective experience of isolation. Two other concepts are also relevant: 'being alone' (time spent alone) and 'living alone' (description of a household type).

One of the key socio-demographic trends over recent decades is a marked shift towards older people living alone (McCarthy and Thomas, 2004). This is the case for 36 per cent of all people aged 65 years and over and nearly half (49 per cent) of all those aged 75 years and over; the majority are women (ONS, 2013; Age UK, 2017). Although living in your own home is associated with enhanced independence, autonomy and choice, one of the negative consequences is the heightened risk of isolation. Those living alone spend between 70 and 90 per cent of their time on their own at home.

Evidence suggests that levels of isolation for those aged 65 years and over range from 13 per cent to 15 per cent (Victor et al, 2009) with rates being much higher in deprived inner city areas and inaccessible rural areas (Victor and Scharf, 2005). Seventeen per cent of older people have 'less than weekly' contact with family, friends and neighbours; 11 per cent have 'less than monthly contact' and half of all older people report that the TV is their main form of company (Griffin, 2010). The changing nature of the family – including people having fewer children and families being geographically dispersed – is a key factor as well as the more privatised nature of modern life (ONS, 2013). Paradoxically, as a result of feeling 'trapped' at home many older people find it difficult to make the connections that may reduce their sense of isolation. This lack of visibility undermines the potential for links to be made and reinforces a sense of being excluded from opportunities for social engagement (Mental Health Foundation, 2011b).

In terms of evaluating the extent of loneliness in the UK most data have been generated from surveys that ask respondents to 'rate' their feelings of loneliness on a Likert scale from 'never' to 'always'. Surveys have consistently shown that between 6 and 13 per cent of older people report that they are 'often' or 'always' lonely; the overall prevalence of loneliness appears to be similar in 1999/2000 and 2007/2008 (Campaign to End Loneliness, 2011; Victor and Bowling, 2012). Rates are higher among those aged 80 years or over; 46 per cent of this cohort reported being lonely in the 2013 wave of ELSA (Beaumont, 2013). Compared with other age groups more older people report being 'persistently lonely'.

Being alone, isolation and loneliness are all associated with reduced quality of life. Loneliness, especially persistent loneliness, is associated with increased vulnerability to mental health problems, especially depression and risk of suicide (Women's Royal Voluntary Service, 2012). Chronic feelings of loneliness are also implicated in the development of a number of physical health problems and damaging health behaviours, notably increased alcohol intake, impaired sleep, increased blood pressure and cardiovascular disease (Bolton, 2012). A recent systematic review identified that loneliness can increase the risk of coronary heart disease[4] by a third (CHD) (Valtorta et al, 2016). It also appears to shorten lifespan; the Marmot review identified that lonely people are up to five times more likely to die prematurely than those with strong social ties (Marmot et al, 2010; Luo et al, 2012; Steptoe et al, 2013a). Persistent loneliness has been identified as being as harmful to your health as smoking 15 cigarettes per day or being an alcoholic, and twice as harmful as obesity (Holt-Lunstad et al, 2010).

There is additional evidence that living alone, isolation and loneliness are associated with reduced cognitive function (Wilson et al, 2007; Shanker et al, 2013). A longitudinal study in Finland found that people aged between 50 and 60 years who lived alone were twice as likely to develop dementia as those who were married or co-habiting (Håkansson et al, 2009). The risk for those who were widowed or divorced was three times as high. The study identified 'a substantial and independent association between (couple) status in mid-life and cognitive function in later life' (p 6). Although this link is ill understood at present – and more work is needed – it is thought that cognitive health is undermined by lack of social stimulation, enhanced stress levels and that coping mechanisms are not reinforced (Fratiglioni et al, 2004). In terms of evidence relating to loneliness, a 2010 study suggests that self-perceived loneliness doubles the risk of Alzheimer's disease (Amieva et al, 2010). The Welsh Assembly's 2017 'Inquiry into Isolation and Loneliness' concluded that loneliness is associated with increased risk of *both* depression and dementia (Welsh Assembly Health, Social Care and Sports Committee, 2017).

In terms of factors associated with loneliness there is consistent evidence of associations between loneliness and key socio-demographic characteristics (living alone, being female, not having any surviving children, being aged 75 years or over); material resources (poverty, limited education); health status (disability, self-assessed poor health, cognitive function, anxiety, depression); social resources (satisfaction/expectations of social contact, time spent alone, presence of a confidante) and adverse life events (recent bereavement, transitions, widowhood) (Victor et al, 2000). Age-related losses of all kinds have long been identified as linked to experiences of loneliness. Although many of these variables are interrelated and cause may be bidirectional, there is limited understanding of their specific associations (Victor and Bowling, 2012). Some researchers make a distinction between social loneliness and emotional loneliness: the former being the lack of a social network while the latter is the absence of a 'significant other' with whom a close emotional attachment exists (Burholt, 2011).

Evidence suggests that older people in residential care have higher levels of loneliness than those living in the community (Bolton, 2012); some of the loneliest people in UK society are care home residents (The Residents and Relatives Association, 2010; Campaign to End Loneliness, 2013). Little is known about its specific nature although the importance of social activity as a key dimension of good quality care is increasingly recognised (Milne, 2016). What is known is that people admitted to long-term care are vulnerable to feelings of 'existential loneliness' arising from loss of home, independence, role and (for some) meaningful relationships (Dening and Milne, 2011; 2020). A well-managed transition from home to a care home can reduce the risk of loneliness as can ongoing contact with relatives and friends, and familiar objects in the resident's room (Tanner et al, 2015).

People living with dementia, especially those who live alone, are at significant risk of social isolation and loneliness (Kane and Cook, 2013). Dementia carries an inherent risk of 'self-isolation': people with symptoms tend to avoid family and friends, and communication difficulties may make it difficult to sustain interests and/or relationships. Further, a person with dementia may not remember that a friend has visited, amplifying their sense of loneliness (Alzheimer's Society, 2013). The fact that those with more advanced dementia may struggle to make use of social media such as Facebook is also a factor.

Despite the headline statistics, it is noteworthy that the majority of older people appear to be *neither* isolated *nor* lonely. That higher numbers of younger people than older people may be lonely is also interesting and runs counter to the assumption that loneliness is an 'older person's condition' (Griffin, 2010). The factors that protect older people from isolation and loneliness are reviewed in Chapter 10.

One of the key problems with most of the research on loneliness is its static state: it measures loneliness at one point in time taking no account of its nature: transitory, situation-specific, time-bound or long term; whether it is a new or existing state; and/or whether the individual has ever been lonely before. In other words, we do not understand loneliness through the lens of a social model nor evaluate it inside the person's life course. Work by Victor and colleagues (2005) identified a fourfold typology of loneliness: those who have never been lonely; those who have always been lonely; those for whom loneliness is a new experience; and those whose level of loneliness has decreased. It can be speculated that: the 'continuity' of loneliness – or lack of it – into later life reflects the influence of personality traits and life course factors; a new experience of loneliness is likely to be a response to a life event or trigger (for example bereavement); and those whose level of loneliness has decreased have either addressed the condition or had a change of situation (for example moved close to an adult son or daughter). This typology may be helpful in informing how risks and protective factors are understood and how the former may be ameliorated and the latter bolstered. Its capacity to accommodate dimensions of the life course and take account of structural dimensions of risk such as class and gender are particular strengths.

Social exclusion

Social exclusion has evolved as a concept over several decades. Individuals are considered to be socially excluded when they suffer from a range of problems which 'endanger their relationship with society' and access to ordinary goods and services (Kneale, 2012). Other definitions understand social exclusion to be 'exclusion from participation in common and popular social experiences, groups and pastimes' (Alcock, 2008, p 44). Although there is no single figure for the proportion of excluded older people between 5 per cent and 16 per cent appear to experience two or more 'risk characteristics'. Drawing on data from ELSA Barnes and colleagues (2006) found the following risk factors to be associated with social exclusion: advanced old age, single-person household, poor mental and/or physical health, lack of access to private transport, living in rented accommodation and having a low income; taking on caring responsibilities are also implicated. There appears to be a bidirectional relationship between social exclusion and isolation and loneliness; depression is also a predictor of exclusion as well as being a cause of it. The roots of exclusion often lie in the older person's earlier life course. Age, particularly frailty and disability, may exacerbate risks but, for many, the causes already exist.

Older people living in deprived urban areas face multiple risks of exclusion, including exclusion from social relations and limited access to material resources (Scharf et al, 2004). There tend to be: few or no local shops, services or public spaces; higher levels of crime and perceived vulnerability to crime; and limited access to public transport. The lack of amenities within the immediate environment not only affects how easy it is for an older person to sustain independence but also reduces the number of informal opportunities for social interaction (Godfrey and Denby, 2004). Older people living in rural areas may also be socially excluded as a consequence of limited opportunities for community engagement and few local resources; poor housing and poverty are also contributory factors (Milne et al, 2007).

'Social detachment' is a concept linked to social exclusion, defined as 'failing to take part in social activities'. It resonates with Alcock's (2008) definition of social exclusion noted earlier. Evidence from ELSA suggests that 7 per cent of older people experience social detachment. Those particularly at risk are older people who live alone and/or do not have a partner; older men and people living on a low income are more likely to experience 'sustained social detachment'. There is considerable intersection between the concepts of social detachment, exclusion and isolation *and* the groups that experience them.

Policy issues

None of the four nations that make up the UK have adopted a single strand of policy relating to older people's mental health. There are specific policies relating to dementia on the one hand and policies relating to preventing and treating functional mental health problems on the other. The former tends to be older age focused while the latter extends across the whole adult age range.

Key emphases in dementia-related policy are: early diagnosis and intervention; improved quality of care in general hospitals; living well with dementia in care homes; and reduced use of anti-psychotic medication. In England, these aims are reflected in the 2009 *National Dementia Strategy* and subsequent policies including the *Prime Minister's Dementia Challenge(s)* of 2012 and 2015 (Department of Health, 2009d; 2012a; 2015b; 2016). Scotland, Wales and Northern Ireland also have dementia policy initiatives with very similar aims (Scottish Government, 2009; 2010; Welsh Assembly Government and Alzheimer's Society, 2011; Department of Health, Social Services and Public Safety, 2012).

Within the last few years all four governments of the UK have made specific policy commitments regarding mental health for their jurisdictions. In England the NHS published its *Five Year Forward View for Mental Health* in 2016 (NHS England, 2016) building on the government's 2011 policy *No Health without Mental Health*. One of its main aims was to achieve parity between physical and mental health and to ensure good mental health for people of *all* ages (HM Government, 2011). The Mental Health Taskforce, which devised the *Five Year Forward View*, recognised the need to develop a life course strategy regarding mental health with a focus on public health, prevention and early intervention and engagement with sectors beyond the health service, such as community services and housing.

Together for Mental Health published in 2012 is the Welsh Government's ten-year strategy for improving the mental health of the Welsh population including older people who use mental health services and their families (Welsh Assembly Government, 2012). The Scottish Government's *Mental Health Strategy 2012–2015* (Scottish Government, 2012) incorporates a number of core themes that are relevant to later life, including working more effectively with families and carers; enhancing the rights of people with mental health problems; and developing an approach to service delivery that engages with personal and social issues as well as clinical outcomes. In Northern Ireland reforms to mental health care include an emphasis on mental health promotion, community-based care and the development of specialist services for groups with particular needs, including older people (Department of Health, Social Services and Public

Safety, 2012). It is noteworthy that there is a definitive policy shift towards 'good mental health' for people of all ages across the UK.

The Care Act 2014 is also relevant to older people with mental health problems, and their carers, in England. It extends rights to information and advice; offers greater rights to an assessment of need for both service users and carers; and imposes a duty on local authorities to meet 'eligible needs', promote well-being among 'at risk' groups in their area, and prevent needs for support from health and social care services arising. The Care Act also places emphasis on the role of communities and universal services in providing support to older people with care and support needs (Department of Health, 2010a). The devolved policy context is a noteworthy and relatively recent change to UK policy making. This is largely due to the decentralisation of political and administrative powers to the legislatures of Scotland, Wales and Northern Ireland. One of the main drivers of devolution was to bring powers in relation to key public services, including health and social care, closer to the citizen so that national (as opposed to UK-wide) factors were better recognised in policy development. It is unsurprising that divergent social policy trajectories have emerged across the UK with a different set of implications for issues relating to older people with mental health problems, or at risk of developing them, and their family carers.

Conclusion

The UK is an ageing society, and there are growing numbers of older people with mental health problems. There are also a range of issues on the boundary – social exclusion, loneliness and alcohol misuse – that affect significant numbers of older people and threaten their mental health. Although an emphasis on mental health problems and psychological issues has the effect of amplifying their prevalence, it also makes visible the number of older people who do *not* have a mental health problem. Even for dementia and depression the proportion of those affected is relatively small. Among those aged 85 to 89 years, for example, under a fifth have dementia, and 'depressive symptomology' affects only about a third of all older people (Larkin, 2013). As 'ageing' is often regarded as intrinsically bound up with 'deteriorating health' this data would suggest that, in fact, the majority of older people are mentally well (Victor, 2010). What being 'mentally well' means and how 'mental health', and related concepts, are understood, conceptualised and captured is the focus of Chapter 2.

2

Mental health, psychological well-being, successful ageing and quality of life

This chapter will explore two key areas: it will discuss the definitions, dimensions and links between four intersecting concepts – mental health, psychological well-being, successful or active ageing, and quality of life. It will also review older peoples' perspectives about quality of life, the meaning they attach to 'good mental health', and research evidence about quality of life in the older population.

Introduction

There is increasing recognition that positive mental health is a prerequisite for a good quality of life across the life course, including later life. That it is more than simply the absence of mental ill health and is a separate and distinctive concept is now widely accepted. The promotion of mental health is also recognised as an important goal for social policy and a legitimate focus of public health intervention (Cattan, 2009). It is a complex overarching concept, which intersects with a number of related concepts. These include psychological well-being, successful and active ageing, and quality of life. It also subsumes, and interacts with, a wide range of sociological and psychological issues, including resilience, morale, agency and self-efficacy. The chapter begins with a review of what is known and understood about mental health before turning to its 'sister' concepts.

Mental health

Essentially mental health is the core resource that enables us to function; it relates both to thinking and feeling so that it includes both happiness/contentment and the positive thinking and skills that allow us to take action, maintain relationships and value ourselves. Our mental health influences how we think and feel and our ability to communicate and to manage change (McCulloch, 2009). Good mental health is increasingly understood as a combination of internal factors, including intrinsic attributes, and external factors; it is also conceptualised as a dynamic process rather than a static state (Williamson, 2008; McCormick et al, 2009).

Despite its common usage, a coherent and widely adopted definition of mental health remains elusive. The World Health Organization (WHO) 2003, p 7) defines it as: 'a state of wellbeing whereby individuals recognise their abilities, are able to cope with the normal stresses of daily life and are able to make a contribution to their families and communities'. Older people themselves consider that good mental health is characterised by the following: a sense of well-being, the capacity to make and sustain relationships, the ability to meet the challenges which later life brings and the ability to continue to contribute both economically and socially as family and/or community members (Mental Health Foundation, 2003).

Most definitions of mental health suggest that it is underpinned by a number of core dimensions. Older people highlight the importance of: resilience and coping, remaining active and involved, having a purpose or role, being able to engage in social relationships, keeping fit, having an adequate income, self-worth, and social capital (Age Concern England, 2003; Health Scotland, 2004). A prominent research finding is that mental health is regarded by older people as an equally important dimension of overall health as physical health (Bowling, 2005). It also appears to be closely tied to self-perception; how an older person views their mental health is as significant as any objective or clinical assessment (Office for National Statistics, 2004).

Keyes (2005) suggests that 'mental illness' and 'positive mental health' form two psychometrically distinct but correlated continua, making it possible for a person with a diagnosed mental illness to experience positive mental health. It is important to note, for example, that people living with dementia routinely report 'good mental health' (see Chapter 8). The two-dimensional model developed by McCulloch (2009; see Figure 2.1) illustrates this point well.

Figure 2.1: The two-dimensional model of mental health and mental illness

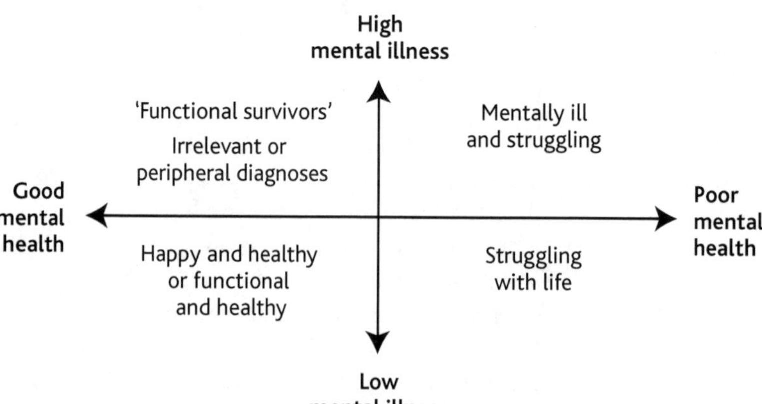

Source: Adapted from McCulloch, 2009

Psychological well-being

Psychological well-being is widely identified as important to quality of life at all stages and ages (Bennett and Soulsby, 2014). It is usually conceptualised as a combination of positive affective states such as happiness and feeling full of life (the hedonic perspective) and functioning with optimal effectiveness in individual and social life (the eudaemonic perspective) (Ryan and Deci, 2001). As summarised by Huppert (2009, p 137), 'Psychological wellbeing is about lives going well. It is the combination of feeling good and functioning effectively'. It tends to be viewed as a more 'clinical' concept than mental health and one that has psychometric properties that can be assessed and tested (to be discussed later).

Ryff (1989a) – one of the most significant contributors to this field – considered psychological well-being to have six core dimensions: self-acceptance; personal growth; purpose in life; environmental mastery; autonomy and positive relations with others. NHS Health Scotland (2010, p 9) defined the closely aligned concept of mental well-being as encompassing '... psychological feelings of life satisfaction, optimism, self-esteem, mastery and feeling in control, having a purpose in life (and) a sense of belonging and support'. There is some evidence that higher levels of psychological well-being are associated with improved overall health (Ryff et al, 2004; 2006). It may also reduce the risk, or delay the onset, of a number of physical and mental health problems including depression and cardiovascular disease (Keyes 2004; Steptoe et al, 2015).

Assessing and measuring psychological well-being

Defining and assessing psychological well-being is conceptually and methodologically complex; it is much easier to measure psychological morbidity.

There are a small number of well-established overarching measures of psychological well-being. One commonly used measure is the General Health Questionnaire (GHQ); the GHQ comes in a 60-, 30-, 28- and 12-item form. The 12-item form focuses on three domains: anxiety and depression, confidence and social function. It is widely used in research studies, and 'population norms' are available for a range of different groups (Bun Cheung, 2002; Victor, 2010). In Scotland a measure, called the Warwick–Edinburgh Mental Wellbeing Scale (WEMWBS), has been validated for use alongside the GHQ in both Scottish and UK-wide surveys (NHS Health Scotland, University of Warwick and University of Edinburgh, 2006). It is a 14-item scale with five response categories, summed to provide a single score ranging from 14 to 70. The items are all worded positively and cover both feeling and functioning aspects of mental well-being; they include positive affect (optimism, cheerfulness, relaxation), satisfying interpersonal relationships, and positive functioning (energy, clear thinking, self-acceptance, personal development, mastery and autonomy). Ryff (1989b) developed a theoretically grounded instrument to measure psychological well-being – the 'Ryff Scales of Psychological Wellbeing' – which assesses each of the construct's sub-dimensions (noted earlier). There are also a number of specific scales that measure some of the dimensions of positive psychological well-being, including resilience, self-esteem, self-efficacy, optimism, life satisfaction and sense of coherence (Martz and Livneh, 2016).

Psychological well-being among older people

In Bowling's (2005) large-scale survey exploring older people's quality of life conducted in the early 2000s, 84 per cent of those aged 65 to 74 and 79 per cent of those aged 75 years and over had 'good psychological wellbeing'. Psychological well-being was measured using the 12-item GHQ (Bowling, 2005). Evidence from the 2008 Health Survey for England[1] (HSE) – which also employed the 12-item GHQ – supported these findings suggesting that only a tenth (10.5 per cent) of those aged 65 and over demonstrate 'psychological morbidity', that is, had a GHQ score of four or more (indicative of possible depression and/or anxiety) (Office for National Statistics, 2008; Victor, 2010). Although the 2016 HSE report showed a rise in psychological morbidity – with 15 per cent of people aged 65 or over scoring four or more on the GHQ – it is noteworthy that in the HSE surveys for both 2008 *and* 2016, those aged 65 to 74 had the highest level of psychological well-being of any age group. However, numbers do start to fall for those aged 75 and over, and people in the 85 and over age category report the lowest levels of well-being for all age groups (NHS Digital, 2017a).

The English Longitudinal Survey for England (ELSA) (Banks et al, 2012) collected information about the psychological well-being of a large sample of older people from 2002 to 2011. The study gathered data on three aspects of psychological well-being: evaluative well-being, that is, people's satisfaction with life; hedonic or affective well-being, that is, measures of feeling, such as happiness, sadness and enjoyment; and eudaemonic well-being, that is, judgements about the meaning or purpose of one's life (Huppert, 2005). Evidence from ELSA suggests that older individuals are shown to have a better subjective well-being than those who are younger for each well-being measure, except at the oldest ages (Jivraj et al, 2013). In the government's National Psychiatric Morbidity Survey 2007, people living in the community were asked about how happy they were (Cooper et al, 2011). The great majority of older people considered themselves to be 'fairly or very happy', with less than 10 per cent reporting being 'not too happy'. There were limited differences between the older age cohorts of those aged 60 to 69, 70 to 79 and 80 years and over. Additional evidence drawn from the same survey distinguishes between hedonic and eudaemonic well-being. Weich and colleagues' (2011) analysis suggests that while levels of hedonic well-being appear to decline with age, levels of eudaemonic well-being increase across the lifespan, albeit with a slight decrease among the oldest group, that is, those aged 85 years and over.

ELSA data identified a pronounced socio-economic gradient with higher levels of psychological well-being evident among older people with higher incomes. This pattern is reinforced by data from the 2016 HSE (NHS Digital, 2017a). This identified that 24 per cent of men and 27 per cent of women in the lowest quintile of equivalised household income reported a GHQ-12 score of 4+ compared with 13 per cent of men and 17 per cent of women in the highest income quintile. There is a strong association between psychological well-being, being active and physical health; older people with chronic illness and/or disability tend to have lower levels of psychological well-being. It may also have a protective role in terms of survival; a higher level of eudaemonic well-being is associated with longer life (Banks et al, 2012). These findings underscore the interconnected nature of physical and mental health noted earlier; it is difficult to sustain a feeling of well-being without the ability to function, but equally it is difficult to function 'normally' without a feeling of well-being.

In 2016 in England the WEMWBS scores for people aged 65 to 74 were 52 for both men and women, and in 2015 WEMWBS scores for people aged 65 to 74 in Scotland were 51; in both, these were the highest scores for all age groups (Braunholtz et al, 2007; Scottish Government, 2016; NHS Digital, 2017a). For those aged 75 and over living in Scotland – the oldest age group for whom data was collected – the scores were also above 50. The maximum WEMWBS score is 70. Lower scores were associated with poorer physical health, lower productivity and more limitations in daily living (NHS Health Scotland, 2010). In both surveys there was a very strong association between WEMWBS scores and self-reported general health.

In general, evidence suggests that older people report higher levels of psychological well-being than their younger counterparts (Allen, 2008; ONS, 2016b). This is especially the case for those aged between 65 and 74 years. In part this pattern may reflect the influence of the 'contrast effect'. Most survey questions ask respondents to compare themselves with 'most people of the same age'. As with all other age groups older people are negatively influenced by stereotypical images of older people as ill and dependent; they tend to respond to questions about health in a way that 'distances' them from this image. Thus, respondents may enhance their evaluation of their own psychological well-being (Victor, 2010). Similar arguments apply to quality of life, an issue discussed later in this chapter. Alongside this it is important to recognise that research consistently shows that many older people, including those aged over 85 years, continue to mature, both intellectually and with regard to skills and that later life is often associated with increased self-acceptance and confidence (Kunzmann et al, 2000). These factors contribute positively to psychological well-being.

Resilience

While there are a range of issues relating to psychological well-being in later life, the most relevant are coping strategies, self-efficacy (mastery and control over one's life), morale and self-esteem. Taken together these dimensions can be understood as resilience. Resilience is defined as 'the process of effectively negotiating, adapting to, or managing significant sources of stress or trauma' (Windle, 2011, p 152). It is considered particularly important in later life in supporting adjustment to common challenges and transitions, for example retirement, ill health and/or bereavement.

Defining resilience and exploring how it 'works' is not straightforward. As a review by Windle (2011) notes, this largely depends on which disciplinary perspective one takes. Developmental psychology defines it as 'good outcomes in spite of serious threats' to ongoing development (Windle, 2011). It facilitates optimisation of subjective well-being, reducing or neutralising the negative impact of life events; it is often referred to as positive adaptation or 'coping well in the face of adversity' (Bartlam and Machin, 2016). Self-efficacy – a dimension of resilience – has specifically been shown to diminish the negative impact of impaired functional capacity on depressive symptomology (Knipscheer et al, 2000).

Some commentators view resilience as a personality trait; whether it is a fixed trait or one that can be acquired is the subject of ongoing debate (Ong et al, 2006). More recent work conceptualises resilience as a process, rather than an intrinsic characteristic, that is influenced by a range of external factors (Friedli, 2009). Resilience is reinforced by the older person's context; protective factors may moderate risk and mediate outcomes. A helpful conceptual model is a framework developed by Windle and Bennett (2011) which draws on Ecological Systems Theory (Bronfenbrenner, 1994). Although developed for work with children it has been gaining increasing attention in the gerontological literature. The framework aims to understand people in situ, taking account of personal, social, economic and environmental assets that an individual has at their disposal (Ottmann and Maragoudaki, 2015).

This model also accommodates a lifespan perspective (Windle, 2012). Not only does the experience of resilience vary across the life course but it also fluctuates (Luthar, 2006). A late life divorce, for example, may threaten a person's resilience as the loss of a partner may reduce both their financial and social resources. It may also have an impact on self-esteem, a key component of resilience. The 'arms' – or elements – of resilience in later life have been described as 'health, wealth, and social' (Age UK, 2014a). It is the intersection of these elements that promotes or undermines resilience. If an older person has good health, is financially secure and has a strong social network then they may well be very resilient, but if one or two of these elements is undermined their resilience may be challenged.

Work from health psychology also suggests that a person's ability to 'bounce back' from threats they have experienced earlier in life is indicative of their ability to do so again. Broadly, a person who has had to deal with stresses throughout their formative years and learned to adjust develops a more effective way of coping with change and stress in later life (Hamilton-West, 2011). Overall, it is suggested that the impact of adversity on an older person's mental health is mediated by psychological and social resources developed, or acquired, throughout life (Rogers and Pilgrim, 2014). It is noteworthy that older people themselves tend to view resilience as a situated construct: it is a dynamic resource that develops over time and is embedded in both a life course and a socio-environmental context.

Research suggests that resilient older people have high(er) levels of physical functioning and autonomy, believe they have control over their life and have high levels of life satisfaction. Resilience tends to be positively associated with optimism and extraversion and negatively associated with neuroticism; survey research by Bowling (2005) in the early 2000s identified that 70 per cent of older people consider themselves to be 'optimists'. Resilience is also consistently linked to positive emotions. In turn 'positive emotions' have been found to facilitate adaptive responses (Aminzadeh et al, 2007). Research with older people echoes a number of these themes, highlighting the importance of strengthening, or at least maintaining, resilience-enhancing assets (Becker and Newsom, 2005).

Salutogenesis

Resilience is a core dimension of Antonovsky's (1979) model of salutogenesis. He identified an interaction between what he called 'generalised resistance resources' – typically money, social support, knowledge, experience, intelligence and traditions – and a 'sense of coherence' – the ability to make use of these. A salutogenic environment is one which promotes a sense of coherence (SOC) and makes it easier for people to deal with the challenges of later life. It focuses on the factors that promote positive health and beneficial change rather than on the factors that cause illness and ill being (Antonovsky, 1987). Adapted and refined over the years the model has found its way into health promotion and community development initiatives relating to mental health (Billings and Hashem, 2009).

Antonovsky (1979, p 10) defined SOC as a 'global orientation that expresses the extent to which one has a pervasive, enduring though dynamic, feeling of confidence that one's internal and external environment are predictable and that there is a high probability that things will work out as well as can reasonably be expected'. He considered that three types of life experience shape a person's SOC: comprehensibility (life has a certain predictability and can be understood), manageability (enough resources to meet personal demands) and meaningfulness (life makes sense, problems are worth investing energy in). More recently a fourth concept has been added – emotional closeness – which refers to the extent to which a person has emotional bonds with others and feels part of the community. The value of the salutogenic model is twofold: it provides an explanatory framework for positive mental health, especially among those who manage to maintain theirs in the face of adversity, and it may inform a strategy to promote mental health in later life. However, it is important to note that Antonovsky himself developed the model as a theoretical one offering a way into understanding health and illness rather than as a professional or practice tool.

There are other salutogenic perspectives. Lundman and colleagues (2010), for example, developed a construct of 'inner strength' – a combination of resilience, hardiness, purpose in life and SOC – to explain positive health status. A number of studies focusing on older people have applied a salutogenic approach. Rena and colleagues (1996) found that SOC was significantly related to how well older people and their carers adjusted to a disability even in contexts where the disability was severe. In another study of carers of older people with mental health problems, those carers who had a strong SOC required lower levels of support from services (Chumbler et al, 2008). A strong SOC is correlated with higher levels of good or positive mental health; negative correlations have been found in relation to psychiatric symptoms, notably depression (Nygren, 2006). The relatively recent concept of health capital also draws on salutogenic concepts (see Chapter 10).

Wild and colleagues (2013) extend the salutogenic perspective further, locating resilience inside a broader framework that has a number of dimensions (see Figure 2.2). This model shifts the perspective away from

Figure 2.2: Multi-dimensionality of resilience

Source: Wild et al, 2013

viewing resilience as an individual characteristic towards an understanding of it as a broader construct that is a product of a person's household and family, neighbourhood, community and wider society (Richardson and Chew-Graham, 2016).

It is noteworthy that 'successful ageing', the third of my meta concepts, shares a number of the psychosocial dimensions identified in salutogenic approaches.

Successful ageing

Successful ageing has gained considerable prominence as a concept and as a policy goal over the last 20 years. Whereas the three concepts already reviewed are applicable across the life course successful ageing is specifically focused on later life.

Some of the older literature defines successful ageing as the avoidance of physical or cognitive impairment. By this rather narrow definition relatively few older people age 'successfully' (Torres, 2003). Taking account of the views of older people themselves, more recent work has adopted a broader view defining it as the process of effectively adapting to functional, social, material and personal losses (Depp and Jeste, 2006). The modifiable nature of factors such as social support and home adaptations and their subsequent capacity to ameliorate the negative impact of widowhood or mobility problems is a key aspect of this body of work (Bowling and Dieppe, 2005).

Baltes and Baltes's (1990) model of successful ageing extends this conceptual purview constructing ageing as the product of a 'dynamic interplay of gains and losses'. The model involves three interrelated processes: selection, compensation and optimisation. These work together to support the attainment of valued goals, the minimisation of losses and the maximisation of gains (Baltes and Carstensen, 1996). Baltes and Baltes (1990) recognise that older people are actively engaged in trying to make sense of, and adapt to, the physical, social, interpersonal and psychological changes that accompany ageing and that this is informed by a lifetime of accumulated knowledge and expertise. They also acknowledge that finding meaning is an integrative process. Ryff (1989b) builds on this further suggesting that 'meaning of the experience' subsumes the following dimensions: self-acceptance, positive relations with others, autonomy, environmental mastery, purpose in life and personal growth. That this model can accommodate heterogeneity and variety is a key strength; it also links with psychological models of ageing, that is, that finding personal meaning is the primary developmental task of old age (Erikson et al, 1986).

In 2001 Godfrey elaborated on the Baltes and Baltes model (1990) developing a socio-cultural model of successful ageing (see Figure 2.3). This model extends the original by locating ageing in its broader cultural and economic context and by recognising that ageing is mediated through the lens of life course experience and is influenced by social and structural issues. It also integrates agency and structure: two of the core elements of successful ageing.

Figure 2.3: Socio-cultural model of successful ageing, 2001

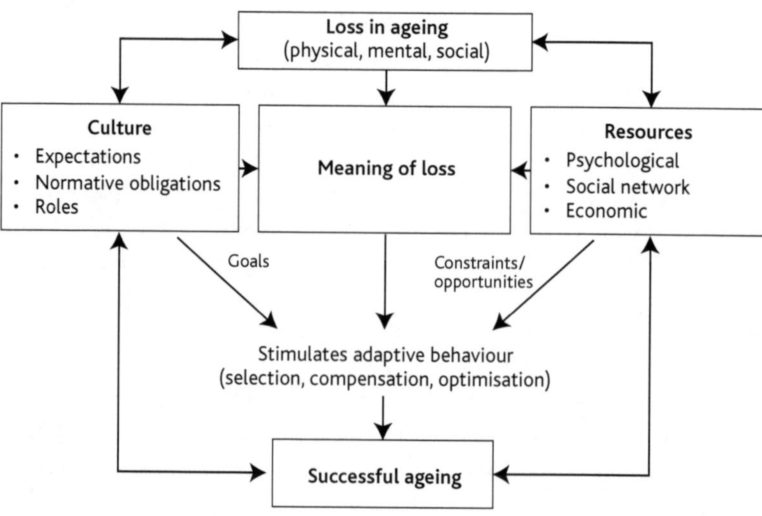

Source: Godfrey, 2001

Although the term 'active ageing' is often used synonymously with successful or even positive ageing, its focus is narrower. Active ageing, as a concept, was intended to challenge the traditional 'decline and loss' paradigm and promote a positive view of old age as a period of opportunity and development (Bowling and Iliffe, 2011). It is underpinned, historically at least, by activity theory (Boudiny, 2013). The WHO's definition of active ageing emphasises 'optimising the dimensions of physical, mental and social wellbeing as a means of maintaining autonomy and independence in old age' (Victor 2010, p 136). While offering a helpful counterweight to negativity an overly positivistic perspective brings problems of its own. It has a tendency to bifurcate later life into those who 'actively age', that is, who are independent, autonomous and fit, and those who have failed to do so. It denies the harsher realities of (often) very old age marginalising those who are frail and reinforcing negative evaluations of chronic illness and dependency (Lloyd, 2012). Issues relating to frailty and the fourth age are explored in Chapter 7. It also tends to construct active ageing as an individual responsibility rather than a responsibility shared with policy makers, communities and wider society.

A third issue is that top-down definitions of active ageing may not resonate with the views of older people themselves (Tate et al, 2003; Bowling, 2008). Current evidence suggests that older people tend to adopt a short temporal horizon in evaluating both 'active' and 'successful' ageing; taking 'one day at a time' rather than conceptualising these issues in a longer-term way (Stenner et al, 2011). Work drawn from psychology indicates that older people operationalise successful ageing in terms of life satisfaction, morale and subjective well-being and that what matters is the *quality* of their daily lived experiences (Bowling, 2009a). This point is picked up later in the section on quality of life. A fundamental issue relates to the fact that older people's own relationship with terms such as 'active' or 'successful' is a much more nuanced subjective one than global constructs suggest. How ageing is experienced and managed by the individual older person in their – often changing – context and life course strongly influences how 'activity' is operationalised or 'success' defined. Models tend to be based on relatively linear objective links between cause and effect occluding the relevance of the subjective dimension emerging as so important in research with older people (Stenner et al, 2011; Timonen, 2016). The active ageing agenda has also been criticised for excluding black and minority ethnic elders and those who are economically and/or socially marginalised in favour of those who have access to resources and have a higher social status (Patel, 2016).

One approach, drawn from psychological theory, that attempts to accommodate the perspectives of older people is gerotranscendence. Its architect, Tornstam (1987), argues that older people's meta perspective shifts from an externally facing, competitive, materialist '... view of the world to a more cosmic, contemplative and transcendent one'. The approach emphasises change and growth as well as adjustment; it suggests that the self continues to develop psychologically throughout the life course and that 'gerotranscendence is the final stage in a natural progression towards maturation and wisdom' (Tornstam, 2005, p 46). One of its advantages is that it offers different, more age appropriate, perspectives on common late life experiences. For example, social withdrawal may be reinterpreted as opting for a smaller number of meaningful relationships, and loneliness may be reframed as positive solitude (Tornstam, 2005). While useful, it has limited purchase in the wider world of psychology and has struggled to achieve a foothold in the gerontological sphere.

A significant shift may be required in our thinking if we are to develop a lens of analysis that can meaningfully accommodate the views and experiences of older people. The way forward, argues Tanner (2005), is for frameworks to reflect later life as a time of both opportunity and growth *and* loss and decline. Especially for the very old, that is, 90 years and over, it may be more helpful to employ a perspective that emphasises autonomy, adaptation and a sense of purpose over that which emphasises absence of disease, activity, and social participation. This argument dovetails with that made by Stenner and colleagues (2011) who identified three principles as consistently emerging in work exploring the meaning of successful ageing: adaptability, meaningful relationships, and agency. Resisting imposed meanings is also important; '... setting one's own norms rather than being 'normed' by others' (Stenner et al, 2011, p 474). Bowling and Dieppe (2005) consider that successful ageing as a concept '... should be placed on a continuum of achievement rather than subject to simplistic normative assessment of success or failure' and that the adoption of a broader perspective needs to have relevance for older people themselves.

Despite the distinctions researchers make between successful ageing and quality of life, they are routinely conflated in the minds of older people. It is to this fourth concept that I now turn.

Quality of life

Quality of life is a multi-dimensional concept encompassing emotional, social, psychological and health-related domains; broadly it encapsulates 'how good' a person's life is overall (Thompson and Kingston, 2004). Like mental health there is no accepted definition of quality of life; the term is often used interchangeably with that of well-being.

A review of research with older people suggests that the main factors regarded as important for quality of life are: family relationships,

relationships with others (friends, neighbours), happiness, religion/spirituality, independence, mobility, autonomy, good health, social/leisure activities and standard of living (Brown et al, 2004). The Age Concern and Mental Health Foundation Inquiry (2006) into 'Mental Health and Well Being in Later Life' distilled a wide range of evidence, including capturing the perspectives of older people themselves. The report highlighted five key dimensions of quality of life: freedom from discrimination, participation in meaningful activity, social relationships, physical health and financial status (Age Concern and Mental Health Foundation, 2006). A 2009 review by McCormick et al highlighted resilience, independence, health, income and wealth, having a role and having time. For many older people having a positive attitude and 'making the best of things' are viewed as important for sustaining quality of life; a positive attitude to ageing has been specifically linked to lower rates of depression and higher rates of satisfaction with life (Bryant et al, 2012). Research with very elderly people highlights 'not being a burden', interdependence, and reciprocity as important factors (Tanner, 2010). Reduced capacity to perform activities of daily living, impaired mobility and long-standing illness are routinely identified as significant factors in reducing quality of life in research with older people (Victor et al, 2009). Evidence further suggests that it is the loss of control and independence associated with chronic ill health that undermines quality of life rather than the illness per se (Bond and Corner, 2004).

A large-scale survey supplemented by in-depth interviews identified the following dimensions as the building blocks of good quality of life: having an optimistic outlook and good psychological well-being; having good health and physical functioning; having positive social relationships and preventing loneliness; maintaining social roles, activities and interests; living in a neighbourhood with good facilities and services; feeling safe and secure; having an adequate income; maintaining a sense of independence and control over one's life; and acceptance of circumstances which cannot be changed (Bowling, 2005, p 221). Bond and Corner (2004) add 'subjective perception' to this list referring to it as an individual's evaluation of their own well-being. They emphasise not only the pivotal importance of this element to the overall construct but offer a definition, '… the meaning that individuals give the quality of their later life is probably determined by their life context: by the political, economic, and cultural influences of the society in which they live; by individual lived experiences across the life course; by their current expectations, attitudes, and values and by the context in which they reflectively provide this account' (Bond and Corner, 2004: p 104).

The core elements of most quality of life measures are: psychological well-being; health and functional status; social networks, support and activities; and neighbourhood social capital (see Box 2.1). Work reviewing how theoretical and lay models of quality of life compare finds that although a number of dimensions are shared, older people tend to emphasise health, instrumental activities of daily living and the ability to get out and about to a greater degree than measures developed by researchers. Older people also emphasise financial circumstances, self-efficacy, autonomy and independence and prefer a focus on the *ability* to do things rather than the *inability*. They frequently comment on the multifaceted nature of quality of life and the interdependency of its components. They also observe that it reflects both the objective and subjective, both macro and micro issues, both societal concerns and those of individuals, and reflects a lifetime's accumulation of resources and skills. For these reasons, it is important that quality of life as a concept, and measures to assess it, are grounded in the experiences and views of older people and take a holistic perspective (Gabriel and Bowling, 2004). A tension remains between the objective and subjective approaches to the conceptualisation and measurement of quality of life (see next subsection).

Box 2.1: Taxonomy of models of quality of life

- objective indicators
- subjective indicators
- satisfaction of human needs
- psychosocial characteristics and resources
- health and functioning
- social health
- social cohesion and social capital
- environmental context
- idiographic approaches

Source: Bowling, 2005

There are a number of approaches to assessing quality of life. These range from basic, objective needs-based approaches derived from Maslow's (1954) 'hierarchy of needs' to instruments based on psychological well-being, happiness, morale, life satisfaction, and social and cognitive competence. More traditional measures tend to reflect biomedical models of ageing focusing on physical function and health while more recent measures attempt to move beyond 'professional centrism' accommodating broader lay informed perspectives (Bowling, 2005, p 42). Three of the most prominent and trusted measures of quality of life are outlined in Box 2.2.

Box 2.2: Measures of quality of life in old age

Older People's Quality of Life Questionnaire (OPQOL)

- looks at life overall, social relationships and participation, independence, control over life, freedom, home and neighbourhood, psychological and emotional well-being, financial circumstances and religion/culture;
- 32-to-35-item measure with 5-point Likert scales.

Control, Autonomy, Self-realisation and Pleasure Scale (CASP-19)

- looks at control, autonomy, self-realisation and pleasure;
- 19-item measure with 4-point Likert scales.

The World Health Organization Quality of Life Measure for Older People (WHOQOL-OLD)

- looks at sensory abilities, autonomy, past, present and future activities, social participation, death and dying, and intimacy;
- 24-item measure with 5-point semantic differential scales.

Source: International Longevity Centre, 2011

It is noteworthy that of these three only the 'Older People's Quality of Life Questionnaire' has a specific domain relating to psychological well-being (Bowling, 2009b). Interestingly, psychological well-being is one of the domains of the quadripartite quality of life instrument developed by one of the original architects of quality of life instruments – Lawton – working in the 1980s (1982; 1983).

In terms of evidence about quality of life among community dwelling older people, in a 2008 national survey 11 per cent of respondents rated their quality of life as 'very poor', 'quite poor' or 'neither good nor poor' with the remaining 89 per cent rating their quality of life as 'good' or 'very good' (Harrop and Jopling, 2008). In Bowling's (2005) survey, conducted in the mid 2000s, over three quarters of older people reported having a good quality of life; this remained the case at follow-up 18 months later despite some reduction in the physical health of many respondents. Bowling developed a new measure – the 'Older People's Quality of Life Questionnaire' (OPQOL – see Box 2.2) – drawing on this research which involved in-depth work with older people (Bowling and Stenner, 2011). In three subsequent surveys using the OPQOL, over a third (36 per cent) of a large representative sample of older people were rated as having 'good' or 'very good' quality of life (2011). This was the case for over a tenth (12 per cent) at follow-up. Far more of the ethnically diverse sub-sample had poor quality of life (International Longevity Centre, 2011).

Research on quality of later life has been criticised for excluding older people with complex needs and/or dementia. Work that has been done exploring what quality of life means for older people with high dependency needs highlights the importance of security, reciprocity, meaningful relationships and being treated as an individual (Blood, 2013). Specific quality of life measures have been developed for people with advanced dementia; these are discussed in Chapter 8 (Warner et al, 2010).

Objective versus subjective factors and quality of life

One of the key challenges in assessing 'quality of life' is capturing the intersection of objective and subjective factors. One reason for the relatively low predictive power of objective variables such as income is limited understanding of its subjective impact. Work by Ehrhardt and colleagues (2000), for example, showed that greater happiness is associated with better living conditions, affluence and income. However, as affluence and education increase, people's relative expectations and potential for dissatisfaction also increase. This complexity is compounded by the mediating role played by income in relationship to independence, poor health and social participation, which are themselves dimensions of quality of life. Although the overall importance of income decreases with age, as it reflects both life course and present status, it is important to capture it objectively and to explore its subjective influence on quality of life.

Research with older people has long recognised that individuals may experience good quality of life in objectively adverse circumstances, for example situations marked by disadvantage or poor health (Windle and Woods, 2004). The fact that people with chronic illnesses consistently rate their own quality of life highly has been termed the 'disability' or 'wellbeing' paradox (Albrecht and Devlieger, 1999). This includes people with Alzheimer's disease (Livingstone et al, 2008). In his research with older people experiencing chronic illness, Bury (1991) identified the employment of what he termed 'cognitive processes' (or cognitive coping mechanisms) whereby the individual learns to tolerate the effects of illness (Tanner, 2005). Johnson and Barer's extensive study (1997) of people over the age of 85 revealed that cognitive processes play a greater role in assessment of quality of life as 'objective' challenges increase. Greater levels of disability, loss of friends and a reduced sense of control over life can be counter-balanced by good relationships with care providers, closer links with adult children and security provided by moving to a smaller, more modern home. Of course the opposite can be true. A move to warden controlled, 'all services provided' sheltered accommodation near relatives may impose restrictions on someone who has enjoyed solitude and the freedom to choose to see their family when they wish. This evidence regarding adaptation and balance dovetails with the dimensions of the model of successful ageing discussed earlier and how late life transitions may be navigated (see Chapter 7 for more on transitions).

As this chapter has focused on those constructs of most relevance to mental health it has inevitably excluded others, for example in-depth exploration of concepts such as self-esteem and life satisfaction (Diener et al, 1999).

A note: successful ageing and longevous groups of older people

Various research groups have proposed that our understanding of successful ageing can be advanced through the study of populations of long-lived individuals, typically centenarians, particularly where they have few serious health problems. A recent study of older people living in the Sardinian Blue Zone suggests that they have substantially lower levels of depressive symptomology compared with their peers from other parts of Sardinia and much higher levels of psychological well-being (Hitchcott et al, 2018). That these findings apply to community dwelling older people and those living in institutional settings *and* to those with, and without, physical ill health is especially striking (Weich et al, 2011). The higher levels of psychological well-being appear to be associated with a number of socio-cultural factors, including high levels of religiosity, social connectivity, having a role, and engagement with leisure activities; a tradition of 'respect for the elderly' may also be relevant. These factors also appear to be associated with a significantly reduced risk of developing dementia as noted in Chapter 1. I explore issues that promote mental health and well-being in Chapter 10.

Policy issues

For well over a decade there has been an emphasis in national and international health and well-being policies on successful (or active) ageing and promoting quality of life and well-being among older people (DH, 2005; Lloyd, 2012). A campaign was launched by WHO in 1999 to promote the benefits of active ageing. In the subsequent policy – *Active Ageing: A Public Policy Framework* – WHO (2002a) sets out a rights-based life course approach that recognises diversity in ageing. A key goal is the prevention or postponement of mental ill health: '... promoting positive mental health throughout the life course and challenging stereotypical beliefs about mental health problems and mental illnesses' (WHO, 2002b, p 48). This was reinforced by the fact that 2012 was designated 'European Year for Active Ageing'. The overarching theme was the promotion of health and well-being of older people.

In the main, policy adopts a broad purview recognising the multi-dimensional nature of 'success' and 'well-being' in later life. Initiatives have focused on a range of issues: maintaining independence, engaging with community and society, and accessing educational opportunities. A life course perspective features strongly in policy approaches albeit framed as an individual responsibility to 'take action'. Examples include the drive to 'encourage young adults to prepare for old age in their health, social, and financial practices' (WHO, 2002a, p 52), and promoting healthy lifestyles, including protecting mental health, across the whole life course (Royal College of Psychiatrists, 2010; Knapp et al, 2011).

More critically, and perhaps inevitably, policy tends to treat older people as if they are a single homogeneous group, that 'one size fits all' and that ways to promote well-being are universal. Not only does this overlook heterogeneity but its top-down nature fails to draw upon the often complex and nuanced strategies devised by older people for actively managing their lives and maintaining or promoting their mental health (Tanner, 2010). This mirrors the limited engagement researchers have with older people's definitions of active ageing, noted earlier.

Despite its centrality as a policy goal and a key dimension of successful ageing, few studies have explored the meaning of 'independence' (Secker et al, 2003). Policy places considerable emphasis on self-reliance, autonomy and recovering or maintaining 'good health' (Ray et al, 2015). This rather narrow lens on independence speaks more to older people with short-term treatable conditions than to very elderly people with long-term chronic conditions, for example dementia, who are 'necessarily dependent' on others to care for them (Lloyd, 2010). Research with older people makes clear that although avoiding reliance on others for help with everyday activities is an important aspect of independence, so too are choice and the retention of a meaningful role (Tanner, 2010). Bland (1999) defines the core values of independence as 'privacy, dignity, choice, autonomy and fulfilment' (p 539). The maintenance of 'identity' and of 'home' are noted elements and appear to be important to older people throughout the whole of their late life course (Lloyd, 2015). In research with older people interdependence has been identified as a more accurate and meaningful concept than independence. This both underpins a life course perspective and is reflected in the 'reciprocity and exchange' nature of older people's social and family networks (Godfrey et al, 2004).

Conclusion

As can be seen from this review, there is considerable common ground between the constructs of mental health, psychological well-being, successful ageing and quality of life. Although the concepts explored in this chapter are hierarchical to some degree, that is, mastery is a subset of resilience, and resilience is a dimension of psychological well-being, they also intersect in ways that render a 'Russian doll' approach redundant. This is complex terrain. That mental health is as much a *product* of quality of life as it is a *component* is an important observation.

Mental health appears to be a product of a number of intersecting dimensions of an individual's personality, life course and environment. To be mentally well requires positive psychological functioning, which is itself a product of a person's personality traits and life events and resources such as self-esteem, control, resilience and social relationships. Positive psychological functioning is strongly influenced by the multiple factors that contribute to overall quality of life (Windle, 2009).

An overarching challenge of reviewing this large literature is the widespread use of terminology and concepts that overlap. 'Self-efficacy' and 'adaptability' are – variously – elements of successful ageing, quality of life and/or mental health. One of the problems of this flexibility is that universal definitions remain elusive. That is not to suggest that refinement of concepts is not positive, and it is inevitable that they *do* intersect, but establishing where key domains 'belong' and where the boundaries of each construct are situated is an issue. Establishing the prevalence of 'good mental health' or 'good quality of life' is an associated challenge (Bowling and Stenner, 2011).

Three other issues characterise this literature. There is often disagreement between the lay and professional definitions of the key concepts, especially in relationship to very elderly people with dependency needs. Older people tend to emphasise subjective issues while professionals tend to be more interested in objective elements that can be more easily measured. This is not just a matter of emphasis; it is about meaning: what matters to older people may not concur with what professionals think matters to them. Accommodating differences arising from gender, sexuality, race, culture, or age, which profoundly influence mental health, is also a challenge for instruments focusing on individuals' life trajectories. A third point relates to the fact that most research has been conducted, and most instruments developed, with the mainstream community-based older population. Much work remains to be done with populations that challenge researchers such as frail older people, people living with dementia, long-term care residents and older people from black and minority ethnic communities.

Exploring the life course and age-related determinants of mental health outcomes in later life is an important next step in enhancing our understanding of this multi-dimensional issue. These determinants and related inequalities are the focus of the next five chapters.

3

The life course, inequalities and mental health in later life

Chapters 3 to 7 intersect. Each chapter explores and offers analysis of a group of, often connected, issues that contribute to deepening understanding of, and explaining, mental health outcomes in later life.

Chapter 3 will explore three key issues. Firstly, it will foreground the importance of taking a life course approach to understanding health outcomes and the contribution of social gerontology to extending this perspective. Secondly, it will explore the nature of health inequalities, their implications for older people and how inequalities impact on health outcomes, particularly mental health outcomes. A part of this makes visible the intersection between health and risks associated with belonging to an unequal society. Its third focus relates to links between later life health and experiences, and exposure to adversity earlier in the life course particularly childhood. In attempting to bring these perspectives together my aim is to: illuminate the different ways in which life course inequality and adversity create and/or amplify risks to mental health in later life; draw out mental health issues from the broader category of 'health'; and expose the embedded and structural nature of causative mechanisms.

Experiences common to later life (such as bereavement, ill health), their intersection with age-related inequalities and their impact on mental health is the focus of Chapter 4. Chapters 5 to 7 explore the impact of age-related risks that are relevant to particular subpopulations of older people: Socio-economic disadvantage and poverty; Abuse, mistreatment and neglect; and The fourth age, frailty and transitions. As these are risks that have powerful implications for mental health they warrant exploration in their own right.

All five chapters focus on functional mental health issues; issues relating to the mental health of people living with dementia and links between mental health and how we conceptualise dementia are explored in Chapters 8 and 9.

The life course approach

There is growing evidence that later life health is a product of the life course. A life course perspective seeks to identify how health outcomes are shaped 'independently, cumulatively and interactively' by biological, psychological, social, historical and environmental factors throughout a person's life, as well as those that impact on it in old age (Kuh et al, 2002; Whalley et al, 2006). It draws attention to both continuity and change and locates an older person's life inside its broader context. It is also an approach which seeks to integrate the major factors that have been empirically linked to health outcomes but have often been considered in isolation (Ben-Shlomo and Kuh, 2002).

The life course perspective arose out of the confluence of several theoretical approaches (Marshall and Clarke, 2010; Bengtson et al, 2012). A predominant theme is that stages in life are not necessarily standardised or chronologically or biologically fixed but are subject to a variety of social, historical and cultural influences. Katz and colleagues (2011a, p 10) defined the life course as a 'sequence of age-linked transitions that are embedded in social institutions and history'. It is the linkage between the individual experience of ageing, on the one hand, and the social and historical contexts within which individual ageing occurs on the other, that differentiates the life course approach from the individual-level life cycle or lifespan approach (Lloyd, 2012). Human development is a lifelong process, and the relationships, events and behaviours of earlier life stages influence subsequent stages.

Later life outcomes, especially those relating to health, are conceptualised as an interaction between biographical time – the influence of personal biography; historical time or cohort effect – the influence of living in a specific time period; and calendar or period time – the influence of historical events experienced by many people (Bengston et al, 2012). 'Biographical time' refers to the features of an individual's personal biography such as childhood abuse, education and employment trajectory (Pilgrim, 2007). 'Cohort effects' are those that impact on a specific birth cohort, for example the baby boomers, and 'period' effects are events such as a world war or economic recession that impact all those living at the time of that event. The fundamental premise is that what may have affected a generation or cohort is located in historical events or circumstances rather than chronology or biology. Ageing is both an individual and a collective experience. As such it needs to be explored through the lens of the individual as well as the cohort; it is a central feature of the social structuring of the life course (Dannefer, 1987).

As Victor (2010) points out this issue presents a significant challenge to gerontological research. Comparisons through time cannot distinguish between the influence of age, period or cohort; this is because we are comparing the characteristics of people of different ages who reflect different experiences of historical time in terms of period and cohort effects. Longitudinal study design – whereby data is collected at regular intervals on the same cohort over a long time span – makes attribution more likely. It strengthens the validity of links between time period, cohort, age (and other key variables) and health. The 1946 cohort study[1] is one such example (Kuh et al, 2016). The health status of older people reflects the influences of the historical period into which they were born and subsequent experiences across the life course.

In proposing a life course approach to understanding variations in health outcomes, Kuh and Ben-Shlomo (2004) identify the importance of both the accumulation of risk factors and levels of exposure. At its simplest level, exposure to risks across the life course will damage health; conversely, exposure to good habits and health-promoting behaviours will enhance health. It is argued that both biological events, for example smoking, and sociological events, for example redundancy-related stress, have an effect on health. They also argue for recognition of the role played by 'critical events' in explaining the distribution of disease across, and within, specific populations. An example of this is exposure of a baby *in utero* to the drug thalidomide[2] in the late 1950s/early 1960s which had a profound and permanent effect on the health and development of at least 2,000 people in the UK. This issue illustrates one of the tensions in the life course arena: the relative influence of genes and biological factors on the one hand and social factors on the other (Lloyd, 2012). The controversial 'Barker hypothesis' – that health and illness have their origins in the womb – was criticised for overlooking the role played by structural and social factors in shaping outcomes and heralded a move towards a broader more socially oriented perspective (Commission on the Social Determinants of Health, 2008). As well as being influenced by genetic factors, patterns of ageing and health outcomes are recognised as fundamentally dependent on an individual's social circumstances, opportunities and experiences over prior decades.

This conceptual change marked a paradigmatic shift away from viewing ageing as an '… immutable process of organismically governed change' towards recognising it as a multi-faceted sociological process (Dannefer and Settersten, 2010, p 3). This has had profound implications for our understanding of later life. It fundamentally challenges the biomedical model of ageing that dominates health care, that is, that old age is a 'disorder' or at very least a set of symptoms to be treated. It also questions the extent to which 'old age' should be managed by health professionals, the dominance of the (often) pathological discourse about ageing and the view that there is a single cause of an illness which is treatable by a medical intervention (Bowling and Dieppe, 2005). It 'complexifies' health outcomes engaging with causative mechanisms rooted in social structures, social processes and history. This is a perspective that fits ill with the traditional medical model and is an issue to which I return later in the chapter.

This paradigm also challenges the view that old age embodies a number of universal features or that there is such a thing as 'normal ageing' (Phillipson, 2013). Rather, it comprises a set of experiences that are highly diverse and varied; increasing diversity is a product of the magnitude and rapidity of social change witnessed during the 20th century (Dannefer and Settersten, 2010). While continuity remains a predominant feature of contemporary pluralistic societies, the ever increasing fluidity of the life course produces huge variation in later life trajectories (Crystal and Shea, 2003). This intersects with evidence about the role of choice and agency and 'the extent to which individuals both negotiate their own lifecourse' and shape their own biography (Larkin, 2013, p 10).

De-institutionalisation of the life course

It is suggested that the recent growth of individualism may have reduced the predictive potential of the life course approach (Higgs and Jones, 2009). De-institutionalisation of the life course is resulting in an uneven and 'ragged' relationship between chronological age and work/life transitions such as retirement (Heinz, 2003). The 'do it yourself' biography that now characterises many people's lives is evidence of the extent to which later life is differentiated (Kohli, 2007). For some, the loosening of traditional constraints offers freedom: those with adequate economic resources, good health and a planned retirement (Gilleard and Higgs, 2005). But for others the individualised life course carries a host of 'new' risks associated with being on a path that is not predictable and which relies on personal economic, social and psychological resources rather than institutionalised structures (Settersten, 2003). The current erosion of the welfare state, for example, threatens those who are vulnerable due to poverty and/or age-related ill health (Centre for Social Justice, 2010). Low income and isolation in later life is constructed as a 'personal failure' when, in fact, the major contributors are a change in state pension provision and the withdrawal of community, health and support services.

This shift in emphasis from the public to the private and from the collective to the individual particularly dis-benefits those whose life course is characterised by disadvantage. In the future it is likely that job insecurity and economic instability will increase inequality in midlife with all the attendant, amplified, risks for later life (Higgs and Jones, 2009). Although there is some evidence of the uncoupling of links between social class and later life outcomes there is parallel evidence of persistence of the influence of early life inequalities on lifelong health (Ferraro et al, 2009). One of the most influential lenses brought to bear on this dynamic discourse is that of critical social gerontology.

Critical social gerontology

As a discipline critical (social) gerontology is strongly influenced by the life course perspective (Phillips et al, 2010). It is concerned with exploring the dialectical nature of the relationship between individual and social factors across the life course (Ray et al, 2009). What it brings to the gerontological sphere is recognition that life experiences, which are inevitably organised by social relationships and embedded in socio-economic contexts, powerfully influence how people grow old. It also emphasises the power of linked lives – the ways in which the lives of individuals are intimately affected by the circumstances and actions of others – and shines a spotlight on the significance of age, not only as a property of individuals but also as a product of social structure. It explicitly sets out to explore, and expose, the situated nature of ageing and old age and the social, economic and political forces that shape it as an experience and as a life stage(s).

Critical gerontology grew out of its parent subject of gerontology in the 1980s; gerontology is itself a relatively new field of study having been established in the early 1900s. Critical gerontology is defined by Phillipson and Walker (1987, p 12) as, 'a more value-committed approach to gerontology – a commitment not just to understand the social construction of ageing but to change it' and critically analyse it. Ray (1996, p 675) defines it as 'a critique of the social influences, philosophical foundations and empirical methodologies on which gerontology as a field has been historically constructed'. It specifically challenged the 'decline and loss paradigm' that underpinned much of the (pre)existing gerontological literature and questioned taken for granted assumptions about ageing and old age (Phillipson, 2013).

Critical gerontology is predicated on a number of premises, that: older people occupy a marginalised political and economic status; societal beliefs and attitudes towards older people are negative and reductionist; traditional theories and methods employed to study ageing are narrow and biomedical in nature; and ageing is a social process as well as a biological one (Holstein and Minkler, 2007). A critical gerontological perspective seeks to make visible the often opaque, historically embedded and socio-political processes of oppression, engage with the perspectives of older people including the 'hard to reach' groups, for example people with dementia, and address issues that have largely been ignored by mainstream gerontology, such as poverty (Baars, 1991). Critical gerontology can be viewed as 'a set of perspectives that draw attention to the need to look at issues that go above and beyond conventional concerns and analyses' (Ray et al, 2009, p 24).

Early work in this field focused on the elements of what Townsend (1962) referred to as the 'structured dependency' of older people: a product of forced exclusion from the labour market, passive forms of community care and the impact of poverty. This was supported by growing evidence of the poor living conditions and mistreatment of a significant number of older people living in care homes and psychiatric hospitals, and surveys about the circumstances of older people living in the community (Phillipson, 2013). However, it was not until the 1970s that those working from within – what became known as a political economy perspective – began to raise crucial questions about how growing old was being experienced by older people themselves (Townsend, 2006). This work also highlighted the role of public policies and health and social care services in not only reinforcing and deepening the dependent status of older people but limiting their opportunities for self-determination, participation and agency.

Work generated from within the political economy domain was further developed in the 1980s and 1990s in relation to research on social inequality (Estes et al, 2003). Critical gerontologists employed the lens of the life course perspective to explore the socially structured processes of inequality; a particular focus was the role played by social class in extending and amplifying inequality in later life (Binstock, 2004). Feminist thinkers drew attention to the nature and impact of lifelong gendered inequalities on the lives of older women (Arber and Ginn, 1991; 1995a; 1995b). This 'led to a greater examination of diversity and difference encompassing racial and ethnic dimensions, disability and sexuality, and the power relationships within and between various groups' (Ray et al, 2009, p 25). Additionally, scholars drawing on the humanist perspective encouraged critical gerontologists to put a human face on the study of ageing and explore questions about 'what makes for a good life in old age' (Minkler, 1996).

The multi-disciplinary field of critical gerontology has made a number of other key contributions to challenging the way we think about, and research, ageing. These include: studying the nature and impact of ageism, age discrimination and intersectionality (Bytheway, 1995); highlighting the strengths and resources people bring to later life (Minkler and Fadem, 2002); and drawing attention to the search for meaning in old age (Cole and Sierpina, 2007). These are issues to which I return in later chapters.

One of the overriding criticisms of critical gerontology is the separation of its two substantive foundational paths, one drawn from the humanities and the other from the political economy perspective (Baars et al, 2014; Age UK, 2017). Both structural *and* individual issues need to be captured for 'a comprehensive understanding of contemporary ageing to take place'

(Estes et al, 2003, p 147, in Ray et al, 2009, p 27). While attempts have been made to organise critical gerontological thinking around key concepts such as empowerment (Minkler, 1996; Bernard, 2000) and human rights (Townsend, 2007), progress to date in combining the two pathways has been limited. What these debates have influenced, however, is a methodological shift away from a focus on the use of quantitative measures to assess a single aspect of an older person's health profile, towards research that engages with the 'lived experiences' of older people, and incorporates narrative and biographical approaches. Holstein and Minkler (2007) call for the adoption of 'methodological bricolage' which they define as 'not ruling out knowledge that is gained from personal narratives, fiction, poetry, film, qualitative investigations, philosophical inquiries, participatory action research and any other method of inquiry ... that yields insights into fundamental questions about how, and why, we experience old age in very particular ways' (p 22). This offers greater opportunity for enhancing understanding about the diversity of later life – including mental health issues – and may also make it more likely that the two aforementioned pathways are brought together in the future (Phillips et al, 2010).

A number of these strands echo work from the mental health field, particularly the role played by social structures and socio-political location in underpinning, or creating, mental health problems (Tew, 2011). The importance of biographical and related methods in research on mental health is also relevant as is an emphasis on subjective experience and service user generated understandings (Beresford et al, 2011).

One of the key contributions of critical gerontology is foregrounding the links between life course inequalities and later life health outcomes. It is to this issue that I now turn.

Health inequalities and later life

The health inequalities agenda has placed particular emphasis on a life course approach to understanding health outcomes. Although this is an expanding field of enquiry most attention has been paid to children and young adults; only recently has the focus turned to links between life course, and age-related, inequality and the health of older people (Marmot, 2005).

In terms of how inequalities themselves are understood a seminal report – The Commission on Social Determinants of Health (2008) – has been highly influential. It stated that, 'social and economic differences in health status reflect, and are caused by, social and economic inequalities in society' (p 16). The report concluded that inequalities in health arise because of inequalities in the conditions of daily life and the fundamental drivers that give rise to them: differential access to power, money and resources (Wilkinson and Pickett, 2006). These social and economic inequalities underpin the determinants of health – the range of interacting factors that shape health and well-being. These include: material circumstances, the social environment, psychosocial issues and biological factors. In turn, these factors are influenced by social position, itself shaped by education, occupation, income, gender, ethnicity and race. All these influences are themselves affected by the socio-political and cultural context in which they are situated.

In broad terms there are two types of research that explore the impact of (mainly) earlier life course influences on later life outcomes. The larger of the two bodies of work charts the impact of very early life and childhood on younger adulthood, and to a lesser extent mid and later life health (for example Barker, 1990). The smaller evidence base focuses on the impact of life events throughout the life course on outcomes in older age. This body of research subsumes two subtypes: those that examine the influence of a number of life course variables and social categories in childhood and adulthood, for example poverty and social class, on later life outcomes (Smith et al, 1997) and those that capture the impact of 'trigger events', such as loss of a spouse (McLaughlin and Jensen, 2000). The impact of age-related inequalities on mental health, including trigger events that tend to occur in later life, is the focus of Chapter 4. The role of inequalities rooted in, or arising, earlier in the life course and their links to physical and mental health outcomes is the primary focus of the rest of this chapter.

Research around social and health inequalities in later life is reflected in the extension of the life course approach by the development of the cumulative advantage and disadvantage model (CAD) through the work of researchers such as O'Rand (2001), Crystal and Shea (2003) and Dannefer (2011). This approach focuses on 'growing old as a collective process of intra-cohort stratification, as social processes allow the accumulation of advantages over the lifecourse for some, but the accretion of disadvantages for others' (Phillipson, 2013, p 42). As Fletcher and colleagues (2002) note, older people '… enter the last decades of the lifespan with the health advantage or disadvantage of earlier experiences cumulated throughout the lifecourse' (p 11). The CAD paradigm supports the popular contention that 'the rich get richer and the poor get poorer'; it explores the role played by social differentiation across the life course and its influence on later life. Dannefer (2003), analysing data from the US, called this process 'trajectories of inequality'. The increased attention paid to the impact of inequality on health outcomes is fuelled, in part, by a rapid growth in inequality in the UK in the 1980s including among older people (Rowlingson, 2011).

Life expectancy and inequalities

A fundamental indicator of inequality relates to life expectancy (Marmot, 2003). Social class exerts a strong influence on the chances of reaching old age. Although (as noted in Chapter 1) average life expectancy has increased significantly over the last century, class differentials remain; there is recent evidence that they may in fact be worsening, widening the class-related difference in all-cause mortality. There is a seven-year difference in life expectancy at birth for both men (80 years versus 73 years) and women (85 years versus 78 years) between the top and the bottom of the social class hierarchy in the UK (Moffatt et al, 2012). Although there are challenges in attributing a 'class' status to older people, work done by Nazroo and colleagues (2009) analysing deaths via English Longitudinal Study of Ageing (ELSA) data, demonstrated mortality differences for people aged 50 years and over using three measures of class: occupational class, educational qualifications, and wealth (Victor, 2010). Their work evidenced a 43 per cent lower mortality rate among managerial and professional workers compared with their counterparts who had done manual jobs. Although these distinctions were reduced they were still present for those aged 75 and over. Bowling (2004) examined evidence from 11 European countries and found that absolute and relative inequalities in mortality exist in old age, even in the oldest cohorts.

These data also demonstrate that the middle and upper classes are the most likely to benefit from health gains, including increased life expectancy (Marmot et al, 2010). For those who reach 65 years of age there is a four-year differential in further expectation of life across the class hierarchy. An advantaged life course not only results in a longer life but also a longer healthy life and a shorter period of ill health at the end of life (Majer et al, 2011). Area-based data reinforces this picture. There is a gap of 16.5 years for healthy life expectancy between men living in the most, and least, deprived areas of England; for women the difference is 12 years (Public Health England, 2015). That this gap appears to be widening is noteworthy.

Other factors that impact on life expectancy include marital status. People who spend most of their adult life being married outlive those who are not. Experience of divorce or widowhood has an adverse effect on the survival of men but not of women (Larkin, 2013).

Morbidity and inequalities

Life course inequalities have profound implications for health (Ratcliff, 2017). There is particularly strong evidence about the extension of the differential impact of socio-economic status into later life (Dorling,

2011). The term 'life course socio-economic status' (SES) describes an individual's journey from the socio-economic environment of their birth family to adulthood and beyond (Marmot and Wilkinson, 2005). Those who experience persistent exposure to low SES, especially when it begins very early in life, have lower self-related health and increased prevalence of chronic conditions in mid and later life (Hayward and Gorman, 2004; Borgonovi, 2010). Of the six major sources of chronic ill health in later life – musculoskeletal; heart and circulatory; respiratory; metabolic and endocrine; digestive; and nervous system disorders – five demonstrate that the lowest SES groupings report the highest disease prevalence rate (Victor, 2010). For example, for musculoskeletal diseases the difference between the lowest and the highest SES group are 30 per cent for men and 22 per cent for women. Recent data from the 1946 Birth Cohort study shows that childhood socio-economic conditions have a significant effect on morbidity among those aged 60 to 64 years, particularly in relationship to cardiovascular illness, cancer and cognitive function (Kuh et al, 2016). A similar pattern is in evidence in relationship to higher incidence of poor nutrition, obesity and accidental deaths (Friedli, 2009). The legacy of life course exposure to socio-economic disadvantage is also strongly correlated with the onset of long-term illness at a chronologically earlier age (Milne, 2009b).

As well as having an impact on physical health, there is strong evidence to show that people from low SES backgrounds suffer disproportionately from depression, anxiety and other 'common mental health problems' across the life course and have lower levels of psychological well-being (Campion et al, 2013; WHO, 2014). Material poverty in childhood is specifically associated with higher incidence of depression in later life (Tampubolon, 2015; Scharf et al, 2017). Survey findings suggest that poor mental health outcomes are 2 to 2.5 times higher among those in the lowest SES groups compared to those in the highest (Goldie et al, 2013). ELSA data consistently finds that people with higher SES have fewer depressive symptoms (Steptoe et al, 2013b). The HSE reports differences of 19 per cent for men and 13 per cent for women in the percentage, rating their psychological well-being as 'good', between manual and non-manual classes (Victor, 2010). Low SES in childhood is implicated in depression in midlife and people in their early to mid-60s (Bann et al, 2015).

Specific data relating to black and minority ethnic populations is also revealing. Morbidity data from the US suggests that African-American men and women are at heightened risk of experiencing a greater number of, and more severe, physical and mental health problems (Jackson and Knight, 2006). These include CVD, stroke and diabetes as well as depression, anxiety, and alcohol and drug problems (Hayward et al,

2000). In part these health disparities can be explained by SES status. Contemporary cohorts of African Americans, including older people, are much more likely than their white counterparts to have had a life course characterised by low SES with all of its concomitant disadvantages. People from minority ethnic groups in the UK tend to have lower SES too across the whole life course (Williams et al, 2010; 2015).

It is additionally relevant that the relationship between mental and physical health is bidirectional. Recent evidence suggests that depression is a risk factor for CHD and stroke; it also appears to be a stronger risk factor for diabetes than the other way around (Mezuk et al, 2008). Depression contributes to poor physical health and ability to function (Steptoe et al, 2015). Older people with low levels of psychological well-being are significantly more likely to report 'difficulties with daily living' than their peers with higher levels of psychological well-being (Evans et al, 2003b). As low SES is a life course risk factor for depression its links with enhanced risk of physical ill health amplify the need to address it through the lens of 'health' as an overarching concept.

Low SES in childhood influences adult health both through its association with adults' SES and through more direct effects on health and development such as poor diet, inadequate nutrition and poor housing (Lynch et al, 2004; Jenkins et al, 2008). It is helpful to make a distinction between the material consequences of low SES and the psychosocial impact. Low SES, especially over the long term, provokes worry, fear of getting into debt, and loss of control over life; it also undermines self-esteem and ability to make choices, access resources and engage socially in family and community life (Zavaleta et al, 2017). Pickett and colleagues (2006) refer to these as the relational or psychosocial features of deprivation. The mental health consequences of psychosocial deprivation include stress, despair, alcohol misuse, anxiety and depression (Friedli, 2009). These issues are explored in some depth later on in this chapter. The relational perspective adopted in this work intersects with the relational approach taken by prominent health sociologists, such as Bury (2005), who foreground the important role played by social and environmental influences on health across the life course. Another argument, made by Mani and colleagues (2013), is also relevant. They suggest that persistently having 'too little' – primarily money and food – narrows the mental 'bandwidth', resulting in people making decisions that go against their long-term interests. For example, not having the time or resources required to adopt 'healthy behaviours', take exercise or prepare meals from scratch.

Although there is some research which suggests that the health-related effects of low SES in childhood can be (partially) modified by upward social mobility, particularly higher earnings in young adulthood and midlife, there is mounting evidence of its persistent negative impact across the whole life course (Crystal, 2006; Tucker-Seeley et al, 2011). Cross sectional studies show that a low level of education, disability and low SES earlier in the life course are important predictors of later life poverty (McGovern and Nazroo, 2015; Allen and Daly, 2016). This reflects both the theme of continuity identified earlier in this chapter and the CAD model. There is related evidence of what Prus (2003) termed the 'divergence hypothesis': that socio-economic inequalities increase and multiply over the life course. Those with low SES not only tend to be exposed to greater cumulative risks to their health than those who are better off but they also have fewer resources or 'buffers' to protect them, for example well-developed social networks (Fawcett and Reynolds, 2010; see Chapter 10). Evidence relating to the impact of low SES and poverty in *later life* on older people's mental health is explored in Chapter 5.

The social gradient of health

These patterns are mirrored, and further explored, in the 2010 *Marmot Review* of health inequalities in England. This review identified a 'social gradient' in health (Marmot et al, 2010). It noted two overarching trends, that: inequalities impact on health across the whole socio-economic gradient and that inequality is sensitive to quite small effects of difference in class status. Figure 3.1 from the Longevity Science Advisory Panel (2011) shows how mortality rates vary by 'occupational grouping'. As can be seen, occupational status and the mortality rate have a linear relationship across the occupational gradient: the higher the occupational status the lower the age standardised mortality rate. It also reinforces evidence about the influence of geographical area. Figures relating to the North East of England, a relatively deprived region, are significantly worse across all occupational groups than those relating to the South West, a relatively affluent region (Bambra, 2016). There is an area-based association between deprivation and higher levels of CVD and diabetes (Larkin, 2013).

Even the comfortably well-off middle classes tend to have poorer health than those who are very well off. This was demonstrated in the so-called 'Whitehall Study' of civil servants conducted in the 1980s and 1990s (Marmot, 2006). This study found that civil servants in the top grade had lower risks of CHD and metabolic syndrome[3] and lower rates of deterioration in mental and physical functioning over a three-year period than those one grade below (De Vogli et al, 2007). Links between SES and mortality indices have also been confirmed in studies utilising panel data sets from the US and Sweden (Adda et al, 2003; Hamilton-West, 2011). It is noteworthy that although SES has been measured in a number of

Figure 3.1: Age standardised mortality rates by socio-economic classification (NS-SEC) in the North East and South West regions, men aged 25–64, 2001–03

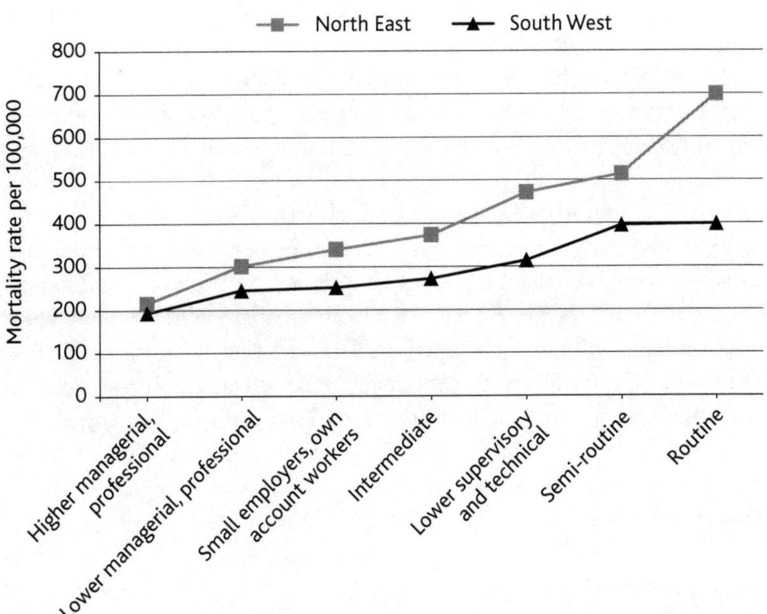

Notes: NS-SEC = National Statistics Socio-Economic Classification
Source: Office for National Statistics

different ways in large-scale studies the social gradient of health persists (Banks et al, 2006).

There is also evidence that common mental disorders are distributed along a social gradient. A review of population surveys in European countries found that higher frequencies of depression and anxiety are associated with low educational attainment, material disadvantage and unemployment, and for older people, social isolation (Fryers et al, 2005). The gradient is more marked for women than men, including older women, and for black and minority ethnic populations across the whole of the life course (McManus et al, 2009).

How inequality impacts on health: expanding the lens and the evidence base

Work on links between inequalities and health outcomes is being extended in two important ways. There is growing evidence about the links between adversity, social status anxiety, biopsychosocial processes and ill health (Adler and Snibbe, 2003). There is, in parallel, evidence about the consequences of living in an unequal society, both for individual members and society more widely. These are important links to unpack because they: strengthen existing arguments about the influence of inequalities on health; suggest that the range and nature of influence is more complex and nuanced than 'traditional' work identifies; and shift the agenda to face towards all of us rather than just those in low SES groups.

Although there is now robust evidence supporting the link between inequality, particularly low SES, and health outcomes the process of *how* inequality and disadvantage actually impact on physical and mental health is less well explored. While the direct effects of some inequalities, for example the impact of poverty on diet, may be relatively straightforward to map, it is more challenging to explain the less visible biopsychological effects. If we are to address the social causes of poor health, including mental health, we need to better understand two relationships: what are the specific dimensions of inequality that affect health and how do these dimensions cause or amplify the risks of poor health outcomes, particularly mental health outcomes? Recent work has identified a link between adversity, social status anxiety and chronic stress and between chronic stress and a number of health problems.

Adversity and chronic stress

There is growing evidence that adversity damages health. Adversity refers to experiences involving hardship or threats to well-being: they may be chronic, isolated or cumulative and may be biological, psychological or social in nature. Adversities can take a number of forms, some of which are linked to personal experiences, such as childhood abuse, and some of which are linked to social inequalities, such as low SES. Low SES is more than lack of money; it means not participating fully in society, having limited control and choices and lower levels of social engagement (Marmot, 2006). It is these factors, particularly lack of control and limited social engagement, that are increasingly implicated in the link between low SES and poor health (Rogers and Pilgrim, 2003). They are sources of chronic psychosocial stress. Although there is some basis to the argument that health may be compromised by stress-relieving, but health-damaging, behaviours such as smoking and drinking, the health gradient is *not* eliminated once these behaviours are taken account of (Steptoe et al, 2002 in Hamilton-West, 2011). This suggests other pathways are involved.

Research in the field of psychobiology looks at how adversity gets 'under the skin' (Steptoe et al, 2005). The strongest evidence identifies that chronic and/or repeated exposure to stress – such as that associated with adversity – impairs 'allostatic processes' and contributes to wear and tear on an individual's biological regulatory system (Hamilton-West, 2011). Allostasis refers to systems that maintain stability during change.

It is proposed that, over time, these regulatory systems no longer operate within normal ranges and recover less effectively from (new or additional) stressful events (Steptoe and Marmot, 2004). This has an impact on coping mechanisms and the ability to adapt to challenge and/or change. This is important as adaptability and effective coping mechanisms are primary dimensions of mental health, good quality of life and resilience. 'Allostatic load' refers to the biological 'cost' associated with maintaining stability during change(s). Another source of evidence suggests that exposure to psychosocial stress and/or trauma in early life can change the 'set point' of the body's stress response systems and predispose the individual to cardiovascular, metabolic and neuroendocrine disorders in adult life (Hamilton-West, 2011).

Cumulative exposure to adversity also causes alterations in stress responses that compromise immunity to disease; its effects have been likened to 'rapid ageing' (Shonkoff et al, 2009). Evidence is particularly well established in relationship to the development of coronary atherosclerosis, the problem underlying coronary heart disease, and also metabolic syndrome. Chronic stress is *strongly* associated with metabolic syndrome (Ryff and Singer, 2002; Friedli, 2009). Although differences observed across the social gradient, in both laboratory and naturalistic settings, are small, if 'assaults' on the system are regular and sustained, they will have a cumulative effect much like the damage done by smoking over many years (Hamilton-West, 2011). There is also emerging evidence about the role played by epigenetics. Work in this field indicates that long-term exposure to adversity may actually alter, most often weaken, the structure of DNA, which, when passed on, renders the individual's children and grandchildren physiologically more vulnerable to poor health (Notterman and Mitchell, 2015).[4]

Of particular relevance to age-related ill health is a study conducted in the 1980s and 1990s related to links between SES, a summary measure of allostatic load and all-cause mortality in older men and women (aged 70 to 79) (Seeman et al, 2004). The findings of this US study – drawn from the well-known McArthur study of successful ageing – found that higher allostatic load accounted for 35 per cent of the difference in mortality risk between those with lower SES and those with higher SES (Hamilton-West, 2011). A major UK study identified a longer recovery time from threats to health among those in lower SES groups compared with their wealthier counterparts (Steptoe and Marmot, 2004).

A review of studies evaluating the impact of chronic stress on immunity in older people concluded that 'stress processes mimic, exacerbate and sometimes accelerate the effects of ageing on immunity' (Hawkley and Cacioppo, 2004, p 118 quoted in Hamilton-West, 2011, p 133). Other work suggests that older people who have suffered chronic stress over a sustained period score worse on measures of physical and cognitive capability than those who have not (Lynch et al, 1997). Chronic stress significantly increases the risk of developing depression and anxiety in later life; people with depression are also at higher risk of developing CVD (Barth et al, 2004). This may suggest that imbalances in brain function increase allostatic load with its concomitant links to risks to physical health. Mentally healthy people appear to have lower levels of cortisol; a stress-related hormone. This reinforces the points made earlier about the bidirectional relationship between mental and physical health.

The impact of adversity in childhood and adulthood on mental health

A recent meta analysis concluded that there is a strong association between exposure to adverse childhood experiences and chronic stress, including impaired cognition, reduced social and emotional functioning and increased allostatic load (Hughes et al, 2017). Very poor mother-child attachment, abuse or neglect, lack of friends and a 'difficult early childhood' have been specifically identified as important markers of psychosocial stress (Weinfield et al, 2000; Shonkoff et al, 2011). Children who have been exposed to multiple adverse experiences are much more susceptible to disease development and the adoption of health-damaging behaviours, for example smoking, and are at significantly higher risk of mental ill health in early adulthood and midlife including anxiety, depression, self-harm and suicide (Hughes et al, 2017). There is a particularly strong association with attempted suicide.

There is a specific link between low SES and abuse and neglect in childhood. The greater the economic hardship the greater the likelihood and severity of abuse and/or neglect (Bywaters et al, 2016). Explanatory models suggest a mix of direct effects through material hardship, and indirect effects through parental stress, but interactions are complex and ill studied. In their 2017 review of evidence focused on the life course effects of child mistreatment, McCrory and colleagues (2017, p 338) concluded that abuse and neglect in childhood 'represent the *most potent predictor* of poor mental health *across the life span*' (emphasis added). Specifically, it leads to 'neurocognitive alterations that may embed latent vulnerability to future psychiatric disorders' (McCrory et al, 2017, p 349) and substantially increases the risk of a wide range of mental health problems developing during both childhood *and* adulthood (Maschi et al, 2013). It is noteworthy that adverse experiences in childhood tend to co-occur, that is, an individual child is often exposed to a number of adverse experiences; this clustering is also evident in disadvantaged communities.

Other evidence suggests that women who have been abused in childhood are four times more likely to develop major depression in midlife, a pattern that may well extend into later life (World Health Organization, 2001; Milne, 2009b). Parental discord, inadequate parenting, parental mental ill health and parental alcohol misuse are well-established risk factors for depression in midlife for both men and women (Maughan, 2002; Evans et al, 2003a). Inadequate or poor maternal attachment is a specific predictor of poor 'adult attachment'; this compromises the capacity of an individual to develop long-term relationships and friendships in adulthood. It also undermines the establishment of social networks. Given the importance of social and support networks for protecting mental health in later life (see Chapter 10) this is a significant issue and one whose legacy has long-term consequences (Fuller-Iglesias et al, 2015).

Teenage pregnancy, being unmarried at first birth and having a large number of children are linked with poor mental health outcomes in both mid and later life, including depression and alcohol misuse (Glaser et al, 2009). Other factors arising in early adulthood or midlife that impact negatively on mental health include: losing a job, being unemployed for a sustained period, working in a low control or passive job, high levels of job-related stress and experiencing redundancy or bankruptcy (Allen and Daly, 2016). There appears to be a bidirectional relationship between employment status and psychological health; poor psychological health is associated with increased likelihood of unemployment and transition to disability benefits or pension (van Rijn et al, 2014). Midlife divorce or separation is associated with higher rates of mental ill health especially depression; rates for women are higher than those for men (Evans et al, 2003b). For women being divorced or widowed at any point in their lives is an important predictor of later life poverty (see Chapter 5).

There is growing evidence of the profoundly damaging impact of sexual and domestic abuse on, mainly women's, mental health. Research reviews and landmark studies (for example Chen et al, 2010) provide 'strong confirmatory evidence that violence and abuse places mental health and personhood at risk' with effects that can be detected across most forms of adult distress and dysfunction. The 2014 UK Adult Psychiatric Morbidity Survey (McManus et al, 2016) identified that more than half of the people who had experienced severe abuse or violence in childhood or adulthood could be defined as clinically depressed or anxious. They are five times more likely than those who have not experienced abuse to develop 'a common mental health problem' and 15 times more likely to have three or more such difficulties (Williams and Watson, 2016). Feelings of anger, helplessness, hopelessness and low self-esteem are also widely reported, and acute anxiety and panic attacks are common (Fisher and Regan, 2006). Sustained abuse is implicated in heightened risk of suicide, psychosis, post-traumatic stress disorder (PTSD) and eating disorders (Williams and Watson, 2016). A 2002 study identified that midlife adults diagnosed with a mental disorder were twice as likely as those without to have experienced three major traumatic life events (Meltzer et al, 2002). These included separation or divorce, serious injury or illness, and sexual or physical assault.

Data from the 2014 Crime Survey for England and Wales[5] suggests that 28.3 per cent of women and 14.7 per cent of men aged 16 to 59 years had experienced domestic abuse 'at some point in their lives' (ONS, 2014). This is equivalent to an estimated 4.6 million women and 2.4 million men (Women's Aid, 2013). Most recently, analysis of the Adult Psychiatric Morbidity Survey, a large-scale general population study carried out in the UK, found that 1 in 25 of the population had experienced 'extensive physical and sexual violence', with an abuse history extending back to childhood (McManus et al, 2016). Women were 80 per cent of this group, nearly all of whom had been assaulted by a partner. Most had been sexually abused as a child and many had also been raped as an adult (Williams and Watson, 2016).

There is very limited work exploring the relationship between abuse experienced earlier in the life course and late life mental health outcomes (Ottmann and Maragoudaki, 2015). It could be argued that this is a gendered deficit as girls are disproportionately exposed to sexual and emotional abuse and women to domestic and sexual violence (Williams, 2005). While there is growing recognition of the prevalence of abuse and of its damaging effects on children's, and to some extent adults', mental health, more attention needs to be paid to its role in undermining late life mental health, especially for older women (Williams and Miller, 2008). Abuse, including domestic abuse and sexual violence, experienced by older women and its effect on their mental health is explored in Chapter 6.

Social status anxiety

Another key source of chronic stress is that linked to 'social evaluative threats' (Wilkinson and Pickett, 2010). These are threats which create the possibility of loss of self-esteem and/or social status. Inequality fuels social evaluative threats, increases the importance of social status and amplifies status anxiety. The larger the difference between those at the top of the social hierarchy and those at the bottom the more pronounced this effect is. Although status anxiety affects most people in an unequal society those with low SES are most affected by the corrosive consequences of marginalisation, exclusion, condemnation, devaluation and insecurity. Wilkinson and Pickett (2010) consider that the insecurities associated with low social status are 'not unlike those we may carry with us from a difficult early childhood' causing similar stress-related responses (Babones, 2009, p 164).

Even after controlling for individuals' income, research suggests the persistence of social evaluative threat. In other words, status anxiety is not (just) about income or material wealth but reflects one's own views, and the views of others, about social status and how successful one's life has been (Subramanian and Kawachi, 2004). Dickerson and Kemeny (2004, p 377) observe that 'Human beings are driven to preserve the social self and be vigilant to threats that may jeopardise their social esteem or status'. There is growing evidence that people are less likely to feel in control of their lives, happy, and optimistic if their (perceived) social status is low. This tendency is amplified among those in low SES groups who are more likely to be deprived of the markers of status (for example cars, possessions) and are thus especially 'vulnerable to the anxieties of being judged by others' (Rutherford, 2008, p 11). The role of the media in portraying certain groups as 'spongers' (for example the 2014 TV series *Benefits Street*) and other groups as unproductive 'consumers' of public resources, for example elderly people, reinforces existing distinctions.

Alain de Botton (2004) describes the failure to attain high(er) status as 'shameful'. Sen's (1992) work suggests that shame erodes self-esteem, self-worth, agency and confidence. As these constitute some of the key building blocks of positive mental health (discussed in Chapter 2), threats to their acquisition and retention is a primary concern. That status anxiety and the drive to 'improve one's position' undermines commitment to the development of family and social relationships is also relevant and links with points made elsewhere in the book about the importance of social relationships in maintaining good mental health.

Because an area reflects the social status of its occupants, a deprived neighbourhood is associated with higher levels of status anxiety (Larkin, 2013). The fact that there are higher levels of crime and violence and limited opportunities for social engagement reflects the evidence reviewed earlier about adversity and low SES (Bann et al, 2015). It also links with the points made in Chapter 1 about risks of social exclusion and isolation being greater in deprived areas.

This body of work identifies two causal pathways underpinning the development of chronic stress and explores the role chronic stress plays in causing or deepening health risks. Importantly, it also adds explanatory weight to the argument already made about links between low SES status and poor health outcomes. People from low SES groups are more likely to experience adversity and chronic stress and the concomitant physical and mental health problems (Wilkinson and Pickett, 2010). They are also less likely to have access to protective resources.

There is growing evidence from the US that black and minority ethnic groups are exposed to the persistent and additive impact of three sets of inequalities: adversity, status anxiety *and* racial discrimination (Turner and

Avison, 2003; Williams et al, 2010). Not only do these have a corrosive effect on individuals' sense of self-worth, value and self-esteem but they play a key role in undermining mental health; the effects may be particularly profound for older people who have had the longest exposure (Sproston and Mindell, 2006). It is also likely that current cohorts of minority ethnic elders would have experienced racial discrimination in multiple forms, some of which are now illegal in the US and UK, for example employment law. Its impact on opportunity and health and well-being was also (largely) unrecognised. Racial discrimination and racism compromise well-being, especially when exposure is long term; they are associated with reduced psychological morbidity, including depression and anxiety (Karban, 2017). These disadvantages are amplified in more unequal societies. Greater inequality increases downward social prejudices elevating risks of racism, for example asylum seekers being described as 'scum', and intolerance of explanatory frameworks that incorporate a structural agenda (Sidanius and Pratto, 1999).

Inequality and the health of communities and countries

There is a third source of evidence linking higher levels of inequality to poorer physical and mental health of communities and whole populations (Wilkinson, 2002). Of particular relevance to older people is evidence from a European Survey – the Survey of Health, Ageing and Retirement in Europe – which suggests that country-wide differences in relationship to rates of late life depression appear, in part at least, to be linked to levels of inequality (Rechel et al, 2013). Scandinavian countries have the lowest levels of late life depression and also have low levels of inequality (Pickett et al, 2006). Higher levels of inequality are also linked to a number of 'societal harms'. There is evidence, for example, that more unequal societies are characterised by higher levels of segregation both socially and geographically, higher rates of discrimination and violence and lower levels of trust and involvement in community life, including voluntary activities (Hall and Taylor, 2009).

Policy issues

Over the last 20 years there have been a range of policies, strategies and reviews that have either wholly, or partially, recognised links between the social determinants of health and poor health outcomes and acknowledged a need to reduce health inequalities. Examples include the 2010 *Healthy Lives, Healthy People* White Paper (HM Government, 2010), the 2013 *Inquiry on Public Health* (House of Commons Health Select Committee, 2013) and, in the mental health arena, the *Prevention Concordat for Better*

Mental Health (Public Health England, 2019) which underpinned the implementation of *NHS England's Five Year Forward View for Mental Health* (NHS England, 2016).

Evidence about the extent to which such policy commitment has been realised suggests a mixed picture. Between the late 1990s and 2010 life expectancy in deprived areas of England increased in both relative and absolute terms, rates of child and pensioner poverty fell considerably and there were improvements in the quality of social housing, particularly in the rented sector (Buck and Maguire, 2015). In short, Marmot's goal – 'to shift the gradient' – was being delivered. However, since 2010 there is evidence that these gains have slowed as measured by gaps in life expectancy and healthy life expectancy by levels of deprivation (Draper and Fenton, 2014). In 2015 an Office for National Statistics report, looking at the 2010–13 period, noted that wide inequality in health not only existed in England but that progress on reducing it had stalled with the most deprived areas and populations experiencing the worst, and worsening, health outcomes (Age UK 2016c; ONS, 2018). In part, this reflects the impact of so-called 'austerity measures' on the social determinants of health. Much higher rates of food poverty is a key example; the Trussell Trust recorded an increase of 170 per cent in the number of people seeking help from food banks in 2014 (Bambra, 2016). The Institute for Fiscal Studies predicts that income inequality will increase between 2015/16 and 2021/22 and child poverty will rise to 4 per cent; those families with larger numbers of children who are dependent on welfare benefits will be the most affected (Hood and Waters, 2017).

Marmot and colleagues (2010) suggest, however, that, more fundamentally, it reflects a lack of political will; the abandonment of specific targets to reduce health inequalities across the UK in 2012 is evidence of this (DH, 2011a: 2015a). It is also evident in the changing nature of policy discourse. Despite officially endorsing a social model of health inequalities, policy makers have increasingly shifted responsibility for health onto the individual and their 'lifestyle choices' in matters such as diet, exercise and smoking (Karban, 2017). This not only obscures the role played by social determinants but allows government, and public agencies, to reframe their role in relationship to addressing inequalities. Investment at a structural level, for example, to reduce childhood poverty, has been replaced by a targeted focus on 'at risk' populations, for example smokers. It also underplays the significance of adopting a life course lens breaking the link between the upstream, that is, what a person has been exposed to earlier in their life, and the downstream, that is, their health status later in life (Lloyd, 2012). Through the lens of Dahlgren and Whitehead's (1991) 'social model of health' policy's primary focus is now on the individual's lifestyle factors (Tier 1), and to some degree social and community factors (Tier 2), but not general socio-economic, cultural and environmental factors (Tier 3) (see Figure 3.2).

For policies that tackle health inequalities to be developed, let alone effective, it has first to be accepted that they exist and secondly that their causes are structurally reproduced. This cannot be assumed. Neo-liberal ideology regards 'variations in health outcomes' between individuals or populations as normal, even desirable, with disadvantage acting as a lever to encourage people to improve themselves and their health (Bambra, 2016). Despite the growing corpus of research which identifies associations between exposure to structurally produced inequalities and poor health, there remains uncertainty surrounding the strength and/or inevitability of causative links. If the relationship is not a definitive one then the role of policy to address life course inequalities may be questioned allowing the locus of policy rubric to be realigned, from life course to lifestyle and from structure to individual choice (Ray, 2016a). This underscores the point made earlier that the policy challenge is a political, not a technocratic, one.

The fact that health policy and practice tend to be dominated by a scientific, biomedical model that foregrounds the role played by individual behaviours is a related issue. As Lloyd (2012) quite rightly points out the complexity and multi-dimensionality of health outcomes, and their embedded nature, is a challenge to a health care system that

Figure 3.2: Social model of health

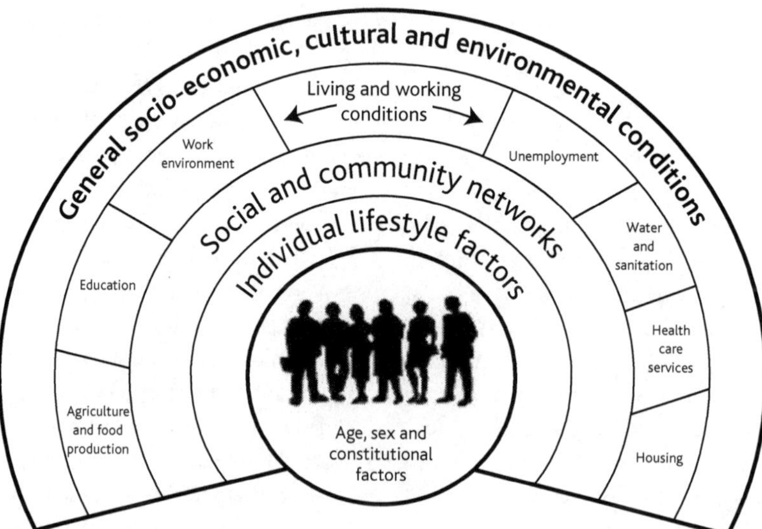

Source: Dahlgren and Whitehead, 1991

deals with the consequences rarely the causes. The fact that causal links are complex, not definitive and that there is (often) a considerable period of time between policy intervention and impact, is a key second challenge. Health-related research tends to reflect the nature of the health care model. Experimental trials predominate with a focus on 'treatments' for individual patients with (usually) one specific condition. There is far less longitudinal research regarding the impact on health of upstream interventions to reduce poverty or improve social housing on cohorts or disadvantaged groups. According to Nutbeam (2003) – quoted in Whitehead (2011) – there is an 'inverse evidence law' in health-related research, that is, the availability of evidence tends to be inversely related to the potential size and significance of the intervention's impact. The role played by commercial interests in influencing the type of research conducted is also relevant. The pharmaceutical industry, for example, has long been criticised for funding research that identifies a need, or at least a potential need, for drug treatments of 'symptoms' (Bell and Figert, 2012).

This perspective chimes with that of Hughes and colleagues (2017) who are critical of the UK's public health policy. They argue that it is driven by a focus on proximal causes of ill health – diet, smoking, lack of exercise – rather than distal causes – poverty, poor education, childhood abuse – and that a great deal more needs to be done to tackle adverse experiences in childhood and early adulthood. Despite increasing evidence about the profound effects of adverse experiences on life course health 'their prevention, and the development of interventions to address them, have been slow to move up the political agenda' (Hughes et al, 2017, p e363). Hughes and colleagues (2017) further argue that if public health policy is to embed sustained improvements in the health of the UK population it will need to shift its focus towards the early drivers of poor health, for example poverty, and adopt a life course lens that can capture the effects of interventions over the longer term (Wickham et al, 2016). These are similar arguments to those made earlier about focusing policy attention on the upstream causes rather than the downstream consequences.

I want to make a final point about the nature of policy. One of the overarching deficits of policies in the health inequalities field is how little attention is paid to links between life course determinants and later life health outcomes. Commentaries and reports rarely extend the lens of 'impact analysis' beyond midlife. For arguments about life course influences on mental health in later life to be made with strength and persuasion this is an issue that needs to be addressed and given the growth in health inequalities in the UK and its ageing profile, sooner rather than later.

Conclusion

Using the theoretical and analytical frameworks afforded by the life course approach and critical gerontology, this chapter has made the case for the role played by life course inequalities in creating, or amplifying, risks to mental health in later life (Vincent, 1995). Causative mechanisms are complex and embedded and there are a number of lenses through which links between inequality and health can be viewed. Marmot (2015), and others, argue for the salience of the socio-economic determinants of health and the role played by social categories such as class as the context for understanding health inequalities across the life course. The case made by Wilkinson and Pickett (2010) emphasises the negative impact of chronic stress and related biopsychosocial mechanisms that, they suggest, are a consequence of living in an unequal society. A third strand, associated with but not always arising from inequality, relates to the role played by exposure to personal adverse experiences, such as abuse, earlier in the life course. In order to distil outcomes relating to mental health and make connections clear, it has been necessary to review and explore evidence relating to physical health and links between physical health and mental health.

Older people 'arrive' in later life with a life course. The life course shapes health outcomes, including mental health outcomes, in profound ways. Older people whose life course has been characterised by low SES have shorter lives and are at increased risk of experiencing a range of mental health problems, including depression and anxiety. They also tend to report lower levels of psychological well-being. That low SES has a direct impact on health, for example poor diet, as well as indirect psychosocial effects, such as worry and reduced ability to socially engage has specific implications for mental health. The fact that common mental disorders are distributed along a social gradient, including in later life, is a reflection of the influential role played by social determinants. Establishing the biopsychosocial mechanisms that are a product of exposure to adversity, chronic stress and social status anxiety helps to explain enhanced risk of experiencing a number of mental health problems. These include depression and anxiety and lowered cognitive capacity. Other psychological consequences – linked particularly to social status anxiety – include limited control over one's life, poor self-esteem and reduced sense of agency; exclusion and isolation are also consequences. Exposure to adverse experiences such as abuse, trauma and/or violence in childhood is strongly associated with poor mental health across the whole lifespan, including depression, anxiety and self-harm. Sexual and domestic abuse at any life stage is also a significant threat to mental health.

That inequality is also linked to higher levels of mental ill health across whole communities and countries is additionally relevant. Specifically, in more unequal societies there are higher rates of depression among the older population. There are also lower levels of trust and community involvement and higher levels of segregation, discrimination and violence.

Overall, the role played by inequalities in creating and/or amplifying mental health problems in later life is considerable: their influence is both direct and indirect, psychological and sociological, and individual and collective. Life course research demonstrates that once embedded inequalities remain part of an individual's life trajectory; they tend to accumulate and deepen over time (Phillipson, 2013). 'Disadvantage is not an event that strikes at a single point' (Graham, 2004; Graham and Power, 2004, p 1). Life course analysis also highlights the relationship between the individual life course and the social process of inequality, they '... relate to each other like lock and key; it is their intersection that needs to be understood if one is to appreciate ... the implications of inequality for mental health' (Wilkinson and Pickett, 2010, p 32). Key dimensions of the constructs outlined in Chapter 2 include self-esteem, agency, resilience, social support, choice and control, and having an adequate income; inequality profoundly threatens these foundation stones of mental health and well-being in ways we are only beginning to unpick.

The role of policy in addressing health inequalities and their social determinants is contested (British Medical Association, 2011). Up until about 2011 this was an embedded dimension of health policy, including mental health policy (Goldie et al, 2013, WHO, 2014). Since 2012, the shift towards neo-liberalism, funding cuts to services and a narrowing of the role of the welfare state has resulted in a reduction of commitment and resources to tackling health inequalities and the social determinants of health. Although there is a link between policy-driven investment in social determinants, for example poverty, and key markers of health inequality such as life expectancy in deprived areas, it is not definitive. Because health inequalities are persistent, their reduction needs to be an explicit and sustained goal of policy. Action is required across a range of policy domains, for example education, housing, as well as in health itself for it to have an impact on health outcomes across the life course (Lloyd, 2012). The role of policy in preventing mental ill health and promoting mental health is discussed in Chapter 10.

Inevitably, by focusing on life course inequalities in this chapter, some issues have received less attention. These include cohort effects, genetic and biological heritage, and environmental factors such as pollution. While these are significant factors, making the case for the role played by inequalities as a relatively underexplored, and yet profoundly influential, issue has greater capacity to enhance our understanding of mental (ill) health in later life. It also acts as a counterweight to the dominant discourse that conceptualises both the cause and resolution of mental health problems as the responsibility of the individual.

A note on methodological and conceptual issues

It is important to recognise that inequalities develop, accumulate and intersect in ways that are challenging to capture and map. It is also shifting terrain. Although the life course perspective offers a dynamic model for exploring the relationship between inequalities, in all their forms, and mental health in later life, it is a considerable methodological challenge to establish the nature of interrelationships (Vincent, 2006; Lloyd, 2012). Even if one establishes a relationship between one or more inequalities and mental health outcomes, it is quite another matter to establish a causal one. One of the weaknesses of much of the data we currently collect is its incapacity to facilitate multiple analysis of disadvantage, especially longitudinally (Jones and Higgs, 2015). Although the evidence base is growing much remains to be done.

A second issue relates to definitions of key social categories. Social class, for example, is no longer the fixed category it once was. This raises a number of questions about how to capture and assess it both between cohorts and through time. There have long been questions about the validity of class as a social category pertaining to later life, and some commentators suggest that the socio-economic lens we use to define class fails to reflect the way it is reproduced. Skeggs (2004) argues that narratives of the 'everyday' are an important way in which class distinctions are maintained. The work of Bourdieu (1984) suggests that class position is constructed and maintained through the accumulation and retention of different forms of economic, cultural and social capital (Jones and Higgs, 2015). Resources in later life offer the opportunity to retain, or even acquire, class advantage (McGovern and Nazroo, 2015). Which class individuals perceive themselves to belong to is also an influence. These more nuanced concepts not only challenge existing definitions and ways to evaluate class but challenge the idea that class is fixed by employment and income status earlier in life and is not amenable to change in later life. It also raises questions about how to evaluate class status; how social class intersects with old age remains a key challenge. In this chapter I have reviewed a lot of evidence relating to SES which is not a proxy for social class but intersects with it. As SES is a relatively fixed unit of analysis it is useful to be able to draw upon data relating to it. Its usefulness does not eclipse the importance of tackling the social class question but, in so doing, the relationship between the two needs to be considered.

However significant earlier life course inequalities may be in influencing mental health outcomes, 'new' inequalities arising in later life, and the extension and amplification of existing inequalities, are also very important. It is these I explore in Chapter 4.

4

The impact of age-related risks and inequalities on mental health in later life

Older people's mental health is a product of both earlier life course experiences and experiences specific to later life. The role and impact of age-related risks and inequalities on psychological well-being and mental health is the focus of Chapter 4. It is important to acknowledge that 'later life' is now positioned as a social category of some significance: a period of life in which 'practices of distinction' take place and risks to mental health can be exacerbated and/or take root (Krekula, 2009, p 8).

In broad terms there are two sets, or groups, of age-related risks. The first set are those arising directly from experiences common to old age and include physical ill health, bereavement and loss. As has been explored in Chapter 3 while some of these risks, for example physical ill health are in part at least, a product of life course exposure to disadvantage, they are risks that tend to be more prevalent as people age. The second set of risks arises from ageism and age discrimination, and their intersection with other structural inequalities, such as sexism for older women.

Individual age-related risks

Most of the evidence relating to heightened risks of developing a functional mental health problem in later life relates to depression. The most significant risk factors for depression are losses as a result of ill health and disability, caring, bereavement, retirement and 'daily hassles' (Godfrey, 2009). As noted in Chapter 2, it is important to recognise that while these issues do not necessarily lead to depressive symptoms they do have a negative impact on psychological well-being and may act as triggers for the development of depression (Steptoe et al, 2015). Some commentators would argue that the boundary between depression and impaired psychological well-being is uneven especially when 'symptoms' may be short term or mild (Keyes, 2002). There is growing evidence that older people will 'suffer in silence' or mask their negative feelings with alcohol or medication.

Physical ill health and disability

As noted in Chapter 1, the prevalence of ill health and long-term conditions increases with advancing age (Age UK, 2016a). Sixty-nine per cent of people aged over 75 have at least one illness or disability. A significant minority of older people experience multi-morbidity: commonly termed 'frailty' (British Geriatrics Society, 2014; frailty is explored in Chapter 7). It is well established that physical ill health and disability are key risk factors for a number of common mental health problems, notably depression (Victor, 2010). Most studies find that rates of depression are approximately double for older people suffering from ill health compared to their healthy counterparts. Estimates suggest that 70 per cent of new cases of depression in older people are related to poor physical health. Older people with mobility problems are particularly at risk, being three to four times more likely to be depressed than those without (Godfrey et al, 2005). Evidence from the 2014 Adult Psychiatric Morbidity Survey suggests that 'sub threshold levels of symptoms of depression' are 'relatively common' among those with chronic physical ill health, the majority of whom are older (McManus et al, 2016).

The general consensus is that it is not illness or disability per se that is key in vulnerability to depression but their *impact*: pain, loss of functional ability and independence, and restrictions in undertaking valued activities, particularly social participation (Godfrey, 2009). There is an interactive and cumulative relationship between ill health, functional ability, social isolation and depression that may in turn lead to increased disability and reduced psychological well-being. Specific evidence of a bidirectional relationship between depression and some physical health conditions noted in Chapters 2 and 3 – namely stroke, IHD and diabetes – adds weight to this argument. There is specific evidence that risk of CVD is directly related to severity of depression: a one to twofold increase for minor depression and three to fivefold increase for major depression (Keyes, 2005). There is also increasing evidence that 'sudden onset events' such as a fall, perceived as a threat to loss of independence by the older person, is a risk factor for anxiety (Godfrey, 2009).

Sleep problems are common in later life and pose a threat to well-being; advancing age is associated with progressive deterioration in quality of sleep. Good-quality sleep is consistently identified as pivotal to older people's ability to engage in daytime activities and participate socially. Chronic sleep disturbance increases the risk of developing depression (Venn and Arber, 2011).

Caring in later life

Over a third of the UK's 6.5 million carers are 'older', that is, aged 65 years and over (Carers UK, 2016). Most older carers support a spouse or very elderly parent. Older carers disproportionately provide intensive levels of care: support that involves physical care, personal care and sometimes quasi medical care (for example, monitoring intravenous medication) and requires many hours. Dementia care is a defining dimension of late life caring (Henwood et al, 2019). Providing intensive care is strongly associated with reduced physical and mental health, including heightened risk of cardiac and back problems, hypertension, sleep problems and fatigue (Hirst, 2005). Two thirds of older carers have health problems of their own which may be exacerbated by caring (Henwood et al, 2019). Many older carers find it difficult to attend hospital appointments or take care of themselves due to care-related demands.

There is specific evidence that caring, especially over the longer term, is correlated with depression and other psychological morbidity, for example a third of people who provide care to a relative with dementia suffer from depression (Henwood et al, 2019). The factors distinguishing those who develop depression from those who do not appear to be related to: higher levels of behavioural problems in the person with dementia, the carer being physically and/or emotionally depleted by caring activities, and 'feeling trapped' (Larkin and Milne, 2014). Similar findings emerge from studies of carers of people who have had a stroke or suffer from heart disease. Carers may also be victims of assault or abuse, for example being hit by their relative with dementia and may themselves become abusive often as a consequence of frustration, fatigue and/or lack of support (see Abuse and mistreatment of older people in Chapter 6). Long-term intensive carers also report feeling isolated and being 'in a state of constant worry' (Larkin et al, 2019). They are also at risk of falling into poverty as a consequence of the combined impact of living on a fixed income, higher household expenses, for example extra laundry associated with incontinence, and paying for social care services for the person they look after.

Bereavement and loss

Bereavement is a common experience in later life. Older women are especially vulnerable to the loss of a spouse (or partner); this is a reflection of men having shorter life expectancy and a historical tendency for women to marry a man older than themselves. Currently, about half of older women are widowed compared with a fifth of older men, a gender gap that widens with age (Victor, 2005). Widowed men are at greater risk of poor health outcomes and of premature death than widowed women particularly during the first year post-bereavement (Isherwood et al, 2017). Bereavement is certainly one of the most widely cited causes of isolation; combined with disability and functional impairment, it significantly increases the risk of loneliness (Victor et al, 2009). A larger mixed social network can ameliorate this risk; older women tend to have access to larger networks made up of friends and relatives whereas men tend to rely on their wives alone (Green, 2010; Grundy and Tomassini, 2010). Some widows develop a new sense of freedom and purpose; this is especially the case for those who have been caring for a partner with dementia (Larkin and Milne, 2014).

Loss of key relationships, especially the death of a spouse, is implicated in the development of acute depression, anxiety and excessive alcohol consumption (Byrne, 2013; Bartlam and Machin, 2016). As noted in Chapter 1, a significant minority of older people, between 10 and 20 per cent, suffer complicated grief reactions. The loss of a confidante is specifically associated with reduced psychological well-being. The existence of an 'intimate, confiding relationship' is a major factor in ameliorating the impact of age-related losses, including widowhood (Bowling et al, 2002). Older people without confidantes report higher levels of psychological distress and higher rates of depression (Prince et al, 1997).

Losses that impact on mental health are not only linked to people. The loss of home and security contingent upon admission to hospital or a care home can be very traumatic especially if ill managed, related to a crisis or linked to another loss, for example of a family carer (Dening and Milne, 2011; Tanner et al, 2015). The death of a family pet can also represent a profound loss (McNicholas, 2014).

Loss of loved ones, home and social networks are implicated in the (re)emergence of symptoms of PTSD. It is thought that losses may make coping with memories of earlier trauma(s) more challenging and that the 'coping mechanisms' used in early adulthood and midlife, for example heavy drinking, may no longer be available or as effective (Ong et al, 2006). A particular cohort that experience PTSD in later life are (mainly male) war veterans (Durai et al, 2011). Women who have been exposed to domestic and/or sexual abuse, including rape, are another group; this is an issue, and population, that is explored in Chapter 6.

Retirement and (re)employment

'Retirement' from paid work has become an embedded life course transition in all industrialised societies (Kohli, 1987). Although the average age of retirement in the UK is 64.5 for men and 62.4 for women this figure hides a wide variation: manual workers tend to retire much earlier often due to work-related health problems while professionals and white-collar workers tend to work for longer (Ní Léime et al, 2017). Most people spend at least two decades in retirement. As discussed in Chapter 3 the increasingly de-institutionalised life course is producing much greater variety of retirement patterns and is uncoupling chronological age from retirement (Heinz, 2003).

While, overall, retirement is associated with improved psychological well-being, to a large extent the post-retirement phase of life is a product of pre-retirement circumstances (Mein et al, 2003; Vickerstaff, 2006). Those who leave well paid jobs in good health with an occupational pension are in a much stronger position to enjoy a positive retirement compared with those on low incomes who are dependent on the state retirement pension (McCormick et al, 2009). For those who gained benefits related to working, such as a valued role, status and identity and opportunities for social engagement, retirement is more likely to be associated with reduced psychological well-being, increased alcohol consumption and isolation (Djernes, 2006).

Women's retirement patterns tend to be very different from those of men (Phillips et al, 2010). It is often noted that women 'never retire' as most continue to do domestic work in the home post-employment. For some midlife women, retiring from paid work may be a response to an increased need to provide family care for a disabled older relative (Larkin and Milne, 2014). This is often associated with reduced current and future income.

There is mixed evidence about the role played by 'early retirement'. Similarly, to the broader point made earlier, those who wish to retire and have resources to do so (generally) benefit while those who retire 'reluctantly' and with no or limited access to an occupational pension tend to fare badly (Larkin, 2013). Psychological problems, including mental health problems, in childhood and adulthood has been specifically identified as a key predictor of premature,[1] and often involuntary, labour force exit (van Rijn et al, 2014). Poor psychological health at *any life stage* significantly reduces the likelihood of being in paid work in later life (Clark et al, 2017). Only 40 per cent of those with long-term depression aged between 50 and state pension retirement age (SPA) are employed; the figure is 20 per cent for those with a long-term mental health problem (Department for Work and Pensions (DWP), 2014). Once this group of older workers leave the labour market they tend to remain outside of it permanently. (Vickerstaff et al, 2013).

Currently about a half of all those over SPA continue to work (DWP, 2014). While this may be positive for more advantaged workers such as professionals, working beyond the SPA is much less attractive for those who have physically and/or emotionally demanding jobs such as labourers or care home staff (Ní Léime et al, 2017). These workers also tend to face a higher level of competition from the core-age workforce reducing their opportunities to remain in employment (Lain, 2012).

It is noteworthy that a small, but growing, number of employers are actively recruiting older workers: workers aged 50 years and over (Centre for Ageing Better, 2019). Evidence drawn from a study of B&Q (DIY chain) – a long-standing champion of employing older staff – suggests that older workers not only help to reflect the diversity of the company's customer base but also directly contribute to improving profitability, the quality of customer service, and reducing staff turnover and rates of absenteeism (Healthy Working Lives and Chartered Institute of Personnel and Development, 2012).

Daily hassles

The psychological literature on coping and adjustment makes a helpful distinction between so called 'daily hassles' such as changing light bulbs and sorting out bills, and major stressors such as deteriorating physical health or bereavement (Godfrey and Denby, 2004). Daily hassles emerge, or become visible, when an older person has limited social contacts to call upon for help; they also act as a constant reminder of reduced functional ability. There is evidence that daily hassles are more strongly correlated with stress and reduced psychological well-being, at least in the short term, than major life events (Kanner et al, 1981). The implication of this finding is that addressing the daily hassles that challenge older people may be a useful way to improve psychological well-being; drawing on older people's own strategies for dealing with these may also be instructive.

Age-related lifestyle

Some aspects of older people's lifestyles directly threaten their physical and mental health. These are often behaviours and/or patterns that have been developed earlier in the life course that extend into later life.

Overconsumption of alcohol is one such issue (McCormick et al, 2009). The proportion of older 'problem drinkers' is rising, especially among women. As noted in Chapter 1, older people are more susceptible to alcohol-related health problems than younger adults and are also more prone to falls (Hallgren et al, 2010). Heavy drinking is a risk factor for a number of health problems, particularly heart disease, stroke, gastrointestinal cancers, liver cirrhosis, cognitive deficits and sleep problems. It may also be both a cause and a consequence of isolation, loneliness and depression and a way to manage loss and anxiety (Byrne, 2013). More positively, smoking among those aged 60 and over has consistently been the lowest of all of the adult age groups for over 40 years and those who stop smoking between the aged of 60 and 75 can reduce their risk of dying prematurely by up to 50 per cent (Livingstone et al, 2017).

Being overweight is also an issue. Those aged 65 and over tend to have higher rates of obesity and are less likely to address weight-related risks than younger adults, partly because they tend to underestimate their weight. In 2008, almost three quarters of those aged between 65 and 74 years and over two thirds of those aged 75 years and over were classified as obese or overweight (ONS, 2010). Obesity is an important public health issue; it not only damages health directly, for example mobility problems, but reduces the likelihood of an older person engaging in health-promoting activity. There is also evidence that being overweight impacts negatively on psychological well-being and is implicated in depression (Public Health England, 2013).

Physical inactivity in later life has been linked to increased mortality, 'cardiovascular disease, diabetes, obesity, osteoporosis, musculoskeletal problems, several cancers and depression….' (Victor, 2010, p 137). In 2015, among those aged 65 years and over in England, 43 per cent of men and 34 per cent of women reported taking 'at least 30 minutes of moderate to vigorous physical exercise on at least five days per week'; this compares with a 56 per cent population average (Age UK, 2016a). Although increasing numbers of older people appear to be engaging in 'moderate physical activity' the numbers are still low, and the proportion decreases with advancing years (Audickas, 2017).

It is worth noting that lifestyle factors often interact with each another deepening risks to health. For example, overconsumption of alcohol is linked with both poor diet and obesity with lack of exercise.

Age-related structural inequalities: risks to late life mental health

The role played by structural inequalities is also a risk to mental health in later life. A powerful example is that of ageism and age discrimination and their intersection with other structural inequalities such as sexism and racism. It is important to explore this issue in some depth as ageism and age discrimination have an impact on all older people and are exclusive to experiences in later life.

Ageism and age discrimination

Ageism is defined as a 'process of systematic stereotyping of older people because they are old, just as racism and sexism accomplish this for skin colour and gender' (Butler, 1969, p 243). It is '… a matrix of beliefs and attitudes which legitimises the use of age as a means of identifying a particular social group … it portrays the members of that group in negative terms and generates and reinforces a fear of the ageing process and a denigration of older people' (Hughes, 1995, p 42). Old-age stereotypes are almost universally negative and are associated with ill health, dependency, isolation, limited social and personal lives, and incapacity to exercise choice, control or self-determination (Victor, 2005). 'Old age' is constructed as a differentiating variable conferring a fixed and homogenous social identity upon *all* older people, obscuring differences arising from race, gender and/or disability and between groups, cohorts and individual older people. Ageism also disconnects old age from earlier phases of life thereby failing to acknowledge the influence of life course experiences, including inequalities, on later life outcomes.

Ageism manifests directly and indirectly in every sphere of life and in the macro, meso and micro domains of UK society (Sargent-Cox, 2017). It is visible in social and economic policies, in the media and in attitudes towards older people. Exclusion from membership of juries for those aged over 75 years (in England and Wales) and the welfare benefit, the 'Personal Independence Payment', only being available to those aged up to 64 years are prominent examples. Other examples include few opportunities for older women actors in TV and film and widespread use of demeaning terminology to describe older women – 'old dear' or worse, 'old bag'. In Victor's (2005) view ageism 'condones and sanctions the subordination and marginalisation of older people within society and legitimises (or at least ignores) poor quality care, neglect, and social exclusion' (p 156). Ageism is also internalised by older people themselves who may accept negative stereotypes.

Ageism also serves to reinforce age-related norms (Bytheway, 1995). 'Age norms' are social prescriptions for, or proscriptions against, involvement in 'inappropriate' activities or roles at particular ages. Social norms relating to older people tend to constrain behaviour, restrict choice and opportunity and (re)produce ageist stereotypes. Age-appropriateness is not a characteristic of the individual but a social and historical construction; what older people are 'allowed' to do now may be more permissive than was the case 25 years ago. For example, older women going on cruises alone and some acceptance that older people have fun and may even have sex. The regulatory power of age-related norms is realised in the course of everyday interactions and experiences in families, communities and services (Settersten, 2003).

Ageism intersects with sexism, racism and prejudice against members of the LGBTQ+ communities and/or those with lifelong disabilities in ways that extends its impact. Older women report that they feel 'ignored', 'sexless' and 'useless', a manifestation of the 'double whammy' of sexism and ageism, and black older women report being exposed to the 'triple jeopardy' of sexism, ageism and racism (Moriarty and Butt, 2004; Ray et al, 2015). The double and triple jeopardy thesis advances the belief that older women and black elders are exposed to repeated and multiple negative social experiences that combine and intersect to amplify the effects of ageism (Phillips et al, 2010). There is certainly evidence that perceived age discrimination is more prevalent among women than men and, as noted in Chapter 3, racial discrimination extends across the whole life course for people from black and minority ethnic groups (Lee and Turney, 2012).

Age discrimination, a manifestation of ageism, is defined as 'an unjustifiable difference in attitude, response, or treatment based solely on age' (Centre for Policy on Ageing, 2009a; 2009b). It is widely viewed as taking two forms: acute and chronic. Evidence suggests that acute age discrimination is experienced by older people in relation to: access to employment, health and social care services, welfare benefits and in financial, insurance and retail services (Help the Aged, 2004; Age UK, 2016c). A specific example is women aged 70 years and over being excluded from England's national breast cancer screening programme.[2] Age discrimination in relationship to employment and health and social care services is explored in more detail later. An example of 'chronic' age discrimination is persistently being treated with less respect than younger adults: older people commonly report feeling undervalued, disrespected and ignored (Age Concern and Mental Health Foundation, 2006). Acute and chronic age discrimination often co-occur. A 2013 survey suggested that in England 37 per cent of people aged 65 years and over perceive themselves to be the subject of age discrimination with many viewing it as 'a multi-level barrier to opportunity and inclusion' (Rippon et al, 2014). The UK has been ranked lowest overall on the 'Experiences of Ageing' matrix developed for a European survey in 2011 (Women's Royal Voluntary Service, 2012). Older people in the UK are more concerned about age discrimination than their counterparts in the Netherlands, Germany and Sweden (Abrams and Swift, 2012).

Ageism and age discrimination represent important elements of the way in which older people experience later life and gain access to, or not, socially valued roles and resources. They underpin and foster a culture that tends to overlook their views and contributes to their oft-reported sense of being cast aside. As discussed next, ageism and age discrimination have a corrosive effect on mental health.

The effects of ageism and age discrimination on psychological well-being and mental health

It is well established that those who are subject to discrimination in any form are more likely to experience compromised psychological well-being and are at greater risk of developing mental health problems (Yuan, 2007). Discrimination is associated with fear, frustration, helplessness, hopelessness, low self-esteem, anxiety and depression (Williams et al, 2003; Jackson et al, 2019). It is also linked to exclusion, marginalisation and abuse (see Chapter 6) and, as identified in Chapter 3, undermines a person's overall 'capacity to flourish' (Sen, 1992). In 2007, an NHS Health Scotland report identified harassment as one of the direct effects of age discrimination, and exclusion from activities as one of the indirect effects; both have mental health consequences associated with feeling unworthy and rejected (NHS Health Scotland, 2007). Lee and Turney (2012) argue that the effect of perceived discrimination on mental health is similar in magnitude to the effect of more commonly studied psychosocial stressors such as job loss, divorce and the death of a loved one.

Ageism has specifically been identified as having a pernicious negative impact on older people's mental health (Age Concern and Mental Health Foundation, 2006). It contributes to feelings of worthlessness, despair, increased feelings of loneliness, depression and anxiety; it is also associated with lower levels of subjective well-being (Age Concern and University of Kent, 2005; Sargent-Cox, 2017). Older people themselves refer to 'everyday ageism' as 'an assault' on their sense of self (Adams et al, 2013). There is also some evidence that 'holding negative age stereotypes' may be associated with Alzheimer's pathology such as greater accumulation of neurofibrillary tangles and amyloid plaques (Levy, 2016). Conversely, positive age stereotypes are associated with positive health outcomes including lower cortisol levels and 'feeling valued and useful' (Levy, 2016).

Internalised ageism may also contribute to lower levels of engagement with health protective behaviours. For example, work by Wurm and colleagues (2013) – referred to in Sargent-Cox's 2017 editorial – found that older people who held negative age stereotypes were less likely to use strategies that promoted recovery following a serious health event. Negative attitudes have also been shown to manifest as barriers to seeking treatment, particularly for conditions that are considered age-related (Sargent-Cox, 2017). A 2003 study, for example, found that older people who viewed depression as a 'normal part of ageing' were four times less likely than those who did not to consider discussing their concerns with their GP (Sarkisian et al, 2003).

This evidence dovetails with two related sets of evidence discussed in Chapter 3. The first refers to the role of chronic psychosocial stress in undermining mental health. The second relates to the damage done to the mental health of people from black and minority ethnic groups as a consequence of intersecting inequalities – persistent exposure to adversity, status anxiety and racial discrimination. While the nature of age discrimination is very different from racial discrimination, its omnipresence, chronicity and capacity to intersect with other types of discrimination are shared characteristics. There is growing evidence, for example, that age discrimination has an amplified negative impact on the psychological well-being of older women, black and minority ethnic elders, LGBTQ+ elders and older people with disabilities (Ray et al, 2015). As Morrow and Weisser (2012) note, 'experienced and enacted intersectionality' is likely to compromise health and well-being especially mental health. That these groups are also more vulnerable to poverty and low SES links to the points made in Chapter 3 about 'exposure to adversity'. They are situated on the experiential nexus of discrimination, oppression and disadvantage.

It is important to acknowledge that women, people from black and minority ethnic groups, gay men and lesbians and those with lifelong disabilities are exposed to a lifetime of discrimination. Age discrimination may be new to them but being discriminated against is not. For some other groups, for example professional white men, later life may be the first time they experience discrimination. As Calasanti and Slevin (2001, p 193) observe '… ageism is the one oppression that we will all face' if we live long enough. The interrelationships between inequalities, psychosocial stress, racial discrimination, age discrimination and mental health in later life have been the focus of limited work; it is ill understood and warrants further attention.

As ageism and age discrimination in the workplace and in health and social care services are relevant to significant numbers of older people these warrant particular attention.

Ageism and age discrimination in the workplace

Despite the fact that age discrimination in the workplace has been outlawed in Britain since 2006 it is well documented that ageism negatively affects older workers' job security, retention, training and promotion (Hurd-Clarke and Korotchenko, 2016). Employers are often reluctant to hire and retain older workers as they are assumed to be less flexible, competent, skilled, productive and adaptable than their younger counterparts; older workers frequently experience involuntary early retirement (Loretto and White, 2006). Gendered ageism results in older female employees being subject to the 'double jeopardy' noted earlier: they tend to be viewed as less competent than either men *or* younger women (Walker et al, 2007).

It is challenging to find evidence about the impact of ageism in the workplace on mental health. What we do know is that 'younger' older workers, that is, 45 to 54 years and workers with low SES appear to be particularly at risk of mental health problems and that stress at work is now one of the most common forms of psychological distress in the UK (McManus et al, 2016). It is likely that ageism and age discrimination at work have similar effects to those identified earlier in relationship to age discrimination more widely. The employers who are actively recruiting older workers (discussed earlier) offer an important counter narrative to ageism in the workplace.

Ageism and age discrimination in health and social care services

Whether in an emergency, or helping to manage a long-term condition, the NHS is vital to the lives of many older people. Despite a downward trend until 2010, since then the overall number of hospital admissions has risen significantly; it is up by 9 per cent from 14.9 million a year in 2010/11 to 16.2 million in 2015/16. Older people account for almost two thirds of – both general and acute – admissions to hospital and up to a quarter of these are people with dementia. Older people's hospital stays are on average of 2.5 times longer than those of younger adults (NHS Benchmarking Network, 2016).

In 2010/11, nearly two thirds of the 885,000 adults receiving community-based services were aged 65 years and over (Health and Social Care Information Centre, 2011; Humphries et al, 2016). Older people accounted for nearly 60 per cent of the £16.1 billion spent on social care by English local authorities in 2010; in 2014/15 the proportion of the overall figure of £22.09 billion was 42 per cent (DH, 2010a; Department of Communities and Local Government, 2014). In part, this proportional reduction reflects definitional changes but it primarily represents an actual reduction in overall spend on older people as a group. This is especially significant if one takes account of the ageing population profile of the UK and rising levels of need for care. Local authority support is targeted, through stringent eligibility criteria, on those with the highest levels of need so older service users who are 'eligible' are likely to have complex needs and to require help with activities of daily living (Humphries et al, 2016).

The fact that two thirds of NHS patients are aged 65 and over and yet receive only two fifths of total expenditure suggests the existence of structural discrimination in the allocation of health care resources (Age UK, 2016c). Some would argue that it is built into health care decision-making by the widespread use of the notion of quality-adjusted life years,[3] such as in the approval of prescription medication (Bywaters, 2009; Swift et al, 2017). Age discrimination also underpins the allocation and nature of medical treatments. One example is evidence from a 2012–14 study by the Royal College of Surgeons that treatment rates drop rapidly for most types of surgery for people aged over 70 years (Royal College of Surgeons, Age UK and MHP Health Mandate, 2015). The national breast screening programme excluding women aged 70 years and over is a second example (noted earlier), and men aged 75 years and over being far less likely than younger men to receive radical forms of treatment for non-metastatic prostate cancer is a third (Fairley et al, 2009). A primary care-based study in London identified that patients aged over 84 years are prescribed fewer recommended coronary heart disease drugs such as beta blockers than those aged 45 to 54 years (Mathur et al, 2011). Evidence of the impact of 'double jeopardy' suggests that women aged 75 and over are a tenth as likely as a woman aged 40 to 64 to receive the best standard of treatment for a heart attack and half as likely as an older man (Shaw et al, 2004).

In terms of the mental health field, the 2009 *New Horizons* strategy identified, '... indisputable evidence that older people experience widespread discrimination' in the planning, allocation and delivery of mental health services and persistent variations in their quality and availability' (DH, 2009b, p 71; Healthcare Commission, 2009; Mental Health Foundation, 2009). A key example is that 85 per cent of older people with depression receive no help at all from the NHS (Royal College of Psychiatrists, 2018). Of those who do access treatment far more are offered drugs such as tranquillisers than talking therapies compared with younger patients; older people with depression's support packages are routinely of much lower cost too (Beecham et al, 2008; Hirst, 2009; Melzer et al, 2012). That far fewer older people are offered therapy via the 'Improving Access to Psychological Therapies'[4] service (IAPT) is also discriminatory, despite evidence that IAPT can be a *more* effective treatment for older people than younger people (DH, 2011b; Age UK, 2016b; Pettit et al, 2017). While calls for older people to be offered the same range of services as younger adults have been made, a separate but equally strong, argument has been made for specialist services which can cater for the complex intersecting needs that older people with mental health problems – and their families – often have (Humphries, 2015; Age UK, 2016b). These specialist mental health services are under significant threat (Royal College of Psychiatrists, 2018).

Mental health services tend not to be sensitive to the needs of older women. There is limited acknowledgement of women's exposure to life course and age-related inequalities and links between these and mental ill health, particularly depression (Williams and Watson, 2016). That older women may present with a different set of 'symptoms' than younger women *or* older men also tends to go unrecognised; these include higher rates of irritability, sleep problems and loss of interest in the activities they usually enjoy (Whiteman et al, 2016). They may also be reluctant to come forward for help as a consequence of their responsibilities, for example caregiving. As older women are the primary users of mental health services it is a neglectful at best, and discriminatory at worst, that much better account is not taken of their particular needs (Whiteman et al, 2016).

Discriminatory patterns are mirrored in social care services too. Lack of investment in innovative provision, the assumption that older people's needs can be met by 'practical services' and limited involvement of professionally qualified staff in work with older service users are prominent examples (Centre for Workforce Intelligence, 2012; Ray et al, 2015). The fact that older people tend to be allocated smaller personal budgets[5] than other user groups is overtly discriminatory (Hatton and Walters, 2012). Discrimination may also play a role in decisions relating to direct payments[6] as fewer older people are in receipt of these relative to other user groups, for example younger adults with disabilities (Fenton, 2015). It could also be argued that the welfare benefits system is discriminatory; people aged 65 and over are not able to make a new claim for Disability Living Allowance.

In terms of evidence about the specific impact of age discrimination in services, there is evidence that older people who are exposed to care which is '… unintentionally disempowering and deprives them of agency and control' is damaging to psychological well-being (Edmondson, 2013). 'Acceptance', or more likely acquiescence to, sub-optimal treatment and care induces stress and reinforces a sense of non-desert (Golub and Langer, 2007). That some services are abusive and/or neglectful is, some would argue, the end of a continuum that begins with inadequate care. This issue is explored in Chapter 5.

A note about cuts and related changes

Recent reductions in spending on NHS and publicly funded social care services amplify the risk of age discrimination. As older people are the largest, and growing, group of service users negative changes are likely to affect them disproportionately. A recent study provides robust evidence that, since 2010, the combined effects of cuts to health care and social care have resulted in '120,000 excess deaths';[7] the groups particularly affected are those aged 85 years and over living in the community and in care homes (Hiam et al, 2017). The study also estimates that by 2020 there will be at least 150,000 more excess deaths. The vast majority of these will be older people (Watkins et al, 2017). Cuts to Pension Credit are also life-threatening. Loopstra and colleagues (2016) examined annual percentage changes in mortality rates of people aged 85 years across 324 local authorities in England between 2007 and 2013. They concluded that each 1 per cent decline in Pension Credit spending per beneficiary was associated with an increased mortality rate of 0.68 per cent.

The total level of real term spending cuts to social care budgets between 2011 and 2013 was £2.8 billion; spending decreased by 1.19 per cent annually between 2010 and 2014 (National Audit Office, 2014). In England, the percentage of the older population receiving support from local authority funded social care fell from 15.3 per cent in 2005/06 to 9.2 per cent in 2013/14 (Humphries, 2013; 2015). Analysis by Fernandez and colleagues (2013) identified that in 2012 English councils were supporting half of the older people they were in 2010. In 2016, Age UK reported that nearly 1.2 million people aged 65 years and over did not receive the help they needed with 'essential daily living activities' such as dressing and bathing; a significant proportion received no help at all (Age UK, 2016d). As there is an association between poverty and disability – see Chapter 3 – it is likely that this group are the most disadvantaged. Fernandez and colleagues' analysis (2013, p 8) concluded that 'although reduced access to (social care) services affects a lot of older people, the poor will be the biggest losers'. The operation of the 'inverse care law' is also relevant; current models of local government funding systematically disadvantage people in deprived areas compounding already entrenched health inequalities (Oliver, 2018).

Increasing emphasis on allocating direct payments to service users may, paradoxically, threaten older peoples' mental health. Evidence suggests that older people in receipt of direct payments have higher levels of mental ill health and lower levels of well-being than those who did not opt to have one, that is, they retain the local authority organised services (Moran et al, 2013). One of the main causes was the anxiety created by being responsible for managing a budget and organising their own support.

Of linked relevance is the state-driven shift away from publicly funded to privately funded care. In 2012 it was estimated that 300,000 older people wholly, or partially, funded their own community-based care in England; this figure is much higher now although actual figures do not exist. In terms of care homes, in 2014, 44 per cent of all residents were self-funders in England (LaingBuisson, 2014; House of Commons, 2017). There is growing evidence that self-funders cross-subsidise those funded by the local authority and that care homes are increasingly relying on this subsidy in order to generate sufficient income (Forder and Fernández, 2010; LaingBuisson, 2017; NHS Digital, 2017b).

While cuts to health and social care services, and related funding changes, are not overtly discriminatory they combine to disadvantage and exclude older people who are ill and who often have profound levels of need for care and support. This is axiomatically damaging to physical and mental health and is particularly harmful to those older people who have the fewest resources.

Care practice

In terms of delivery of care in 2012, 21 per cent of older inpatients reported that they were not always 'treated with respect for their dignity and privacy' by hospital staff (Care Quality Commission, 2013). The fact this figure is the same as was the case when the survey was first conducted in 2002 is particularly concerning. Health and social care staff are routinely reported as using derogatory language about older patients, for example, 'bed blockers'. There is also a tendency, fuelled by a narrow biomedical model of ageing, to emphasise 'functional deficits' in health and social care assessments disconnecting physical health from psychological well-being and 'symptoms' from the person (Grenier, 2006). Risk reduction is often a primary goal of assessment rather than promotion of quality of life of the older person (Marshall and Tibbs, 2006). There is a related tendency for practitioners to construe ordinary personality traits in a negative way; for example, assertive behaviour may be viewed as 'stubbornness' or unwillingness to consider admission to a care home as 'resistance' (Thompson, 2005).

Reductions in time spent with older patients is one of the key consequences of recent cuts. In 2013, a Royal College of Nursing survey of community nurses found that although they were supporting older people with more complex needs the time spent with them had reduced; only 6 per cent considered that they had 'sufficient time to deliver the care the patient needed' (Ball et al, 2014). Documented consequences include less opportunity to build up a trust relationship and limited engagement with the concerns of the older person (Fawcett and Reynolds, 2010). Shorter visits to older service users by home care workers, as a consequence of cutbacks in local authority commissioning budgets, is another example. This shift is widely regarded as discriminatory and potentially abusive (see Abuse and mistreatment of older people in Chapter 6). In 2011 the Equality and Human Rights Commission reported that it is 'commonplace' for older people to be excluded from decisions about their own care, and a recent report commissioned by the Fawcett Society suggests that patients are increasingly being made to 'feel like a commodity' on a conveyer belt (Hayes, 2013, p 119). The development of inappropriate and unsustainable support is also more likely in contexts where due weight is not given to the older person and their family's perspective (Richards, 2000).

As women account for over two thirds of older users of community care services, and many carers are female too, women are disproportionately affected by these changes. There is evidence, for example, that older people who experience marginalisation in service settings and lack of involvement in their own care are at heightened risk of depression and anxiety (Milne, 2016). In its Convention report relating to discrimination against women the United Nations (2010, p 8) concluded that 'unfair resource allocation, limited access to services and neglect' by health and social care workers have a direct impact on the mental health of older women. That these issues tend to go unrecognised by policy makers, the 'care system' and staff within it is, of itself, an additional assault on older women's sense of self-worth and well-being.

Policy issues

In this section I will offer a brief overview of policies that are relevant to addressing age-related risks to mental health.

Policy and older people with health-related needs

As Ray (2016a, p 30) notes policy for older people is neither developed nor implemented in a rational or linear way but is 'rather developed incrementally and its progress is shaped and influenced by numerous factors'. Health and welfare policy illustrates this pattern well; it tends to be fragmented and atomised with an, often considerable, gap between policy rhetoric and policy action. It is vulnerable to political vicissitude and economic concerns about funding and tends to be accorded much lower priority than policy for other groups, for example children.

There are in fact very few policies that focus on older people; they tend to be included in wider policies such as those relating to care and support and/or mental health. The Care Act 2014 is a key example (see Chapter 1). In recent years there has been a thrust in mental health policy for older people to achieve parity with younger adults, also for policies relating to physical and mental health to be joined up to a greater degree. Examples include *No Health without Mental Health* (HM Government, 2011; see Chapter 1) and *Let's Get Moving* which highlights the benefits of physical activity for both physical *and* mental health (DH, 2009c). It is noteworthy that despite the parity claim the *Five Year Forward View* – which built on *No Health without Mental Health* – allocated no dedicated funding to meeting the needs of older people (Royal College of Psychiatrists, 2018).

It is important to acknowledge that there have been some improvements in mental health services for older people, mainly in the dementia arena (Ray, 2016a). Much greater attention being paid to dementia by policy makers has resulted in significant changes to commissioning and to service development and design (see later chapters). There have also been some system-wide improvements. For example, a 2016 NHS benchmarking project found that, 91 per cent of participating Trusts providing acute services have 'a protocol for accessing specialist mental health services for older people' and that 'depression was routinely assessed for in older people in 62 per cent of participating organisations' (NHS Benchmarking Network, 2016). Concerns remain that developments in this arena are slow and uneven; progress is also threatened by recent cuts (Humphries et al, 2016).

Encouraging the 'care system' to work better and more efficiently is a long-standing policy concern. A key focus of *Improving Care and Saving Money* (DH, 2010b) was to shift the care and support system for older people towards prevention and early intervention. While promoting a model of care that targets the development of difficulties at an early stage is self-evidently positive, critics would argue that the policy's primary emphasis is on the avoidance of use of expensive services such as hospitals, and saving public money and not about 'improving care'. More recently and with more urgency, commentators have described the care system as 'broken', especially in England. The 2014 Commission on the Future of Health and Social Care in England (aka the Barker Commission) concluded that the challenges of an ageing population in 21st-century Britain cannot be effectively met by 'muddling through' and that the existing model of care is 'unsustainable'. The Commission proposed a ring-fenced budget with a single commissioning function and free care for all of those whose needs are complex and challenging to separate into 'health' or 'social' care; this is especially relevant to older people with dementia and/or frailty (Humphries, 2015). These proposals were rejected as 'too expensive' but the issue of squaring the circle of affordability and sustainability in care remains a significant public and policy challenge.

Ageism and age discrimination

Drawing attention to the endemic age-based discrimination in policy is an important first step in addressing it. Lloyd and colleagues (2014b) suggest that a number of policies directed at older people are, paradoxically, inherently ageist. 'Active ageing' policies are a prominent example (Boudiny, 2013). They place responsibility on the individual older person advising them to 'adopt a healthy lifestyle' in order that they do not make 'excess' demands on health services. The OECD policy on 'healthy ageing' specifically urges older people to 'take more exercise' and 'eat a better diet' (Oxley, 2009). The related policy focus on self-care, maximising independence and reducing use of costly services is also relevant. The moral agenda underpinning these policy messages is inextricably linked with questions of entitlement to health care and the costs of care. They also link to points made in Chapter 3 in relationship to health inequalities and underscore the shift towards a neo-liberal discourse away from structural and/or social explanations for health problems. This is a particularly problematic, and some might say unjust, message in relationship to older people for both the reasons outlined in Chapter 3 and in this chapter.

An overarching observation about most policies relating to care and support for older people is their limited focus on older people with chronic comorbid health problems and/or a mix of physical and mental health problems. Responses relating to, and services to help address, the long-term effects on mental health of some of the key challenges that often accompany later life are oddly absent from the very policies that one might imagine are developed precisely with these issues in mind. This is in part a reflection of the nature of policy making which tends to focus on a single issue; it struggles to deal with comorbidity and complexity and is usually developed with a short-term horizon in mind. It may not be ageist as such but paying limited attention to those issues that are more likely to emerge and co-occur in later life while at the same time reducing access to, and investment in, care services for those older people who need support from such services is at the very least an abdication of public responsibility (Royal College of Psychiatrists, 2018).

There is, at the same time, evidence of explicit attempts to address ageism and age discrimination in the policy-making arena. They take two main forms. The development of policies to combat (mainly direct) age discrimination and attempts to embed equity in policies and services that older people access. The cornerstone of the Equality Act 2010 is the public-sector equality duty, which requires all public bodies, and those performing public functions, to eliminate 'unlawful discrimination, advance equality of opportunity and foster good relations between groups' (p 96). Public bodies such as local authorities, transport authorities and the police service have a duty to take account of the needs of people with protected characteristics, including older people, when carrying out their functions and planning their activities. For example, if a transport provider is considering cancelling a rural bus service and that service is used by a significant number of older people to access health and community services, their needs would have to be considered in making the decision (Women's Royal Voluntary Service, 2013).

Outlawing age discrimination in employment is one of the other key provisions of the Equality Act 2010. In 2012, the default retirement age of 65 was abolished. This coincided with a policy shift towards 'extending working lives', driven partly by a need to raise the age at which state retirement pensions will be paid in the future and partly by the financial benefits of working for both individuals and the economy (Vickerstaff et al, 2008; Phillipson et al, 2016). In the last quarter of 2014 there were 1.13 million people aged 65 and over in employment; 643,000 men and 460,000 women (DWP, 2014). This primarily represents retention of older workers in existing employment rather than (re)employment (Kanabar, 2012). Although evidence to date suggests that working for longer is psychologically beneficial, as this only reflects the profile of the healthier, better off workforce it needs to be treated with caution. There is concern that once working beyond SPA becomes a universal requirement of all employees, including those with health problems, the psychological health of the older workforce will significantly worsen (Di Gessa et al, 2017). Phillipson and colleagues (2016) also warn that enthusiasm for 'flexible working', which many older workers interpret as phased retirement, needs to tempered by the reality that for many employers this equates with zero hours contracts and shift systems that entrench already poor employment conditions for (many) older workers. This may be especially bad news for those people with mental health problems. One of the related risks arising from the collision between the deinstitutionalisation of retirement in the mid to late 20th century and extending paid work for as long as possible, is that people may find themselves caught between insecure work on the one side and increasingly insecure retirement on the other (Dewilde, 2012; Phillipson, 2013). The mental health consequences of this assault on security and certainty have yet to be explored.

A third plank of the Equality Act 2010 is outlawing age discrimination in health and social care. Although this legal duty reinforced a long-standing policy commitment to addressing age discrimination in mental health services, progress has been slow. In good part this relates to cost. In 2008, it was estimated that 'eliminating age discrimination in mental health services' would require extra expenditure of around £2 billion (Beecham et al, 2008). I have already highlighted areas where (some) improvements have been made (but many commentators consider that mental health services for older people retain the 'cinderella status' they had in the 1980's (Centre for Policy on Ageing, 2009b).

There is a broader policy role in relationship to raising public and media awareness about the importance of recognising and addressing age discrimination and ageist attitudes. This includes undertaking campaigns to increase knowledge about the range and diversity of the 'ageing experience' and ensuring that a balanced view of ageing is presented in the media. In 2016, on the International Day of Older Persons the World Health Organization ran a campaign exposing the extent of discrimination and negative attitudes towards older people worldwide and the impact of these on their mental health and well-being (WHO, 2013; Officer et al, 2016). The United Nations is under growing international pressure to establish a Convention for the Rights of Older People; one of its key dimensions is addressing ageism and age discrimination globally (HelpAge International, 2015). Local and national older people's organisations also play an important role. In 2017, for example, Age UK launched a London-focused campaign called 'Age Allies'. It aimed to help make London a more age-friendly city; its activities include delivering free workshops to businesses and organisations promoting inclusion of older people.

Family carers

Carers are the focus of a number of intersecting policies whose collective aims are to: recognise their role and contribution; identify and address their needs; help them to live a fulfilled life outside caring; and support them to remain in paid work (Larkin and Milne, 2014). The Care Act 2014 consolidates previous legislative requirements relating to carers and introduces a 'parity of esteem' between carers and service users, strengthening carers' rights to an assessment of need and placing a new duty on local authorities to fund support to meet carers' eligible needs, as well as entitling them to information and advice. Despite their enhanced public and policy profile studies show that many carers – including many older carers – are routinely overlooked and unsupported (Pickard et al, 2016; Henwood et al, 2019). There is specific evidence that carers' willingness and ability to care is often assumed by assessors and few carers receive a separate assessment (Moran et al, 2012; Carers UK, 2016). Paradoxically, the introduction of parity of esteem may have made more visible the challenges inherent in balancing the interests and well-being of carers with those of the cared for person. Some would argue that it exposes an uncomfortable tension between policy claims regarding the importance of support for carers on the one hand and an austerity fuelled policy drive that expects families to pick up the ever increasing 'tab for care' on the other.

Conclusion

This chapter has brought together evidence relating to the role and impact of two sets of age-related issues on mental health in later life: experiences common to old age and the structural inequalities of ageism and age discrimination.

A number of risks to mental health present for the first time, and often in combination, in later life. Ill health and disability, long-term caring, bereavement and loss, retirement and 'daily hassles' are much more prevalent in older age than earlier in the life course. They are all, to varying degrees, implicated in reduced psychological well-being and increased vulnerability to common mental health problems, particularly depression. Some aspects of older people's lifestyles also undermine physical and mental health. It is important to recognise that a number of age-related risks have roots in the life course and, while age amplifies them, they often have structural causes, for example vulnerability to ill health.

Age-related risks are intertwined with, and compounded by, the structural inequalities of ageism and age discrimination. These twin processes serve to systematically stereotype older people portraying them in almost wholly negative terms and generate a fear of the ageing process. Ageism and age discrimination are embedded in, and permeate, structures, care services, workplaces and public attitudes. They take direct and indirect forms and are overt and covert in nature.

Ageism and age discrimination have a corrosive impact on older people's mental health and act as a multi-level barrier to opportunity, participation, inclusion and ability to access socially valued resources. Older people report feeling ignored, undervalued and disrespected in daily encounters, and ageism is implicated in increased risks of exclusion, isolation, lower levels of subjective well-being and depression. Ageism intersects with sexism, racism and prejudice against gay men and lesbians and/or those with lifelong disabilities in ways that amplify its negative psychological impact.

Policies that are relevant to older people with health-related needs have been developed in a piecemeal and incremental way. Despite the specific inclusion of older people in policies on mental health and the inclusion of mental health issues in policies relating to older people there is limited evidence of improvement. There is widespread concern that the goals of prevention, integration and raising the quality of care are being undermined by cuts to welfare services and fragmentation of the system. This is particularly bad news for older people with chronic comorbid conditions and/or whose needs straddle the 'physical' and 'mental health' domains. The neo-liberal discourse, that permeates policy thinking, also places emphasis on reducing demand on expensive care services and shifting responsibility for care onto the individual and their family. Policies to address ageism and age discrimination have had mixed success. While it is important to acknowledge the role of the Equality Act 2010 in outlawing age discrimination in care services, the workplace and the public domain, much work remains to be done in terms of ensuring that older people at risk of, or with, mental health problems gain timely access to care and support, that older people are not discriminated against by employers and that negative attitudes and stereotypes are challenged.

One of the weaknesses of policy making and policy thinking in relationship to older people's mental health, including mental ill health, is the lack of joined-up whole systems cross-government thinking. This in part reflects its complexity. The issues explored in this chapter suggest that age-related risks to mental health are a mix of those events that are more prevalent in later life and the impact of structural inequalities of (mainly) ageism and age discrimination. Their intersection is an added third dimension. That some age-related risks are, in part at least, a product of the life course is an important, but often obscured, dimension of the causative arguments that link Chapters 3 and 4 and that make visible the plural interconnected nature of risks to mental health in later life.

There are also a number of risks that affect the mental health of subpopulations of older people. These risks are the focus of Chapters 5, 6 and 7.

5

Socio-economic disadvantage and poverty

In addition to the issues explored in Chapter 4 there are a number of risks and inequalities that affect the mental health and well-being of particular groups of older people. The nature and impact of three prominent issues are explored in Chapters 5 to 7: socio-economic disadvantage and poverty; abuse and mistreatment; and the fourth age, frailty and transitions. While not experienced by all, or even the majority of older people, these are risks that have powerful implications for mental health and, as such, warrant specific exploration.

It is important to note that the three sets of risks are conceptually distinctive. Socio-economic disadvantage affects a particular subpopulation of older people (usually) across the whole trajectory of their later lives; abuse and mistreatment affects a number of particular groups of older people in both service settings and the community; and issues arising from the fourth age and transitions affect all of those older people who achieve very late life. In each chapter I offer a summary of the key issues before focusing on evidence about how they impact on older people's mental health and well-being; policy issues are also discussed. At the end of Chapter 7 I offer a conclusion drawing together the key threads of all three chapters.

Age-related socio-economic inequalities

Despite growing interest in the intersection of life course inequalities with late life mental health outcomes, surprisingly little work has been done on exploring the role played by socio-economic inequalities in late life itself. While most late life inequalities have roots earlier in life, the difference is that once a person reaches later life s/he has limited (or no) opportunity to significantly alter their socio-economic status (SES). If you are poor at 65 years old you are very likely to be poor until you die. This could be a period of 40 years. There is of course huge diversity between groups, cohorts and social categories and a great variety of individual experience but key stratifications appear to be, at least partially, fixed; late life tends to amplify what is already present.

While there can be little doubt that socio-economic inequalities affect well-being, distilling connections is complex. The evidence base is uneven. Most evidence relates to the damaging role poverty plays;

being poor in later life compromises mental health and well-being in a number of profound ways. Poverty's concomitants, including poor housing and living in a deprived neighbourhood, also undermine mental health deepening the impact of poverty. There is much less evidence about how older people manage on a low income or how links between socio-economic disadvantage and health outcomes are made by older people themselves.

Income-related poverty

The economic position of older people in the UK has improved significantly since the end of World War II. Older people hold more assets than ever before. In 2016, 76 per cent of older households were owner-occupiers; of these 71 per cent owned their homes outright (Pannell et al, 2012; Age UK, 2016a). In 2014, Age UK (2014b) estimated that older people contribute £61 billion a year to the economy.

Although pensioner poverty has halved since the 1970s, many older people still live on low or very low incomes (Department for Work and Pensions (DWP), 2017a; 2017b). Forty-six per cent of pensioner couples and 16 per cent of single pensioners have no source of income other than the state retirement pension and related benefits (Hancock et al, 2016). Figures show that in 2016/17, 1.9 million older people were living in poverty;[1] of this group 1 million were living in severe poverty and a further 1.2 million had incomes just above the poverty line (DWP, 2017a). Since records began older people have consistently been one of the largest groups of UK citizens living in long-term poverty (Price, 2006). It is instructive to note that the risk of poverty for an older person in the UK is almost 2.5 times higher than the risk of poverty elsewhere in Europe and the fourth highest of the European Union (Zaidi et al, 2006; European Commission, 2009). Retirement from paid work, loss of a spouse – and thereby loss of marital status – and the onset of disability are the key 'triggers' for poverty in later life (Joseph Rowntree Foundation, 2016).

One of the main reasons pensioner poverty fell in the first decade of the 2000s was increased uptake of pension credit. That even small improvements to an older person's income can have a significant impact on quality of life including promoting independence and facilitating social participation suggests that one of the key mechanisms to reducing poverty is to improve uptake of benefits (Smale et al, 2000). The government estimates that in 2014–15, up to £3.8 billion of low income benefits to older people (Pension Credit and Housing Benefit) went unclaimed (DWP, 2017b). About one in three of those eligible (4 million older people) are still not claiming these despite regular campaigns by Age UK and other agencies to raise public awareness. There are a number of reasons for this. Many older people regard claiming benefits, including disability benefits, as stigmatising; the confusion and complexity of the benefits system is also a barrier (Moffatt and Higgs, 2007).

The role of disability-related benefits is to compensate for the additional costs that disabilities often create. These may include care needs, for example help with cleaning, shopping and cooking, additional transport costs and/or adaptations to the home such as installing a stair lift. In 2015, 8 per cent of the population aged 65 years and over received Disability Living Allowance and 14 per cent claimed Attendance Allowance.[2] While there is some evidence that these benefits protect those with less chronic forms of disability from poverty, those with longer-term and/or more severe disabilities – which tend to be more expensive to manage – are not protected. As older people are more likely to have chronic and/or long-term disabilities they are particularly disadvantaged by this model (Hancock et al, 2016).

State-funded sources of income (state retirement pension and welfare benefits) remain crucial to maintaining living standards among older people. In 2012/13 state benefits accounted for 44 per cent of the overall income of UK pensioners; they represented more than half of the incomes of retired households in the bottom three income quartiles and 79 per cent of the incomes of the poorest segments (Phillipson et al, 2016).

Two overarching income-related trends are important to highlight. Although the numbers of older people living on low incomes fell substantially until about 2010, progress has now stalled; numbers have been static in recent years. Sixteen per cent of pensioners lived in poverty in 2015/16, a rise of 3 per cent since 2011/12 (Barnard et al, 2017). This is partly a reflection of changes to welfare benefits and reductions in overall allowances. In the 1980s and 1990s the value of the state pension fell and it continues to fall; this is especially problematic when there have been significant increases in energy and food prices (Barnard et al, 2017). It is also a reflection of growing numbers of older people in the 'at risk' groups (to be discussed later). A lack of political will to prioritise this issue is an additional factor.

The second trend is an overall shift towards greater inequality within the older population; the gap between those who are better off and those living on low incomes is growing (Scharf et al, 2017). Income inequality in later life is greater now than it was in the 1970s; socio-economic differentials are widening with age (Mishra et al, 2004). Current pension policies, which are downgrading the role of the state pension and emphasising private pension arrangements, reinforce pay inequalities creating 'two nations' in old age (Victor, 2005; Phillipson, 2011). There is linked evidence of widening inequalities in relation to social class, gender, ethnicity and, as noted earlier, disability (Moffatt et al, 2012).

The impact of living on a low income

A fundamental challenge for older people living on low incomes is paying for essentials. In 2009, 42 per cent of older people reported that they 'struggled' to afford items such as food and fuel. In 2012, 22 per cent (3 million) of older people skipped meals to cut back on food costs, and in 2015, Age UK reported that one in five older people were denying themselves food to pay for heating (Age UK, 2016a; Purdam et al, 2016). Recent estimates suggest that 1.3 million older people (the majority of whom live in the community) suffer from malnutrition (Age UK, 2016a). This number has trebled in the decade between 2005–06 and 2015–16 (Forsey, 2018). As an inadequate diet impairs health – at all stages of the life course – and contributes to premature death these figures are very concerning (Adler et al, 2016; ONS, 2017b). That the situation is also likely to get worse as food prices increase is an additional issue.

Socio-economic deprivation in later life is often reflective of life course SES status. It is axiomatic that living on a low income forces individuals to make choices which ultimately inhibit their ability to save or contribute to a pension, thereby diminishing financial security in older age. The role played by the narrowing of the mental bandwidth referred to in Chapter 3 is also relevant.

Socio-economically vulnerable groups

The pattern of unequal ageing particularly disadvantages certain groups. People aged 85 years and over, frail and/or disabled older people, single people living alone, long-term carers, private tenants and older people from minority ethnic populations are at enhanced risk of living in poverty, including severe and long-term poverty (McGuiness, 2018). For example, 18 per cent of those aged 85 years and over live in poverty compared to 12 per cent of those under 70 years (Age UK, 2014b). These groups also have the fewest accumulated material resources.

Women predominate in many of the 'at risk' groups. Most poor older people are female. Although women outnumber men by just less than two to one in the over 75 years age group, among single pensioners in this cohort poor women outnumber poor men by almost four to one (Price, 2006; Phillipson et al, 2016). Single pensioners have less than half the earnings of married pensioners; over a quarter of single female pensioners have no savings at all (Allen, 2008; DWP, 2017a). Married women who are divorced or widowed in later life are particularly at risk of becoming poor (Scharf et al, 2017). For women late life poverty is primarily a consequence of gender-related inequalities across the life course. These include: greater likelihood of fragmented work histories and reduced opportunity to build up an occupational pension, time out to raise children and/or care for elderly relatives and long-term exposure to pay inequalities (Milne and Williams, 2000; Williams, 2005). Recent evidence suggests that the gender pay gap is worsening not improving which will have significant implications for the SES of older women (Elming et al, 2016). A number of these issues were explored in Chapter 3.

Older people from black and minority ethnic groups have also been exposed to a set of intersecting life course risks. They are more likely to have been in unskilled poorly paid jobs, have fragmented employment histories and have limited access to occupational pensions (Vlachantoni et al, 2017). Forty-eight per cent of Pakistani and Bangladeshi pensioners live in poverty compared to 24 per cent of their white counterparts (DWP, 2012).

Poor housing, fuel poverty and deprivation

Older people living on low incomes also tend to be disadvantaged in other material ways (McCormick et al, 2009). They are more likely to experience fuel poverty,[3] occupy inadequate housing and live in environments that can feel unsafe, such as run-down housing estates (Scharf et al, 2004; Office of the Deputy Prime Minister, 2006; Social Exclusion Unit, 2006).

Six million older people (3.5 million households) were estimated to live in fuel poverty in 2011 (Age UK, 2015). On average, 75 years and over households spend much more of their annual income on fuel: 45 per cent compared to an all-age average of 5.3 per cent. The UK has the highest rate of fuel poverty in Europe (Association for the Conservation of Energy, 2013). In 2012/13, over a quarter of all older households[4] in the UK (26.1 per cent) lived in 'inadequate housing' and one in eight 75 years and over households were identified as having substandard heating and insulation (Garrett and Burris, 2015). 'Inadequate housing' means homes that lack adequate heating, are damp, have faulty or unsafe wiring and/or are located in a deprived neighbourhood (Department of Communities and Local Government, 2013). Older people in privately rented accommodation are at the greatest risk of living in inadequate housing.

The UK has the highest rate of 'excess winter deaths'[5] in Europe; the rate is above those of much colder countries, for example Siberia (Pannell et al, 2012). It has been estimated that between 25,000 and 50,000 of excess winter deaths in the UK are the result of the combined impact of difficult to heat housing and fuel poverty (ONS, 2017d). A higher proportion of UK-based older people 'dread the winter' than is the case in Sweden, and in 2013, 28 per cent (3 million) of older people reported that they were 'worried about staying warm in their home' in cold weather (Age UK, 2016a).

It is noteworthy that poor housing and excess cold are primary, and very expensive, causes of admission to hospital of a significant number of older people (Balfour and Allen, 2014; NHS Benchmarking Network, 2016). Age UK (2016a) have estimated that the cost of cold homes to the NHS in England is around £1.36 billion per year. In addition to issues relating to 'inadequacy' there is evidence that there are shortages of specially adapted accommodation. Over three quarters of a million people aged 65 and over need specialised housing because of a medical condition or disability; in 2013, 145,000 of this group reported living in homes that did not meet their needs (Department of Communities and Local Government, 2013).

In 2016, 2,420 older people were recorded as homeless. Unofficially, the number is considered to be much higher; a figure of 42,000 has been estimated for England and Wales (Warnes and Crane, 2006). A recent report by the Local Government Association (LGA) suggests that there has been a 130 per cent increase in the number of older homeless people over the last eight years in England and Wales; among those aged 75 years and over the increase has been 155 per cent (Leng, 2017). Nearly ten people aged 60 years or over are accepted by councils every day as 'vulnerable' and thereby have a right to be housed; this is a figure predicted to double by 2025 (Leng, 2017). For two thirds of this older population homelessness is a new experience. The cause is often a combination of adverse events primarily relating to: marital breakdown or loss of a close relative, health problems and/or accommodation issues such as the property needing repairs or being in rent arrears (Crane and Warnes, 2010). More older homeless people are male than female. Being homeless is self-evidently bad for an older person's health and is strongly correlated with heightened risk of morbidity and premature death (Leng, 2017).

A note on socio-economic status in later life

There are a number of challenges relating to assessing and measuring SES status in later life. 'Occupational class' as a definitional category is certainly much less theoretically robust once people reach state pension age; SES status appears to have most effect via the accumulation of material resources and cultural and social capital (Jones and Higgs, 2015). It is noteworthy that not all commentators agree that earlier life course SES has the influential role suggested here. They argue that deinstitutionalisation of the life course is destabilising the link between earlier and later life SES, and that one's late life SES status is more amenable to change than has hitherto been the case (Ferraro et al, 2008). While SES may not intersect with health in the way it does earlier in the life course it remains a major axis of social differentiation in older age and one whose dimensions, and relationship with health, has been the subject of limited analysis. A number of these points link with the discussion pertaining to social class and later life at the end of Chapter 3.

Socio-economic inequalities in later life and mental health

While exploring the impact of late life socio-economic disadvantage on physical and mental health is instructive, it is important to recognise that, for many older people, their health may have already been damaged by life course exposure. Impact is likely to be cumulative *and* additive; disadvantage rarely travels alone. Inequalities develop, deepen and intersect in later life in ways that are ill understood. Capturing the impact of a multi-dimensional issue is a complex challenge and one that researchers have yet to address in a coherent way. The evidence reviewed here builds on that explored in Chapter 3.

There is a significant correlation between poverty and lack of social participation, limited social support, marginalisation, isolation and exclusion (Killeen, 2008). In surveys, 'having enough money to meet my needs' is persistently correlated with capacity for social engagement (Ipsos MORI, 2015). A report by the Centre for Social Justice (2010) identified that at least 2 million older people were living on incomes so low that they 'failed to ensure participation in society to any meaningful degree'. Poverty is also implicated in the development of loneliness and depression which is, interestingly, associated with a heightened risk of malnutrition (Eskelinen et al, 2016). Recent evidence that older people on low incomes are much less likely to be 'digitally included' than either their better off peers or younger adults is also relevant as more and more services are moving to online platforms, and internet-based communication plays an ever-greater role in all of our lives (Age UK, 2016d).

Living in poverty, particularly severe or persistent poverty, is linked with worry, loss of control over life, lack of choice and limited independence (Victor et al, 2009). Being in debt, or on the edge of falling into debt, is not only anxiety provoking but is associated with shame and lack of self-worth (McNeill, 2014). It is chronically stressful and profoundly undermines psychological well-being (Grundy and Sloggett, 2003). Huisman and colleagues (2013) argue that, 'socioeconomic adversity is among the foremost fundamental causes of human suffering and this is no less true in old age' (p 84). Recent analytical modelling of data from a large-scale survey reinforces these findings concluding that 'socioeconomic position has a significant direct influence on wellbeing' as well as a strong indirect effect which is mediated by health status and lifestyle (Pratschke et al, 2017, p 1770).

Poor older people are especially vulnerable to stress-related mental health problems such as anxiety; many are reluctant to ask for help partly because they feel they should have made 'provision for their old age' (Howden-Chapman et al, 2011). Secondary analysis of ELSA data suggests that older people with low SES are at much higher risk of reporting depression than those with high SES (Steel et al, 2014). Work by Williams and colleagues (2015) suggests that, for older people from 'the Black Caribbean community, heightened risk of depression is largely explained by their (lifelong and later life) exposure to, and experience of, socioeconomic disadvantage' (p 40). There is specific evidence that baby boomers are at heightened risk of depression as a consequence of the so-called 'disappointment paradox' (Grant, 2013). Unlike their predecessors, the baby boom generation(s) have been (largely) protected from financial adversity throughout their lives; when exposed to poverty for the first time in later life they have few coping skills to deal with it and struggle to adjust (McKee and Stuckler, 2013).

Draughty, damp and/or 'hard to heat' housing contributes to older people becoming isolated (Larkin, 2011). In 2011, 36 per cent of people aged 60 or over in the UK '... lived in just one heated room' to save money and rarely invited friends or relatives round (Age UK, 2011, p 4). Housing quality has consistently been identified as a very significant contributor to older people's psychological well-being (Howden-Chapman et al, 2011). In part this is a reflection of the fact that older people are more likely than other age groups to spend long periods of time in their own homes. There is specific evidence that inadequate housing contributes to depression, anxiety and stress (Evans et al, 2003a; Evandrou et al, 2015).

Insecurity linked to living in a deprived area also undermines psychological well-being (Buffel et al, 2013). Fear of assault, or of falling over without anyone around to help, contributes to a sense of vulnerability and reluctance to go out and thereby to a heightened risk of social exclusion. As older women are more likely to be living alone and not to have access to a car they are particularly affected. Marshall and colleagues (2014) identified an association between depression and living in 'the most deprived neighbourhoods' of England. They estimate that 10 per cent of the variability in depression among older people can be explained by neighbourhood environment. Living in an increasingly unequal society, including unequal ageing, is an additional pervasive stress (see Chapter 3) (Wilkinson and Pickett, 2007).

Homeless older people are much more likely to experience both depression and dementia as well as alcohol and substance misuse problems than their peers (Leng, 2017). They are both a cause and a consequence of homelessness (Crane and Warnes, 2010). It has been shown that mental health problems in homeless populations are linked not only to recent experiences but often have causes relating to earlier life course experiences such as childhood abuse or trauma (Kim et al, 2010). This underscores the points made in Chapter 3.

Policy issues

There is an overarching need for policy to appreciate the nature of late life poverty as a product of a number of intersecting inequalities. Some of these are embedded in the life course, some arise in later life itself and some have structural roots exposing particular groups of older people to a heightened risk of poverty and its mental health-related consequences.

The UK has a poor record compared to other developed countries in sustainably and coherently addressing poverty in later life. The fact that this has been a consistent issue across time and governments of different hues, suggests a systemic policy failure to understand its dimensions, causes and consequences. One of the underpinning issues is a widely held, but tacit, belief that reduced resources in later life are inevitable and normal. The strength of the link between 'economic' productivity and what is socially and politically valued is an underpinning factor (Walker, 2009). Not only does this narrow lens fail to value the non-economic contribution of older people, such as family caring, volunteering and community-related activities, but it also fails to acknowledge the role played by life course *and* age-related low SES in undermining health, including mental health.

Given that there is increasing evidence that socio-economic disadvantage, especially poverty, damages the mental health and well-being of a growing number of older people, addressing it is a key dimension of tackling inequality. It is also considered by some policy commentators to be an issue of social justice (Walker et al, 2011). One of the cornerstones of addressing poverty in later life is a continued commitment to funding the basic state pension as a 'fundamental building block of a secure old age' (Phillipson, 2011, p 211). By providing the state pension, the government not only protects those older people most at risk of poverty but, implicitly, accepts that some groups – primarily women and low-paid workers – are less able to access continuous full-time employment and/or a private or occupational pension than others (Price, 2006). Although, in the longer term more women are likely to benefit from reforms to the pension system (particularly the reduction in the number of 'qualifying years'), in 2015 over 46 per cent of women were still not entitled to the full state retirement pension (Price et al, 2016). The 'gendered occupational life course' is, in any event, more complex and women are vulnerable to the impacts of other changes to the care and welfare system, for example women carers are affected by cuts to services for older people and carer-related benefits. The current financial crisis is directly implicated in changes to the way that pension providers are now encouraged to operate, for example closures of final salary pension schemes. As discussed in Chapter 4 removal of the compulsory retirement age may be a positive move for advantaged groups of workers but is, generally, bad news for those in employment contexts characterised by physical demands, precarity, low pay and no access to an occupational pension (Ní Léime et al, 2017).

Phillipson (2011) argues for a new discourse on pensions, one that challenges the view that government provision should be reduced and reliance on the private market increased. Evidence to date suggests that market provision has led to a deepening of inequalities among pensioners and that the volatility of the market is in 'direct contradiction to the need for security and certainty in old age' (p 212). A second issue, in Phillipson's view, is the need for more radical policies directed at the poorest and most disadvantaged groups of older people, particularly in areas experiencing social and economic dislocation (Bambra, 2016). Older people are especially vulnerable to the loss of local services such as post offices, libraries, shops, pubs and community policing as they spend a lot of time in their neighbourhoods; an under-recognised issue is the important role these play in enhancing older people's sense of inclusion and safety (Barrett and McGoldrick, 2013; see Chapter 10). The extent to which 'age friendly cities' and 'ageing in place' policies take account of these wider issues is moot. Most urban developments have confirmed inequalities rather than challenged them, ignoring for the most part, those groups who do not directly contribute economically (Buffel et al, 2013). The role played by housing also needs to be more prominent. Accessing affordable adaptations to housing as a way of keeping disabled older people in their own homes and communities is one such example.

A third issue relates to intergenerational issues. Instead of positioning generations as competitors, that is, 'old' versus 'young' for a slice of the welfare cake, much greater emphasis needs to be placed on developing a framework of 'social solidarity' (Vincent, 2003, p 108). This would accommodate a life course perspective that recognises the uneven and unequal nature of access to employment across a lifetime and a concomitant need to protect all of those who are disadvantaged by this pattern whether they are young, middle-aged or elderly, male or female, able-bodied or disabled. It also recognises the life course-related, multi-dimensional and cumulative nature of poverty. A fourth issue is that of disability. Policy discourse relating to poverty in later life fails to take account of the fact that disability is particularly prevalent in the older population and that it generates additional costs. Traditional income analysis tends to ignore these extra costs giving a distorted picture of older peoples' financial status. For poverty in later life to be coherently addressed policy makers need to take full account of the, often incrementally increasing, costs related to managing ill health and/or disability (Hancock et al, 2016).

6

Abuse, mistreatment and neglect

The focus of Chapter 6 is the abuse, mistreatment and neglect[1] of older people. It is a cross-cutting issue that spans settings and contexts and is self-evidently damaging to well-being and to physical and mental health (Milne et al, 2013). Prevalence and incidence of abuse will be discussed first before reviewing what is known about its causes, nature and impact. It is important to note that mental ill health intersects with abuse and mistreatment in at least two overarching ways: older people with mental illness, especially dementia, are at heightened risk of abuse; and older people who are victims of abuse are at risk of poorer mental health.

Prevalence and incidence of abuse and neglect of older people

Due to the fact that abuse of older people occurs 'behind closed doors' and often goes unreported, accurate statistics about its prevalence and incidence are difficult to obtain. Current estimates suggest that between 2 per cent and 10 per cent of older people suffer 'some form of abuse'. Randomised, community-based epidemiological studies have reported annual rates of between 2 per cent and 4 per cent in the United States, Canada and Europe (Sethi et al, 2011). The *2007 UK Study of Abuse and Neglect of Older People* identified that 8.6 per cent of older people (those aged 66 years or over) living in the community experienced some form of 'mistreatment' (O'Keefe et al, 2007). 'Mistreatment' was defined as physical, psychological, sexual or financial abuse or neglect. The survey identified that the prevalence of mistreatment increased with declining health of the victim; it also noted the particular vulnerability of very elderly people who have complex comorbid health conditions (O'Keefe et al, 2007). Action on Elder Abuse (a charity) estimates that at least 500,000 older people are abused each year in the UK (2004). Data drawn from 'adult safeguarding systems' suggest that older women make up the vast majority of victims (Milne et al, 2013).

Studies focusing on older people dependent on family carers report that approximately a quarter have experienced significant psychological abuse and a fifth neglect (Hirsch and Vollhardt, 2008; Association of Directors of Adult Social Services, 2011). In studies with well-defined target populations, 11 to 20 per cent of family carers reported physically abusing the relative they support and 37 to 55 per cent reported verbally abusing or neglecting them (Cooper et al, 2008). Some studies also show high rates of co-abuse, that is, abuse by both members of a dyad (Compton et al, 1997).

Although abuse of older people in long-term care settings[2] is well documented and widely regarded as commonplace, prevalence studies are few (Royal College of Psychiatrists, 2000; Garner and Evans, 2002; Francis, 2013). A groundbreaking study conducted in the late 1980s reported that 80 per cent of care home staff had observed abuse (Pillemer and Moore, 1989); a 2008 study identified that 16 per cent of staff reported 'committing significant psychological abuse' (Cooper et al, 2008). In 2012/13 over a third of all adult abuse alerts in England arose in a care home setting; this equates to more than 39,000 investigations (National Institute for Health and Care Excellence, 2015a). Specific issues that constitute abusive – or at the very least poor – practice in care homes include covert administration of drugs, for example crushing up pills into food, the routine use of physical restraints, for example cot sides, and electronic tagging (Wetzels et al, 2010; Brooker, 2011; Owen et al, 2012).

Rarely are older people themselves asked about abuse. In a 2011 study, a group of older participants were asked what they considered to 'constitute abuse'; they included 'withdrawal of respect' and 'reduction of roles and opportunities for participation' as examples (O'Brien et al, 2011). Other work suggests that the following are, or contribute to, abuse of older people: violations of human, legal and medical rights; social exclusion; deprivation of liberty; reduced choice and agency; and lower status (WHO and the International Network for the Prevention of Elder Abuse, 2002). It is noteworthy that these definitions are closely aligned with the dimensions of ageism explored in Chapter 4; that they are not included in most formal definitions, or understanding, of abuse or mistreatment by policy makers, practitioners or in care settings is also interesting.

Causes of abuse and neglect

Evidence relating to cause(s) of abuse tends to be generated around domestic settings *or* service settings.

Domestic settings

In family contexts evidence suggests that while there is no single cause, abuse tends to either be a continuation of a long-standing pattern, for example domestic violence (see later in the chapter) or it is related to changes in living situation, declining health and/or increased dependency

(De Donder et al, 2011). Prominent features of abusive situations are: social isolation; a poor-quality long-term relationship between the abuser and the older person; and dependence on the abuser by the victim (Lachs and Pillemer, 2004). A shared living situation is a risk factor for all types of abuse except financial where victims disproportionately live alone (Lachs and Pillemer, 2004; Green, 2010). Evidence indicates that people with dementia are particularly vulnerable, with challenging behaviour often cited as a 'trigger' (Dyer et al, 2000).

Evidence on perpetrator characteristics suggests that in domestic settings, abusers are more likely to be male, primarily sons, dependent on an older relative for financial support (Milne et al, 2013). The risk of abuse may be increased by difficulties, such as stress, mental health problems or substance use, in the life of the abuser (Choi and Mayer, 2000). Risk of abuse is also heightened in contexts where the carer has been subject to abuse *by* the cared for person; this is not an uncommon experience for elderly spouse carers of partners with dementia (Cooper et al, 2006; De Donder et al, 2011). While there is limited evidence of this, the 'new' caring demands placed on carers, particularly older carers, are likely to raise additional issues of abuse (as noted in Chapter 4) (Henwood et al, 2019).

It is important to place this issue in its wider context. The benefits of family care are strongly promoted in public discourse over admission to long-term care. Keeping an older person at home where they are 'naturally best placed' is presented as virtuous and economically sound (Manthorpe and Iliffe, 2016b). Although there is significant policy emphasis on supporting family carers – see the Care Act 2014, for example – this is underpinned by an expectation that 'support' is provided to help carers to continue caring (Larkin et al, 2019). That fewer carers received support from publicly funded services in 2012/13 (354,000) than they did in 2009/10 (387,000) is noteworthy and is particularly discomforting when situated next to the well-established fact that a person with dementia is at least 'twenty times more likely to be admitted to a care home if they do *not have* a co-resident carer' (emphasis added) (Banerjee et al, 2003, p 1316; Humphries, 2015). Manthorpe and Iliffe (2016b) suggest that there is a cruel, rather dark, side to the increased expectations placed on carers, that '… the effects of poorly resourced care (services) become framed as a moral failure on the part of family carers who may be accused of being abusive or neglectful of the person they care for' (p 22). These pressures are likely to increase the risk that carers will 'lash out' or make a mistake with medication as a consequence of overwork, fatigue and/or the complexity of care tasks (Henwood et al, 2019). This raises questions about the lenses through which we view and understand abuse, an issue to which I return later in the chapter.

Service settings

Most evidence about abuse in services relates to long-term care. Inquiries into abuse in care homes[3] and hospitals, for example the Commission for Health Improvement (2004) and the Francis Report (2013) – into the failures of hospital care – identify a number of common features of abusive settings. These include: institutionalised environments, low staffing levels, routine use of temporary staff, limited training, ignorance, poor leadership and supervision and a closed culture (DeHart et al, 2010; Parliamentary and Health Service Ombudsman, 2011). Limited recognition of the challenges of care work, the complexity of the needs of residents and the 'off the radar' status of care homes are additional factors (Dening and Milne, 2011).

Most abuse or neglect develops insidiously. Although frontline staff are most often the 'perpetrators' the causes tend to lie in the care home's regime, culture and practices. Inquiries and serious case reviews[4] often uncover situations in which the least powerful individuals are held responsible for abuse inside very powerful and profitable organisations which have failed to resource the care home adequately and who have put profits before the needs of residents (Brown, 2011). The model of efficiency that underpins care practices sets the context for the enforcement of institutional regimes and for conflicts of interest between care workers and residents, and increases the risk of abuse (Lloyd, 2012). Ageism plays a role here too; at the very least it normalises discriminatory attitudes and practices and, at most, actively contributes to their development or amplification (WHO, 2011). Further, 'negative attitudes towards older people and the low value attributed to caring for them, inside and outside care home settings, contribute to a denigration of residents' experiences and the experiences of frontline care staff' (Brown, 2011, p 120).

Although the Francis Inquiry (Francis, 2013) was focused on an NHS Hospital and not a care home it also concluded that most of the causes of the '1200 unnecessary deaths' and preventable harm done to very vulnerable elderly patients were structural and reflected institutional imperatives, for example to keep ward costs down. The Report specifically identified 'insufficient numbers of qualified nurses' caring for elderly patients as contributing to the neglect of patients with dementia. This included failing to recognise when patients were starving to death or dying of dehydration. The limited work that has been done with care home residents identified that they consider a number of structural issues to be the cause of inadequate care; these include limited time spent with residents and families, high staff turnover and inadequate pay (Hyde et al, 2014). Despite policy actions to regulate care homes, establish care quality standards and improve the training of care workers, abuse is a regular feature of long-term care (Care Quality Commission (CQC), 2017).

It is instructive to remind ourselves about the current profile of care home residents (Dening and Milne, 2020). Older people are likely to move into a care home at a later stage in their life course and illness trajectory than they did in the past and they are also more likely to be admitted in a crisis, that is, following an emergency hospital admission (Lievesley et al, 2011). At the point of admission most residents have complex comorbid conditions and unpredictable clinical trajectories; they have become markedly more dependent over time (Forder and Caiels, 2011; Quince, 2013). It has been estimated that four fifths of care home residents have dementia and/or a hearing impairment, are in receipt of seven or more medications, and a significant proportion live with depression, mobility problems, pain and/or incontinence (Cohen-Mansfield and Taylor, 2004; LaingBuisson, 2014; 2016). Dementia is the biggest health-related determinant of care home admission; incontinence is also a trigger.

There is some evidence about which factors reduce the likelihood of abuse. Research from the US demonstrates that when more professionally qualified nurses are employed in care homes the quality of care improves. One of the reasons for this is that professional registration engages workers with a set of accountabilities that are both external *and* alternative to those that are embedded in the home's regime (Lloyd, 2012). These may offer a challenge to 'taken for granted' practices and provide staff with a rationale for resisting collusion with poor-quality care. Better pay, a well-trained workforce, a reflective culture, a commitment to staff spending time with residents, supervision of staff, and staff retention are all associated with lower levels of abuse and higher standards of care (Dening and Milne, 2013; 2020).

In community-based care settings, domiciliary care staff are the most commonly cited perpetrators, particularly in relationship to financial abuse (Ismail et al, 2017). In part this reflects the isolated nature of the care activity, that is, it takes place in the older person's own home, in part the dependency of the older person on the carer, that is, it is difficult to challenge the person upon whom they rely for their survival, and in part the lack of formal oversight by their employing agency (Milne et al, 2013). There is recent evidence that direct payments amplify the risk of financial abuse, positioning the service user (even further) outside the protective purview of the local authority (Manthorpe and Samsi, 2013).

The wider context of care is also relevant. Within health and welfare services the focus is on care as 'a commodity' with funding issues driving decision-making in procurement and commissioning. Money and time become linked to care via a unitised system that tends to reduce it to a set of tasks (for example, bathing, preparing food) thereby allowing them to be commissioned from agencies and 'allocated' to care workers. This tendency inevitably privileges tasks over less visible – so-called 'softer' – dimensions of care, such as the importance of the relationship with the care worker, kindness, communication issues, or enhancement of the older person's well-being (Lloyd, 2010). When the pressure is on to keep costs down, as is the case with cuts to public services, home care visits become shorter or the time permitted to do a set of care tasks is reduced. Risks of abuse are greater in this market-driven model of care for three reasons. It reduces service users to 'objects of care' marginalising the issues that face towards the human experiential dimensions of care. It also encourages a default approach to care provision – one size fits all – limiting the capacity of workers to individualise care, change the package of activities or vary the length of visits. There is also a tendency to view workers as interchangeable, resulting in a number of different workers visiting the same service user: it is not unusual for an older person who needs four visits a day to see 20 different workers in any given week (Woodward et al, 2004). Opportunities for the older person to develop a relationship with a particular care worker are very limited. These issues combine to dehumanise the older person, put distance between them and the care workers and erode staff retention (Ayalon, 2008). As with care home staff, community care workers are less likely to act in an abusive way if they are better paid and trained, supervised regularly and there is a commitment by the employing agency to allocating fewer workers to support each service user (Cooper et al, 2008).

Another facet of the neo-liberal welfare state is reduced regulation and inspection. The CQC[5] was heavily criticised by the Francis Inquiry for its part in the scandal (Francis, 2013). Its 'light touch' approach to inspection was identified as one of the main features of structural failure. This is important to note as the Inquiry took place at the end of a decade-long policy-driven shift away from what the government called 'unnecessary and intrusive' over-regulation of care services. It was particularly concerned that state agencies did not 'intrude' on the independent sector's 'commercial freedom' in relationship to care homes and other care services and did not threaten their capacity to make market-driven decisions (CQC, 2017; Dening and Milne, 2020). Concerns about the financial stability of for-profit community-based and residential services have been identified as 'damaging to the lives and wellbeing' of vulnerable older people, creating feelings of uncertainty, insecurity and fear (Leyland et al, 2016). In 2011, the collapse of Southern Cross which supported 30,000 residents and in 2019 the threatened collapse of Four Seasons which supported 17,000 residents, are two examples.

A number of the issues relating to the profile of victims of abuse in care settings are reflected in the profile of victims of domestic abuse and sexual violence. It is to these issues that I now turn.

Domestic abuse and sexual violence

Domestic abuse is a complex and largely hidden phenomenon. The Crime Survey for England and Wales referred to in Chapter 3 excludes those aged 60 years and over (ONS, 2014). This not only means that we know very little about domestic abuse and older people, primarily women, but that we (continue to) construct it as a 'younger women's issue' (Women's Aid, 2013). This is an example of structural age discrimination. The fact that it is subsumed under the generic term 'elder abuse' serves to hide it as a distinctive type of abuse and a profoundly gendered issue. This is mirrored, some commentators would argue, in the lack of attention paid to gender issues in elder abuse discourse (Penhale, 1999).

A recent study by the domestic abuse charity SafeLives (2016) estimated that in 2014/15 approximately 120,000 people aged 65 and over experienced at least one form of abuse in the UK. This report highlights the particular nature and profile of domestic abuse of older people. Older victims of domestic abuse are much more likely than younger victims to: be abused by a family member (44 per cent versus 6 per cent) or intimate partner (40 per cent versus 28 per cent); live with the abuser (32 per cent versus 9 per cent); and have a disability (48 per cent versus 13 per cent). On average older victims experience domestic abuse for twice as long as younger victims before seeking help and are less likely to leave the situation. Many have lived with domestic abuse for a long time; the SafeLives (2016) survey identified that over a quarter of victims had experienced abuse for at least 20 years.

Factors that influence reluctance to disclose abuse include: reliance on the perpetrator, fear about the consequences of reporting the abuser, and reluctance to give up a lifetime's investment in a marriage, a family and a home. Internalisation of a traditional gendered view that you 'put up with it because it's your duty to do so', a feeling of non-desert and lack of awareness of support services also act as barriers to help-seeking (Scott et al, 2004). Financial dependency is a particular factor for the current cohorts of older women as they are less likely than younger women to have independent sources of income (Phillips, 2000).

Lack of coordination between services is also an issue: an 'ideological gulf' between safeguarding services, primary and secondary health care, older people's services and domestic abuse services has been identified (Hester, 2011; SafeLives, 2016). The fact that domestic abuse services tend to focus on younger women, and their children, is an additional factor as is the unsuitability of (much) refuge accommodation for meeting the needs of older women with mobility issues (Blood, 2004). We know practically nothing about domestic abuse and older men. Among professionals, embedded stereotypes about domestic abuse 'not affecting older people' and confusion about the differences between abuse of older people and domestic abuse is also a concern. The discourses have evolved along parallel conceptual and experiential tramlines undermining the potential to pool evidence and knowledge and make links that will benefit older people, especially older women.

There is a similar profile in the field of sexual violence. Despite a greater focus on preventing and addressing sexual violence against women, we know very little about its prevalence among older women or men. In part this reflects a widely held perception that sexual violence only happens to attractive young women and that older women are asexual and thereby immune from 'sex' crimes. That feminist literature has largely ignored this as an issue reinforces its invisible status (International Longevity Centre, 2013). This view is further supported by the fact that when rape cases relating to older women (the vast majority are female) are reported it is the 'vulnerability' of the victim that is highlighted rather than the violent act. The perpetrator is often characterised as mentally ill rather than as a criminal (Bows and Westmarland, 2015).

A recent piece of work analysing sexual offences data in the UK[6] reveals that about 0.75 per cent of all those recorded relate to women aged 60 years or over (Bows and Westmarland, 2015). The proportion is small compared with those aged under 60 and is lower than that reported in the only other similar study conducted in the UK which exposed a rate of 3.1 per cent[7] (Ball and Fowler, 2008). These low figures can partly be explained by the known reluctance among older people to report sex offences; they also reflect differing methodologies and structural resistance to exploring sexual offences against older people. Bows and Westmarland's (2015) study identified that most perpetrators were known to the victim although a higher proportion were 'acquaintances' than is the case for younger women; at least 20 per cent were a partner or husband. In a significant minority of cases the perpetrator was a paid carer. Some of the evidence suggests that sexual violence is a feature of a long-standing intimate relationship; this mirrors evidence relating to younger women. A 2011 study identified that 28.1 per cent of older women in Europe had experienced 'at least one kind of violence and/or abuse' by someone who is close to them over the last 12 months (De Donder et al, 2011).

Constructing domestic abuse and sexual violence as 'a safeguarding issue' not only removes the gendered element, which is a defining feature of both types, but it also uncouples it from the life course where, for many, its roots are located. It also tends to foreground old age as the defining dimension of the abuse rather than its other dimensions. Further, it denies older people access to support systems developed to protect and support victims of domestic or sexual abuse (Scott et al, 2004). Ageism is a prominent but largely invisible feature of these patterns which not only serves to exclude older people, especially older women, from rights-related discourses but also reinforces the separation of abuses experienced in later life from those experienced earlier in life.

Re-thinking abuse: (some) ways forward

An overarching criticism of statutory responses to all forms of abuse of older people is the nature of the adult safeguarding system. There is a tendency to rush to categorise abuse according to a typology which not only constructs the older person exclusively as a 'victim' but fails to engage with their own perspective on their experiences or accord them any agency. Many adult women, including older women, resist the label of victim regarding themselves as survivors of abuse and as employing coping strategies in the face of adversity (Kelly, 2010). Donovan and Hester (2010) note that this purview is almost completely overlooked in safeguarding discourse and suggest that the existing 'administrative' model of dealing with abuse of older people may be, in part at least, a reflection of systemic ageism (Biggs and Haapala, 2013). As noted earlier older people's own views about abuse are liminal in research; this is mirrored in service responses and systems. A related criticism concerns the dominance of the binary approach that infuses current models of abuse of older people – victim versus perpetrator, dependency versus independency, illness versus health – and the limitations this imposes (Daniel and Bowes, 2011).

One of the lenses suggested as helpful in moving understanding and responses forward is that provided by the life course. A life course approach offers an opportunity to engage with a more nuanced discourse allowing for the perspective of the older person to be foregrounded and for alternative narratives to the 'procedural model' to find purchase. It also offers a route into bringing together analysis at the micro level of the individual with that relating to macro structural issues of disadvantage and inequality and engages with issues that persist across the life course creating vulnerability to abuse. These issues include: poverty, long-standing domestic abuse and/or chronic ill health. Further, it may expose the complexities inherent in abuse including those arising from systemic sources, promote more individualised responses to need, engage with a rights-based discourse and enhance our understanding of the consequences of abuse, including those relating to mental health (Daniel and Bowes, 2011; Dow and Joosten, 2012).

A second, linked, lens is that offered by an ethic of care (Barnes et al, 2015). This is concerned with promoting an understanding of care as an integral part of human relationships and a product of interdependence and reciprocity; care is both an activity *and* a disposition (Barnes, 2012). In the context of abuse an ethic of care approach would start from an understanding of the experiences of the people involved in abusive relationships so that 'choices about appropriate interventions and resources can be better informed' (Lloyd, 2012, p 6). An ethic of care is a form of 'political ethics' in which an enshrined notion of social justice can be achieved through awareness of social systems and practices, for example adult safeguarding, and the way these are influenced by dominant discourses that construct abuse in a particular way. Most policy-related literature on abuse does not refer to frailty, socio-economic disadvantage or issues of power; rather it refers to risks and interventions or articulates a set of 'standards'. As power lies at the very heart of abuse of older people in all contexts this is a profound oversight.

Mental health consequences of abuse and sexual violence in later life

Violence, in all its guises, has profoundly negative mental health consequences. There is surprisingly little specific evidence about the impact of abuse on older people, although a recent systematic review concluded that the most prevalent psychological consequences are depression, anxiety, learned helplessness and post-traumatic stress disorder (PTSD) (Dong et al, 2013). Unsurprisingly, compared to non-victims, older people who have experienced abuse are more likely to report 'high levels of psychological distress' and fear (Williams and Watson, 2016).

There is robust evidence that domestic and/or sexual violence undermines health and well-being (Women's Aid, 2013). This is especially the case if it is sustained (Trevillion et al, 2013). It is linked to increased morbidity and premature death. Physical health problems include: hypertension, trauma-related injuries, musculoskeletal and genitor-urinary disorders including incontinence, as well as sleep problems and persistent nightmares and/or flashbacks (McGarry and Simpson, 2011). Sexual assault in later life is specifically associated with anxieties and fears about leaving the home, or if attacked in the home, fear of living in the property after the attack (Jeary, 2005). As discussed in Chapter 3, the effects of long-term trauma, which often includes exposure to abuse throughout the adult life course is associated with significantly increased risk of depression, anxiety and other mental health issues (Scott et al, 2004). Older women who have experienced abuse at an earlier time in their lives – and have not resolved the related trauma – experience anger, frustration, helplessness, hopelessness and low self-esteem (McGarry and Simpson, 2011). Re-victimisation, or an extension of existing abuse, compounds and deepens existing damage to mental health (Johnstone and Boyle, 2018). Loss of identity and sense of self are additional issues (McGarry et al, 2016).

In terms of service usage one US study evidenced that for a significant proportion of referrals of older women to mental health services, domestic abuse was an underlying factor. Reluctance to acknowledge the abuse on the part of staff amplified the women's sense of isolation and powerlessness, and (further) undermined self-esteem and self-worth (Acierno et al, 2010). Related evidence suggests that although training about domestic abuse increased awareness and knowledge health professionals remain reticent about actually engaging with the issue with older women. Given the limited nature of both appreciation of complexity *and* service provision in the 'safeguarding arena' it is unlikely that services address mental health problems arising from abuse nor engage meaningfully with the older person's perspective on their experiences or potential ways forward.

Policy issues

There are a number of relevant policy arenas. It is a complex field. Policies are characterised by different foci, target groups and/or issues, geographical purview, statutory remit and aims. Space does not permit a lengthy discussion about the myriad policies related to abuse; it is reserved for those that have most resonance with the arguments made in this chapter and the UK context.

The human rights of older people are self-evidently important. The World Health Organization (WHO) defines abuse of older people as a human rights issue declaring that 'countries need to ensure that older people can live with dignity, integrity and independence and without maltreatment' (WHO, 2011, p 3). The WHO explicitly supported the 2002 *Toronto Declaration on the Global Prevention of Elder Abuse* (WHO, 2002c) and in 2010 the UN General Assembly established a working group on strengthening older people's human rights. Reports to this group identified that the abuse and neglect of older people, particularly older women, is a widespread international phenomenon not limited to any particular context or region (UN, 2010). In May 2016 the World Health Assembly adopted a *Global Strategy and Action Plan on Ageing and Health*; a part of this strategy focused on preventing abuse of older people through initiatives that help to identify, quantify and respond to the problem (WHO, 2016). Both of the WHO strategies underscore the responsibility that public bodies have to ensure that the human rights of older people are protected and abuse issues addressed. Although challenging to capture, evidence suggests that the *Toronto Declaration* has had limited impact; it remains to be seen how effective subsequent initiatives will be. It is an issue that has become more prominent in the public domain and on the international stage for which these policies can take some credit.

What is clear, however, is that the human rights agenda continues to be overshadowed by the wider political agenda of resources. One of the main reasons that global strategies have had limited impact on national policies, and an even weaker impact on practice, is that they are conceptualised as separate from, and somehow above, the world of politics (Tronto, 1993). This conceptual differentiation not only 'obfuscates the way in which political considerations influence and shape' responses (Lloyd, 2012, p 6) but contributes to the gulf that exists between policy aims – both global and national – and the operationalisation of those aims. As Lloyd (2012) observes, while the *language* of policies is highly moral in tone, policies in *practice* become subsumed into the political arena where the management of resources is the primary consideration. A good example of this is the UN Convention on the Rights of Persons with Disabilities (UN, 2006) to which the UK is a signatory. The Convention is '... an international human rights treaty intended to protect the rights and dignity of persons with disabilities' including older people and people with dementia (UN, 2006, p 3). In its 2017 report the UN Convention on the Rights of Persons with Disabilities described the UK's policies for disabled people as 'a human catastrophe' (UN, 2016; 2017a). It accused the UK government of 'grave' and 'systematic' violations of human rights, of forcing through welfare reforms with '*no regard* for the rights of disabled people' (emphasis added) and of providing care that has become so basic that many disabled and older people are unable to get out of their homes (House of Lords Select Committee on the Equality Act 2010 and Disability, 2016; UN, 2017b). The UK's abject failure to achieve the Convention's aims is a consequence, primarily, of its prioritisation of reduction in public spending over the protection of the human rights of disabled citizens. A second issue relates to power. While declarations are valuable for articulating public standards and principles they cannot be relied upon as a basis for tackling abuses of power. As abuse of power is a defining feature of all forms of abuse the policy infrastructure needs to engage with this, and by definition its socio-political location, if it is to have meaningful effect (Tronto, 2010).

The fact that abuse straddles the private *and* public domains represents a third challenge. Although policies formally recognise that abuse occurs in both settings, the lens of analysis adopted to understand and respond to the abuse engages with a different set of moral frameworks. In the context of social policy, '... justice is widely regarded as the moral framework for public life, whilst care is seen as the moral framework for private life' (Lloyd, 2012, p 6). While there is emerging acceptance that principles of justice should apply in the private domain, especially around issues of abuse, these tend to be eclipsed by concerns about public resources.

It is in this context that policy relating to 'safeguarding adults' is situated. In England,[8] local authorities have a duty under the Care Act 2014 to promote the well-being of the population in their area; this includes offering protection from abuse and neglect. It requires each local authority to make enquiries if it believes an adult is being abused or neglected, or is at risk of abuse or neglect, and take action to prevent it. These duties apply in relation to adults (18 years and over) at risk of abuse 'because of their needs for care and support' in all settings and includes self-neglect. The CQC has a duty in relationship to preventing abuse or neglect that occurs in service settings and responding to concerns.

There have recently been a number of positive policy shifts in the safeguarding arena. *Making Safeguarding Personal* (2013), for example, is a sector-led initiative which aims to 'develop an outcomes focus to safeguarding work, and a portfolio of responses to support people to improve or resolve their circumstances' (Local Government Association, Association of Directors of Adult Social Services Departments and the Social Care Institute for Excellence, 2013, p 6). It aims to engage with people about the outcomes they want to achieve and working towards realising these, including evaluating what differences have been made to their lives and well-being post the safeguarding intervention. The 'Making Safeguarding Personal development project', which ran for a year in 2012/13 in four local authorities, concluded that the traditional narrow focus on making older people 'feel safe' compromises other aspects of their well-being, such as feeling in control; also that using an asset-based approach to identify a person's strengths can help them and their family to manage complex situations and feel empowered, reducing the future risk of abuse (Pike and Walsh, 2015).

Additionally, there is greater recognition that abuse of older people is a social problem not just an individual one and that it is embedded in a relational context. The role played by structural factors has yet to be incorporated into the policy or practice agenda. The fact that the safeguarding system is most often reactive, that is, it responds to abuse or neglect *after* the event, and focuses on relatively short-term safety issues, is a practical and conceptual barrier. It is important to acknowledge that working in the arena of abuse is complex, requiring practitioners to operate in a vortex of different policies and procedures and resolve potentially conflicting values, such as protection, promotion of independence and self-directed care (Ray et al, 2015). While widening the analytical lens may make the role of practitioners even more complicated, the fact that older people *are* placed at risk by an intersecting mix of 'personal, relational, societal and structural factors' would encourage a practice that more honestly reflects the nature and causes of abuse (Sevenhuijsen, 2004, pp 14–15). It also holds greater potential for creative solutions that lie beyond the confines of the current narrow paradigm and engage with the values of rights and social justice.

7

The fourth age, frailty and transitions

It is important to acknowledge that this chapter has a different tone to that of Chapters 5 and 6. Primarily, this reflects the nature of the literature; there is a well-developed sociological discourse in relationship to the constructs of the fourth age, frailty and transitions. It also reflects the more experiential evidence base; the voices and agency of older people are much more visible dimensions. The fact that it is exploring processes such as transitions also affects its shape and content. Links with mental health issues mirror this difference. There is a mix of specific evidence about the management of a change in circumstance, for example admission to a care home, and the impact on a person's mental health of coming to terms with the changes and losses that accompany the fourth age and 'becoming frail'. There is relatively little on mental illness.

Introduction

One of the implications of an ageing population is the growing number of very elderly people; those aged 85 years and over. Chapter 1 identified that 'later life' is a long life stage, potentially lasting up to 40 years. One of the ways in which later life has been subdivided is into the 'third age' and the 'fourth age'. The idea of the third age emphasises opportunities for freedom and growth in a post-employment life (Lloyd, 2012). The agentic third age lifestyle is constructed around the principle of delaying the mental and physical decline associated with the fourth age by engaging in leisure and fitness activities, holidays and 'healthy lifestyles' (Higgs and Jones, 2009). This links with the discourse on active and successful ageing explored in Chapter 2. It is important to remind ourselves about the role played by the social gradient of health in relationship to mortality and morbidity discussed in Chapter 3. While the most disadvantaged older people may not survive to experience very late life, nevertheless, the impact of inequalities on those who do reach the fourth age remain both relevant and underexplored.

According to Twigg (2006), quoted in Lloyd and colleagues (2014a), optimistic accounts of the third age are possible only 'by projecting into a dark fourth age all the problems and difficulties associated with ageing' (p 2). Limited attention has been paid to the fourth age in part because it is 'a place where our greatest fears reside' (Gilleard and Higgs, 2010a, p 126) and in part because it is close to death and lacks meaning as a life stage (Twigg, 2006). Conceptually, sociologists consider that the fourth age 'demarcates experiences that occur at the intersection of advanced age and impairment' (Grenier and Phillipson, 2013, p 57) and as associated with risk of failure to achieve the socially valued goals of independence, autonomy and self-reliance (Lloyd, 2004). It is also linked with abjection, a term that refers to 'a realm of decay, disease and impurity that embodies the capacity to disgust' (Gilleard and Higgs, 2011, p 135). Psychological literature treats the fourth age as a life stage which represents new developmental tasks of coping, adjustment and adaptation (Baltes and Smith, 2003).

Life course analysts criticise the bifurcatory picture of third and fourth ages on the grounds that the third age overemphasises the absence of illness and the influence of individual agency, and the fourth age constructs older people as dependent, ill and without agency (Phillips et al, 2010). It is noteworthy that for neither group are social categories, such as gender and class, viewed as influential. The dominant construction of illness is problematic because it gives priority to physical functioning ignoring the way in which health outcomes in later life are structured by the life course. The third versus fourth age issue also raises a temporal question. The deinstitutionalisation of the life course discussed in Chapter 3 disrupts the hitherto chronologically defined life stages introducing more fluid definitions of later life and the timings of key transitions.

The life course approach intersects with the concept of embodiment. According to Krieger (2011) we 'literally embody – biologically – our lived experiences' (p 215). Ill health, including mental ill health, is thus a product of a life course characterised by exposure to adversity, hazardous conditions, economic and social deprivation, discrimination, violence and trauma, and poor health care (Karban, 2017). Exposure tends to be cumulative and multiple and its impact is mediated by class, gender, sexuality, ethnicity and age. This argument dovetails with that made in Chapter 3 about the ways in which adversity and chronic stress get 'under the skin'. Embodiment is an especially relevant concept to the fourth age as the biological consequences of the life course *and* of age-related ill health tend to be most visible, profound and felt. As ill health is a common feature of the fourth age it is important that its presence does not obscure the causative role played by life course inequalities and structural issues.

Older people living with frailty

The biomedicalisation of ageing is a dominant dimension of literature about the fourth age. This is particularly true in relationship to the concept of 'frailty'. Although the fourth age and frailty share (some) common conceptual and experiential territory, frailty may be treated as an 'analytic category' in its own right representing a condition or state characterised by multiple impairment, decline and dependency (Manthorpe et al, 2018). The fourth age may be viewed as a category, or stage of life, of which frailty is considered a subset.

The British Geriatrics Society (BGS) describes frailty as a 'distinctive health state related to the ageing process in which multiple body systems gradually lose their in-built physical and psychological reserves' (BGS, 2014, p 1). It is characterised by increased vulnerability to functional decline, dependence, sudden deterioration and reduced ability to recover from health setbacks, for example a fall (Clegg et al, 2013). The BGS estimates that among community-based older people: 9 per cent of those aged 75 to 79, 16 per cent of those aged 80 to 84 and 26 per cent of those aged 85 years and over can be described as 'experiencing frailty' (BGS, 2014). The figure for the oldest category is contested with some commentators considering the proportion to be nearer to 50 per cent (Clegg et al, 2013). Reported prevalence of frailty in care home residents is high but varies wildly from 18 per cent to 76 per cent, suggesting big differences between definitions and methodologies used (Dening and Milne, 2020).

Analysis of ELSA data suggests that there is a close relationship between socio-economic status and frailty (Tomkow, 2018). Older people who live in socially disadvantaged neighbourhoods and who live on a low income are significantly more likely to be frail than those who live in more advantaged neighbourhoods living on high incomes (Lang et al, 2009). In the Hertfordshire (county of England) Cohort Study (Syddall et al, 2009), frailty among men aged 64 to 74 years is associated with older age and socio-economic characteristics such as lower educational attainment and not owning one's own home. Work by Marshall and colleagues (2015), quoted in Scharf and colleagues' (2017) report, identifies some interesting differences between age cohorts. Using five waves of ELSA data (2002–10), their analysis suggests that frailty levels are higher in more recent cohorts (people aged 50 to 69 years in 2002) than in older birth cohorts (those aged 70 and over in 2002). What is particularly noteworthy are the unequal outcomes over time associated with differences in wealth. For the wealthiest groups, there is relatively little change in trajectories of frailty over time, suggesting little difference between younger and older age cohorts. By contrast, substantial cohort differences exist in the least wealthy group, leading the authors to draw the pessimistic conclusion that poorer older people are spending longer periods of later life in a frail state than had previously been the case (Marshall et al, 2015).

Recent evidence suggests that older people aged 75 years or over who are considered to be 'severely frail' are: four times more likely to be admitted to hospital, six times more likely to be admitted to a nursing home and five times more likely to die over a 12-month period than less frail older people (Clegg et al, 2016). Falls and worsening mobility are also much more likely. A 2017 study additionally suggests that frailty *substantially* increases the risk of developing dementia (Rogers et al, 2018). In Rogers and colleagues' research (2018) the frail group of participants were 3.5 times more likely to develop dementia compared to their non-frail peers. That frailty has particular implications for older people's mental health is also relevant (see later in the chapter).

Higgs and Jones (2009) argue that when the body fails, the 'ageing experience' becomes more manifest as caring for oneself may become problematic. Sociological perspectives emphasise the social, emotional and psychosocial dimensions of bodily decline (Phillipson, 2013). The effects of illness and disability change irreversibly a customary way of life and call into question a set of assumptions about one's sense of self, role and value. Loss of confidence *with* your body and loss of agency *over* the body have specific implications for identity and self-worth (Bury, 1991; Lloyd et al, 2014a). It also obliges engagement with notions of dependency, failure and burden (Grenier, 2007). It is noteworthy that the ageing body is largely absent from gerontological literature and when mentioned tends to be associated with dirt, disgust, fear and disparagement (Twigg, 2006). This links with the point made earlier about abjection.

Grenier (2006) makes a clear distinction between *being* and *feeling* frail. Drawing on Archer's (2000; 2003) concept of reflexivity – a combination of concerns about physical well-being (natural order), competence in day-to-day living (practical order) and a sense of self-worth (social order) – Grenier (2007) argues that it is only when this is fractured that an older person *feels* frail. 'Being frail' is usually determined clinically via some form of functional assessment by a health professional. 'Feeling frail' relates to the older person's emotional responses to loss, illness and impairment and is a socially determined experiential status.

Recent work suggests that older people are aware of the psychological and sociological risks of identifying as 'frail' (Goffman, 1963; Tanner, 2010). A 2015/16 study suggests that lower levels of psychological well-being can be both a cause and a consequence of doing so (Warmoth et al, 2016). Respondents reported an iterative 'cycle of decline' in which older people disengage from physical and social activities thereby reducing their physical functioning and social networks, undermining well-being and making future engagement less likely. They also report holding very negative views of frailty; these reflect widely held stereotypes and reinforce a resistance to being described as frail even by older people with high support needs (Nicholson et al, 2016). Labelling someone as frail can be interpreted by the older person, and by those around them, as evidence of 'failing to age well' (Richardson et al, 2011). One of the specific fears is alienation from peers and social exclusion (Gilleard and Higgs, 2017). As Grenier (2012, p 174) warns, notions of frailty risk older people in this group becoming socially and culturally 'othered' both from society and from the older population itself. Frail older people with more assets and higher incomes tend to have better subjective well-being than their poorer counterparts, suggesting that access to financial resources may act as a 'partial buffer against the detrimental psychological effects of frailty' (Hubbard et al, 2014, p 367).

One of the paradoxes relating to frailty is that despite its conceptual emphasis on incapacities, frail older people are often the survivors outliving the majority of their birth cohort (Nicholson et al, 2016). I return to this issue in Chapter 10.

Dignity and agency

It is important to acknowledge that most older people who would be described as frail are likely to suffer from a number of disabilities and/or illnesses, have limited strength and mobility, need help with activities of daily living and may have impaired cognitive capacity; some will be living in long-term care. One of the attendant risks of frailty, especially for those who are 'necessarily dependent' on others for daily living, is loss of dignity (Lloyd, 2010). As the lives of frail older people are often shaped by institutional practices, at least some responsibility for the maintenance of dignity rests with those who fund, commission and provide support and care services (Gilleard and Higgs, 2010a; 2010b). Certainly, there is evidence that dignity, agency and autonomy are routinely compromised in service contexts, especially long-term care, and, as noted earlier, it is a relatively short step from undignified care to abuse and mistreatment (O'Brien et al, 2011; Commission on Dignity in Care for Older People, 2012). Unsurprisingly, care and support that is sensitive to older people's individual experiences is more likely to enhance personal dignity and promote agency (Ray, 2016b).

Findings from a recent study by Lloyd and colleagues (2014a) explored the meaning and maintenance of dignity among a sample of frail older people who need support from services to remain in the community. It identified the importance of perseverance and self-determination and of retaining control and highlighted older people's continuing capacity for agency and identity in a context that poses a threat to their preservation. The pivotal role played by relationships and service's engagement with relational autonomy, for example with a spouse, in promoting decision-making and dignity was a key finding. This reflects issues explored earlier in this book about the embedded nature of long-term relationships and their importance as 'ways in' to unlocking understanding and knowledge about an older person's history, biography and needs. It also challenges bifurcatory notions of dependency. To achieve 'good outcomes' and promote dignified care recognition that dependency is both a normal part of, and integral to, all human relationships appear important. Viewing the self through the relational lens helps to promote and protect dignity. For a frail older person, this may include relationships with paid carers such as care home workers as well as relatives (Tanner, 2016).

This narrative intersects with evidence drawn from the carers literature. Emerging research suggests that family carers, especially spouses, are often engaged in 'emotional work' as well as 'illness specific work' and 'care tasks' (Vassilev et al, 2013). Emotional work tends to be subtle, opaque, and nuanced and includes supporting the person's selfhood and dignity, and protecting the status, character and nature of the dyadic relationship (Knowles et al, 2016). Related work focusing on spouse carers of people with dementia identifies that retaining couplehood, in the face of a deteriorating condition, is a primary dimension of emotional work. Hyden and Nilsson (2015) call this the 'We-ness' dimension of caring. That couples often view their life, and life course, as a shared one is also relevant (Ray and Phillips, 2012).

Evidence from both these domains challenges the widely held view that one of the defining characteristics of frailty is 'negation of individual agency' and loss of selfhood (Gilleard and Higgs, 2010a). Rather than being absent agency may be experienced and manifested differently; it may take a different form, one hitherto not included inside the 'agentic tent' (Grenier and Phillipson, 2013; Tanner, 2016). Traditional conceptualisations of agency made up of the dimensions of physical independence, rational action and/or articulating one's needs unproblematically do not 'match' the profile of a frail older person. However, this does not mean it does not exist. Agency for this group, and perhaps for the fourth age more broadly, requires reworking.

Gubrium and Holstein (1995) suggest a more fluid interpretation of agency in the fourth age echoing Bourdieu's (1984, p 110) view that it is about 'making do with what is available'. In Tanner's case study, for example, the older woman's agency was supported by her 'positive (re) appraisal of situations and events' (2016, p 164). The reworking may also need to accommodate the potential of agency to be embedded in, and re/produced and protected by, a relationship. Understanding agency as multi-shaded or on a spectrum may open up new ways to conceptualise it. Exploring in greater depth, and with a more flexible analytic lens, the strategies that older people adopt to maintain or reframe agency is essential especially among very frail older people who experience dependency, those who live in care homes and people living with dementia. The interwoven nature of agency, identity and selfhood is a subject that warrants specific exploration. These are issues to which I return in Chapter 10 when I explore the promotion of mental health.

Transitions

The losses and challenges that often accompany the fourth age can be characterised as transitions; 'turning points that have implications for an individual's ability to adapt' (Victor, 2010, p 94). Transitions tend to take place over time and seem to follow a series of stages, although these vary depending on the context. Tanner and colleagues (2015) suggest that there is usually a 'before' or antecedent stage, a significant event or trigger, the transition itself and an 'after' stage when the consequences of the change create a new state. Transitions are viewed differently depending on the disciplinary lens adopted: in sociology they are viewed as shifts in role and/or status and in psychology as stages of development or adaptation.

Transitions tend to multiply in the fourth age and may occur in quick succession. They are often complex, involving changes in identity, roles, relationships and abilities as well as, sometimes, changes in place, setting or condition. Transitions are social, emotional and psychological in nature and may be physical too. Older people undergoing transitions are 'experiencing disruption in one or more areas of their lives and may feel they are living through a time of chaos and confusion' (Tanner et al, 2015, p 2060). The situation is often unfamiliar, they may feel disoriented, and challenged to cope. Some transitions reinforce losses common to the fourth age. Being admitted to a care home, for example, is often associated with the diminishment of choice, autonomy and self-expression, amplifying and deepening the 'collapse' of agency, status and citizenship associated with frailty (Higgs and Gilleard, 2016a; 2016b). While most transitions are negative, such as the onset of chronic illness, some are positive, such as the birth of grandchildren. Some are planned for, for example moving near to an adult son or daughter, while others are unexpected, for example, the death of a partner. Transitions vary considerably in intensity and size 'from minor to life changing' (Victor 2010, p 94).

While it is known that transitions can have a profound negative effect on an individual's psychological well-being and that experiencing multiple transitions is problematic, there is evidence that resilience, and its sub-dimensions, can play a key protective role (Victor, 2010). Older people who are resilient tend to react more positively to change and those with higher levels of self-mastery (or being in control of events) manage transitions more effectively (Hamilton-West, 2011). Research with older people themselves suggests that what is important is the 'personal meaning' that the individual attaches to the transition they are facing. For example, as Tanner and colleagues (2015) note, Chambers (2005) explored the diverse ways older women deal with widowhood, and Milne and Peet's (2008) work on responses to being diagnosed with dementia suggest that while some people find it 'biographically shattering' others manage it more positively. Related research suggests that when faced with a transition older people endeavour to preserve goals, values, relationships and selfhood and to adapt by employing cognitive coping mechanisms (discussed in Chapter 2) (Tanner, 2010; 2016).

Despite the fact that the most profound late life transitions tend to occur in the fourth age, limited research attention has been paid to their nature and management. Grenier (2012) identifies the complex subjective and emotional challenges associated with fourth age transitions especially the onset of long-term health problems and disability. One of the key challenges relates to maintaining continuity *while* accepting and accommodating change. They are not mutually exclusive experiences but rather co-exist. As Kuh and Ben-Shlomo (2004, p 5) argue, continuity should be conceptualised as 'the persistence of general patterns rather than as sameness in the details contained within those patterns. Religious values and beliefs may remain the same, but the meaning and interpretation that stand behind them evolve'.

Literature tends to focus on the objective or functional issues linked to transitions not the emotional and psychological ones; for example, capturing the meaning older people attribute to change(s). If we are to understand transitions as a defining dimension of the fourth age and a normative part of the later life course, we need to capture the perspectives and lived experiences of older people to a much greater degree. In particular, Grenier (2012) argues, we need to explore the emotional significance of those transitions that take place 'in the liminal space between health and illness near to the end of life' as this space holds considerable potential to generate new knowledge (p 178).

One of the benefits of understanding more about how older people experience transitions is to inform health and social care workers about how to provide effective support for transitions that involve services. Transition out of hospital or from home to a care home are transitions known to be stressful and are widely reported as ill managed, confusing and damaging to older people's psychological well-being (Tanner et al, 2015). The anxiety and stress caused by delayed discharge from hospital is well evidenced and research clearly shows that service providers are not considering the psychological and social aspects of discharge for the older person (Department of Health, 2014). Care home admission is routinely fraught with anxiety, and research suggests that older people and their families often feel they have limited choice or control over decisions (Fisher et al, 2006). Research also highlights the complexity of the psychological and social process of care home admission for the older person and their family: issues that are often lost, or at best marginalised, in the admission process. Practitioners tend to treat a service-related transition as a physical event rather than a social and psychological one imbued with personal meaning (Fisher et al, 2006). That these transitions tend to affect those older people who are most frail, have dementia and/or whose autonomy is under greatest threat makes it especially important that they are managed in a way that takes full account of their experiences, feelings and views.

The nature and level of support offered to older people and their carers during all stages of transitions can have a significant impact on both the transition process and outcomes, particularly in terms of the older person's adaptation to change (Tanner et al, 2015). The key ingredients of well-managed transitions involve: continuity of relationships with at least one key professional who straddles settings, participates in all stages of the process, can work in partnership and can offer advice and empathetic support to the older person and their family; support that maximises the older person's ability to make choices and retain control; acknowledgement that a service-related transition takes time, planning and expertise; and recognition of the emotional and psychological complexities that experiencing a transition involves including the role of 'critical junctures', for example when key decisions need to be made (Richards et al, 2014; Ray et al, 2015). One of the key routes to improving outcomes is to take meaningful account of older people's perspectives and embed 'what matters' into the care system in a sustainable way.

The fourth age and mental health

Although the fourth age is a contested concept there is growing recognition that those older people who reach very late life are likely to face a number of intersecting and complex challenges that have implications for their mental health; these often include frailty and transitions. Some of these have already been discussed. In this section I will offer an overview of key issues.

What are the distinctive challenges to mental health in the fourth age? Older people's accounts draw attention to the tensions that exist between the desire to maintain continuity and the need to accommodate change; notions of continuity and change may become somewhat fused. Accounts also reference uncertainty, the existence of a more permanent state of decline and impairment, bereavement and, in some cases, proximity to the final transition of death (Grenier, 2012). Fear and denial are commonly reported responses to chronic illness and threats to mortality (Laslett, 1991). Research with older people also highlights loss of identity and role and a reduced sense of selfhood and value. Agency, autonomy, choice and control are threatened by the combined impact of bodily decline, social attitudes, a biomedical and frailty discourse, and withdrawal from activities. As a number of these issues are key dimensions of good mental health and/or psychological well-being – see Chapter 2 – it is axiomatic that their erosion is a primary threat to both. That evidence suggests older people in the fourth age strive to maintain these in the face of multiple threats attests to this (Grenier, 2012). Related evidence identifies the enormous amount of work older people put into protecting a positive sense of self, identity and self-worth (Tanner, 2016).

Grenier (2012) reminds us that the fourth age is embedded in a life course and can be conceptualised as a product of the combined impact of cumulative (dis)advantage and impairment. This approach not only offers a way for earlier life course issues that undermine health and well-being to be made relevant to, and visible in, the fourth age but helps to establish a link between the fourth age and the rest of the life course. This includes links with the third age, a life stage widely regarded as separate for reasons already discussed. It also challenges the dominant narrow biomedical narrative.

This argument is supported by accounts from older people in the fourth age. Evidence from recent research suggests that the 'double whammy' of impairment and cumulative disadvantage has more serious consequences for overall health and well-being than impairment alone (Hu et al, 2018). Effects include: enhanced risks and earlier onset of frailty, fewer financial resources to help manage the effects of impairments such as paying for a carer or buying a walking aid, higher levels of worry and anxiety and a greater risk of being excluded from key decisions (Davis, 2005). This evidence base is, however, limited and we need to know much more about the nature of the intersection of the fourth age, impairment, disadvantage and life course inequalities and their combined impact on mental health in later life.

It is noteworthy that the focus of literature about the fourth age tends to be on those issues that may compromise mental health or psychological well-being as broad constructs; there is relatively little on mental illness, for example heightened risk of depression. This reflects two intersecting agendas. One is that only recently have researchers paid attention to the fourth age as a discrete entity. The second is that the focus of existing work is primarily about exploring what gives value to life in the fourth age and, as part of that, what 'good mental health' might mean and how it might be protected (see Chapter 10). The fourth age is a life stage characterised by multiple changes, impairments, losses and transitions which combine in a complex and mutually reinforcing way. The management of this iterative process poses a profound challenge to mental health and psychological well-being (Victor, 2010). These challenges may amplify existing mental health problems. As many older people manage the challenges well, understanding how mental health is protected is also important; this issue is discussed in Chapter 10.

Policy issues

There is no such thing as a policy for frail older people or those experiencing the fourth age. The policies reviewed in Chapters 1 and 4 relating to older people, and older people with mental health problems, are relevant, and policies which aim to improve the care and support that older people receive are important too.

It is, however, the case that frailty, as an issue, is visible in guidance documents for health professionals and care agencies. Examples include: guidance by NHS England (2014b) on providing *Safe, Compassionate Care for Frail Older People using an Integrated Care Pathway*; and a *Toolkit for General Practice in Supporting Older People Living with Frailty* (NHS England, 2017). There is also some literature on 'good practice' in working with frail older people, and models of care on the websites of the Royal College of GPs, and the BGS. Key features of these documents are: the importance of understanding what frailty is, an emphasis on integrated care and on person-centred care taking into account an individual's circumstances and preferences, and a need to appreciate that terminology – including the concept of frailty itself – is unlikely to be adopted by older people themselves (Allen and Daly, 2016). There is also some recognition of the importance of key relationships with workers and professionals, of timely support and thoughtful time rich communication; also that needs are likely to be complex. There is related and growing acceptance that the health care system struggles to accommodate frailty. Hospitals are particularly poor in this regard (Macdonald, 2001). Health services tend to focus on single conditions rather than multi-morbidities and most do not adequately support the mental health and well-being of frail older people (Oliver et al, 2014).

There is some policy acknowledgement of the role played by a well-managed transition for the health and well-being of older people. For example, the National Institute for Health and Care Excellence (2015b) has guidelines on the *Transition between inpatient hospital settings and community or care home settings for adults with social care needs*. It aims to improve people's experience of admission to, and discharge from, hospital by better co-ordination of health and social care services.

The 'promotion of dignity' – an issue allied to frailty – is identified in guidance for a range of care services, particularly care homes. One example is the Local Government Association, NHS England and Age UK's (2012) 'Delivering Dignity' guidance relating to older people in hospitals and care homes. Research evidence suggests that there are eight key factors that make the promotion of dignity more likely in services and which contribute to a person's well-being: choice and control, communication, eating and nutritional care, pain management, personal hygiene, practical assistance, privacy and social inclusion (Archer, 2003; Dening and Milne, 2013; 2020).

One of the key barriers to any policy-related discussion about frailty is its association, in the minds of many older people and others, with dependency, deficits, loss of autonomy and control, and long-term care. The fact that there are a growing number of scales and measures that 'assess frailty' squarely positions it in the biomedical camp. For example, Rockwood and colleagues (2005) developed a Frailty Index derived from a model based on the burden created by accumulating deficits (symptoms, such as tremor and hearing loss, and disorders, such as arthritis or dementia). Despite the rich nature of sociological discourse in relationship to frailty, dignity and agency and much greater emphasis on frailty as an individual lived experience, most current policy emphasis is on 'managing' it as a health problem and developing guidance to deal with it more effectively as an expensive condition that challenges the care system.

Conclusion

Chapters 5 to 7 have explored three issues that affect particular groups or subpopulations of older people: socio-economic disadvantage and poverty; abuse and mistreatment; and the fourth age, frailty and transitions. While not experienced by all older people these are risks that have particular, and particularly negative, implications for mental health in later life. It is of course the case that a number of older people will be exposed to all three of these issues and others to two of them. Their impact on mental health is thus very likely to be intersecting and additive.

There are a number of overarching points to be made. Although a number of the issues discussed may arise for the first time, and only, in later life itself, for example abuse in a service setting, some are continuations or exacerbations of issues and/or inequalities that originated earlier in the life course. Poverty is a key example. The embedded and cumulative nature of long-term risks is important to make visible. Given both the length of later life as a life stage(s) and the heightened risk of life course inequalities being amplified in older age it is important to expose their distinctive age-related nature.

A second point relates to impact. All three of the issues explored in these chapters have direct and indirect effects on mental health and well-being. A poor diet due to poverty and physical harm as a result of domestic abuse are examples of direct threats; linked indirect threats include those arising from limited choices, exclusion and lack of agency. A third point relates to who is affected. Older women and those who need help from care services are at particular risk of abuse. The fact that this profile tends to be invisible in the way that we think about 'who is poor, and/or 'abused' and/or 'frail' is a noteworthy tendency and one that needs to be countered, as I have attempted to do in all three chapters.

The evidence base underpinning the chapters is fragmented, uneven and partial. That the voices and perspectives of older people are often absent from the discourse is a cross-cutting weakness, especially in relationship to abuse. Although the often opaque and multi-dimensional nature of 'impact' is challenging to capture and record, it is critical that the research community addresses this deficit if we are to prevent and/or address the mental health consequences of socio-economic disadvantage and abuse and mistreatment and those arising from experiences of the fourth age, frailty and transitions.

Thus far the book has focused predominantly on risks to psychological well-being and threats to functional mental health. One of the dominant concerns of older people and their families, and policy makers and services, is dementia. Given its size and complexity as a condition and mental health issue it is important to explore it in some depth; dementia is the focus of Chapters 8 and 9.

8

The mental health and well-being of people living with dementia

This chapter is the first of two focusing on dementia. Chapter 8 reviews four sets of intersecting material: inequality-related risks relating to dementia that are a product of the life course and later life itself; mental health problems among people living with dementia; what we know about the mental health, well-being and quality of life of people living with dementia; and evidence relating to how we understand and measure quality of life and well-being in this growing population. Information about the prevalence of dementia and the different types is covered in Chapter 1.

Research evidence relating to dementia tends to be of two kinds: it either relates to a specific type(s) of dementia or to the broader category of 'dementia'. Where I discuss the latter, more specific evidence does not exist.

Dementia: life course and age-related risks and inequalities

Life course-related risks and inequalities

There is growing evidence of links between a number of life course inequalities and increased incidence of dementia. Low socio-economic status (SES) across the whole life course and lower levels of education in early life have been consistently identified as risks for developing dementia, particularly Alzheimer's disease (Fratiglioni and Qiu, 2013; Livingstone et al, 2017). Specific issues arising from low SES that appear relevant include poor nutrition, inadequate housing, higher levels of alcohol and tobacco consumption, lower levels of exercise and chronic stress; evidence relating to smoking is especially strong (Zhong et al, 2015) (see Chapter 3 regarding links between damaging health-related behaviours and low SES). In part this link can be explained by heightened risk of cardiovascular disease (CVD) which plays an obvious causal role in the development of vascular dementia. The risk factors for CVD – obesity, hypertension and high cholesterol – are life course-related and linked, via the factors noted earlier, to low SES and disadvantage. That recent research also suggests that CVD predisposes people to Alzheimer's disease strengthens and amplifies these links (Alzheimer's Society, 2007). Another health-related risk factor for dementia is diabetes, a condition that has substantially increased in recent years (Azad et al, 2007). This is both an epidemiological and sociological concern (Gregg et al, 2000) and links to points made in Chapter 3 about exposure to life course adversity and chronic health conditions (Friedli, 2009).

Recent work suggests that a number of the risks for CVD are increasing among women, specifically hypertension, high cholesterol, obesity and poor diet (World Heart Federation, 2011). Tobacco and alcohol misuse are also more of a 'women's problem' than they were 20 years ago, especially among baby boomers, with the concomitant health risks to both body and brain (Crome et al, 2011). In terms of education a 2011 meta-analysis of 11 cohort studies found that women who left full-time education early had an increased risk of dementia death; there was no association for men (Brayne et al, 2006; Russ et al, 2013).

A study of links between lifetime principal occupation and dementia found that manual work appeared to increase the risk (Qiu et al, 2003). It has been suggested that this may be due, in part at least, to occupational exposure to bio-material hazards such as pesticides; psychosocial stress may also play a role (see Chapter 3). Other, less well established, risk factors include early parental death, maternal health, exposure to adversity in childhood and working in a low status job (Alzheimer's Disease International, 2014; Regan, 2016). There is emerging work specifically linking childhood trauma, such as abuse, with increased risk of dementia, although it is early days in terms of establishing a definitive relationship (Burri et al, 2013).

A new group of US studies into racial disparities among people with Alzheimer's disease suggest that life course exposure to a cluster of intersecting risks, including low SES, racism, low levels of education, and limited opportunity, substantially increases the risk of developing dementia among African Americans (Gilsanz et al, 2017). Findings suggest that the long-term effects of this cumulative set of social and structural risks create stresses that damage brain health in later life. These risks are independent of those relating to the African-American population's higher rates of diabetes, obesity and CVD. This argument supports the 'accumulation of life course risks' causative model of dementia that will be discussed later.

There is some separate, but linked, research relating to the impact of socio-economic factors on cognitive function. Living in a neighbourhood with high levels of deprivation appears to be associated with 'lower levels of cognitive function', even when controlling for individual socio-economic circumstances (Lang et al, 2009). US research goes further suggesting that neighbourhood disadvantage may contribute to incidence of dementia (Kind et al, 2017). This links with the points made in Chapter 3 about there being an established association between deprivation and higher levels of CVD and diabetes, which are both risk factors for developing dementia (Larkin, 2013).

A number of commentators, most notably Jones (2017), challenge claims that there is a link between low SES and higher incidence of dementia on the basis of measurements used to assess both constructs. The fact that assessments of income and wealth vary and that income fluctuates across the life course makes the establishment of SES status difficult (as noted in earlier chapters). Assessment of cognitive capacity is also a challenge. There is well-established evidence that better educated individuals perform better on cognitive tests than those who are less well educated, undermining the reliability of such tests to objectively assess 'cognitive function'. The extent to which it is reasonable to view SES and education as separate variables, when they tend to be so closely related, has also been raised. This argument can be further extended to incorporate social class, a more complex construct than SES, and the intersection between class and education (Jones, 2017). Despite this criticism, it is nevertheless important to recognise that links *do* exist even if their precise nature is challenging to distil.

It is important to note that a number of life course risk factors are more prevalent among women. Women are more likely to have lower levels of education, to live on a low income and be exposed to chronic psychosocial stress (Buchmann et al, 2008). They are also more likely to be victims of domestic abuse (see Chapter 6) which may cause brain damage, a neuropathological risk factor for developing dementia (Organisation for Economic Co-operation and Development, 2015). The influence of the combined effects of lifelong exposure to sexism and to discrimination on the grounds of age and age-related disability is totally unexplored (Whalley et al, 2006).

Establishing, and then explaining, links between life course factors and dementia is not straightforward. If one accepts that there is a direct causative relationship between specific risk factors and dementia, three possible mechanisms explain the link: first through worsening vascular health, second by decreasing cognitive reserve and finally by increasing Alzheimer's and other neuro-degenerative disease pathology (Barnes and Yaffe, 2011). An alternative explanation, which is gaining purchase, is that dementia is an outcome of accumulation of life course risks over many decades (Mental Health Foundation, 2013; Manthorpe and Iliffe, 2016a). There may be multiple pathological processes at work over a long period of time. The Lancet Commission (Livingstone et al, 2017) on dementia prevention, intervention and care, mentioned in Chapter 1, suggests that 35 per cent of all dementia cases could be prevented if nine modifiable risk factors were fully eliminated: low levels of education, hearing loss, hypertension, obesity, smoking, depression, physical inactivity, social isolation and diabetes. It is noteworthy that these are a mixture of structural issues related to the life course such as poor education; mental health issues such as midlife depression; and physical risk factors such as diabetes and obesity that are part about lifestyle and part about life course. Dementia prevention research is in its infancy, but this evidence suggests that the causes of, or risks of developing, dementia are complex and interact in ways we are only now beginning to interrogate (International Longevity Centre, 2014). It also suggests that simple messages about individuals 'adopting a healthy lifestyle' will not be sufficient to reduce the risk factors for dementia, at least not on their own. Issues relating to protection and prevention are explored in Chapter 10.

It is instructive to observe that the first explanatory algorithm is firmly located in the biomedical domain, conceptualising dementia as a condition with a clear physiological basis, profile and timeline; the second algorithm less so, leaving room to accommodate risks which have a social and/or structural basis, including life course and age-related inequalities. Opportunities to make visible the complex and often reinforcing ways that risks accumulate and intersect are also, theoretically at least, more likely than they would be in the first. The role of conceptual frames of reference in influencing understanding of, and responses to, people living with dementia is an issue to which I return in Chapter 9.

Age-related risks and inequalities

There is a second group of risks relating, either in whole or part, to mid and later life.

There is a relatively robust body of evidence linking persistent depression with a heightened risk of dementia. A large longitudinal study in Holland found that older people who experience depressive symptoms for three years or more are over a fifth more likely to develop dementia (Mirza et al, 2016). There is also evidence that persistent depression experienced in midlife may increase the risk of developing dementia by as much as twofold (Ownby et al, 2006). Longitudinal data from a Norwegian study in 2014/15 confirms this link and additionally suggests that the association is stronger for depression and psychological distress experienced in *early midlife*, that is, under 45 years, compared to *later midlife* (Skogen et al, 2015).

Although the mechanisms explaining this association are poorly understood, if a causal relationship does exist, depression and psychological distress may potentially be modifiable risk factors for dementia. It has been suggested that it may be useful to design a clinical trial to investigate the effect of prevention of mid and late life depression on the risk of developing dementia (Diniz et al, 2013). Recent evidence that certain types of antidepressants appear to be linked to an *increased* risk of dementia complicates the nature of any such trial (Richardson et al, 2018). This evidence also raises the important question of whether it is depression, or its treatment, or a mixture of both that play a causative role. An alternative explanation is that depression is the starting point of the dementia continuum, that is, midlife depression is a prodrome of dementia (Johansson et al, 2010; Barnes et al, 2012; Da Silva et al, 2013). This is an explanatory framework I review in more depth later.

Isolation and loneliness in mid and later life appear to be associated with reduced cognitive function *and* increased risk of dementia (Wilson et al, 2007; Shankar et al, 2013). Of particular note is evidence suggesting that self-perceived loneliness 'doubles the risk of Alzheimer's disease' (Amieva et al, 2010). The fact that loneliness is associated with heightened risk of developing both depression *and* dementia and that these two conditions have an intersecting relationship is particularly interesting (Welsh Assembly Health, Social Care and Sports Committee, 2017). Older women are more likely to experience mid and late life depression and be exposed to a number of the risk factors associated with loneliness: living alone, living on a low income, being aged 75 years or over, caring for a relative with dementia and/or being widowed. These risks, as noted in earlier chapters, reflect both life course and age-related inequalities.

Women are also exposed to (some) biological risks. A number of studies suggest that post-menopausal women may be at slightly higher risk of Alzheimer's disease due to lower levels of oestrogen and other hormonal changes (Maki, 2013). Oophorectomy[1] and other gynaecological surgeries performed earlier in the life course also appear to heighten risk (Rocca et al, 2007). Attitude to life may play a role too (see the paragraph on super-agers in Chapter 1). In a 2011 study, older people with 'more negative attitudes to ageing' performed worse in cognitive testing than their more positive peers (Levy et al, 2011). That a negative attitude could, partly, be a consequence of worries about early signs of deteriorating cognitive and social functioning underlines the complexity of unravelling these multi-directional influences.

An overarching feature of dementia discourse is its gender neutrality (Bamford, 2011). Despite women populating the dementia arena as patients and service users, as family carers and as care staff the profiles, needs, voices, and perspectives of women are almost totally absent. Women are invisible despite their dominance. Some would even argue that it is precisely because of this feature that dementia is marginalised as a political issue and under-resourced as a health and care issue (Bamford, 2011; Scharf et al, 2017). Adopting a gendered lens helps to illuminate the number, range and nature of life course and age-related factors that may contribute to and/or amplify the risk of developing dementia. If there are causative links between at least some of these factors and dementia they not only need to be unpicked but recognised as related to inequality and as socially and structurally produced.

Mental health problems and people living with dementia

Before exploring mental health, well-being and quality of life, I will offer an overview of the prevalence and nature of mental health problems of people living with dementia.

Depression and anxiety

In community-based populations, depression is estimated to affect about a fifth of people with Alzheimer's disease and almost a third of those with vascular dementia and dementia with Lewy bodies (Alzheimer's Society, 2017). Symptoms include diurnal variation of mood, poor appetite and weight loss, tearfulness, calling out, and an expressed wish to die (Penninx et al, 1998). The person's 'usual' dementia-related symptoms may become amplified, that is, they may appear more confused and have greater memory loss (Alzheimer's Society, 2017). Depression may also make existing behavioural challenges worse such as agitation, problems with sleeping, or refusal to eat. Although causal mechanisms are unclear, there does appear to be a definite association between dementia and depression (Huang et al, 2011).

The fact that some of the symptoms of depression and dementia overlap (for example memory problems, difficulty concentrating) disentangling whether an older person has depression, dementia or both can be challenging (Regan, 2016). It is, however, important to assess for the presence of depression, as antidepressant treatment in people living with dementia is evidenced as effective: it can enhance psychological well-being, physical function and overall quality of life (Nelson and Devanand, 2011). Depressive symptoms may arise following a dementia diagnosis. The most robust evidence for non-pharmacological interventions for depression in people with early-stage dementia is cognitive behavioural therapy although validation therapy and cognitive stimulation programmes have also been shown to help in reinforcing positive coping strategies (National Institute for Health and Care Excellence and Social Care Institute for Excellence, 2006; Woods et al, 2006). One of the problems in terms of help-seeking is that depressed mood, especially in later stages, is often dismissed as 'part of the dementing process' and as untreatable. Sometimes the person with dementia may not even be aware they are becoming depressed. Age-related life events such as bereavement or physical ill health can be triggers for depression in the same way they may be for a person without dementia. In terms of evidence about life course risk factors the limited work that has been done suggests that adversity early in life, onset of dementia at a younger age, and being female may all contribute to heightened risk of depression in people living with dementia (Ballard et al, 1996).

Dementia, especially advanced dementia, is identified as an independent risk factor for depression in care home residents (Borza et al, 2015; Giebel et al, 2016). Up to half of care home residents with dementia also have depression; evidence about its nature is mixed. Some research suggests that depression tends to persist and is linked with increased risk of mortality (Midlöv et al, 2014) but there is also evidence that while depressive symptoms are significant post-admission, they decrease over time (Borza et al, 2015). Associations other than dementia include: pain, dysphagia, diabetes, lower levels of function, and heart disease; behavioural symptoms such as aggression; psychological variables, such as loneliness and a previous history of depression; and social variables, such as loss of family and home (Giebel et al, 2016). The depressogenic effect of 'institutional care' is also noteworthy (Dening and Milne, 2020). Particular features include: loss of privacy, noise, institutional furniture and odours, lack of stimulating social contacts and/or close relationships, high staff turnover, cultural dissonance between residents and staff, a medicalised culture and the constant presence of death (Clare et al, 2008). Better muscle strength, balance and higher walking speed are significantly associated with fewer depressive symptoms (Kvæl et al, 2017) and regular access to the outdoors, participation in leisure activities and using a hearing aid all appear to have protective effects (Boorsma et al, 2012). It is perhaps unsurprising that a number of the risks for developing depression are also primary triggers for admission to a care home (Ray and Sullivan, 2016).

One of the key challenges in estimating incidence relates to the difficulty of assessing depression in individuals with, especially advanced, dementia (Bagley et al, 2000). Variability in the use of, and concerns about the reliability of, scales and measures is a linked issue. A number of well-known scales (for example, the Geriatric Depression Scale) are not sensitive for depression in people living with dementia (Kafonek et al, 1989). These points link with discussion later in this chapter about evaluating quality of life and well-being in people with later stage dementia. Assessment issues notwithstanding, in the last few years greater attention has been paid to depression in care home residents increasing the number of people who are being diagnosed and offered treatment (Gaboda et al, 2011). Although high rates of prescribing have been reported – up to 40 per cent – evidence for the efficacy of antidepressant treatment in dementia is weak (Nelson and Devanand, 2011). There is widespread concern that residents who have depression are not being offered antidepressants routinely or consistently (Dalby et al, 2008). There are, paradoxically, parallel concerns that antidepressants are being prescribed to residents without proper assessment of depressive symptoms (Harris et al, 2012). Mixed interventions involving antidepressants and psychosocial interventions, often with a stepped care approach, seem most effective (for example Llewellyn-Jones et al, 1999; Leontjevas et al, 2013; Bosmans et al, 2014). Other interventions that show positive effect include: educational interventions, for example training nurses in nursing homes to recognise depressive symptoms; individualised 1:1 activities; structured group activities; music therapy; bright light exposure and reminiscence therapy (Williams et al, 2006; Huang et al, 2015; Onega et al, 2016; Bailey et al, 2017; Ray and Mittelman, 2017).

The atomised nature of the care home sector means that treatments, interventions and response patterns vary; homes serving more disadvantaged areas appear to provide less support for residents' depression, especially to people from minority ethnic groups (Botsford and Harrison-Dening, 2015). It is important to note that most research relating to the treatment and/or management of depression among care home residents is relatively small scale. Thus, findings need to be interpreted with caution. There remains a great deal of work to be done in this field (Mikelyte and Milne, 2016).

Dementia produces high rates of anxiety symptoms, particularly restlessness, agitation and fear. Studies suggest prevalence rates of between 5 per cent and 21 per cent (Starkstein et al, 2007). It may be higher in those with vascular dementia than in those with Alzheimer's disease and it appears to decrease in severity in the later stages (Ballard et al, 2000; Starkstein et al, 2007; Seignourel et al, 2008). A 2003 study of people with Alzheimer's disease identified that anxiety was inversely related to Mini Mental State Exam scores and was more prevalent among patients with a younger age at onset, that is, aged under 65 years (Porter et al, 2003). Anxiety disorders are strongly associated with depression, stroke, poor vision, pain, limitations in activities of daily living and behavioural disturbances (Smalbrugge et al, 2005; Creighton et al, 2017). In terms of care home populations, Smalbrugge and colleagues (2005) found that in a sample of over 300 residents[2] 5.7 per cent had anxiety disorders, 4.2 per cent had sub-threshold anxiety disorders and nearly 30 per cent had anxiety symptoms. Both depression and anxiety in people living with dementia have been found to directly correlate with poorer self-reported quality of life (Woods, 2012). The fact that anxiety may co-exist with dementia *as well as* depression makes its assessment and diagnosis a significant challenge. As noted in Chapter 1, although effective treatments do exist for anxiety disorders greater efforts are needed to make these routinely available to older people, including those with dementia and care home residents (Dening and Milne, 2013).

Other mental health problems

Delirium is a relatively common disorder in later life, particularly among people living with dementia, and the risk rises as dementia progresses (Hogg, 2013). It is marked by sudden onset of greater levels of confusion, disorientation and memory problems. The cause is most often physical in nature, including urinary tract and other infections, dehydration, untreated pain and heart failure. Some prescribed drugs such as opioids and sleep medication can cause or worsen confusion; hospital admission is often an arena in which delirium presents (Anderson, 2005; Venn and Arber, 2011).

Prevalence of psychotic symptoms, including delusions and hallucinations, among people with Alzheimer's disease is estimated to be over 40 per cent (Ropacki and Jeste, 2005). Visual hallucinations are a known feature of dementia with Lewy bodies and Parkinson's disease dementia; they commonly include animals or people, can last several minutes and may be distressing. Delusions are persistent beliefs that are inaccurate; they are often persecutory in nature and may involve accusations of theft or of deliberate harm. These beliefs may be a result of people living with dementia trying to make sense of their changing world. If they are unable to find familiar items or money that they may have misplaced, they may (reasonably) conclude that they have been stolen (Cullum, 2013). Less commonly, the emergence of delusions may be part of the syndrome associated with dementia with Lewy bodies. Psychotic symptoms can be particularly distressing for both the person with dementia and their family and are cited as a key reason for seeking help from mental health services (Regan, 2016). This evidence suggests that while condition-based factors may be partly responsible, psychotic symptoms may also be a response to feelings of fear, confusion, alienation and/or isolation (Keady and Jones, 2010). Environment is also relevant. In care home settings factors that have been implicated in higher levels of psychotic behaviour among residents include being short-staffed or staff being rushed, low levels of communication between staff and residents and lack of responsiveness to residents' specific needs (Zeller et al, 2009; Eritz et al, 2016).

There is evidence that, for some people living with dementia, post-traumatic stress disorder (PTSD) symptoms – relating to an event much earlier in life – may emerge *for the first time* (Mittal et al, 2001). Others may re-engage with PTSD symptoms they have previously been exposed to (Floyd et al, 2002; Murray, 2005). Both types of experience may result in self-defensive behaviour against the perceived threat, including verbal and physical aggression, upset and/or anger (Martinez-Clavera et al, 2017). People with later stage dementia may already be reliving past events as part of their condition and may no longer have the psychological defence mechanisms to protect themselves against emotional or psychological pain (van Achterberg et al, 2001). Veterans with dementia appear particularly vulnerable to experiencing PTSD symptoms (Borson, 2010). There is an alternative school of thought which suggests that PTSD may be a risk factor for dementia, not the other way around. Data from a large US Veterans cohort study, for example, indicates that individuals diagnosed with PTSD were almost twice as likely to develop dementia than their peers without PTSD (Yaffe et al, 2010). Although this finding is reinforced and echoed by a wider review of evidence conducted in 2011, more research is needed to understand the complex associations between PTSD and dementia (Qureshi et al, 2011).

There is a related need to explore links between traumatic brain injury – relatively common among war veterans – and dementia. A recent study in the US suggests that veterans are at significantly higher risk of developing dementia if they have (ever) experienced concussion, especially if it was associated with loss of consciousness (Kenney and Diaz-Arrastia, 2018). The study identified that rates of dementia for those with moderate to severe traumatic brain injury who lost consciousness were nearly four times higher than cohort-based norms and 2.5 times higher for those who had not lost consciousness (Kenney and Diaz-Arrastia, 2018). How this evidence intersects with that relating to PTSD is, at present, unknown but it seems likely that there is both a bidirectional and potentially additive link.

Most existing work focuses on PTSD in (largely male) war veteran and prisoner-of-war populations. Much less is known about links between other forms of trauma and dementia, for example that arising from rape and/or sexual assault (for example, see McCartney and Severson, 1997). This links with some of the points raised in Chapter 6. An interesting, final, question relates to whether the experience of 'having dementia', especially in its later stages, could be considered to be *of itself* a source of PTSD. For example, if the person is no longer able to understand the reason for receiving personal care they might be traumatised by a care worker undressing and bathing them, in effect 'assaulting' them (James and Jackman, 2017). The experience of trauma may transcend memory – impaired by dementia – and have both immediate short-term impact and cumulative longer-term impact. As far as I am aware no work has been done to explore this issue.

Alcohol issues, isolation and loneliness

The Royal College of Psychiatrists (2011) recently highlighted the fact that alcohol misuse and recreational drug use are increasingly common in older people as the first baby boomers reach retirement age. Both amplify risks of cognitive impairment and confusion. However, there is evidence that their impact can be moderated, at least partially, if drug use and alcohol intake is significantly reduced in later life itself.

People living with dementia, especially those who live alone, are at significant risk of social isolation and loneliness (Kane and Cook, 2013). A 2013 survey identified that 62 per cent of people living with dementia who live alone 'feel lonely' and 47 per cent do not 'feel part of their community' (Department of Health, 2013). As noted in Chapter 1, dementia carries an inherent risk of 'self-isolation': people with symptoms tend to avoid family and friends, and communication difficulties may make it difficult to sustain social networks and interests (Moyle et al, 2011). Further, a person with dementia may not remember that a friend has visited, reinforcing their sense of loneliness (Alzheimer's Society, 2013).

Mental health, well-being and quality of life of people living with dementia

It is important to recognise that a good quality of life and dementia are not opposing or contradictory states. In fact, there is limited evidence that well-being or quality of life worsens as dementia severity increases (Livingstone et al, 2008; Hoe et al, 2009). The relationships between mental health, well-being, quality of life and dementia are much more nuanced and varied and are worthy of detailed analysis.

In this complex arena there are, broadly, two schools of thought around which knowledge is generated and evidence collected. The first school focuses on the development of measures of quality of life (mainly), distilling its key dimensions and evaluating how to enhance the accuracy of assessment (Ready and Ott, 2003). This research is interested in how the meta constructs of mental health, well-being and quality of life intersect with dementia. The second school takes a broader more bottom-up approach to considering what matters to people with dementia and how to 'live well' with the condition. While these two arenas share a number of operational aims, they do not share the same conceptual territory.

Work in this field is at a relatively early stage of development, and evidence is uneven. In part this reflects where investment is made which, in turn, reflects dominant interests. Biomedically oriented research has particular purchase. Although emphasis in this section is placed on those issues that are particular or distinctive for people living with dementia, there is some inevitable overlap with some of the issues explored in Chapter 2.

Quality of life and 'living well' with dementia: dimensions, associations and variations

Two points are useful to make about the nature of the terrain. There is limited material that focuses on mental health as a separate construct from the other two; well-being is often a subset, or dimension, of quality of life.

There is now a substantive body of research, mainly qualitative in nature, that has explored those factors that are important to quality of life among people living with dementia in the community. Key dimensions include: psychological well-being, autonomy, having a meaningful role and activities, acceptance, sense of agency, promotion of selfhood and identity, social interaction and relationships, financial security and religious beliefs (Byrne-Davis et al, 2006). Other work identifies being active, engaged, 'as independent as possible', good physical health, autonomy, choice and control as key factors (Warner et al, 2010). The issues that appear to be particularly important are: 'being of use', life having meaning, security, privacy and self-determination (Warner et al, 2010).

In terms of evidence, although depressed mood is associated with lower quality of life among people living with dementia in all settings, factors such as cognitive function and behavioural symptoms do *not* show any clear association (Menne et al, 2009; Beerens et al, 2014). In the LASER-AD study – a longitudinal epidemiological study of people with Alzheimer's disease in the community – mean well-being scores did not change significantly over time (Livingstone et al, 2008). Further, future well-being was much more strongly associated with mental health (anxiety and depression) and social relationships than either global dementia severity or general health (Hoe et al, 2013).

In their one-year follow-up study of people diagnosed with dementia, Selwood and colleagues (2005) found that 'many people continue to have positive experiences' (p 236) and echo Albert and colleagues (1996) finding that 'dementia is not a psychologically null state' (p 1342). They concluded that the only major predictor of future subjective quality of life for a person living with dementia was quality of life at baseline, suggesting that pre-dementia attributes such as personality type and attitude to life are more influential than having the condition per se. A 2007 two-year follow-up study also identified that quality of life was not determined by cognitive changes alone but by non-clinical variables related to the physical and social environment (Missotten et al, 2007). There is specific evidence that people with an early diagnosis of dementia are 'as satisfied with life' as those without dementia and, perhaps more surprisingly, subjective quality of life is not necessarily impaired by the progression of dementia in care home residents (Moyle and O'Dwyer, 2012).

How well a person adjusts to a change of circumstances, including those relating to dementia, appears to be a pivotal influence on current and future quality of life (Selwood et al, 2005). This finding resonates with arguments made in Chapter 2 about adjustment and adaptation. A higher level of functional ability, well-established social networks and having a positive relationship with relatives or carers are all associated with better quality of life among people living with dementia in the community (Fratiglioni et al, 2004; Clare et al, 2014; Bauer et al, 2018; Martyr et al, 2018). Research also suggests that higher quality of life in people with severe dementia, some of whom may live in long-term care, is 'associated with better functional ability, lack of disability, improved mood status and increased engagement with the environment' (Hoe et al, 2005, p 134).

Over the last decade, there has been an increasing focus on identifying what 'living well with dementia' means to people with the condition. In 2010, the Alzheimer's Society worked with a number of partner organisations to launch a National Dementia Declaration for England; it was updated in 2017 (Dementia Action Alliance, 2010; 2017). The Declaration is underpinned by five statements representing the issues that are most important to people living with dementia:[3]

- Independence/Interdependence/Dependence: we have the right to be recognised as who we are, to make choices about our lives including taking risks, and to contribute to society. Our diagnosis should not define us, nor should we be ashamed of it.
- Community/Isolation: we have the right to continue with day-to-day and family life, without discrimination or unfair cost, to be accepted and included in our communities and not live in isolation or loneliness.
- Care: we have the right to an early and accurate diagnosis, and to receive evidence-based, appropriate, compassionate and properly funded care and treatment from trained people who understand us and how dementia affects us. This must meet our needs, wherever we live.
- Carers: we have the right to be respected and recognised as partners in care, provided with education, support, services and training which enables us to plan and make decisions about the future.
- Research: we have the right to know about and decide if we want to be involved in research that looks at cause, cure and care for dementia and be supported to take part.

The IDEAL project (Improving the Experience of Dementia and Enhancing Active Life) is a longitudinal cohort study exploring people's experiences of living with dementia over time (www.idealproject.org.uk/). It began in 2014 and will continue until the end of 2022. Key (early) findings indicate that: helping people to deal with low mood, anxiety and depression, bolstering resilience and a sense of optimism, and addressing loneliness are important dimensions of improving psychological health. Supporting people to stay fit and independent and engaging with the development of problem-solving strategies to manage day-to-day tasks are evidenced as important to quality of life; supporting carers is also very important to the quality of life of both the carer and the person living with dementia (Lamont et al, 2019). Findings additionally suggest that the ability of people to live well declines as the number of 'other conditions' increases (Clare et al, 2019). The situated nature of dementia is reflected in both the Dementia Declaration and the IDEAL study. Living well with dementia is shaped by the physical, social, cultural and environmental context as well as the effects of the condition on the individual, their family members and their social and support networks (Katz et al, 2011a; 2011b; Clare et al, 2014). Living well appears to be a broad construct, incorporating concepts of psychological health, well-being and life satisfaction and as reflecting the importance of social capital, assets and resources and the potential for social participation. The prominence of the role played by social issues is noteworthy: social connectedness, social interaction, social relationship and meaningful social activities. These findings are mirrored in the Joseph Rowntree Foundation's *Better Life Programme* which explored the meaning of a 'good life' for older people with high support needs, including people with dementia (Bowers et al, 2009; Katz et al, 2011b). They are also relevant to the protection and promotion of mental health among people living with dementia, which is discussed in Chapter 10.

There is no evidence about the prevalence of well-being or quality of life among people living with dementia in the community.

Well-being and the diagnostic window

Research with people with a recent diagnosis of dementia suggests that two key factors influence their well-being: the rate of cognitive deterioration and the person's capacity to adjust to the diagnosis (Gabriel and Bowling, 2004). Capacity to adjust appears to be dependent on whether the person adopts a self-adjusting style that is associated with awareness of cognitive change and help-seeking behaviour, or a self-maintaining style which is associated with minimal acknowledgement of the diagnosis and a 'life as usual' approach (Clare, 2003; Wilhelmson et al, 2005). People who adopt the former style are more likely to access treatments and/or psychological support, make plans for their future and do what they can to bolster their own well-being and that of their families (Beard and Fox, 2008). It is noteworthy that resilient individuals are more likely to adopt a self-adjusting coping style and integrate the illness into everyday life (Milne and Peet, 2008). A self-maintaining coping style is associated with seeking help at a later stage, if at all, when opportunities for early intervention, treatment for symptoms and promotion of well-being may be lost (Aminzadeh et al, 2007).

It is important to focus attention on the diagnostic window because evidence suggests that it offers an opportunity to enhance well-being in both the short *and* longer term and embed skills that can help manage the condition across the whole dementia trajectory (Katsuno, 2005; Carpenter et al, 2008). Key dimensions of early support include: challenging the nihilism that is often associated with dementia; understanding dementia as a social condition and subjective experience not just a biomedical illness; recognising the continuity of personhood; and supporting positive coping strategies (O'Connor et al, 2007).

Care home residents living with dementia

What determines the quality of life among care home residents has been the focus of considerable research (Brooker, 2011). Despite challenges regarding how to meaningfully capture the perspectives of residents with advanced dementia the issues that have been identified as important include: social interaction, psychological well-being, religion/spirituality, independence, financial security, and health (Samus et al, 2005; Byrne-Davis et al, 2006). Themes from research exploring what matters to residents include: the right to make choices, be involved in decisions that affect their daily life, the importance of relationships, having an occupation or role, retaining contact with family, caring for – and being cared for by – others, maintaining identity and 'making the best of oneself' (Surr, 2006; Clare et al, 2008). Unsurprisingly, these mirror the broader findings reviewed earlier.

Although there is mixed epidemiological evidence, most research identifies care home residents as having low levels of well-being and poor quality of life (National Institute for Health and Care Excellence, 2013; 2015a). Issues that undermine well-being are: lack of activity and stimulation, limited access to health services, limited contact with relatives, and care that does not afford the older person dignity or respect (Alzheimer's Society, 2007; Dening and Milne, 2020). These deficits tend to be particularly acute for residents with more advanced dementia. Quality of life among residents is higher in care homes where: staff have higher levels of training; there are specialised workers, for example dementia nurses; residents are involved in care planning decisions; residents are encouraged to participate in everyday activities; physical health care needs are attended to; families are encouraged to be involved in care home life; and residents have a meaningful relationship with at least one member of staff (Edvardsson et al, 2014). Smaller homelike care establishments are correlated with higher levels of quality of life among residents (Mikelyte and Milne, 2016). It is important to note that some research is more positive. For example, a 2007 Dutch study of a group of care home residents with advanced dementia showed that over a two-year period their quality of life improved significantly (Oudman and Veurink, 2007).

When people are very dependent and live in a care home, quality of life becomes inextricably linked to quality of care (Milne, 2011). 'Care' is a multi-faceted construct made up of both elements within the care home, such as staff, and external elements, such as health services. Good-quality care also depends on a range of micro-level (for example satisfied staff) and macro-level (for example financial stability of the provider) factors and their interaction. The quality of life of care home residents is thus not only complex because it is a challenge to capture resident perspectives but, as a consequence of being embedded in the care home environment, is inevitably determined by multiple factors that are situated in this environment (Dening and Milne, 2020). Emerging work exploring micro-cultures in care homes is beginning to engage with these issues (Mikelyete and Milne, 2016).

The National Institute for Health and Care Excellence (NICE, 2013) developed guidance called *Mental Wellbeing of Older People in Care Homes*. It sets out a set of six statements reflecting standards on: maintaining personal identity; recognising signs and symptoms of a mental health condition; support of sensory impairment; support of physical problems; participation in meaningful activity; and access to a full range of health care services. NICE considers mental well-being to include 'issues that are key to optimum functioning and independence' such as life satisfaction, optimism, self-esteem, feeling in control, and having a purpose in life and sense of belonging (Phair, 2016). That the flavour of the guidance is 'treatment' focused and about 'support' cannot be surprising as it has been developed by an organisation tasked with raising care standards and improving health in populations with (mainly) diagnosed conditions. However, two of the standards – maintaining personal identity and participation in meaningful activity – closely mirror the dimensions of quality of life already noted, and the elements of mental well-being also reflect a number of the issues that matter to people living with dementia.

There is a need to take a broad perspective if we are to understand variations in quality of life and are concerned to promote and/or maintain 'an optimal quality of life' for people living with dementia' (Etterma et al, 2005, p 353). This goal has underpinned the development of quality of life measures and assessments of quality of life in people living with dementia; it is to this body of work that I now turn.

Measuring and assessing quality of life and well-being in people living with dementia

There is an overarching tension between the objective evaluation of quality of life and the subjective views of people living with dementia. This reflects the schism referred to at the beginning of this section. It is, however, noteworthy that greater efforts are now being made to incorporate the perspectives of people living with dementia in quality of life research, including in work with people with advanced dementia and care home populations (Cordner et al, 2010). This field is characterised by a number of fundamental challenges. Determining quality of life in a condition that, by its very nature, deteriorates is a scientific problem. Developing a reliable measure across a (potentially) lengthy unpredictable trajectory is a related challenge. There are also practical and methodological difficulties in research with people with advanced dementia, including the credibility of self-reporting and consent and capacity issues (Milne, 2011).

While it is not my intent to review all the dementia-related quality of life instruments that exist, I think it is helpful to offer a flavour of the terrain and demonstrate how research and research tools shape our understanding of quality of life, well-being and mental health in people living with dementia.

It is axiomatic that the domains identified by researchers as important to quality of life *by* people living with dementia are reflected in research instruments to evaluate it. Most measures are health-related quality of life measures (HRQoL), that is, they assess issues relating to dementia alongside broader issues such as well-being and social engagement. Despite the fact that key HRQoL measures vary considerably in nature and type, they share a number of core domains: physical functioning, cognitive abilities, ability to participate in meaningful activities, social engagement and mood (Warner et al, 2010). Most also incorporate a domain that assesses the self and/or identity.

Broadly, there are three types of measure: self-rated tools used mainly for people in mild to moderate stages of dementia (Trigg et al, 2007; Crespo et al, 2013); proxy carer-related tools used by family or formal carers; and tools that use a mix of both. Some measures are questionnaires while others rely on observational data, for example of the person's behaviour, collected by a third party (Ettema et al, 2005; Sloane et al, 2007). Key dementia-related HRQoL measures include: Quality of Life in Alzheimer's Disease scale (QoL-AD) (Logsdon et al, 1999; Hoe et al, 2006), DEMQOL (health-related quality of life for People Living with Dementia measurement; Smith et al, 2005), the DQoL (the dementia quality of life instrument; Brod et al, 1999) and the QUALIDEM scale (dementia-specific quality of life instrument; Ettema et al, 2007).

It is important to make a distinction between measures developed for a community-based population with a range of severity of dementia, for example DEMQOL and measures developed for (primarily) care home populations with advanced dementia, for example QUALIDEM. There is, perhaps inevitably, greater reliance on third-party reports and observational data in research with care home residents. It is important to acknowledge that a direct self-assessment tool is not the same as an indirect observational measure in status or value.

More recently existing quality of life measures, such as QUALIDEM, have incorporated a dimension of 'adaptation'. This addition acknowledges the growing body of evidence that people living with dementia can, and will, attempt to ameliorate the impact of their condition on their physical and/or psychological well-being and protect their quality of life (Clare, 2003). This includes people with advanced dementia (Ettema et al, 2005). It appears that people living with dementia limit the number and nature of their goals to those that are most highly valued, work harder to achieve them and employ alternative strategies to compensate for those that may no longer be effective (Nikmat et al, 2015). This evidence resonates with issues highlighted in Chapter 7 about older people with frailty pursuing goals that are emotionally meaningful and that contribute positively to their well-being (Chung, 2004). The fact that people living with dementia, at all stages, appear capable of 'steering' their resources towards primordial, or vital, areas of well-being additionally confirms the relevance of the SOC model (selection, optimisation, compensation) of successful ageing discussed in Chapter 2. It also opens up new possibilities to explore this, and related constructs, through the lens of dementia.

One of the distinctive features of HRQoL instruments is that they aim to capture a subjective evaluation *by the person* of relevant aspects of their health and well-being rather than offering an external assessment of an objective entity (Warner et al, 2010). This represents two principles: that external assessments of quality of life are regarded as inferior to the person's own evaluation and acceptance that *all* those living with dementia can communicate meaningfully about their quality of life (Byrne-Davis et al, 2006). These trends reflect the increased involvement of people living with dementia in research and greater acknowledgement that people living with dementia are legitimate witnesses to their own lives and have a right to be heard (Woods, 2012). It also reflects greater investment in developing tools or measures that captures what is important to people living with dementia (Lamont et al, 2019). It remains the case, however, that involvement is more easily operationalised in research with people with earlier stage dementia (Williamson, 2012a; see Chapter 9).

It has also been suggested that the validity of the self-evaluation principle may diminish as dementia worsens (Logsdon et al, 2002). How far the subjective assessment of quality of life by a person with advanced dementia can be regarded as credible is contested. On this basis observational scales of quality of life in advanced dementia have been developed, mainly for use in long-term care (Zimmerman et al, 2005). QUALIDEM is one such example. It relies on ratings by care home staff of: care relationship, behaviour, mood, self-image, social relations, having something to do, level of isolation and feeling at home (Ettema et al, 2007). Structured observational methods also exist; Dementia Care Mapping (DCM) is the best known example (Brooker, 2005). Kitwood (1997), who developed the early prototype of DCM, described it as 'a serious attempt to take the standpoint of the person with dementia, using a combination of empathy and observational skill' (p 4). DCM is used as both a research measure and a practice improvement tool. More recently, a shorter tool based on it – the Short Observation Framework for Inspection – has been used by the Care Quality Commission in England, Social Care and Social Work Improvement Scotland, and the Care and Social Services Inspectorate in Wales as part of their evaluation of the quality of life of people with dementia living in care homes (Care Quality Commission, 2017).

Concern to ensure that the perspective of the person with more advanced dementia was captured underpinned the development of a hybrid instrument by Smith and colleagues (2005) for use in community-based settings. The researchers devised two separate but complementary measures: one for the person with dementia (DEMQOL, noted earlier) and one for family carers (DEMQOL-proxy). The measures are administered by an interviewer; they have undergone extensive validation in the UK and are widely used. Although Smith et al (2005) suggest that DEMQOL-proxy should be used mainly with people with severe dementia, it is also a valid instrument for use with people with mild to moderate dementia (Chua et al, 2016).

There are long-standing concerns about differences between the ratings of carers (paid or family) and the rating of the person living with dementia themselves. Self-ratings of quality of life are often higher than those made by third parties (Gräske et al, 2012). It has been suggested that these may arise, in part at least, from a difference of perspective and emphasis. For example, one study found that care home residents' quality of life scores were most affected by the presence of depression and anxiety, whereas staff ratings were more influenced by level of dependency and behaviour problems (Hoe et al, 2006). Family carers' ratings may be influenced (perhaps inevitably) by carer-related burden and their emotional ties to the person living with dementia (Sands et al, 2004).

In addition to instruments intended to assess the quality of life of the person living with dementia, there are also measures that aim to evaluate the quality of life of family carers (Vellone et al, 2008; Larkin et al, 2019). Discussing these is beyond the scope of this chapter, but it is useful to note that this is a growth area predominantly characterised by an emphasis on the negative aspects of caring and on the role that carers' services can play (Rand and Malley, 2014). Carer measures have been criticised for their primarily instrumental focus on supporting carers to continue to care; instruments tend not to take a broader view of carers' quality of life of which caring is a part (Vitaliano et al, 1991). A particular deficit in this field is the development of instruments that can take account of the quality of life of *both* members of the care dyad simultaneously (Milne and Larkin, 2015). The current model, unintentionally, reinforces the view that family carers' quality of life is subordinate to that of the cared for person; their only role, in research terms, is to act as a proxy informant or as a source of information about the impact of caring on their lives.

Conclusion

This chapter has identified a number of life course and age-related inequalities that enhance the likelihood of developing dementia. This not only reinforces the growing body of evidence which suggests that dementia risks are more complex and situated than has traditionally been believed but it also underscores the 'accumulation of risks' thesis. This challenges the neuro-degenerative disease model and opens up the possibility of a discourse about links between the life course, inequalities and dementia that takes us in a different conceptual and operational direction. Links between mental health problems and dementia intersect with this analysis in ways that are only partially understood. Some mental health problems appear to be a product of, or at least are very common among, people living with dementia, for example delirium. With others, such as depression, a strong association with dementia appears to exist but its aetiology is unclear. Researchers are only now beginning to explore the nature of the links between mental health problems and dementia. There are multiple factors at play, and much remains to be done.

Research regarding quality of life and well-being among people living with dementia is located along three interrelated axes: the stage of the condition, the setting, and the nature of the research. Most work capturing the perspectives of people living with dementia has been done with people in the earlier stages of the condition living in the community, although more efforts are now being made to include people in the later stages. Existing work on those with more advanced dementia tends to focus on people who use services, primarily long-term care (Beerens et al, 2014). The inclusion of care home residents living with dementia is a distinctive feature of research in this field.

Research aims and methods also differ reflecting these distinctions. The former body of work tends to be qualitative in nature, capturing evidence about the lived experience and gathering data directly from people living with dementia. Understanding what enhances and undermines quality of life and well-being are core aims. Research with people with more advanced dementia tends to rely on validated instruments to evaluate quality of life; the perspectives of people living with dementia are less prominent and are often supplemented, or substituted, by input from a third party. This type of research is often focused on care outcomes, the effectiveness of a service and/or changes in quality of life over time.

In terms of epidemiological evidence, we know most about those groups of people living with dementia in receipt of (public) services, particularly long-term care. There is (almost) no work on the quality of life and well-being of people with dementia living 'ordinary lives'. People with dementia tend to be excluded from large-scale community-based surveys. This suggests that, despite claims to the contrary, people living with dementia are conceptualised as separate from 'the mainstream'. There is also little research focusing on the dimensions of quality of life *across* the dementia trajectory (Cordner et al, 2010). Research tends to take a snapshot at one point in time or of one service setting rather than adopting a dynamic lens of analysis that can accommodate change and temporality (Hughes and Williamson, 2019). Longitudinal evidence is needed to clarify causal relationships and identify ways of maintaining or improving quality of life over time. The mixed body of evidence we have at present suggests a need to reconsider approaches to understanding and assessing living well with dementia at all stages and in all contexts (Martyr et al, 2018). That a single instrument *could* possibly be used to assess quality of life across the trajectory of a variable and unpredictable condition is a scientific conundrum as well as a conceptual one, adding to the complexity of the research challenge.

The fact that no account is taken of the role played by social inequalities and life course determinants is an overarching deficit of existing dementia research. Having dementia does not eclipse what has gone before, it does not eradicate the influence of social class, gender, race, sexuality, age or disability on mental health and well-being and nor does it necessarily dominate older people's evaluation of their life's quality. The issues that seem to matter to people living with dementia are similar to those that matter to people without dementia (Wilhelmson et al, 2005; Banerjee et al, 2006; Bowling and Gabriel, 2007). While dementia-related symptoms may play a role other factors appear to be as, or more, significant.

While some work has been done to explore the intersection between dementia, quality of life, well-being and mental health, it remains a neglected area in policy and research (Aminzadeh et al, 2007). A fundamental influence on the discourse is how dementia, and people living with dementia, are conceptualised and treated, the extent to which current models take account of life course issues and inequalities, and the implications of current frameworks for the mental health and well-being of people living with dementia. This literature is reviewed in Chapter 9; dementia-relevant policy issues are also explored in some detail.

9

Conceptualising dementia

Introduction

This chapter reviews links between the ways we conceptualise and construct dementia and treat people living with dementia, and explores the extent to which existing frameworks and models take account of life course issues and social and structural inequalities. The implications of adopting a broader lens for the mental health and well-being of people living with dementia, and for understanding and responding to their needs, is also explored. The intersection of relevant policy with this discourse is discussed too.

Understanding and conceptualising dementia

The chapter begins with an overview of the different approaches taken to conceptualising dementia and how these inform the way that people living with dementia are viewed and supported. Figure 9.1 is a pictorial representation and timeline of the key models.

Figure 9.1: Conceptualising dementia: the widening lens

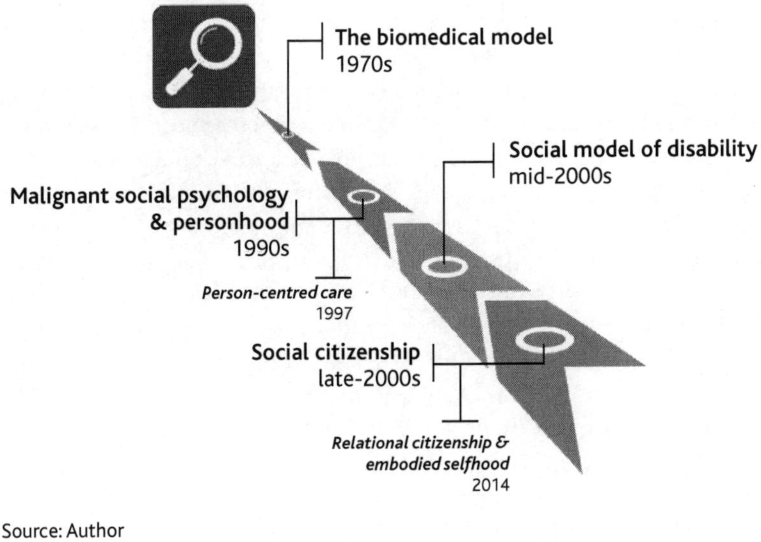

Source: Author

Biomedical model

The dominant approach to understanding dementia is located in the biomedical paradigm. The 1970s and 1980s heralded a shift away from regarding 'deteriorating cognitive function' as a normal part of the ageing process and relabelled it a 'pathological condition', most notably Alzheimer's disease. This lens assumes irrevocable decline related to neuro-pathological changes and predicts that over time the person with dementia will become progressively more dependent and in need of care (for example Mitchell and Shiri-Feshki, 2009). Although the medicalisation of dementia has some benefits, including investment in pharmacological treatments and the development of (some) health services, it encourages a focus on disease and fatalism (Bond, 1992). It also positions the person living with dementia as a victim of chronic illness with a particular set of symptoms and a distinctive trajectory. Further, it tends to be accompanied by clinical and service-oriented language and an ageist nihilistic set of assumptions about lack of potential and ability.

That this approach eclipses all other facets of the person's biography, life and personality is a long-standing criticism (Killick and Allan, 2001; Milne, 2010a). Understanding of the individual's subjective experiences, life course, relationships and nature is lost beneath, or at least marginalised by, a primary focus on dementia as a medical condition and a 'master status' (Goffman, 1963; Milne 2010b). It 'relegates the person's qualities, skills and capabilities behind their deficits and difficulties' (Morris and Morris, 2010, p 159), restricts our understanding of the emotional world of people living with dementia and tends to 'render meaningless their actions' (Beard, 2004, p 418). A number of these dimensions resonate with arguments relating to frailty; its intersection with dementia is explored later in the chapter.

It is noteworthy that the biomedical approach continues to dominate understanding of dementia in the UK, and internationally, and infuses how people living with dementia are treated in the policy, service and practice domains and by the public. For example, in the health care system there is much emphasis on early diagnosis and treatment of dementia, a focus on 'the patient' as the passive recipient of care and on managing challenging behaviours (Parker, 2001). The number of Mental Capacity Act 2005 assessments of people living with dementia suggests that the care system struggles to accommodate the complexity of their needs and/or cannot manage to support them without recourse to, often restrictive, legislative mechanisms (Boyle, 2008).

As there is growing evidence that neurodegenerative change alone does not account for the path dementia takes and – as we saw in Chapter 8 – that it intersects with other elements of the person's life, roles and context in ways that are far from standardised, the explanatory capacity of the biomedical model is limited. Other models and frameworks offer 'ways in' to developing new thinking and different approaches.

Malignant social psychology and personhood

The importance of relationships, the situated nature of dementia and a drive to extend understanding of dementia beyond its biomedical confines lies at the heart of seminal work done by the psychologist Tom Kitwood in the 1990s. Kitwood (1993a; 1997) developed the concept of 'malignant social psychology'. This refers to the role played by attitudes and the environment in amplifying the impact of losses commonly experienced by people living with dementia and creating a self-reinforcing spiral of 'depersonalisation' in which people living with dementia are ignored, dismissed, marginalised, misunderstood and (often) mistreated (Kitwood and Bredin, 1992; Kelly, 2010). Stigma and discrimination are related features, including self-stigmatisation (Tzouvara et al, 2018). Kitwood (1997) theorised that at least some of the deterioration seen in people living with dementia is caused not by neuro-pathological deficits but by depersonalising processes and responses. Sabat (2002; 2005) agrees, suggesting that 'dysfunctional treatment of the afflicted person' such as talking negatively about them in their presence is not only harmful in its own right but, when the person reacts with righteous anger and this is labelled as irrational, they are doubly wounded and become less and less able to manifest healthy behaviours and abilities.

It is axiomatic that such treatment has a profoundly negative effect on the mental health and well-being of people living with dementia. It undermines their self-esteem, confidence and sense of security (Reeve, 2002). Specifically, it has been linked with increased risk of depression, anxiety, diminished social opportunities and loss of motivation to engage in relationships or occupation (Sabat, 1994; Sabat et al, 2004; Brannelly, 2011). It is also implicated in heightened incidence of so-called 'challenging behaviours' including agitation and wandering (Moniz-Cook et al, 2003; Langdon et al, 2007; Chaudhury and Cooke, 2014). Depersonalising cultures in long-term care settings are associated with higher levels of neglect and abuse; the more a person with dementia is constructed as a 'bag of symptoms' or a 'set of tasks' the greater the risk of their not being regarded as fully human and of being vulnerable to poor care and abuse (see Chapter 6 regarding abusive cultures in care homes; also discussion on infrahumanisation later in this chapter). Stigma and discrimination are implicated in increased risk of isolation and exclusion and reduced sense of self-worth and value (for example Link and Phelan, 2001).

Kitwood (1993a) stressed the influence of interpersonal relations on the well-being, mental health and treatment of people living with dementia (O'Connor et al, 2007). They form the cornerstone of 'personhood' and, later, the development of person-centred care (Nolan et al, 2002). Personhood brought psychosocial understanding to bear on dementia; 'it revisioned dementia as socially constructed by, and within, a person's interactional environment' (Bartlett and O'Connor, 2010, p 19). Kitwood defined personhood as, 'a standing or status that is bestowed upon one human being by others in the context of particular social relationships and institutional arrangements. It implies recognition, respect and trust' (Kitwood, 1997, p 8). He argued that a person with dementia retains an enduring sense of self, preferences and personality characteristics as well as meaningful connections with family members and care staff. Kitwood placed great emphasis on the 'social nature of the self and interpersonal encounters that (have the potential to) support wellbeing' (Kitwood, 1997, p 69). For example, he suggested that identity can be supported by those around the person with dementia 'holding it in place' (Kitwood, 1997). Keeping 'a particular narrative going' and 'integrating individual biography with external events' is another related role external agents can play in bolstering personhood (Giddens, 1999, p 54).

Kitwood's (1993a; 1997) work led to a paradigm shift in the dementia field. Since the mid 1990s dementia has been increasingly seen as a complex interaction between neurological impairment, personality, biography, physical health status and social psychology (Bruens, 2013). This approach not only extended understanding of dementia but engaged with ways that quality of life for people living with dementia could be appreciated and promoted, especially in service settings. It opened up the possibility that by adjusting the social context and creating a more nurturing environment cognitive capacity and function could be better maintained and the impact of disability limited.

A focus on personhood and person-centred care: benefits and limitations

Bartlett and O'Connor (2010) argue that at a micro level personhood in dementia can be credited with developing dementia practice and research in three important ways. Firstly, it has engaged with a more holistic and hopeful understanding of dementia and promoted a shift of focus from the disease process itself to the interpersonal and broader environment. This approach is supported by the growing evidence that psychosocial interventions, environmental changes and assistive technologies can mitigate the extent of disability and improve quality of life (Fossey et al, 2006). Examples in care homes include: the introduction of meaningful activities, regular access to a garden and supporting the use of game consoles which encourage communication, coordination and sociable fun (Phair, 2016).

Person-centred care – a practice framework drawing on the concept of personhood – can be seen as the process that operationalises it. Wilberforce and colleagues (2017) recently provided a threefold definition of the principles of person-centredness summarised as: understanding the person and their unique interpretation and experience of dementia; service user empowerment in choice-making; and placing relationships at the heart of support and care (Manthorpe and Samsi, 2016). Person-centred care (PCC) has acted as a fulcrum in improving recognition of the individual needs of people living with dementia, for challenging established narrow cultures of care and practice and promoting the rights of people living with dementia to make decisions about their life (Allan, 2001). Other, related, frameworks are also relevant. For example, Brooker's (2011) VIPS model which highlights the importance of **V**aluing people and promoting their rights, **I**ndividualised care and support, appreciating and working from the **P**erspective of the person living with dementia and facilitating a **S**upportive social environment.

A second positive impact of personhood is that this lens 'offers an important strategy for beginning to individualise the experience of dementia by contextualising it within a broader lifecourse perspective' (Bartlett and O'Connor, 2010, p 20). At least three of the factors that contribute to the dementia experience – personality, biography and physical health status – are a product of, and are embedded in, the life course. With this link continuity between previous and current life experiences and dementia is made and an emphasis on understanding a person's life course in order to understand their experience of dementia is explicit. It also underscores the importance of knowing about the person living with dementia in order to provide effective support and care. I return to these issues later.

Thirdly, an approach that respects personhood has meant that the way people living with dementia are spoken about, and to, has improved dramatically in the last decade. It has encouraged the incorporation of the perspectives of people living with dementia into both research and practice (Williamson, 2012b). There is now a burgeoning body of work that clearly demonstrates that people living with dementia *can* contribute important insights about their experiences and needs (for example Clare et al, 2005; Whitlatch et al, 2005). This work is informing policy and practice, for example helping to develop innovative ways to communicate with people living with dementia who have impaired capacity to do so. People living with dementia are also increasingly involved in research as co-designers and co-researchers, reviewers of research bids and as partners in national initiatives such as the Dementia Engagement and Empowerment Project (DEEP). DEEP aims to connect groups of people living with dementia who have an 'influencing' or 'involvement' role in order to capture their work and impact. There are over 50 groups who are members of the DEEP network (Williamson, 2012a; dementiavoices.org.uk, 2018).

More critically, both personhood and PCC have limitations. Bartlett and O'Connor (2007) suggest that while personhood raises the possibility of improving support for people living with dementia in the immediate interpersonal environment it does not: engage with the wider socio-political context; recognise that people living with dementia matter but not that the person with dementia has the capacity to exercise agency; and limits itself to individual health and well-being without examining how power shapes relationships. Further, personhood is a concept that assumes passivity in the face of external forces – malignant social psychology; it is a static status conferred on a person rather than an ongoing dynamic process of recognition and realignment (Dewing, 2007).

Higgs and Gilleard (2016b) suggest that personhood is a rather ill-defined concept; its achievement is opaque and its components a challenge to pin down. This is a concern as it has become one of the defining features of contemporary policy and practice in dementia care and is invoked in a range of settings, particularly long-term care. Higgs and Gilleard (2016b) further suggest that, paradoxically, its lack of concrete form may undermine, rather than enhance, the fundamental moral imperative of care that they argue is central to the social realities of a disabled, and disabling, old age.

There are also a number of criticisms of PCC as a framework. As with personhood PCC tends to be described in rather abstract ways (Manthorpe and Samsi, 2016). PCC, especially in the later stages of dementia, is complex and makes considerable cognitive and emotional demands on those receiving care and family carers. PCC is not just a transaction but is about a meaningful relationship that enables compassionate care to flourish, dignity to be respected and consistency to be assured. There is some confusion about whether PCC is a process or an outcome. There is limited research on which aspects of PCC are effective or what is required to deliver it. For example, does its achievement rely on the attributes of individuals or organisational structures or both? Outcome measures also remain elusive and, despite persuasive rhetoric, there has not been widespread improvement in practice since the adoption of PCC as a core element of 'good dementia care' (DH, 2012a). The evidence that does exist suggests that well-funded PCC can deliver improved levels of participation and the maintenance of personhood for people with dementia living in the community (Gladman et al, 2007). It is difficult to see how cash-strapped services will accommodate such costs, especially in an era of austerity.

A failure to contextualise personhood and PCC has also led to assumptions of homogeneity that have 'effectively muted differences and limited the development of a textured understanding of the experiences' (Bartlett and O'Connor, 2010, p 23). In particular, it fails to engage with issues relating to social location or take account of structural inequalities arising from gender, age, race, SES, sexual orientation and/or disability (Doyle and Rubinstein, 2013). As we tend to describe the dementia *experience* rather than the dementia *experiences* the myriad ways that other sources of disadvantage impact on living with dementia are obscured. Due to the fact that there is growing evidence that these issues profoundly influence the experience of dementia this is a significant oversight. Hulko (2009), for example, found that privileged people tend to be more devastated by the losses that often accompany dementia than those from more disadvantaged backgrounds who have previously faced profound challenges in their lives, for example poverty.

Relationship-centred care was developed to redress the focus on the person with dementia to the exclusion of those who provide support (Ryan et al, 2008). The impetus of relationship-centred care is to 'fully capture the interdependencies and reciprocities that underpin caring relationships' (Nolan et al, 2002, p 203) and to make explicit the centrality of relationships to family and formal care. This model made two key contributions to dementia care (Kontos et al, 2017). Firstly, it shifted the nexus from autonomy and independence – that underpin personhood and PCC – to interdependence and relationality; '... the model makes explicit the importance of interconnectedness and partnerships' (Bartlett and O'Connor, 2010, p 25). Secondly, it foregrounds an expectation that the person with dementia will retain status as an active partner in the dementia care experience and that they have, at least some, agency.

However, it retains a rather narrow focus on interpersonal care relationships thus overlooking the role and influence of other relationships the person with dementia may have 'such as those with the state and its institutions' (Kontos et al, 2017, p 183). Further, the person living with dementia is solely conceptualised within their personal environment and in need of care context. By confining the focus to the interpersonal there is a danger that responsibility for supporting a person with dementia is located in the immediate care environment. There are two problems here. One is that the 'significant other' now assumes power over the person with dementia (Bartlett and O'Connor, 2010). Secondly, responsibility can be neatly assigned, usually to poorly paid frontline care staff, and there is no requirement to capture how wider social processes and profit-driven systems influence what is, or is not, done. Poor treatment remains the 'fault' of the care worker not of the organisational priorities that lead to poor treatment nor the policies that create the conditions for it. This is an issue I explored in Chapter 6.

In the informal sector, another set of pernicious issues emerge whereby responsibility for poorly resourced care is transferred onto stressed and tired family carers (Manthorpe and Iliffe, 2016b in Chapter 6). Micro level interpersonal relationships are treated as if they are unconnected to the wider social and economic world and to the power differentials embedded in it. They are presented as quite separate from the macro policy, socio-political and societal context that shapes the nature of care, funding issues and how people living with dementia and paid and family carers are perceived and supported.

A note on biographical approaches

Although biographical approaches are aligned to personhood and PCC they have a distinctive profile. Biographical approaches include life history, life review and reminiscence work (Williams et al, 2014; Ray, 2016b). When these models first became prominent in the 1990s, they represented a significant development in dementia care (Murphy, 1994; McKeown et al, 2010). Recognition of the importance of life course issues and the potential interventions offered to enhance the well-being of people living with dementia were positive; they also challenged the therapeutic nihilism that permeated dementia care (Gibson, 2004). They explicitly draw on psychological models and thinking, including narrative therapy principles, preservation of self in storytelling and identity maintenance (for example Surr, 2006; McAdams, 2008).

Biographical approaches have been employed in a range of service settings such as long-term care (Moos and Björn, 2006), psychological therapy for couples where one person has dementia (Ingersoll-Dayton et al, 2013) and day-hospital settings (McKeown et al, 2010). Actively engaging with an individual's biography is reported to enhance care workers' ability to regard the person living with dementia as a unique human being with an individual life course, experiences and relationships (Clarke et al, 2003). Adopting a biographical approach can also act as a memory aid and can help bolster identity. Research has also identified that understanding significant events in the person's life, for example a war experience, can help to interpret behaviours which may appear unusual (Gibson, 2004).

The development of a new dementia paradigm

Since Kitwood's (1993a; 1993b; 1997) work there has been a slow but steady move away from viewing dementia solely through the biomedical lens (Sabat, 2014). This has, importantly, included an increased understanding of the ways in which social dimensions can influence the experience and has helped re-focus policy, care and research on the person rather than the condition (Gilliard et al, 2005).

It is important to acknowledge the contribution of three key drivers in shifting the agenda forward. These are: the elevation of the voices of people living with dementia in service and policy development and research, the (re)emergence of a politically framed 'rights-based' optic on the lives and well-being of groups of people who have historically been marginalised, and a number of legislative measures that – collectively – aim to enhance the inclusion of people living with dementia and ensure that those in need of support from services receive it.

Challenges to existing models and frameworks are emerging from six sources located in two arenas. The first arena relates to the conceptualisation of dementia. In this arena there are three frameworks that offer potential to extend understanding of dementia as a condition, a socio-political issue and as linked to human (and other) rights: the social model of disability; social citizenship; and relational citizenship. Issues relating to the life course and inequalities are more visible in this new paradigm and are a more prominent dimension of dementia discourse as a consequence. The intersection of sociological analysis with dementia is the second arena and includes frailty and the processes of infrahumanisation and precarity.

The social model of disability and dementia

Constructing dementia as a 'disability' is a thesis that is beginning to gain traction, particularly in relationship to policy and legal rights (Thomas and Milligan, 2015). Although the social model is well established in the disability field it has only recently been brought to bear on dementia discourse. Disability rights are powerful levers for change; it is this capacity that makes it attractive to those who wish to secure rights for people living with dementia. The role that the social model has played in challenging the 'individual tragedy' model is also relevant, reframing disability as a set of systemic and societal barriers that impede the capacity of people with impairments to fulfil their potential and live full lives.

There can be no question that people living with dementia are disadvantaged in profound ways and excluded from participating in mainstream society, utilising ordinary services and public areas, accessing good-quality care and treatment and contributing to family and community life. Space does not permit a lengthy exposition on this issue but key barriers include: lack of engagement by shops, leisure centres, GPs and other services with meeting the communication needs of people with (more advanced) dementia, being excluded from decisions that affect them, being 'assumed' to lack capacity to make choices and being offered less valued treatments, that is, drugs rather than psychosocial support (Cantley and Bowes, 2004; Benbow and Jolley, 2012). People with advanced dementia are at particular risk of being excluded, isolated and institutionalised prematurely.

The social model of disability has much to offer (Thomas and Milligan, 2015). By framing dementia as a disability the 'problem' of dementia is transferred from the individual and their family to wider society, locating responsibility for addressing barriers to participation and involvement in social and economic policies, the environment, public, political and professional attitudes and services (Mental Health Foundation, 2015). It highlights the disabling consequences of a society organised around the needs of non-disabled – non-demented – people, incorporates at its core the experiences and perspectives of people living with dementia and challenges notions of dependency and passivity (Barlett and O'Connor, 2010; Manthorpe and Iliffe, 2016b).

Pursuing a social model challenges deficit-based thinking and the social construction of dementia as a wholly negative condition shaped by fear, stigma and exclusion (Sabat et al, 2004). It engages with reframing public understanding of dementia, promotes higher levels of inclusion of people living with dementia in communities and society, helps shift the 'care system' towards the achievement of more ambitious goals than those focused on reducing hospital admissions and safeguarding, and encourages a much more nuanced personalised approach to care and support (Gilliard et al, 2005; O'Connor and Purves, 2009). The social model reframes the clinical arena too. It demands that professionals learn to communicate meaningfully with service users with dementia, ensure that the service user is placed at the centre of any encounter and is valued and respected as an individual with feelings, a personality, a biography and a right to be fully involved in decision-making (Ward et al, 2008).

Locating dementia inside the social model also offers an opportunity for people living with dementia to act as catalysts for change and to have their voices heard. Examples include DEEP (see earlier) and the *Scottish Dementia Working Group*, both of whom directly engage with people living with dementia, campaign to improve rights, services and attitudes, raise awareness about dementia in communities and society, and offer a space for people living with dementia to support one another, fight for justice and contribute to policy making, research and national debate (Alzheimer Scotland, 2018; dementiavoices.org.uk, 2018). Another issue relates to language. The social model challenges negative labels used to describe dementia, for example as a 'tsunami', and people with dementia as 'senile' (Cahill, 2018).

Further, (re)framing dementia as a disability and positioning it inside disability legislation would increase its status and engage policy makers in a different kind of discourse (Hughes and Williamson, 2019). It would challenge the current 'chronic incurable illness' narrative and shift the lens towards a more overtly political perspective underpinned by notions of inclusion and rights (Downs, 2000; Gilliard et al, 2005). In facing towards the social model, policy makers would, importantly, be acknowledging a need to address the social, economic and physical barriers facing people living with dementia mirroring the drive, which began in the 1980s, to address similar barriers facing disabled people (Oliver, 2013; Shakespeare, 2013; Slasberg and Beresford, 2016).

In terms of broader issues, recognising that people living with dementia, as is the case for some people with disabilities, are pejoratively positioned in relationship to what is valued by wider society is an issue that the social model makes explicit. For example, the emphasis placed on economic productivity as the only meaningful type of productivity and the 'failure' of people living with dementia to achieve the desired policy goals of independence and autonomy (Michalowsky et al, 2016). This intersects with arguments relating to the fourth age and frailty, which were explored in Chapter 7 and are also discussed later in this chapter.

Challenges and limitations

There are, however, a number of key challenges in terms of operationalising these goals and delivering an effective social model of disability for people living with dementia. Its meaningful implementation would require significant societal and cultural changes at both micro and macro levels, and there is work to be done about the precise nature of the dimensions of the model. Shakespeare (2006) argues that the social model has a number of deficits, which may be particularly problematic for people living with dementia. It tends to reduce the complexity of disability to crude environmental determinism and ignores the personal experiences of those living with a disability (Shakespeare, 2006). It was also developed with a static condition in mind and fails to accommodate pain, frailty and degeneration, especially if they are associated with ageing. Additionally, it struggles to make space for mental health conditions and pays little heed to life course issues or structural inequalities. The social model was – in effect – developed by, and for, younger adults with physical disabilities and was designed primarily to address their exclusion from paid work, decent incomes, public transport, relationships of equality, political power and socially valued roles (Priestley, 2004). Its capacity to accommodate the complex and variable nature of dementia may be more limited.

Another issue relates to what matters to people living with dementia and their families. Many people living with dementia view it as a disease which needs a medical solution, and in its later stages, support from health and social care services (Steeman et al, 2007). A related question is how far people living with dementia perceive themselves to be 'disabled'. Many older people regard dementia as a condition 'linked to old age'; few conceptualise it as a disability. Evidence certainly suggests that people living with dementia are less likely than younger adults with a physical or learning disability to identify with the term disabled (Kelley-Moore et al, 2006). Nor are people living with dementia generally regarded by the public, professionals or other disabled people as members of the disabled community, and the dementia community has, up until recently, not been part of the disability movement (Shakespeare et al, 2017). Some older people even feel that being considered disabled is more stigmatising than having the label of dementia (Gilliard et al, 2005).

From the perspective of the disability community there are also a number of tensions. Dementia challenges disabled people to take account of the impact of a deteriorating condition and multiple impairments on daily living and the role played by relationships in maintaining the well-being of the person with dementia (Shakespeare et al, 2017). The relational lens highlights the interdependent nature of the lives of many people living with dementia, a message which runs counter to one of the original aims of the social model for disabled people: to promote independence (Sabat, 2008; Hughes, 2014). The fact that people with – mainly advanced – dementia are routinely viewed as less than human and treated accordingly is also a challenge to the disabled community who have fought hard to secure their status as citizens with rights to live full lives (Miron et al, 2017). That dementia activism is in its infancy and is not aligned with the well-established disabled rights movement is also an issue (Bartlett, 2014a; 2014b). A reluctance to acknowledge the intersectionality of ageism and discrimination relating to mental illness with disablism for people living with dementia and its 'manifestation in institutional and other socio-structural forms' is also relevant (Thomas, 2010, p 37). Thomas (2015) refers specifically to the damage inflicted by 'psycho-emotional disablism', stating that it, 'operates along psychological and emotional pathways to injure disabled individuals' self-esteem, personal confidence and ontological security' (p 6). Thomas and Milligan (2018) argue that this process plays a particularly pernicious role in the interpersonal relationships upon which people living with dementia depend and may be implicated in abuse.

Shakespeare (2006) suggests that due to the nature of dementia as a medical condition *and* a lived experience, applying the social model of disability requires a new approach in which appropriate weight is given to both neurological symptoms *and* the social relations in which people with dementia are embedded. Dementia is a multi-dimensional phenomenon and requires a response that addresses its different dimensions including the clinical, psychological, social and political. Shakespeare and colleagues (2017) argue for the development of a stronger more politically oriented model which recognises that people living with dementia are an oppressed social group who are poorly served in most environments and who are routinely exposed to exclusion, stigma, prejudice and discrimination.

The Mental Health Foundation proposes a similar hybrid model that can accommodate the personal, the medical and the social. Its report *Dementia, Rights and the Social Model of Disability* (2015) refers to an approach which 'gives greater credence to the personal experience of having a disability, in conjunction with the political and social contexts' (p 15). The authors conclude that the 'social model needs to take account not only of the external barriers but also of the social and psychological obstacles that exclude or restrict full participation in society' (Mental Health Foundation, 2015, p 15). Disability arises from the interaction of a health-related condition with environmental and personal factors (WHO, 2003). The Mental Health Foundation calls for a dual approach whereby biomedical research into treatments and action to remove social, attitudinal and environmental barriers to participation are pursued in parallel.

Policy, 'disability status' and people living with dementia

There are a number of advantages to incorporating people living with dementia under the disability umbrella in terms of international and national law and policy. For example, Article 19[1] of the UN Convention of the Rights of Persons with Disabilities (CRPD) (United Nations, 2006) could, theoretically at least, extend their rights to live in the community and to receive personalised services. Issues of agency, autonomy and dignity would also be accorded higher and more visible status. The CRPD explicitly includes people with dementia (The Dementia Policy Think Tank, the DEEP Network and Innovations in Dementia CIC, 2017). It called for stronger protection for disabled people from abuse and neglect and unlawful deprivation of liberty; this included specific reference to the treatment of people with dementia living in care homes. This prompted the All Party Parliamentary Group on Dementia (APPG) to launch an inquiry into dementia and disability in 2018. The APPG considers that regarding dementia as a disability 'helps to recognise the barriers that exist in society that prevent people living with dementia being able to live independently and provides a framework for action' (Alzheimer's Society, 2019a). It helpfully highlighted a link between dementia and the social model of disability that could, potentially, extend well beyond the boundaries of the inquiry. The international call for the UN to establish a Convention on the Rights of Older People is also relevant and strengthens these arguments (Age International and Age UK, 2015; HelpAge International, 2015).

The fact that dementia, certainly in its later stages, constitutes a disability under the Equality Act 2010 is also noteworthy. The Act states that 'a person is disabled if they have a physical or mental impairment that has a substantial and long-term negative effect on their ability to do normal daily activities' (p 4). A key aim of the Equality Act is to outlaw 'less favourable treatment' based on disability. As with the CRPD this sounds like good news. The fact that people living with dementia continue to experience widespread discrimination in community and service settings and (often) poorer treatment than other groups suggests that the Act's capacity to extend legal benefit to them has yet to be realised (Alzheimer's Society, 2015).

The Equality Act 2010 and the *Prime Minister's Dementia Challenge(s)* (DH, 2015b) both recognise a need to address the stigmatised status and exclusion that people living with dementia routinely experience. As this is a well-established threat to the mental health and well-being of people living with dementia (see Chapter 8) such high-profile policy goals are to be welcomed. A specific initiative is the 'dementia friendly community', introduced as part of the *2012 Prime Minister's Dementia Challenge* (DH, 2012a; Crampton et al, 2012). Despite its popularity – 152 dementia-friendly communities were set up by 2015 – it has been criticised for being, what Shakespeare and colleagues (2017) call, 'a nice sounding but conceptually weak' idea. Exactly what they are, and are not, is difficult to define, and how they actually benefit people living with dementia is largely opaque and untested. Cahill (2018) argues that as dementia-friendly communities, and similar initiatives, are not embedded in a rights-based framework, it is impossible for a person living with dementia to claim any entitlement to its benefits or identify, with any certainty, how these may have failed to take meaningful form.

Overall, the status of people living with dementia in policy is not that of a disabled person with the rights and advantages that a 'disability' status may bring (Hughes and Williamson, 2019). Unlike policies for disabled people, dementia policies tend to have very limited legal traction, are not reflective of a social model nor are they couched in the language of rights (DH, 2012a, 2015b). In terms of acquiring a robust legal platform and access to stronger policy levers, it would serve people living with dementia well to be included in the disability-related legal framework. It represents an important, if contested, mechanism to improve their status and rights.

Whatever the benefits of constructing dementia as a disability may be, some commentators argue that this framework does not go far enough. Conceptual thinking, rights and benefits for people living with dementia may be further extended by the social citizenship model which incorporates, at its heart, issues of social justice and human rights.

Social citizenship and dementia

Social citizenship is fundamentally about the relationship between the individual, society and the state (Turner, 1993). It goes beyond citizenship in so far as it is about attaining equality of status, that is, more than participation in a community or a society (Marshall, 1950) and draws on the principles of critical gerontology. Bartlett and O'Connor (2010) define social citizenship as: 'A relationship, practice or status, in which a person with dementia is entitled to experience freedom from discrimination, and to have opportunities to grow and participate in life to the fullest extent possible. It involves justice, recognition of social positions and the upholding of personhood, rights and a fluid degree of responsibility for shaping events at a personal and societal level' (p 37).

It is a broader, integrated, more politically oriented lens of analysis than those based on personhood or relationships and is 'attuned to issues of power, agency, marginalisation and disempowerment' (Bartlett and O'Conner, 2010, p 70). It differs from the social model of disability in that it explicitly recognises that the person with dementia is embedded in, and shaped by, a range of influences. These include: social policies, organisational policies and practices, social location (gender, socio-economic status, race and other structural dimensions), and broader societal processes such as discrimination, how we understand 'dementia' as a condition, and how we view issues such as agency, autonomy and independence for people living with dementia (Race Equality Foundation, 2016). Dimensions of social location and risks that pre-exist dementia, for example socio-economic disadvantage and being a victim of abuse, are recognised as retaining relevance; in fact dementia may amplify risks. This more granular multi-dimensional lens is defined by Bartlett and O'Connor (2010) as 'the socio-cultural context' (Figure 9.2). The model attempts to combine the personal, the social and the political. It positions personhood at the nexus of subjective experience (SE), interactional environment (IE) and socio-cultural context (SCC).

One of the key benefits of this model is that it accommodates, rather than replaces, the personal and the relationship focused frameworks. It enriches and expands our understanding of how dementia as a lived subjective experience is shaped by social location and structural inequalities. It also 'draws attention to the dynamic and multi-directional

Figure 9.2: A multi-dimensional model for contextualising dementia – a social citizenship approach

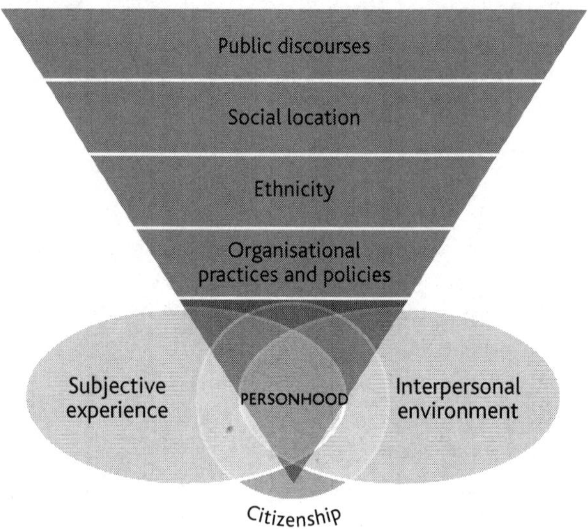

Source: Bartlett and O'Connor, 2010

nature of the relationships' between the different elements. While the concepts of personhood and PCC recognise the importance of including the voices of people living with dementia, 'the social citizenship model makes explicit their capacity for agency and rights to have influence and control over decisions that affect their lives and wellbeing' (Bartlett and O'Connor, 2007, p 115).

An underpinning principle of the social citizenship approach is a commitment to criticality, a challenge to 'the unreflective acceptance of established positions', normative assumptions or ways of understanding the world 'in relation to their social, historical and political contexts' (Bartlett and O'Conner, 2010, p 54). This might include: reframing reductionist responses to poor services as inadequate public funding rather than 'better staff training', limited access to support and care for people living with dementia as discrimination and 'carers doing their duty' as the state reneging on its responsibilities to support families affected by dementia. Challenging oppressive use of language is another example. There is a widely noted tendency to construct people living with dementia as 'other'. This not only distances 'us' from 'them' but positions 'having dementia' as the only, or most prominent, aspect of the person's identity (as noted earlier) and portrays dementia as a single homogeneous experience.

The model's acknowledgement of the role played by power is a third dimension. This is considered to be a stronger and more apposite focus for improving the status and treatment of people living with dementia than a politically 'softer' model whose focus is on the person and their localised environment. One of the key issues this agenda brings to the fore is the profound lack of power that most people living with dementia have; this recognition encourages engagement with a discourse that 'politicises' dementia, including campaigning and the acquisition of legal rights (Williamson, 2012b; Litherland, 2015).

Recognition of the importance of social justice is a fourth issue. Much of the discourse relating to dementia focuses on care and support. While it is important to acknowledge the contribution of services, it is also important to challenge common understandings about the need for care and related notions of dependency. Kittay (1999), Barnes (2012) and others argue 'that the myth of independence is damaging to the pursuit of political and social practices that embody an understanding of inequality' (Bartlett and O'Conner, 2010, p 61). Those working in the field of disability studies have challenged the simplistic bifurcation of dependence/independence and refocused attention on the concept of interdependence. This helps – theoretically at least – to reframe the concept of care, acknowledge its (often) reciprocal nature, and normalise it as a dimension of all human relationships 'removing some of its pejorative connotations' (Bartlett and O'Conner, 2010, p 63). This is not to suggest that for family carers, later on in the dementia trajectory, reciprocity may be lost but it is important to disrupt dichotomous thinking and foreground the relational interdependent nature of (most) care (Lloyd, 2012).

Social citizenship, services and care practice

Ideas about social citizenship demand new forms of critical practice in health and social care. While space does not permit a detailed discussion of ways this can be achieved, given its importance to the lives, mental health and well-being of people living with dementia, a number of key issues will be highlighted. A social citizenship approach in practice is grounded in certain principles (Box 9.1). These give rise to a much broader conceptualisation of people's capacity to participate and are 'predicated on the need for a fundamental shift in onus from person with dementia to society at large' (Bartlett and O'Conner, 2010, p 70).

Box 9.1: Principles underpinning a social citizenship approach

- Active participation by people living with dementia in their own lives and society at large must be valued and maximised.
- The potential for growth and positivity within the dementia experience must be recognised and promoted.

- Individual experiences and circumstances must be understood as inextricably connected to broader socio-political and cultural dynamics and structures.
- Solidarity between people living with dementia achieved through the fostering of a sense of 'we' and community building is a realistic goal that must be nurtured.

Source: Bartlett and O'Connor, 2010

Bartlett and O'Connor (2010) suggest that in the services arena it is important to make the case for ensuring that people living with dementia 'get what they are entitled to and/or have a right to expect as an equal citizen' (p 108). They argue that social citizenship is *defined* by the degree to which an individual's rights are recognised and upheld through care practices, policies and institutions. Examples include: being supported to fully participate in assessments and care-related decisions (Österholm and Hydén, 2018); engaging with a human rights lens in relationship to deprivation of liberties and other restrictive interventions (Cahill, 2018); providing opportunities for expressions of self in care interactions (Baldwin, 2008); and reconceptualising behaviour that challenges as responses to powerlessness, frustration and marginalisation (Behuniak, 2010). Brannelly (2011) offers an example where, following care home admission, a woman with dementia made it clear she did not like her new living arrangements. Her preferences were taken into account by practitioners who knew her well and who made it possible for her to return home with a personalised care package.

At a more structural level examples include: addressing inequity in service provision for people living with dementia and (where relevant) their family carers and, more recently, cuts to those services (Kelly and Innes, 2013; Manthorpe and Iliffe, 2016a). The purposeful employment of more rights-based language – in place of care-oriented language – not only (re)positions the person with dementia as a citizen, rather than a service user, but engages with notions of entitlement and justice. People living with dementia and their carers find it easier to access services if they perceive themselves to have a legitimate right to them rather than a 'need' for them (O'Connor, 1999, in Bartlett and O'Connor, 2010).

While the concept of social citizenship is attractive to many individuals and organisations, what it actually means for people living with dementia and their families is less clear. It is particularly challenging to translate into actions in relationship to people with more advanced dementia. The 'practice of social citizenship' lacks definition and substance; the model has also been criticised for being under-theorised (Kontos and Martin, 2013).

Cognisance and citizenship

That most of the literature on social citizenship conceptualises citizens as having full cognisance represents another challenge (Erevelles, 2002). There are difficulties in operationalising the rights and obligations of social citizenship for groups who do not meet this key criterion, such as people with more advanced dementia (Marshall, 1950). This discourse intersects with that relating to the user movement which assumes a link between citizenship and the 'user as consumer'. Historically, people living with dementia have been excluded from politicised service user activism – for example in the mental health field – because they were seen as antithetical to the notion of the 'pro-active, rational consumer of services' (Smith et al, 2011, p 1466). Although this has been challenged by the campaigning activities of organisations like DEEP these primarily involve people with mild or early-stage dementia and, unintentionally, promote a model of citizenship premised on the ideological construct of self-cognisance (Bartlett and O'Connor, 2007; Bartlett, 2014a). This deepens the social devaluation of those with more severe dementia who may not be able to make recognisable public contributions and tend not to be 'good copy' for public engagement activities and campaigns. Bartlett and O'Connor (2010) observe that as a consequence of the degenerative nature of dementia, temporality is an inevitable feature of dementia activism. The dementia user movement has yet to address this issue and the related issue of how to include people with more advanced dementia.

It is important to note, however, that DEEP, and similar organisations such as the *Scottish Dementia Working Group*, have demonstrated that people living with dementia *can* effectively unite, advocate and influence (University of Edinburgh and the Scottish Dementia Working Group, 2014; Litherland, 2015). For example, DEEP contributed to the British Psychological Society's (BPS) guidance on psychosocial interventions for people with early-stage dementia (BPS, 2014), a House of Lords Select Committee (2014) *Review on the Mental Capacity Act* and participating in dementia-friendly conferences, for example Alzheimer's Europe's Annual Conference. DEEP members also contribute to enhancing standards of care and support and to the training of care workers and health and social care professionals (Williamson, 2012b).

Human rights issues and people living with dementia

Greater involvement in political activism and engagement with rights-related discourse has generated interest in dementia as a human rights issue (Bartlett, 2014a; 2014b; Hare, 2016; Hughes and Williamson, 2019).

One of the key aims of Dementia Alliance International is to develop human-rights-based policy in the dementia field (Dementia Alliance International, 2018). This includes making full use of the United Nations Convention on the Rights of Persons with Disabilities (Nuffield Council on Bioethics, 2009). In terms of the extent to which human rights have penetrated UK policy, the most recent policy statement on dementia in England – *Prime Minister's Challenge on Dementia 2020* (DH, 2015b) – directly refers to the 'human rights of people living with dementia', albeit in a relatively peripheral way (p 20). Scotland has gone further and incorporated a human-rights-based approach into its national dementia strategies, guidance and practice standards. For example, the *Scottish Charter of Rights for People Living with Dementia and their Carers* is underpinned by an approach known as *PANEL*. It emphasises the rights of people with dementia to:

- *P*articipate in decisions which affect their human rights;
- *A*ccountability of those responsible for the respect, protection and fulfilment of human rights;
- *N*on-discrimination and equality;
- *E*mpowerment to know their rights and how to claim them; and
- *L*egality in all decisions through an explicit link with human rights legal standards in all processes and outcome measurement (WHO, 2015; Cross-Party Group on Alzheimer's, 2009).

While a human rights agenda holds significant promise, there are concerns that its individualistic approach contradicts the lived relationality of people living with dementia. The Convention on the Rights of Persons with Disabilities for example, has almost nothing to say about families and carers; it 'essentially promotes the individualist fiction rather than the complex messy interdependent reality of life and of dementia' (Shakespeare et al, 2017, p 13). This oversight is mirrored in UK policy too (DH, 2009d). The *Dementia Challenge* policies (DH, 2012a; 2015b) pay very limited attention to carers. Additionally, actually securing rights to services or care that recognises the human rights of a person with dementia is very difficult (Cahill, 2018). Some commentators argue that however prominent 'rights' are in policy, they are only made meaningful when they are operationalised in services and in practice.

Relational citizenship and dementia

Relational citizenship grows out of the concepts of the self, selfhood and embodied selfhood and builds on social citizenship as a model and concept. It also intersects with personhood and PCC.

For some time, it has been observed that 'the self' persists throughout the whole of the dementia trajectory and that this depends, to a lesser or greater degree, on the way that the person with dementia is related to and treated by others (Hampson and Morris, 2016). Sabat's (2002) work is especially influential in this arena. He developed a '1–3 framework': a lens for conceptualising the enduring self in dementia. Self 1, expressed in terms such as 'I' and 'me' is the least vulnerable to the perspectives of others. Self 2, comprising personal characteristics and attributes, is vulnerable to others' perspectives; the extent to which they are regarded positively or negatively can be enhanced or eroded by the way others respond to the manifestations of dementia. Self 3, expressed in public roles and social identities, is the most vulnerable to erosion when others fail to co-construct the self and the person's social identity, a concept known as selfhood.

In support of this argument Sabat (2002) and others suggest that the responses and judgements of others are key influences in determining selfhood. They refer to examples of demeaning interactions in care settings such as care homes or hospital wards where staff do not recognise (any of) the Selfs 1–3 of the person with dementia and do not promote selfhood (Sabat et al, 2004). This argument dovetails with those made earlier in relationship to personhood and PCC; they also amplify the points made in Chapter 6 in relationship to lack of priority placed on relationships between staff and residents and on residents' biographies in care services (Eriksson and Saveman, 2002; Brooker and Latham, 2015). Dewing (2002) argues that current models of care that claim to be rooted in the principles of personhood ignore the importance of the self; for personhood to be meaningful it needs to be rooted in the 'embodied self and manifested through social relations based on a concern for others' (p 160).

These arguments engage with the idea that selfhood resides beyond the mind and may be expressed in bodily dispositions (Kontos, 2005). Bourdieu defines a disposition as a 'way of being, a habitual state … a tendency, propensity or inclination' developed and refined over a lifetime's exposure to certain social conditions (1977, p 214 in Kontos, 2014). In practice these materialise as corporeal expressions including postures, gestures, movements and actions; they are part of a modus operandi of which the individual is not the producer and over which, for the most part, s/he has no conscious mastery (Bourdieu, 1977). They are ways of being in the world that support and convey humanness, individuality and identity; they are the embodiment of selfhood (Kontos and Martin, 2013).

Embodied selfhood takes understanding of selfhood to another level, permitting it to take form and be expressed and 'reproduced non-discursively' even in the most advanced stages of dementia (Kontos,

2004, p 845). This is important because if the 'coherence of selfhood and its generative spontaneity' has the capacity to persist despite the neurodegenerative changes associated with dementia it must 'reside below the threshold of cognition and in the pre-reflective level of experience' (Kontos, 2004, p 845). This recognition challenges the presumed loss of selfhood that tends to be associated with dementia and uncouples notions of agency from being inevitably, and only meaningfully, connected to cognition. This is mirrored by the presumed loss of citizenship status, also associated with cognitive decline, discussed earlier.

Embodied selfhood also offers the potential to engage with and enhance selfhood in new and different ways. Current models of care tend to treat the mind and body as separate entities failing to conceptualise the body as a source of intention that persists throughout the dementia trajectory (Kontos and Naglie, 2007). It may also strengthen arguments for care to become more humanistic, ethical and relational. Kontos (2014) argues that recognising and appreciating the importance and relevance of bodily expressions of selfhood could achieve more positive care outcomes, especially in populations that challenge paid and unpaid carers, such as care home residents and people with advanced dementia supported by relatives in the community (Kontos and Naglie, 2009). That a person with advanced dementia is embedded in at least one relationship is axiomatic. Selfhood is thus both embodied and relationally situated.

Kontos and colleagues (2017) advocate the need for a new model of citizenship – relational citizenship. It is a model premised on the central tenets of relationship-centred care, that is, interdependence and reciprocity, and the support of people with dementia as active partners in their own care (Nolan et al, 2002). It offers a theoretical and applied connection between embodied selfhood and social citizenship. Kontos and colleagues (2017) and others (Baldwin, 2008; Bartlett and O'Connor, 2010) suggest that it has the capacity to extend citizenship entitlements to people living with more advanced dementia as it challenges the erosion of selfhood and loss of agency and makes visible the connection a person living with dementia has to a citizenship status (Kontos et al, 2017).

Making visible the role and relevance of the life course and inequalities

Traditional dementia discourse tends to obscure the relevance of life course issues and ignore the role played by social and structural inequalities. As these issues are prominent features of mental health discourse and exert a powerful influence on mental health outcomes in later life, there is no reason to think they do not influence dementia both as a condition and lived experience. One of the key contributions made by the new paradigm is making these issues (more) visible and exposing their links with dementia (Bartlett and O'Connor, 2010).

The social citizenship model, in particular, considers the situation of people living with dementia from an explicitly socio-political and socio-cultural perspective. As Bartlett and O'Connor (2010) note, understanding of dementia has evolved a great deal over the past 30 years from viewing it as an inevitable part of the ageing process, to recognising it as a biomedical phenomenon, and then towards an approach that acknowledges and supports *the person* living with the condition. As understanding has extended, so has the capacity of conceptual models to incorporate both individual and interpersonal issues, life course issues and, latterly, issues relating to social location and the broader socio-political context. This wider lens of analysis, inevitably, offers more room to accommodate diversity, heterogeneity, complexity and multi-dimensionality. It also engages with an entitlement narrative shifting the fulcrum of debate towards legal, political and human rights, an arena which holds considerable potential to improve the status and well-being of people living with dementia (Cantley and Bowes, 2004).

Recognition of social and structural inequalities is intrinsic to the theory and practice of the social citizenship model. It foregrounds, and attempts to expose, intersections between life course-related disadvantages such as low SES and dementia *and* the role played by socio-political structures that create and/or amplify disadvantage, stigma and discrimination. It also 'draws attention to how systems of discrimination, including sexism, ageism, racism and ableism, may work in tandem' to exclude and damage people living with dementia and their families' (Bartlett and O'Connor, 2010, p 126; Milne, 2010a). It aims to reframe understanding(s) of dementia and, importantly, to (re)locate the 'problem' of dementia from 'the person with dementia' to societal structures, attitudes, policy and services. In so doing it shifts the focus of 'what needs attention' to addressing the inequalities, structural disadvantages and discrimination that many people living with dementia are often exposed to and which profoundly undermines their mental health and well-being. This frame of reference may be especially potent for people in the later stages of dementia when the risks of marginalisation, oppression, abuse and poor-quality care are highest and when people tend to have the least power to influence their situation.

Both selfhood and embodied selfhood – the conceptual foundations of relational citizenship – speak to life course and inequalities issues. These include the relevance of life course exposure to advantaged, or disadvantaged, social conditions and the role played by the life course *and* inequalities in influencing expressions of selfhood in people living with dementia. Its capacity to extend citizenship entitlements to those with advanced dementia and, implicitly, to challenge their mistreatment and impoverished political and social status are also noteworthy.

The contribution of feminist thinking to the new paradigm is important to acknowledge, for four reasons. One is that most people affected by dementia are female (see 'Women and Dementia' later in the chapter). The second is that feminist literature and analysis provides a critical lens that accommodates stigma, power and oppression and has engaged with issues related to social positioning and intersectionality, all of which are relevant to the dementia arena. Specific contributions include the ethic of care noted in Chapter 6 (Lloyd, 2010; Barnes, 2012); this not only draws attention to the dynamic relational nature of care but also challenges its existing narrow dichotomous construction. The importance of life course issues in shaping, often negatively, the lives, health and well-being of women is a third contribution (Williams and Watson, 2016). Fourthly, as Bartlett and O'Connor (2010) point out, feminist literature offers 'analytic strategies for making the links between lived experiences and broader societal structures and systems' (p 9).

Although progress has been made much remains to be done to make the role and relevance of the life course and inequalities more visible in, and meaningful to, the dementia field; it is a work in progress.

Sociological constructs and dementia

While much of the discussion in this section, and the new dementia paradigm itself, integrates sociologically oriented perspectives it is additionally instructive to explore the contribution of three sociological constructs to the debate. The rationale for their inclusion is that their penetrative negative influence on thinking, care and treatment is both opaque and persistent and their damaging implications for the mental health and well-being of people living with dementia is profound.

Frailty, infrahumanisation, precarity and dementia

Frailty is a sociological construct of key relevance to dementia discourse. As Higgs and Gilleard (2016a) note '... the prospect of becoming demented represents a major fourth age fear more profound than any other infirmity, as it seemingly risks undermining any claim to be ageing well' (Higgs and Gilleard, 2016a, p 45). Extending the arguments made in Chapter 7, when mental frailty – primarily dementia – combines with physical frailty the person moves from occupying a status of being 'capable of at least potential agency to a state of thorough abjection' (Higgs and Gilleard, 2016a, p 63). The person's incapacity to 'unfrail' themselves then renders the person doubly abject, having become 'irretrievably frail'

(Gilleard and Higgs, 2010a). Grenier and colleagues (2017) go further, observing that the fourth age and frailty intersect with dementia to produce a status 'beyond frailty' into failure: a 'failed' old age (p 319). It is a particularly toxic negative status: one associated with fear, 'burden, pity and weakness' (Pickard, 2014). Dementia amplifies the capacity of frailty to disenfranchise, delineate and marginalise people living with dementia, a process that brings with it a range of damaging consequences for their mental health and well-being.

A linked construct is that of infrahumanisation. Infrahumanisation is 'a tacitly held belief that one's ingroup is more human than an outgroup' (Cortes et al, 2005, p 243). It is a process by which outgroups are stripped of the status of being fully human. Attributes that differentiate ingroups from outgroups include intellect, language, communication skills and being less able to experience exclusively human emotions such as shame, hope or love (Leyens et al, 2001; Haslam and Loughnan, 2014). The process of infrahumanisation is amplified when members of an outgroup share more than one feature of 'failure', for example they are cognitively impaired *and* have communication difficulties, are visibly dependent or institutionalised (Leyens et al, 2000; Baranski, 2016). Infrahumanisation is especially pronounced with groups who are viewed negatively, induce disgust and/or fear, do not contribute economically and belong to a specific illness category (Loughnan et al, 2014; Miron et al, 2017). Goffman's (1963) work is also relevant. He observed that losing one's mind is one of the 'most pervasively threatening things that can happen to a self in our society' (Goffman, 1961, p 131). Referencing Sullivan (1956) Goffman noted that it is essentially 'a failure at being human – a failure at being anything that one could respect as worth being' (1961, pp 184–5).

The process of infrahumanisation is aided and extended by the language used to describe dementia and people living with the condition (Zeilig, 2013). Terms such as time bomb, threat and burden are common. Haslam and Loughnan (2014) discuss the particularly powerful representation of people living with dementia as 'shuffling zombies' (p 400); dementia has also been described as a 'living death' or a liminal state between life and death (Peel, 2014). Such terms are particularly applied to care home residents with dementia, reflecting their marginal social and physical location as well as their separate conceptual status.

Infrahumanisation permeates political, social and clinical narratives about dementia and feeds into negative perceptions and attitudes. It infiltrates the views and everyday treatment of people living with dementia and those who support them, especially in service settings. It is linked to the process of depersonalisation, referred to earlier, and to the promotion, or at least tolerance, of dehumanising care practices

(Cahill, 2018). Recent research by Featherstone and colleagues (2018) on acute hospital care for people living with dementia describes 'desperate ward landscapes of dehumanisation' where patients are restricted from moving around, are routinely restrained and display high levels of anxiety, disorientation, anger and difficulties in communicating their needs. These arguments dovetail with those made in relationship to institutionalised cultures, Kitwood's (1997) malignant social psychology and heightened risk of abuse.

A third construct, that of precarity, may further extend understanding of a frailed late life, especially one marked by dementia. Butler (2009) and Standing (2010) argue that precarity, and the structures of inequality that underpin it, need to be made visible if they are to be addressed. Butler (2009) considers precariousness to be political; '… precarity is a politically induced condition in which certain populations suffer from failing social and economic networks of support' and become differentially exposed to illness, neglect, abuse and marginalisation (p 25). Older people with long-term conditions, particularly dementia, and/or who have few resources, are prominent examples. One of the main dimensions of economic precarity is reduced social protection: lower state pensions, limited welfare benefits and a paucity of publicly funded good-quality care services. These create conditions of uncertainty, insecurity and fear among people living with dementia and their families; many report feeling 'abandoned' by the care system (Lloyd, 2012; Phillipson, 2015). For Standing (2010) a precarious life is characterised by a 'truncated status' whereby people become 'denizens' rather than citizens defined as lacking at least one group of basic rights: civil, political, economic, social and/or human (p 146). As this chapter has outlined, the lack of rights people living with dementia have is a key dimension of their impoverished status and treatment.

Grenier and colleagues (2017) suggest that, '… the social and political conditions which shape a devaluing of subjects by means of their physical and/or cognitive impairments, can serve to reinforce precarity and deflect attention from the disadvantages that accumulate (across the lifecourse) and affect late life, the experiences of living with dementia and the practices of providing and receiving care' (p 325). Precarity draws attention to life course, and late life, risks and inequalities and challenges the ways that people living with dementia are conceptualised and treated (Phillipson, 2015). That the usual calamitous discourse relating to dementia is amplified in conditions of economic austerity confirms its status as a socio-political issue.

Unequal access to services and the role inequalities play in this domain is the focus of the next section.

Services and treatments for people living with dementia: the role of inequalities

A fundamental inequality relates to the care system itself. The so-called 'Darzi report', *Better Health and Care for All*, observes that if people living with dementia need support they (usually) have to pay for it, that is, it is means-tested social care, while those with cancer receive NHS care, free at the point of delivery (Institute for Public Policy Research, 2018). 'People rightly expect an elderly friend or relative to receive the same care with the same entitlements whether they have dementia or cancer'; this pattern disproportionately affects people living with dementia, particularly those with high levels of need (Institute for Public Policy Research, 2018, p 36). Combined with this is the shift – discussed earlier in the book – that an ever growing number of social care services are being means-tested. As a high proportion of those in care homes and in receipt of community-based services are people living with dementia this 'double whammy' has a particularly pronounced impact on them (National Audit Office, 2009). Those people with the fewest resources tend to be additionally disadvantaged. Not only do they have to rely on an ever-shrinking pool of public services but, if they cannot fund their own care home, they tend to have much more restricted choice and the quality of the care provided may also be lower (Bond et al, 2005; Alzheimer's Society, 2018). It is important to point out that there is considerable variation across UK jurisdictions. In Scotland, for example, the local authority does make a contribution to the care home fees of all residents whose needs meet its definition of 'personal care' (regardless of income). This is not the case in England, Wales or Northern Ireland where local authority funding for care home fees is only available to those who have limited income and/or savings.

Iliffe and Manthorpe (2016) argue that this is an issue of rights. While there is a universal right to free health care at the point of need, rights to publicly funded social care are *conditional* depending on the situation of the individual, the severity of their need and the socio-economic context. For this reason, they suggest that people living with dementia need legal instruments and mechanisms of redress to secure their rights to all care services. This dovetails with some of the broader points made earlier about strengthening the rights-based agenda.

In work exploring self-directed care, evidence suggests that people living with dementia may be disadvantaged (Manthorpe and Samsi, 2016). As noted earlier in the book personal budgets for most older service users are considerably smaller than their equivalents were a decade ago; the older person also needs to be in a high level of need to be eligible (Lewis and West, 2014). There is a separate argument about the suitability of the consumer-oriented model itself. It may ill fit the needs and situations of people living with dementia. They often require help from social care services when in crisis, for example at the point of hospital discharge, their needs are multiple, their mental capacity to manage a budget may be compromised and their carer may be a frail older person themselves (Lloyd, 2010). The processes of making informed choices and decisions are time rich and complex and tend not to be compatible with these circumstances. As Tanner (2001) observes, there is 'a central contradiction between being 'in need' and functioning as an autonomous, articulate and solvent consumer' (p 266).

The evidence that does exist suggests that where a carer does take on a management role for their relative's direct payment it significantly increases their workload and does not necessarily result in improved outcomes (Moran et al, 2012; Netten et al, 2012). This is amplified for service users and carers who are socio-economically disadvantaged (Ferguson, 2007). There are also concerns about risks, for example of financial exploitation (Samsi et al, 2014; Ismail et al, 2017). Although direct payments appear to improve outcomes for *some* people living with dementia it is by no means a model that suits everyone; more nuanced research is needed to explore who benefits in what circumstances and also who does not (Mental Health Foundation, 2011a; 2011b).

In terms of differences between groups of people living with dementia, Jones (2017) suggests that social class plays a role in diagnosis and treatment. There is evidence that people from a lower SES are more likely to get diagnosed with dementia but are less likely to receive drug treatment (such as cholinesterase inhibitors) than their middle-class peers. This is supported by work by Cooper and colleagues (2010) who found that people living with dementia who own their own homes are four times more likely to be prescribed drug treatments than either those who rent or live in more deprived areas (Cooper et al, 2016). Middle-class educated patients are also more likely to be referred to a memory service and have greater access to both mental health and physical health services than their working-class counterparts (Barrett and Savage, 2012; Cooper et al, 2016). Another facet of inequality relates to research; most work is done with white middle-class people privileging their perspectives, priorities and needs (Hulko, 2009).

Women and dementia

Women have been described as the 'marginalised majority' in the dementia field (Alzheimer's Disease International, 2015). As noted in Chapter 7, dementia disproportionately affects women as those living with the condition, as patients and users, and as paid and unpaid carers.

Women bear the overwhelming level of responsibility for dementia care, both family and formal. Despite this, the dementia agenda is constructed as gender-neutral (Alzheimer's Research UK, 2015; Women's Health and Equality Consortium and Age UK, 2016). This invisibility mirrors, and masks, a number of gendered processes: the invisible nature of women's labour in the home, their status as 'natural carers' justifying lack of support to family carers and low pay in services, and normative assumptions that older women are unproductive, particularly economically (Barnes, 2012). These processes interleave with a number of life course and inequality issues which are also, usually, presented as gender-neutral, including poverty, psychosocial stress, likelihood of living alone, risk of abuse, and family-related responsibilities. They are also amplified by the twin forces of life course sexism and late life ageism (Fawcett and Reynolds, 2010). These have been discussed earlier in the book and their gendered nature highlighted.

The 'default position' of the discourse is to de-genderise and homogenise dementia and, as with most narratives, that default position is a male one. Gender affects the lived experience of dementia but our care system is designed around the needs and perspectives of men. How services are designed and what they respond to is a case in point. Older women with dementia place emphasis on empathy over efficiency, emotional support over instrumental support and talking over doing (Tanner, 2012). The 'female attributes' of kindness, care and prioritising relationships are not viewed as important, and certainly not worth paying for, in the development of services or the resourcing of the care workforce. Home care is illustrative of this model; it offers instrumental support with personal care, toileting and/or dressing rather than with the emotional and psychological challenges relating to living with dementia or the relational issues confronting a family carer. The emotional costs of care home work also reflect some of these tensions with many, predominantly female, workers reporting insufficient time to perform their roles with due care or to a standard that protects the dignity and feelings of residents with dementia (Erol et al, 2015).

Another issue is that for many women caring *is* integral to their life course embedded identity. This not only influences how a woman living with dementia manages her condition but whether, and how, she adopts the role of carer. There is evidence that women are diagnosed later in the dementia trajectory than men partly as a consequence of their caring and domestic responsibilities. They tend to continue to perform domestic and household tasks even in the later stages of dementia. They also describe their 'symptoms' in emotional and relational terms rather than about a failure of cognition and/or function (Tanner, 2010). Services struggle to manage this profile favouring the management and 'treatment' of cognitive problems and/or behavioural symptoms and allocating resources accordingly.

There are also gendered barriers to help-seeking. Many older women, with or without dementia, feel they don't have a right to ask for help, complain, be seen or have their feelings acknowledged (Beaulaurier et al, 2008). Older women's lack of visibility, power, choice and control is especially profound when they have advanced dementia; as they are less likely than a man to have a family carer to advocate for them they are at considerable risk of being discounted, excluded from decision-making and to have their rights compromised (Savitch et al, 2011). In terms of family caring, there is evidence that older wives are much less likely than older husbands to seek help from services; service providers tend to be more inclined to offer male carers support than their female counterparts (Eley, 2003). These patterns reflect the persistence of life course and age-related gendered inequalities.

It has been acknowledged, to a degree at least, that gender matters in the context of illness, disability and caregiving (Bartlett et al, 2018). 'Forms and impacts of disablism are always refracted in some way through the prism of gender, gendered locations and gender relations' (Thomas, 1999, p 28). There is a growing call to explore the gendered nature of dementia too. In terms of research a number of issues are prominent (Alzheimer's Disease International, 2015). We know little about the long-term impact of dementia on women with the condition, unpaid carers for relatives with dementia or members of the paid care workforce. We also need to know more about both non-modifiable and modifiable risk factors for dementia taking account of life course issues and the effectiveness of treatments and care services for women (Erol et al, 2015). Women, in all their roles, need to be more involved in research as advisors, reviewers and co-researchers, and women's perspectives and concerns need to be much more embedded in the aims, design and delivery of research (Litherland, 2015). Dementia and related policies and strategies need to incorporate a gender dimension in their development, delivery and evaluation (Alzheimer's Disease International, 2016). Professionals and the care workforce need to be aware of gender issues too in assessment, care planning, intervention and care practice with women living with dementia; there may even be a case for women-only dementia services (Fenton, 2015). Recognising the gendered nature of responding to dementia is part of the wider social justice and human rights agenda (Bamford, 2011). Bringing a feminist discourse to bear on the dementia debate is also important in foregrounding women's rights and their intersection with the socio-political location of dementia.

As Bartlett and O'Conner (2010) helpfully remind us the lives of people living with dementia are shaped by social divisions other than gender; namely race, ethno-cultural group membership, social class, sexual orientation and religious affiliation (Hulko, 2011). Lesbian women and gay men, for example, face particular issues related to stigma within care environments that are heteronormative (Westwood, 2016). All of these social categories are important dimensions of the dementia debate. They warrant specific attention in their own right; also how they intersect with gender and with one another (Truswell, 2018).

While space does not permit that to happen here, I want to highlight two points. The first is that one of the most profound consequences of being exposed to multiple jeopardies is the risk of silence, erosion of the right to be heard and to have an influence over your life, care and choices. This is a particular issue – as has become clear in Chapters 8 and 9 – if you have dementia. Secondly, one of the main aims of highlighting the relevance of gender to the dementia debate is to explore the issues that are invisible and occluded and yet omnipresent and influential. By doing this one uncovers a web of assumptions and norms that need to be exposed in order to address the deficits of existing 'default position(s)', highlight the role played by the life course and challenge the creation, perpetuation and amplification of inequality.

Policy issues

Unlike the rest of the book, a number of policy issues have been interwoven into this chapter where they have best fitted. Other relevant policies such as the Care Act 2014 have been discussed in other chapters. An overarching point about policies relevant to the dementia field is that few efforts are made to integrate them or explore how their intersectionality impacts on the lives and well-being of people living with dementia. While there are dementia-specific policies in the UK, these tend to have limited legal traction; those policies that do have legal traction tend not to be specific to dementia (Innes and Manthorpe, 2013).

It is evident from the number of policies that have been developed over the past decade that dementia is an issue of considerable political interest. It is also clear that over time not only have policies began to accommodate models other than the biomedical but they have increasingly accepted that people living with dementia have needs beyond those arising from dementia and rights to support from services, including mental health services (DH, 2015b; 2016; All Party Parliamentary Group on Dementia, 2016; Mental Health Foundation, 2016b). There has been a greater focus on recognising and addressing discrimination and stigma including changing public attitudes to dementia and improving access to universal services (Scottish Government, 2010). This suggests that the social model of disability is penetrating the dementia policy arena although this may be, in part at least, the government bowing to pressure from European and international organisations who have been highly critical of the UK in promoting the rights of disabled people (UN, 2016). Explicit engagement with rights issues in relationship to people living with dementia remains limited, and recognition of the role played by life course and structural issues is wholly absent from policy.

There are policy and legal variations across the UK. The Scottish Government, for example, offers a guarantee, entitling anyone diagnosed with dementia to a year's post-diagnostic support. This does not exist elsewhere. It seems likely that distinctions will become greater in the future as powers are further devolved to individual nation states (Rees, 2014). There is also variation in relationship to what family carers are entitled to although interestingly, despite a great deal of policy 'talk' about carers, they have very few legal rights. Governments are slow to provide funding to support carers, preferring to 'enrol them in the production of care' as observed earlier. Increasing reliance on family care is part of the neo-liberal turn in the political economy. This expectation assumes that families will 'naturally' wish to provide care, that caring is in their and their relative's best interests, and that the quality of the care provided is of good quality (Larkin et al, 2019). These are untested assumptions.

In addition to financial issues, there are a number of psychosocial consequences for carers of this transfer of responsibility. It does not permit 'guiltless grieving' by family members who are enmeshed in managing and providing care (Davis, 2004) nor does it acknowledge the loss and boundary ambiguities that can occur in caring for a relative living with dementia (Lloyd and Stirling, 2011). Carers may feel a guilty ambivalence towards the person with dementia dreading his or her death while longing for the closure that the person's death would bring. Trapped in a state of cumulative ambiguity and/or invalidated grief, carers can become overwhelmed, perceiving themselves as powerless to make decisions that could lead to positive change in their daily lives (Lloyd and Stirling, 2011). Being responsible for care eclipses the carers' own journey and fails to permit space or time for them to adjust to the changed nature of their relationship, or the often profound changes to the cared for person.

My last policy point relates to care homes. Although the infrastructural deficits remain, policy and guidance increasingly recognise that care homes, supported by external agencies, have a duty to meet residents' emotional, psychological and social needs and enhance well-being, including those living with dementia (Alzheimer's Society, 2016). It is acknowledged that in order to achieve this care homes need: a well-trained specialist workforce; consistent and coherent access to NHS primary care and specialist mental health services; and engagement with an inspection regime that is committed to driving up quality (Care Quality Commission, 2017). The publication of the National Institute for Health and Care Excellence's (2013) quality standard – *Mental Wellbeing of Older People in Care Homes* – is evidence of this recognition (see Chapter 8).

However useful these initiatives may be it is important to remind ourselves of the ongoing crisis in the care home sector across the UK, particularly acute in England. Key issues include the increasing rate of care home closures, chronic staff recruitment and retention problems, a number of high-profile 'scandals', underfunding of the sector and the unresolved uncertainty about the future model of paying for long-term care (Dening and Milne, 2020). These systemic concerns tend to eclipse calls for sector-wide improvements and hamper investment in care practice.

Conclusion

Chapter 9 has made three key arguments: that the way we conceptualise and construct dementia informs and intersects with the way we treat and support people living with dementia; that dementia as a lived experience interleaves with a person's life course and with past and present, social and structural inequalities; and that the mental health and well-being of people living with dementia is shaped by a range of micro, meso and macro factors that often combine in damaging and pernicious ways. There are a jigsaw of issues that exert influence; the jigsaw is complex and has many pieces.

Traditional perspectives on dementia tend to limit thinking and narrow responses. As Bailey and colleagues (2013) note, a primary biomedical neuro-degenerative focus 'flattens recognition' that dementia 'is not just a one-dimensional neuro-pathological journey but is criss-crossed with personal histories, social networks and socially contextualised perceptions' (p 394). Critical perspectives informed by social models, and by sociological thinking, challenge this model and extend the focus of analysis beyond the 'patient' to the family and to care settings; account is also explicitly taken of the person as an individual (Ray, 2016b). The new dementia paradigm purposefully adopts a broader lens still. In order to appreciate the impact of dementia on a person's mental health and well-being, understanding needs to accommodate the subjective experience of dementia, the environment and the socio-cultural context in which dementia – as a condition and sociological construct – is embedded.

It is important to recognise that threats to the mental health and well-being of people living with dementia are not only numerous but are direct, that is, discriminatory attitudes, and indirect, that is, the consequence of task-focused models of care. They also take a range of forms and differ in size from the small and relatively ordinary to the gross and abusive: from the use of dismissive labels, through a public discourse characterised by the language of burden and infrahumanisation, to neglectful practices in care homes and the underfunding of social care. There is a third temporal dimension. Threats tend to be greater in size and number the more advanced the condition. Models located in the new paradigm, particularly those informed by the lens of social citizenship, aim to take account of this multi-dimensional perspective and acknowledge the ways in which they influence the lived experience of dementia and undermine mental health and well-being. The new paradigm is overtly political and the social citizenship model is explicitly 'attuned to issues of power, agency, marginalisation and disempowerment'. It is concerned to reframe dementia as an issue of social justice and of human and legal rights. Making visible the ways in which connections exist between a person's life course and experiences and exposure to social and structural inequalities and the mental health and well-being of a person living with dementia is pivotal to making meaningful the principles of social citizenship.

The embedded nature of threats, and the powerful influence the wider socio-political and sociological context exerts on mental health and well-being, is a notable, if underexplored, feature of dementia discourse. Hence its foregrounding here: many texts that purport to adopt a non-traditional stance on dementia fail to engage in any depth with the complexity of the socio-politically informed alternatives.

There can be no doubt that dementia is one of the most feared conditions of later life. It tends to be viewed as very different from other (functional) mental health problems and as an age-related condition about which 'little can be done'. There is much in this chapter to challenge this nihilistic assumption and encourage ways to engage with, and extend, approaches to understanding dementia that can incorporate life course issues and inequalities and reduce risks to the mental health and well-being of people living with dementia.

Thus far the book has focused on mental health problems in later life and their intersection with the life course and social and structural inequalities. The next, and penultimate, chapter turns to the promotion of mental health in later life and to enhancing well-being, including among people living with dementia.

10

Promotion and prevention

This chapter reviews what is known about the prevention of mental ill health in later life and the protection and promotion of mental health. This includes research evidence and, importantly, the perspectives and lived experiences of older people. The relevance of conceptual issues, of models of ageing, and frameworks for understanding mental health promotion and prevention are also explored, as is their intersection with policy. Services and/or interventions are identified where useful.

Introduction

Before reviewing the material in the complex area, it is useful to make a number of overarching points about its nature and scope.

A key observation is that the literature on 'good' or 'positive' mental health among older people tends to focus on late life itself, that is, what promotes mental health *in* later life rather than what contributes to its promotion across the life course. Some of its determinants are life course linked, for example the availability of social support, but those links are rarely made in any robust way. This is a deficit even for those commentators who are committed to adopting a life course lens (Marmot et al, 2010). Given that we are beginning to unpick some of the links between childhood adversity, early life inequality and midlife mental ill health, it is timely to explore extending these links into later life. Arguably, longitudinal data should be able to contribute to building a stronger evidence base in this underdeveloped field (Understanding Society and Economic and Social Research Council, 2009; Hamer et al, 2014).

A second issue relates to distinctions between, and evidence about, promotion and prevention. While much of the literature considers these issues separately, they are often viewed as two sides of the same coin, particularly by older people; they also intersect with the notion of protective factors. For both prevention and promotion, it can be challenging to establish a relationship between inputs and outcomes: the role played by promotional activity in enhancing mental health or a preventive intervention in reducing risks is hard to prove. If the issue being targeted is a social one, for example decent housing or education, as opposed to a narrower health-related issue, for example a healthy diet, links are very difficult to establish.

Where the promotion of mental health in later life 'belongs' from a policy and services perspective is a third issue. Is it the role of age-related, mental health or public health policy to address it, or all three? This is significant as it not only determines responsibility for developing and funding strategies and services but it also makes overt policy makers' understanding of the causes and thus responses. Public health ownership of mental health promotion has the capacity to take us down a very different path than that of ageing or mental health; one that acknowledges that the challenges are about life course rather than lifestyle, about social determinants not individual behaviours, and that adopts a preventive perspective on health. One could argue that one of the reasons for shifting statutory responsibility for public health from the NHS to local authorities is to simultaneously narrow the focus of interventions and reduce funding for public health services.

A fourth point is about the nature of the late life cohorts(s), especially those in the fourth age. These populations are viewed, by some commentators, as 'survivors' and tend to have a particular profile. It is important to acknowledge that the majority of those in late life who have good health, including good mental health, have had a life course characterised by socio-economic advantage and lower levels of exposure to chronic adversity and inequality. It is also the case that the majority of very old people are women. Old age itself is, of course, replete with inequalities, and risks of Alzheimer's disease *do* increase with very old age, but it is also the case that life course embedded social determinants retain their influential potency in either undermining or promoting mental health well into later life. As Thompson and colleagues (1990) quite rightly note, '… inequality is one of the fundamental continuities of later life' (p 224). Much of the literature renders this important continuity invisible; once you reach later life what has gone before becomes largely irrelevant. It is this dimension that I have strived to make visible throughout this book.

Fifthly, it is important to remind ourselves that good health, including good mental health, is graded by socio-economic status across the life course and that this pattern persists into later life (McGovern and Nazroo, 2015). Also, that socio-economic inequality in the older population is widening. A sixth point is about listening to older people themselves. What can we learn from those who have maintained or achieved good mental health in later life and how can we develop life course and age-related policies and interventions that take account of these lessons? We need to celebrate the capacity of many older people to reach later life with positive mental health and to understand more about this achievement. This chapter aims to achieve a balance between this celebratory tone – alongside recognition of the profile issue noted earlier – and ensuring that those older people who develop mental health problems are not 'blamed' or stigmatised. A linked seventh point is also relevant. It is pivotal to appreciate that older people are contributors to their own mental health and well-being and retain agency throughout their lives, including in the later stages when frailty and/or dementia may be present.

The first substantive section of this chapter offers a review of conceptual and theoretical issues, including outlining a number of relevant models drawn from the fields of prevention and promotion, ageing and mental health. The subsequent section(s) summarises what is known about the factors that promote and protect mental health in later life and prevent mental ill health among older people, including people living with dementia. Policy issues are discussed where appropriate.

Prevention, promotion and protection: conceptual issues

Prevention

Traditionally, prevention has been conceptualised as operating at primary, secondary or tertiary levels. It has been widely deployed in the health care domain, the level of intervention being dependent on whether the strategy prevents the disease itself, the severity of the disease or the associated disability. A primary intervention may be focused on changing behaviour and lifestyle and/or improving the quality of the socio-physical environment. At the secondary level the emphasis may be on identifying and treating a condition in its early stages such as dementia. Tertiary interventions focus on reducing disabilities, for example by the use of medication, rehabilitation or helping the older person manage a chronic condition (Godfrey, 2001).

Prevention is easier to conceptualise in relationship to physical health issues than it is for mental health partly because it is clearer what is being prevented, for example diabetes, and its symptoms are easier to identify and assess, for example frequent urination. When a medical condition such as diabetes begins can also (usually) be determined; it tends to have a known aetiology and trajectory. To even determine the 'onset' of a mental health problem is a challenge; it is usually only with hindsight that this is clear, if it ever is (Hamilton-West, 2011). Prevention is de facto about ill health not health; without a definition of an illness it is impossible to know what is being prevented. This is a fundamental problem in the mental health field as evidencing the effectiveness of preventing something is widely acknowledged as very challenging; it is rarely definitive, tending towards the probabilistic rather than the deterministic.

In the mental health field Goldie and colleagues (2016) define the three different levels of preventive activity thus:

- Primary prevention: intervening to stop the causes of a mental health problem arising in the first place, for example reducing levels of social isolation and loneliness, well-known risk factors for depression.
- Secondary prevention: identifying early signs that mental health is being undermined and ensuring that the development of more serious problems is prevented, for example providing support for long-term dementia carers who have some symptoms of depression and/or anxiety.
- Tertiary prevention: working with older people with established mental health problems to ensure access to services and support, ameliorate symptoms and reduce its negative impact on health and well-being.

The concepts of 'causes' and 'interventions' are also a challenge in the mental health field. Causes may be multiple and not directly related to health per se and certainly not viewed as the responsibility of health services to address, for example poverty, abuse. The primary/secondary/tertiary model works less well for conditions whose causes lie in a mixture of the personal, social and environmental and where risks are situated in the life course and/or linked to inequalities (Scott et al, 2013). Risks also tend to be understood as linear and static and as amenable to change by means of a 'single intervention'. These definitional and conceptual issues do not fit easily into the mental health domain and struggle to engage with its causal pathways and correlates (Leamy et al, 2011; Wistow et al, 2015).

Despite there being recent policy emphasis on prevention, for example the Care Act 2014 duty to '… arrange services that help *prevent* people developing needs for care and support or *prevent or delay* people deteriorating such that they would need ongoing care and support' (emphasis added), services are often focused on the later tertiary end of the preventive continuum. Social services departments are increasingly obliged to target their shrinking resources on those 'in greatest need' and prevent the use of intensive expensive care such as hospital admission (Allen and Glasby, 2013; Humphries et al, 2016). One of the obvious consequences of this is that fewer households receive primary or secondary level preventive support with the concomitant consequences (Fernandez et al, 2013). Budget cuts to local authorities are at odds with the policy drive to offer low-level preventive services (Tanner, 2007). There is a related, already identified tendency, for policy makers to locate responsibility for 'care and support' with the individual, and/or their families and communities and not with the care and support system.

The issue of targeting is an important dimension of the prevention discourse. Preventive investment, particularly in public health, is commonly focused on universal interventions targeted at whole populations, selective interventions targeted at vulnerable groups, or individuals who are deemed to be 'at risk' (Zechmeister et al, 2008). The scope of preventive intervention intersects with these target groups. Primary interventions tend to have a broad set of aims and are targeted at a population or large group, for example a campaign to reduce loneliness among all older people in England (Bolton, 2012); secondary interventions tend to have a selective focus on specific groups who may be at risk of ill health, for example dementia carers (noted earlier); and tertiary interventions tend to be targeted on older people who fulfil a number of 'need criteria', for example s/he requires support with activities of daily living. A secondary tier intervention is described in Box 10.1; its target group is isolated older people. The Brighter Futures programme attempted to work 'with the grain' of both individuals and communities.

Box 10.1: The Brighter Futures programme – preventing social isolation

In developing effective services to prevent or reduce social isolation, taking account of what matters to older people is key to success. Between 2007 and 2009 the Mental Health Foundation (2011a), working in partnership with NHS Health Scotland, supported the development of a peer mentoring service aimed at improving the mental health and well-being of isolated older people in a number of areas with different socio-demographic profiles. The programme adopted a peer mentoring model whereby – after training – older people themselves worked to enhance the social networks and facilitate meaningful community engagement of isolated older people. They specifically focused on what the older people thought would help them re-engage, for example picking up an old interest or attending a community group. All of the 96 service recipients reported improvements in self-esteem after nine months, many also described having a much more positive mood; 74 per cent noted a reduction in perceived social isolation and lower levels of loneliness. The programme also delivered a number of mental health benefits to the peer mentors; they felt they were 'giving something back', were performing a socially valued role and had developed a larger social network.

Source: Mental Health Foundation, 2011a

The scope of the preventive intervention also tends to reflect the nature of the conceptual frame adopted by policy makers. If the role of the welfare state is conceived narrowly then only those people in the tertiary category with established symptoms of a mental health condition will be included in the 'preventive tent'. The opposite is the case for policy makers who conceptualise the role of the welfare state in broad terms and its preventive capacity as being primary, secondary *and* tertiary. The latter lens will include a focus on reducing and addressing inequalities acknowledging their role in creating vulnerability to mental ill health and amplifying risks (Friedli, 2009).

These points are illustrated well by a model developed by the Association of Directors of Social Services/Local Government Association in 2003. They suggested an 'inversion of the care triangle' where resources are shifted from downstream acute interventions for the few to upstream preventive interventions for the many (see Figure 10.1). Despite it being well over ten years old it has clear resonance with the arguments I am making here; it also dovetails with a public health approach to mental health (Faculty of Public Health and Mental Health Foundation, 2016).

Marmot and colleagues (2010) advocate an approach that combines a commitment to both targeted *and* universal services. They argue that 'to reduce the steepness of the social gradient in health, actions must be universal, but with a scale and intensity proportionate to the level of disadvantage' and need: proportionate universalism (p 9). They suggest that a focus solely on the most disadvantaged or vulnerable will fail to reduce the social gradient of health and that proportionate universalism achieves a balance between focusing on the many and targeting the few. This is an approach to which I return in the conclusion.

Promotion and protection

Whereas prevention is concerned with avoiding or reducing the impact of a mental health condition, promotion is about improving mental health and well-being. Protective factors are events or conditions that reduce or mediate the negative impact of disadvantage and/or that bolster mental health (Rogers and Pilgrim, 2003). These factors are reviewed in later

Figure 10.1: Inverting the Triangle of Care

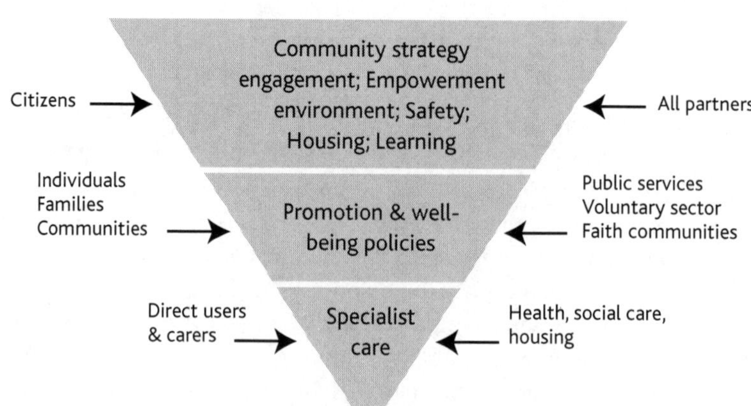

Source: Association of Directors of Social Services/Local Government Association, 2003

sections. Promotion and protection are widely regarded as complementary concepts, and activities, to prevention.

The World Health Organisation (WHO) (1998) defines health promotion as 'the process of enabling people to increase control over, and improve, their health', and health promotion interventions as 'any action that addresses the potentially modifiable determinants of health' (p 1). WHO (2014) regards mental health as an integral part of overall health and adopts a wide lens on the role and remit of health promotion. It would include the alleviation of poverty as a 'modifiable' determinant and access to education as a key mechanism to promoting good mental health across the whole life course. WHO (2003; 2015) considers mental health promotion to be a human rights issue and suggests not only that it is fundamental to the well-being of individuals but that it increases the mental health and well-being of whole populations.

Mentality (2004) conceptualises mental health promotion as any activity or action that strengthens or protects mental health. It operates at three levels; these may helpfully be conceptualised as concentric circles with individuals at the centre:

- Strengthening individuals: for example, by increasing coping skills or resilience among people with dementia (Moniz-Cook et al, 2011; Subramaniam et al, 2014; Oyebode and Parveen, 2016);
- Strengthen communities: for example, by improving access to universal services and enhancing opportunities to socially participate (Ichida et al, 2013);
- Reducing structural barriers: for example, by promoting access to welfare benefits among older people (Mentality, 2001; Age Concern England, 2007); Age Northern Ireland ran a campaign to tackle pensioner poverty (Age NI, 2018).

The levels of promotion activity dovetail with the size and scope of the target group. In this sense it shares both conceptual and actual territory with preventive initiatives and foci. This model also links with that proposed by Tanner (2010) who suggests that resources – and threats – to the mental health and well-being of older people exist in the personal *and* community domains; she also adds a social dimension, for example the nature and quality of social and family relationships. While her analysis does not explicitly identify a category of 'structural issues' she incorporates factors such as health inequalities, poverty and ageism through the prism of older people's lived experiences.

Knapp and colleagues (2013) make the economic case for investment in three promotional initiatives: time banks, befriending and community navigators for older people in need of support. Specifically, there is some evidence that these services have the capacity to improve the mental health and quality of life of older people, reduce levels of depression and enrich the social capital of the local community (Younger-Ross, 2008). Befriending services, in particular, may represent good value for money; they reduce demands on primary care and more intensive support services especially in relationship to depression; they also help to facilitate older people's engagement with neighbourhoods in ways that often save money, for example volunteering.

Older people's views

Most older people regard prevention, promotion and protection as conjoined elements of any strategy or policy (Age Concern and Mental Health Foundation, 2006). As we know they also tend to regard mental health as an embedded dimension of overall health. There *is* recognition that some threats to mental health require specific attention, including loneliness, bereavement and carer stress but for the most part older people view promotion of mental health as intrinsic to the promotion of overall health and well-being (see Chapter 2).

Evidence also suggests that most older people conceptualise prevention and promotion broadly. Prevention is 'preventing the loss of independence' or 'preventing isolation' and preventive support is defined as activities or services that 'prevent excess disability' or 'becoming a burden' (Stenner et al, 2011; Allen and Glasby, 2013). Promotion includes interventions to help older people 'achieve self-determination and choice', continue to be active members of their communities and be enabled to remain at home (Tanner, 2001). Libraries, walking groups and social clubs would all be viewed as performing a protective role (Taylor and Donoghue, 2015). While older people also value more intensive services such as home care and respite care and appreciate that these aim – in part at least – to prevent the use of more intensive resources, research consistently identifies that they regard prevention as operating at primary and secondary levels, not just at the tertiary level (Theander and Edberg, 2005). When older people are invited to determine the shape and nature of services to promote their mental health, or prevent its erosion, they routinely emphasise the importance of small amounts of support that will be titrated to meet their (often increasing) needs, the importance of relationships, and of services that are sufficiently nuanced to work with their coping strategies and skills and that promote self-efficacy and control. In this sense, their views are profoundly at odds with those of policy makers and commissioners both in terms of approach and level of intervention (Lloyd et al, 2014b; Tanner, 2016).

Research with older people also identifies a distinction between issues that are fundamental to creating vulnerability to mental ill health – causal factors – and those issues that prompt a slide into it – trigger factors. Some of the causative issues are linked to the life course and may include abuse, long-term physical health problems and chronic poverty. Triggers may also have life course links but they are more likely to be experiences common to later life such as bereavement. Promotion of mental health may thus require a two-tier approach: one that appreciates the nature of the 'fundamentals' and recognition of life course challenges and the other that is responsive to trigger factors and can step in flexibly at short notice with appropriate support. Both may be needed particularly for an older person with complex needs and/or dementia and their elderly spouse carer.

Research by Bernard (2000) emphasises the importance of understanding health and health promotion from the perspective of older people. She argues for a focus on older people's own strategies for health and mental health promotion and learning from their approaches to achieving optimal levels of functioning. This argument links with those made by Tanner in her research exploring the 'ageing experience' (to be discussed later).

Mental health – promotion, protection and prevention: theoretical issues and models

Given that older people regard mental health promotion and protection and mental ill health prevention as overlapping issues there is an intuitive logic to combining the concepts and approaches. This section will review theories and models drawn from both arenas. Priority is given to material that is relevant and has purchase; one of the deficits of work in this area is its abstract, and at times, reductive nature. However useful a theoretical model may be, if it has not been operationalised in practice its value is difficult to evaluate.

Ageing and (mental) health promotion

There is a, perhaps obvious, link between theoretical position and models. As has been discussed in Chapter 3, there are a number of theories of ageing. They differ along a range of dimensions including the weight they place on individual as opposed to broader social or life course-related explanations for mental health outcomes and the extent to which they accommodate temporality. Some appreciate the influence of the life course on mental health; others concern themselves only with the here and now. How they conceptualise the process of ageing is also a, linked, defining distinction. Social gerontology, for example, promotes the view that ageing is not simply about loss and decline but is also about growth, personal development and adjustment to age-related challenges.

Social gerontology informs the model I outlined in Chapter 2, the socio-cultural model of successful ageing (Figure 2.3). In 2004, Godfrey and Denby adapted this model to reflect a focus on mental health and well-being (see Figure 10.2). The model was accompanied by a Framework of risk and protective factors in securing mental health and well-being in later life[1] (see Box 10.2). Drawing principally on evidence about depression the framework conceptualised risks and protective factors as being located in three domains – individual, community and national/societal – and as acting to undermine, or secure, core dimensions of well-being. In the 'individual domain' issues such as opportunities for social participation and adaptive coping strategies offer protection; in the 'community domain' they include a safe local environment; in the 'national/ societal domain' action to reduce structural inequality is identified. A number of these elements resonate with the resilience framework also outlined later in the chapter (Figure 10.3: Wild et al, 2013).

One of the framework's key strengths is that the factors located at different levels interrelate with one another, for example needing material resources for a comfortable later life and anti-poverty strategies, levels of social participation and the nature of community networks. The role played by the life course and inequalities in the creation of risks and/or protective factors is also recognised (Godfrey et al, 2005).

Related work, by Tanner (2007; 2010) and others incorporates consideration of *both* barriers/threats (things to be reduced or prevented)

Figure 10.2: Socio-cultural model of successful ageing, 2004

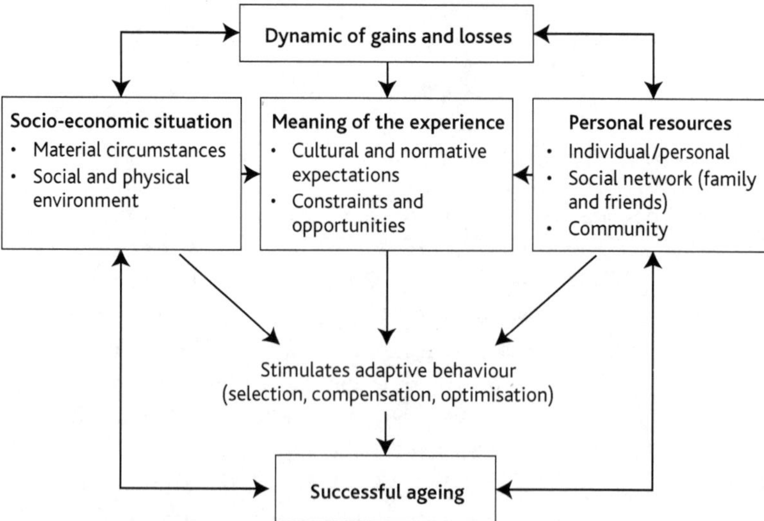

Source: Godfrey and Denby, 2004

and strengths/resources (things to be developed or strengthened) in parallel. An older person can be exposed to a risk, for example physical ill health alongside a protective factor, for example having a good income. Research by Hill and colleagues (2009) exploring older peoples' experiences of change and continuity observe that older people use their resources (of all types) in two ways: as a 'managing mechanism' that helps them to cope with change when it occurs and as a 'protective force' whereby resources act as a buffer to mitigate the negative impact of change.

Effective mental health promotion requires understanding of how the goals pursued by older people at the micro level, for example retaining contact with friends or responding to loss of mobility, are shaped by the familial, community, environmental and socio-economic context of the individual and how these dimensions have been, and continue to be, influenced by the life course (Tanner, 2010). In other words, to appreciate the micro issues relating to mental health one must not only take account of the macro, that is, the wider context, but also how the resources and protective factors that are located in that context have been developed over the individual's life course. They are intrinsically connected; one is both a product of, and is embedded in, the other. Income and social relationships are two examples.

Box 10.2: Framework of risk and protective factors in securing mental health and well-being in later life

Domain	Elements of well-being	Risk factors	Protective factors
Individual and family	• Physical health • Personal/social relationships • Social activities	• Loss of function/ mobility • Loss of role/ connectedness • Social isolation	• Regular exercise • Volunteering • Retaining hobbies • Having a confidante • Seeing friends and family members regularly
Community	• Participation and engagement • Quality of physical and social environment	• Poor physical/ social environment • High levels of crime • Poor public transport	• Engaging with community groups/activities • Having access to neighbourhood resources and outdoor space • Crime prevention initiatives

(continued)

National/ society	• Material resources • Inclusion • Equality • High-quality support from health and care services	• Poverty/poor housing • Exclusion/ marginalisation • Age discrimination • Limited access to health and care services	• Protection of universal state pension • Social inclusion policies/ initiatives • Addressing age discrimination • Accessible and available health and care services

Source: Adapted from Godfrey and Denby's framework, 2004

It is important to note that some of the key dimensions of the models discussed in this section – social networks, coping skills, environmental mastery – are core elements of a number of the constructs explored in Chapter 2 – mental health, psychological well-being and resilience. In relationship to resilience I highlighted a model developed by Wild and colleagues (2013) (Figure 2.2). This model conceptualises resilience as a product of a person's household and family, neighbourhood, community and wider society (Richardson and Chew-Graham, 2016). A second model, developed in parallel by Wild and colleagues (2013), views resilience as being made up of a number of separate but linked 'areas': psychological, mobility, financial, environmental, physical, social and cultural (see Figure 10.3). The authors acknowledge that a person may be resilient in one area of their life, for example income, but not in another, for example physical health, and that this balance may vary through time and in response to circumstance. This is a similar point to that made earlier in relationship to the co-existence of risks *and* protective factors.

This relatively accessible conceptual model has been used by agencies to help them think about mental health promotion. In its report on *Improving Later Life* for example, Age UK (2015) conceptualises resilience as having three 'legs': wealth, health, and social networks and support. The report acknowledges that resilience is broader than an individual personality trait and that the 'system' around the older person – family, universal services, the environment and care services – needs to be resilient to provide effective support.

Another example of how models have influenced action is the Age Concern (now Age UK) and Mental Health Foundation (2006) inquiry into *Mental Health and Well Being in Later Life*. The inquiry highlighted five key areas which should be the focus of policy and public investment: maintaining relationships; participation in meaningful activity; physical

Figure 10.3: Areas of resilience in later life

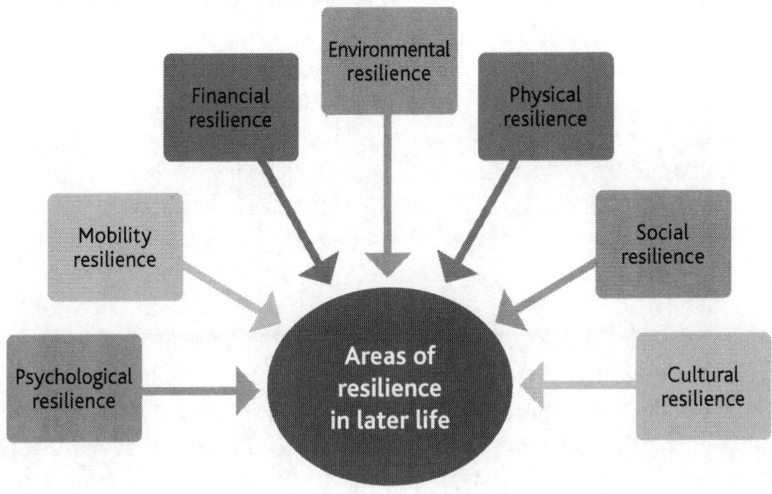

Source: Wild et al, 2013

health; discrimination; and poverty. Each of these areas are conceptualised as needing to be addressed at a structural, community and individual level.

Contributions from mental health promotion

In addition to those drawn from the ageing field, theoretical concepts and models drawn from the mental health promotion arena are also relevant.

Social capital is one such concept; it is commonly identified as an 'untapped resource'. The *Mental Health and Well Being* report (part of the Foresight project) makes a strong case for 'unlocking' the social and mental capital of older people in terms of mental health promotion (Government Office for Science, 2008). Yusuf (2008) defines social capital as four sets of intersecting resources: social resources, for example neighbours you can call upon; collective resources, for example self-help groups; economic resources, for example income; and cultural resources, for example libraries. While older people make use of these resources proponents of social capital suggest that they also contribute significantly to it, benefitting their own mental health and that of other older people.

The aligned principle of 'collectivity' is also relevant. It is embedded in Beattie's model of health promotion (2002). This model distinguishes between types of mental health promotion intervention on a scale from 'fully negotiated through to professionally determined', and the focus of practice ranges from 'the individual to the collective'. Although examples of collectively oriented interventions are relatively popular, community groups for example, Tilford (2009) wryly observes that most mental health promotion activity locates responsibility for mental health squarely with the individual and the mode of intervention as a state endorsed call to 'make better lifestyle choices'. Examples include campaigns targeted at older people urging them to 'keep fit' and 'join a social club' (Age UK, 2018).

A public health perspective tends to take a broader approach, acknowledging that there is a complex picture of causality. Hertzman and colleagues (1994) argue – as has been identified earlier – that the older population is highly diverse and heterogeneous as a consequence of exposure over time to a range of life course influences including structural and social inequalities (Crosland and Wallace, 2011). Individuals become increasingly different from one another as they get older. The multi-dimensionality of this perspective offers us a number of 'ways in' to reducing threats to mental health, including tackling childhood poverty, addressing domestic abuse, creating safe neighbourhoods and ensuring that community and health services are accessible to older people and are well resourced. A public health agenda also engages with a commitment to ensure that universal initiatives such as policies to address social exclusion, neighbourhood safety programmes and regeneration strategies, take proper account of older people's needs and interests (Age Concern and Mental Health Foundation, 2006). For example, Neighbourhood Watch (2009) invested in an initiative focused specifically on supporting older neighbours. The bringing together of public health and mental health in the policy arena is an issue I explore in the concluding chapter.

Although it has not been operationalised the *Foundations of Mental Wellbeing in Later Life* (FUEL) model is important to include (Cattan, 2015: see Figure 10.4). This model was developed to bring together evidence about what underpins mental well-being[2] for the National Institute for Health and Care Excellence's guidance on *Mental Wellbeing and Independence for Older People* and related quality standard (NIHCE, 2016). The FUEL model (also) adopts a multi-dimensional lens on mental well-being and recognises it as a dynamic state affected by both context and life course. Cattan (2015) suggests that four main pillars provide the foundations of mental health across the whole life course: functional ability, psychological attributes, social connectedness, and power and resources. The model was co-produced by a group of stakeholders including older people and explicitly draws on the concepts and theories of salutogenesis, resilience and flourishing (Billings and Hashem, 2009; Ottmann and Maragoudaki, 2015). It also recognises the strong intersectional links between mental well-being and quality of life. Cattan (2015) acknowledges that some issues, such as culture, are less visible; also that it does not clearly differentiate between the micro, meso and macro levels of factors that affect mental well-being. The explicit acknowledgement of the role played by power, and its connection

Figure 10.4: Multi-dimensional, theoretical model of the foundations of mental well-being in later life

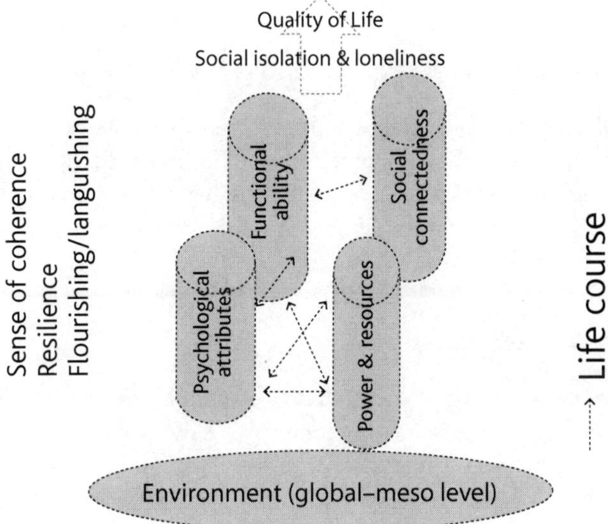

Source: Cattan, 2015

to resources, is a distinctive feature of the FUEL model and one that resonates with issues of inequality. It is also echoed in subsequent work in the mental health field which foregrounds the role played by power in understanding and responding to the needs of people who use mental health services (Johnstone and Boyle, 2018).

It is noteworthy that the NIHCE guidance itself has a much narrower focus than the evidence review. The *Mental Wellbeing and Independence for Older People* quality standard covers 'interventions to maintain and improve the mental wellbeing and independence of people aged 65 or older who are at risk of decline'; its accompanying three quality statements require that these groups are identified by service providers, offered tailored, community-based physical activity programmes and a range of activities to develop or maintain social participation (NIHCE, 2016).

Despite the number and range of models that exist in both the preventive and promotional arenas they are challenged to accommodate the multiplicity of dimensions that influence mental health in later life. They particularly struggle to take account of dynamism, intersectionality and inequalities. A conspicuous omission from much of this literature is older people's perspectives although this is not universally the case. The FUEL model directly incorporates the views of older people and the *Socio-cultural Model of Successful Ageing* draws on evidence from work *with* older people. Another overarching point relates to the absence of theory.

As many of those who work in the health promotion field consider that 'effective practice depends on good theory' this is an important, if under-recognised, deficit.

Mental health in later life: protective factors

In this section of the chapter I will explore what is known about the factors that protect and promote the mental health of older people facing common age-related challenges. There is an inevitable overlap with some of the material reviewed in Chapter 2 in relationship to what older people consider 'good mental health' to be.

Personal attributes and resources

A range of personal attributes including positive self-esteem, self-efficacy, a sense of security and resilience are protective of mental health. Resilience, in particular, helps an older person to adapt to age-related challenges, 'bounce back' from adversity and cope with stress (Windle, 2012). As noted in Chapter 2, resilience is broadly understood to mean 'the process of effectively negotiating, adapting to, or managing significant sources of stress or trauma' (Windle, 2011, p 152). Older people who use coping strategies that include problem-solving approaches have better mental health than those who use avoidant strategies. Two psychosocial processes that promote mental health are highlighted in the literature: positive reappraisal whereby challenging or adverse events are successfully integrated into 'normal life', and self-enhancing social comparisons. Those people who make comparisons 'upwards' with those whose status and excellent physical health is out of their reach are more likely to have poorer mental health than those who compare 'downwards' with people who are worse off than themselves (Bowling and Dieppe, 2005).

The effect of an illness or loss is mediated by the psychosocial resource of mastery: having a sense of control over one's life (Bowling, 2005). A higher level of perceived self-mastery and an optimistic outlook are related to better coping mechanisms and fewer depressive symptoms in older people with deteriorating conditions (Wurm and Benyamini, 2014). In Chapter 2, the mechanism of 'cognitive coping' was noted whereby an individual learns to tolerate the effects of chronic illness (Bury, 1991; Tanner, 2005). This is clearly a useful attribute for those who develop long-term health problems.

So-called 'flourishing' individuals perform better in a range of key areas than their non-flourishing peers and have better mental health. Flourishing is defined by Keyes (2002, p 207) as 'a state of positive emotion, positive psychological functioning and positive social functioning'. Flourishing individuals have often been exposed to a number of life course advantages, including good parenting, a stable childhood and positive attachment with parents; they also tend to display prosocial behaviour (Keyes, 2007). This supports arguments about the foundational role played by early life in developing good mental health whose reach extends across the whole life course.

One of the challenges of reviewing evidence in this area is that it is difficult to disentangle cause from effect. It is perhaps not surprising that optimistic people are more likely to have positive mental health and thereby manage age-related challenges more effectively. Resilience is consistently linked to positive emotions. In turn 'positive emotions' have been found to facilitate adaptive outcomes and enhance coping skills (Aminzadeh et al, 2007). There is cyclical quality to these links. This observation does not invalidate them but their connectivity is to be expected. Methodological complexity in terms of disentangling the direction and nature of influence(s) is an ongoing issue.

Physical health, exercise and activity

There is a well-developed evidence base demonstrating the positive psychological and social benefits of participation in group activity for older people. Specifically, it promotes social interaction, engagement and inclusion (Victor, 2010). It can also offer a source of identity and support and can enhance self-esteem (Fox, 2003). The European *Better Ageing Project* found that regular exercise, especially in a group, enhanced overall well-being, improved mood, reduced stress and anxiety and alleviated depressive symptoms (Warburton et al, 2006; Benyamini et al, 2010). 'Regular exercise' need be no more than ten minutes of moderate exercise a day as evidenced by Age UK's *Keeping Fit and Well* and *Fit as a Fiddle* programmes (Age UK, 2012). Walking clubs and exercise classes are particularly popular activities. Interventions to promote physical health among care home residents such as chair-based exercises also show positive results for both physical and mental health (NIHCE, 2015a).

As noted in Chapter 3, there is growing evidence of a bidirectional relationship between mental and physical health (Edmunds et al, 2013). There are two sets of intersecting research: the first relates to mental health problems and the second to the protective role of positive mental health. Depression contributes to reduced physical health and well-being (Steptoe et al, 2013a), and older people with low levels of psychological well-being are significantly more likely to report 'functional difficulties', for example with activities of daily living (Evans et al, 2003b). Keyes's (2005) work suggests that the risks of developing a range of specific conditions, including stroke, arthritis, diabetes and cancer, is much lower among people with positive mental health. Interventions to promote mental health also appear to improve a range of physical health outcomes, including stroke incidence and survival (Ostir et al, 2001), lower risk of heart disease and lifetime mortality rates.

Research identifies that having access to affordable exercise facilities, for example at a local leisure centre, and accessible green spaces is key to engaging older people in regular physical activity (Belza et al, 2004). As is the case across the life course older people belonging to higher income groups tend to take more exercise than those in lower income groups (Clark, 1999).

Religiosity and spirituality

Greater attention is now being paid to the role played by religion and spirituality in the lives of older people (Narayanasamy et al, 2004). Research indicates that membership of an accepting faith community has a positive effect on mental health; identity, purpose and self-worth are validated by religious belief (Mentality, 2004). Resilience, coping abilities and sense of connectedness are also bolstered by religion *and* by being part of a religious group (Mental Health Foundation, 2006). Building and sustaining relationships is an important element of the role religion can play in promoting mental health as is the 'religious environment' – familiar people, patterns, places and rituals, and shared values and moral codes. Religious belief and regular attendance at a house of worship can also represent a constant in a person's life that may span the whole life course, reinforcing an older person's sense of self and belonging (Krause and Bastida, 2011).

Social relationships, social networks and social participation

There is a large literature on the nature, value and benefits of social relationships, social networks and social participation, and social capital. For this reason, the evidence will be reviewed in two blocks – the first three issues followed by the fourth; it is important to acknowledge that all four are connected.

Positive social relationships play a critical role in enhancing well-being and sustaining mental health (Gabriel and Bowling, 2004; Pratschke et al, 2017; Bruggencate et al, 2018). They can bolster coping abilities and resilience, moderate stress, provide a sense of continuity and security and reinforce 'purpose in life' (Forsman et al, 2013). There is recent evidence that regular face-to-face contact with friends and family reduces current, and future, risk of an older person developing depression (Teo et al, 2015). Older people identify 'meaningful engagement' as an important facet of social relationships. Specifically, that having a role and helping others promotes an older person's identity and purpose and increases levels of personal satisfaction; it also reinforces a sense of belonging to a family or group (Godfrey et al, 2005). Feeling valued, respected and understood by others contributes, unsurprisingly, to positive mental health; there is even evidence that it can counter the impact of age discrimination (Age Concern and Mental Health Foundation, 2006). Social relationships are prominent dimensions of the models reviewed in Chapter 2.

Litwin's study (2001) found that diverse social networks encompassing both friends *and* family are associated with higher levels of positive mental health among older people than networks made up exclusively of relatives. It has been suggested that this may be because friends permit greater feelings of autonomy and facilitate integration into a broader set of networks than relatives do (Soulsby and Bennett, 2015). Long-term friendships play an especially important role in the networks of older people who are widowed, childless or single (Isherwood et al, 2017). Having a confidante is specifically evidenced as highly protective of mental health across all age groups and is important for the maintenance of morale, self-esteem and prevention of loneliness (Holt-Lunstad et al, 2010; Schwarzbach et al, 2014). Older women are more likely to have a confidante than their male peers and tend to have larger and more mixed social networks too. People in lower socio-economic groups report weaker friendship ties but stronger links with relatives (Steptoe et al, 2013a).

Marriage appears to have a protective effect on mental health, especially for men across the life course (Evans et al, 2003b). Older never married adults have poorer mental health than their married counterparts (Blomgren et al, 2010). Divorce in later life often has a long-term negative effect on psychological well-being (Bennett, 2005). Part of this effect is indirect and is a consequence of both partners, particularly the woman, being worse off post-divorce in terms of income, housing and other material resources. If divorce is a desired outcome self-reported distress levels fall significantly in the years post-divorce (Hughes and Waite, 2009).

Older peoples' social networks shrink, especially among those aged 75 years and over; this is primarily a consequence of friends and relatives dying. Kahn and Antonucci's (1980) social convoy model suggests that the 'convoy' of relationships also changes in later life; contact with friends may diminish while links with family members increases. The social convoy model is made up of three concentric circles reflecting degree of attachment and closeness of relationships: the inner circle contains partners and children, the middle circle contains confidantes and long-term friends, and the outer circle is made up of (ex)work colleagues, neighbours and formal carers (where these exist). Over time older people have reduced social contact with those in the outer – and subsequently middle – circles relating increasingly to members of their inner circle. This evidence is echoed in Tanner's (2010; 2016) work relating to older people's lived experiences of 'sustaining the self' to be discussed later. In 2012, a Women's Royal Voluntary Service survey (2012) identified that over three quarters of all older people (78 per cent) see their children at least once a week with a quarter (25 per cent) of those aged 75 to 84 years and 20 per cent of those aged 85 years and over, seeing their children on a daily basis. Ageing without children, higher levels of divorce, and social mobility makes it likely that non-kin relationships may play a more prominent role than relatives in the future (Spencer and Pahl, 2006). This appears to be the case too for same-sex older couples who may be alienated from their families (De Vries, 2007).

Social networks are also a major resource in terms of providing social support and in mitigating the negative impact of illness and disability on mental health (Bisschop et al, 2004). Positive social relationships, especially with family members, have consistently been identified as a primary source of *both* emotional and instrumental support for older people with dependency needs. They facilitate adaptation to late life transitions such as becoming ill or needing to move to a smaller house and promote a sense of control, dignity and self-worth (Pinquart and Sörensen, 2000).

What appears to be important is the quality of key relationships and how the support is valued by the older person rather than its quantity or type (Umberson and Karas Montez, 2010; Yang and Victor, 2011). Support that is provided in a respectful way that appreciates the older person's lifestyle, views and feelings, understands what is important to them and is underpinned by reciprocity is associated with high levels of satisfaction and psychological well-being and reduced stress (Fiori et al, 2006; Amieva et al, 2010). It is also linked to health-enabling behaviours such as eating well and/or taking part in a group activity. A study of people aged 85 years and over in Finland highlighted the positive effects of social networks and support on mental health, especially on preventing depression (Nyqvist et al, 2006).

Social relationships also foster good mental health through encouraging social participation (Holt-Lunstad et al, 2010). Social participation is associated with reduced risk of isolation, loneliness and depression and better self-reported health (Cornwell and Waite, 2009; Litwin and Stoeckel, 2014). Participation can take a number of forms: economic, educational, social, cultural, political and/or civic. Examples of activities include: a book group, arts classes, citizens forums, adult education classes, pub quizzes, bingo and volunteering (see the section on 'Meaningful Occupation' later in this chapter). Participation is often local especially for older people who have health or mobility issues, although it is important to recognise that growing numbers of older people are participating in online groups and networks (Gatto and Tak, 2008).

Social capital

It has been suggested that 'social capital' – an umbrella term incorporating social networks, social support and social participation – may be regarded as a mental health resource for older people (Le Mesurier and Northmore, 2003). Although variously defined there are two broad camps. A distinction can be drawn between Bourdieu's (1986) conceptualisation of social capital, which is focused on the individual level, and Putnam's (2000) community-level conceptualisation. Bourdieu (1986) defined social capital as '... the aggregate of the actual or potential resources which are linked to possession of a durable network of more or less institutionalised relationships of mutual acquaintance or recognition' (p 241). This includes material resources such as money. Putnam (2000) distinguishes three types of social capital: bonding (strong ties between people, for example families, friends); bridging (weaker ties with ex-work colleagues, acquaintances); and linking (connections between those with different levels of power). Putnam's model has a 'structural' dimension, for example participation in neighbourhood activities and a 'cognitive' dimension, for example level of perceived trust. Although both models share conceptual territory with, respectively, social networks and the social convoy model, their lenses are broader and represent a fusion of issues; relationships are regarded primarily as a resource rather than as of value in their own right. They also incorporate some elements of the wider environment, that is, there is recognition that relationships are embedded in social and physical spaces.

The social capital of older people is strongly connected to the area they live in. In good part, this is because they spend a significant amount of time in their own homes and neighbourhoods. This is especially the case for older people in the fourth age who are more likely to have health and mobility problems (Nyqvist et al, 2006). The nature of the community, neighbourhood and environment are intersecting influences (Milligan and Wiles, 2010).

'Community belonging' is positively associated with mental health and well-being (Kim and Kaplan, 2004). It can take four forms: attachment to place (community attachment); being in tune with the social and physical characteristics of place (community identity); being involved with others in the community (social interaction); and walkability of the community environment (pedestrianism). There is specific evidence that attachment to place is protective of mental health (Bambra, 2016). Community and neighbourhood facilities, civic and social opportunities and accessible leisure and educational resources all protect against isolation, enhance opportunities for participation and promote mental health (Age Concern England, 2007). Protective features of the environment include accessible spaces such as parks and places to 'stop and chat' (Clarke et al, 2007). A Japanese study found longevity of older people in urban areas increased in accordance with the access to proximity of walkable green spaces (Takano et al, 2002). This dovetails with earlier evidence relating to physical activity. 'Environmental mastery' – having some control over one's home and neighbourhood – has been linked to positive mental health (Knight et al, 2011). Research by Knipscheer and colleagues (2000) found that 'feeling able to influence one's (local) environment' decreased depressive symptomology in older people with poor functional ability.

As discussed in Chapter 3, communities with high levels of social capital are characterised by norms of trust, reciprocity and participation; they bolster the potential for individual resilience, promote a sense of belonging and offer more social support (Hall and Taylor, 2009). They are also associated with higher levels of positive mental health, including among older people (McKenzie and Harpham, 2006; Bambra, 2016). The processes involved are only partially understood but are thought to involve the capacity of social capital to enhance self-esteem and self-efficacy and reduce anxiety and fear, for example about isolation and/or crime (Curtis, 2010). Such communities are sometimes referred to as 'resilient communities'.

The concept of social capital intersects with the concept of 'health capital' (Bergland and Slettebo, 2015). This is an umbrella term incorporating a cluster of health resources; these are a mix of social assets and individual attributes. They include: adaptability, activity, reciprocity in relationships, social connectivity, making a positive contribution, coping well with change, positive health-related behaviours, for example good diet, being part of a supportive social network and having access to social and community resources. High levels of health capital contribute to positive mental health and well-being. It is understood to be a dynamic construct that is a product of a life course, not a static state; as such it can be depleted or augmented by life course experiences and inequalities (Gerdtham et al, 1999). It is noteworthy that the positive psychological well-being experienced by a high proportion of older people living in the Sardinian Blue Zone (discussed in Chapter 2) is associated with a number of the key elements of both social and health capital (Hitchcott et al, 2018).

Despite the prevalence of policy discourses on the dependency of older people, it is increasingly recognised that older people are not simply passive recipients of the benefits of social and health capital but actively contribute to it, even in the fourth age (Lloyd, 2012). Boneham and Sixsmith (2006), for example, identified the important role played by older women in a community in the north of England in creating and maintaining social capital. Brighter Futures is another example (see Box 10.1, earlier in the chapter). A need to protect social capital is now imbued with a sense of urgency arising from concerns about its erosion and the consequent negative impact on the mental health and well-being of older citizens (Scharf and Keating, 2012). In the US, a substantial portion of a 30-year decline in happiness is explained by a reduction in social connectivity and lower levels of social participation across all age groups, particularly older people (Bartolini et al, 2013). In New Zealand, there is ongoing research exploring how to protect older people from the negative consequences of the shrinking of their social networks (Wiles et al, 2009). In the UK the *Campaign to End Loneliness* was launched in 2011 and a Minister for Loneliness was appointed in 2018 in response to political and public concerns about the loss of social capital (Bolton, 2012).

Social capital is an attractive concept for policy makers because it holds out the possibility of improving community and individual well-being, through means which appear to be both more intuitively appealing and cheaper than traditional publicly funded services (Skidmore et al, 2006). It could be argued that its rather opaque and ill-defined nature is also a useful terminological smokescreen for policy makers to hide behind. There is, in fact, very limited evidence that policy has a positive impact on the development of social capital. In part this is because top-down models tend to mix badly with locally grown bottom-up initiatives and in part because one of key ingredients of social capital for older people are community facilities such as parks, libraries and buses which require public investment (Boeck and Fleming, 2005).

It is noteworthy, however, that policy can be effective. One such example, albeit rather out of date now, is the UK-wide *A Sure Start to Later Life* policy of 2005/6 (Social Exclusion Unit, 2006). Its focus on working with the grain and priorities of local communities, providing funding for initiatives, and a requirement that its adoption, implementation and evaluation be 'owned' across all government departments were hallmarks of its success. It also explicitly acknowledged the role played by poverty, disadvantage and deprivation in undermining well-being and eroding social capital. One of the projects originally funded via *Sure Start* is 'Gloucester's Village Agents'; it offered face-to-face information and support to people over 50 years, signposted them to services and carried out practical safety checks on people's homes. It is still operational today, has been extended to any age group and renamed 'Community Wellbeing Agents' (Darch, 2014).

Meaningful occupation

Having a meaningful occupation is consistently identified as important to older people's mental health and well-being (Bruggencate et al, 2018). Although education and learning can fulfil this role (Allen, 2008) most research in this area – that does not relate to paid employment – is associated with volunteering. It is a relatively popular activity (Humphrey et al, 2011). Thirty-one per cent of people aged 65 to 74 and 21 per cent of 75 and over in England participated in volunteering in the 12 months to June 2013 (Wave Trust, 2013).

Both befriending and volunteering are associated with a range of benefits, including higher levels of social participation, a sense that one is 'making a contribution', having a purpose, and being stimulated (Walsh and O'Shea, 2008). Older people who regularly volunteer have been shown to have higher levels of psychological well-being, reduced stress levels, improved morale, better coping skills, greater confidence and larger social networks (Nazroo and Matthews, 2012). It has specifically been associated with a reduction in symptoms of depression which is interesting as other evidence suggests that it is mainly older people with positive mental health who volunteer (Lum and Lightfoot, 2005). Volunteering by older people is usually undertaken locally thereby contributing to the social capital of their community.

Socio-economic and life course-related resources

Having access to a reasonable income, particularly an occupational pension, is evidenced as having a positive impact on mental health in later life (Grant, 2013). It provides a degree of comfort and the means to make choices, participate in enjoyable activities, for example going out for a meal, and feel part of ordinary society. This has a direct and positive effect on levels of anxiety and stress. Money can also cushion the impact of some age-related losses. The negative impact of a disability, for example, can be mediated to some degree by the ability to purchase aids, adaptations and private treatment (Milne, 2009a). As noted in Chapter 5, higher income in midlife is protective of mental health in later life (Bryant et al, 2001; Eikemo et al, 2008). Higher levels of education also appear to be protective, especially for women (Ploubidis and Grundy, 2009; Yang and Victor, 2011).

Choosing to work beyond the statutory retirement age tends to be associated with positive mental health, particularly for those who are self-employed or in valued occupations, for example doctors (Vickerstaff, 2006). Flexible and/or part-time work in preparation for retirement is evidenced as helpful to psychological adjustment (Age UK, 2015). This issue was explored in Chapter 4.

Older people with a reasonable income also tend to live in greener better kept neighbourhoods and own their own homes. Housing can play an important role in promoting mental health (Evans et al, 2003a). For many older people housing is much more than bricks and mortar; it is in, and around, the home where most social interactions take place, interests are pursued, TV is watched and relationships are nurtured. The quality, security and comfort of the older person's home is therefore especially important particularly as they are more likely than other age groups to spend a lot of time at home (Sixsmith et al, 2014).

A note on psychosocial stress

In Chapter 3 I explored in some depth the intersection between exposure to psychosocial stress and mental health problems. In terms of factors that reduce the adverse effects of chronic stress, evidence is mixed. Although some research suggests that 'restorative processes' such as sleep have a positive impact on stress levels (Hawkley and Cacioppo, 2004), other evidence indicates that the damage of prolonged exposure to stress cannot be undone (Lupien et al, 2009). Related research suggests that the stressful impact of an adverse event, for example midlife redundancy from paid work, may be mediated by a level of 'psychological robustness' that has been developed earlier in the life course (Rogers and Pilgrim, 2003). In terms of specific evidence social connectedness, social support and positive relationships are all factors that reduce allostatic load.[3] They also appear to aid the generation of protective physiological defences against illness, lower risks of cardiovascular disease and improve sleep (Ryff et al, 2004). This evidence dovetails with the protective capacity of social participation and social support reviewed earlier.

Learning from older people: managing the ageing experience

There is limited, but growing, research exploring older people's views on the meaning and promotion of good mental health. In broad terms this body of work highlights two issues: that there are a number of 'mental health positives' relating to later life and that the existing narrative does not take sufficiently nuanced account of how older people manage late life challenges, including frailty. Both offer an important counterweight to the medically dominated discourse that focuses on mental health deficits (Bryant et al, 2001).

Older people identity a number of benefits related to later life. These include: increased self-acceptance and confidence, the easing of domestic responsibilities and having more time to pursue interests, have fun and enjoy life (Help the Aged, 2004). Many older people – including those aged over 85 years – continue to mature, both intellectually and with regard to skills (Kunzmann et al, 2000). Research with older people underscores the fact that a person's capacity for well-being does not necessarily decline with age.

Tanner's (2007; 2010; 2016) seminal work exploring how older people manage 'the ageing experience' has much to tell us about mental health in later life. By focusing on the strategies that older people develop Tanner's work adopts a positive approach to ageing, recognising older people as active agents and as resourceful and resilient in the face of declining abilities. 'Sustaining the self' is a pivotal element of managing the changes that later life brings, achieved by pursuing the twin practical and psychological goals of 'keeping going' and 'staying me' (Tanner, 2010). Important issues are protecting identity and retaining the things that matter, including relationships (Phillipson and Biggs, 1998). Tanner (2010) emphasises the highly individualised interaction between the 'objective' and the 'subjective': for example, between the loss of a spouse and the interpretation of that loss. Although some assumptions can be made about bereavement, each person's experience of it is different; meaning making is a personal process mediated through the lenses of a life course and a context.

Tanner's (2010) work highlights the important role played by continuity in protecting mental health. In adapting to change older people rely on the continuities that have helped them manage life's challenges, including tried-and-tested coping strategies; long-standing relationships that affirm autonomy, identity and agency; money; home; and environment. The degree of an older person's success in achieving continuity is influenced to a significant degree by their access to physical, emotional and economic resources thus entwining the individual and the structural. This underscores the role and relevance of the life course and the embedded nature of continuity.

In her 2016 paper, following up on one of the original case studies from her 2010 study, Tanner revisits the factors that impact on Harriet's[4] mental health and well-being. Harriet is by now 97 and quite frail. Harriet integrates changes, mainly health issues, into the 'ongoing story of self' in way that maintains her life narrative (Giddens, 1999). Tanner (2016) notes that the 'essence of her subjective well-being seems to reside in the threads of continuity she is able to preserve' (p 164). The issues that protect mental health take on a different form in the fourth age; they do not go away but they are reframed (Baltes, 1998). Harriet's previous efforts to maintain independence have been replaced by an acceptance of her altered situation; she acknowledges her worsening health, reliance on others and narrowed world but does not dwell on these changes (Milne and Williamson, 2016). As might be expected a number of these themes resonate with those raised in Chapters 7 and 9 relating to frailty, and frailty and dementia, respectively.

Older women's voices

The work of Tanner (2010; 2016) and others highlight the absence of women's voices in the fourth age discourse. As most of those who survive into the fourth age are women their invisible status is a notable deficit. This echoes the point made in Chapter 9 about women and dementia.

Three issues need to be highlighted. The first is about survival. Feminist literature from the mental health field acknowledges midlife women as survivors: survivors of a life course (often) marked by abuse and disadvantage, of injustice and inequality, and of damaging mental health services (Williams and Watson, 2016). Older women are survivors too; often of a number of these challenges *alongside* those relating to age, ill health and loss. I am not going to repeat points made earlier in the book but it is nevertheless instructive to remind ourselves that the women who have been exposed to abuse, domestic violence, lifelong poverty and ageism are those who, in the fourth age, become frail. Being frail does not delete what has gone before, if anything it amplifies its relevance. It may help us adopt a life course lens on the lives of fourth age older women to view them as survivors. It may also make it more likely that we listen to their stories and perspectives and learn from them about the protection and promotion of mental health (Boneham and Sixsmith, 2006).

A second point relates to older women as a resource: both as resourceful in terms of their own well-being (see Harriet) and a resource for other women. The importance of long-term friendships, and of a confidante, to the mental health and well-being of older people is noted earlier (Holt-Lunstad et al, 2010; Schwarzbach et al, 2014). What is not particularly visible is the role played *by* women. It is well documented that women's relationships with each other are a source of both instrumental and therapeutic support across the life course *and* in later life. This extends into the fourth age and is amplified at a stage of life when social networks shrink (Hutchinson et al, 2008). Forssen (2007) considers that we need to capture, and take account of, the 'special health promoting knowledge' older women hold as lifelong caregivers, mothers, friends and partners (p 228). These points dovetail with the points made earlier in relationship to older women and social capital.

Thirdly, in Chapters 7 and 9 it was noted that older women (especially) value relationally oriented dimensions of support and care practice. The fact that services are designed around what the neo-liberal market rewards and what male policy makers and commissioners prioritise, for example instrumental care, suggests that we neither listen to older women nor consider what they want to be important.

Promoting cognitive health

In Chapters 1 and 8 I discussed risk factors for dementia. For some of these risks the obverse acts as a protection.

The theory of cognitive reserve suggests that the brain's functional capacity can be bolstered and/or protected by a number of factors that support the development of a 'reserve' or repertoire of cognitive skills; these not only help to prevent the onset of dementia but also act as a buffer to help people cope with dementia-related symptoms (Meng and D'Arcy, 2012; Stern, 2012). There is growing evidence that strong social networks and social engagement contribute to promoting cognitive reserve in both healthy older people *and* those living with dementia (Fratiglioni et al, 2004; Bennett et al, 2006). It is the quality of the social networks, rather than the quantity, that seems to be important, that is, networks made up of members of the inner and middle circles of Kahn and Antonucci's (1980) social convoy model (Clarke et al, 2012). 'Social connectedness' has also been identified as promoting cognitive recovery following a stroke (Glymour et al, 2008). Education may have an independent protective effect (Brayne et al, 2010). Exercising regularly, not smoking and keeping one's weight down and addressing a number of health problems at an early stage including hearing loss, hypertension, diabetes and depression are specifically identified as protective of cognitive health (Public Health England, 2016). Adopting a so-called 'Mediterranean diet' also appears to act preventively (Plassman et al, 2010; Sofi et al, 2010). Older adults who participate in mental exercise can promote 'cognitive vitality', that is, the brain's ability to adapt and learn. This includes brain games such as sudoku and taking up new interests. It is thought that the 'reserve hypothesis' holds considerable potential for dementia prevention and for public health strategies to reduce risk (Fratiglioni and Qiu, 2013). A number of the protective factors noted here are present in the lives, and life courses, of older people living in the Blue Zones whose cognitive health is very good.

Cellular level factors may also protect against dementia, even when brain changes are further advanced. For example, social support and activities increase levels of brain-derived neurotrophic factor (BDNF), which reduces the risks of developing dementia or having a stroke (Hsiao et al, 2014). Vascular endothelial growth factor (VEGF) also promotes brain development and is associated with healthier brain ageing, especially for individuals with the amyloid or tau changes noted in some people with dementia (Zachary, 2005).

Although there is some evidence of short-term benefits relating to 'cognitive training' (Clare et al, 2003; Plassman et al, 2010) the strongest evidence to date relates to the ten-year ACTIVE study which tested the effectiveness of three cognitive interventions in maintaining cognitive health and functional independence; it found sustained improvement in cognitive function among a sample of healthy older participants (McAvinue et al, 2013). The study randomly assigned participants to one of four groups: ten-session group training for memory (verbal episodic memory), or reasoning (ability to solve problems that follow a serial pattern), or speed of processing (visual search and identification); or a no-contact control. At two years follow-up the study demonstrated that cognitive interventions had sustained impact; participants continued to perform better on multiple measures for the relevant cognitive skill. It did not, however, demonstrate the generalisation of such interventions to everyday performance (Ball et al, 2002).

The mental health of people living with dementia: promotion and prevention

There is a mixed literature in this complex arena. Hard evidence about the issues that promote mental health among people living with dementia is limited. This is partly a consequence of the conflation of material on mental health, well-being and quality of life of people living with dementia – an observation made in Chapter 8 – and partly because there is limited investment in supporting, and capturing, the promotion of mental health in a population where care and funding issues dominate the policy and political agenda.

In order to offer a coherent platform upon which to 'hang' this discussion – and extend understanding about the role of the new dementia paradigm, particularly social citizenship (discussed in Chapter 9) – I will focus on four key areas. All hold promotional potential in relationship to the mental health and well-being of people living with dementia. For detailed discussion on social citizenship in action I commend Part II of Bartlett and O'Connor's (2010) book *Broadening the Dementia Debate*.

Tone and language of the new paradigm

Firstly, a word about how the new paradigm might shift the nature of dementia discourse. It is noteworthy that the tone is positive, importing into traditionally nihilistic narratives the possibility of change. It engages with the development of new thinking, understanding and models as well as new structures, interventions and practices. Despite some differences around level of analytical focus, the newer models share a commitment to engagement with improving mental health and well-being. Core dimensions of this frame of reference include: using different language; challenging assumptions, values and beliefs; engaging with issues of social justice and rights alongside issues of care; confronting 'othering' processes and language; and a commitment to critical reflection in practice (Bartlett and O'Connor, 2010). Active engagement with the person living with dementia is a core feature of the new paradigm too, challenging the passive recipient role that characterises the position of most people with dementia, especially those in the later stages and those who live in a care home.

Relationships, identity and continuity

As identified in Chapters 8 and 9, relationships are pivotal to the well-being of a person living with dementia. For people in the later stages of the condition relationships take on particular significance as sources of emotional attachment, comfort and security and as a touchstone for normality, habits and routines (La Fontaine and Oyebode, 2014). The role of key relationships in extending citizenship status is an additional dimension of the argument: facilitating engagement with issues of agency and rights and enhancing the person with dementia's capacity to be involved in decisions (Kontos et al, 2017). For these reasons, relationships with families and friends, and with paid carers, need to be nurtured and supported and their importance foregrounded in practice.

There is growing evidence that it is possible to protect and/or promote identity in people living with dementia, including in the later stages. As identity sits on 'the crossroads of "the personal" and "the social" interactions with, and in the context of, others play a pivotal role' (Tanner, 2013, p 158). Evidence specifically emphasises how family carers can bolster their relative's identity and preserve a sense of continuity (Braun et al, 2009; Westius et al, 2010; Knowles et al, 2016; Tolhurst et al, 2017). For example, 'when you were a headmaster you enjoyed chairing meetings' or 'you loved playing games with the grandchildren at Christmas'. Ways to support care home residents to retain aspects of their identity include preserving links with relatives and friends and promoting continued engagement with interests and routines (Stenner et al, 2011; Ray, 2016a). Life course and biographical knowledge held by family carers may partly explain why they privilege agency over security and paid carers, who know less about the person, tend to do the opposite (Clarke and Heyman, 1998). These points dovetail with those made in the section on 'Dignity and agency' in Chapter 7.

Occupational identity is often viewed as unimportant to a person living with dementia; most care assessments fail to record a person's occupational preferences or interests (Cohen-Mansfield et al, 2000). As being meaningfully occupied is consistently identified as a key dimension of good quality of life this is a significant oversight. Opportunities to remain involved, including in everyday activities such as cooking, gardening or housework, is an important way to promote well-being and support identity both in domestic and care settings. By supporting the continuation of established roles, life course-related issues are reinforced, enhancing well-being, for example an older woman being helped to 'cook dinner for her family at 6pm' as she has done for 30 years of her life (Bailey et al, 2013).

Remaining in one's own home for as long as possible promotes identity in people living with dementia (Milligan and Thomas, 2016). The presence of familiar people, objects, belongings and pets represents what Auge (1995) calls the 'anthropological space'. This space not only promotes a sense of security but also offers familiar visual cues reminding the person of their past life, roles and relationships with others (Milligan, 2009). As a visual manifestation of a person's identity, the home places limits on the extent to which an individual can be objectified and de-personalised, something that is a risk in a new setting, especially an institutional one. Moving a person out of their home and community environment poses a threat to their identity and well-being (Milligan and Liu, 2015; Tanner et al, 2015; Milligan and Thomas, 2016).

Paying attention to communication

People living with advanced dementia have traditionally experienced exclusion from relationships, in good part as a consequence of the loss of 'normal' verbal communication skills (Killick and Allan, 2001). This assumption highlights the deeply ingrained primacy we attach to words, language and speech and how connected they are to issues of engagement, emotion and inclusion and to the achievement of practice-related goals, for example facilitating choice. It also underscores the links between language and cognition and between cognition and (lack of) citizenship status.

Intrinsic to supporting the well-being of a person living with dementia is engagement with their particular forms of communication. It encourages a more nuanced relational approach to care (Hellström et al, 2007). Although greater attention has been paid to developing ways to facilitate communication, such as Talking Mats, sensory approaches and arts-based methods, investment in embedding these in care practice has been much more limited. Providing opportunities for people with dementia to engage in creative self-expression, through means such as music, drama and storytelling, can help to improve communication, social relationships, emotional well-being and self-esteem (Lee and Adams, 2011).

Facilitating meaningful communication between care home residents and staff is evidenced as not only promoting well-being but as reducing levels of agitation and aggression; just one hour a week can make this difference (NIHCE, 2013; Ballard et al, 2018). It is especially effective when care home staff are supported to engage with residents' biographies, lives and views and in contexts where the care home culture rewards the development of relationships as an intrinsic dimension of good-quality care (Mikelyte and Milne, 2016).

The mental health benefits of involvement

A fourth issue relates to the association between the process of involvement – for example in campaigns – and mental health benefits (Bartlett, 2014a; 2014b). Among people with dementia, involvement has been evidenced as helping to reduce isolation, improve feelings of self-worth, self-esteem and confidence, and bolster a sense of engagement, purpose and having a role (Crepaz-Keay, 2016). It also helps to create a sense of solidarity and empowerment and is associated with leaving a legacy for the future (Williamson, 2012b). For many it (re)engages with the skills and knowledge people bring from their years of paid employment and it also draws on their experiences of living with dementia. Some participants in Dementia Engagement and Empowerment Project (DEEP) activities (see Chapter 9) also report a subjective sense that involvement slowed down the actual progress of dementia itself: an experiential example of use it or lose it! Others noted that involvement was 'a form of self-management' of their symptoms (Williamson, 2012b).

There is related evidence that the mental health and well-being of people living with dementia is enhanced by involvement in research (Ross et al, 2005). In Tanner and Littlechild's (2016) study, where people with dementia worked as co-researchers, they reported that the role had encouraged them to engage socially and had improved their confidence levels and feelings of personal and social value. For some it also offered an opportunity to become involved in further research, teaching of social work and medical students and/or speaking at national conferences (Tanner, 2012).

As might be expected, there is a synergy between those issues identified as promoting of mental health among people *without* dementia, particularly frail older people, and the material reviewed here, as well as an intersection with those issues highlighted as important to the mental health and well-being of people living with dementia discussed in Chapters 8 and 9.

Policy issues

In this section I will re-engage with the life course purview and discuss the role of policy in reducing health inequalities and addressing social determinants in order to prevent mental ill health and promote mental health. It builds on arguments made throughout the book and reminds us that the roots of mental health problems – and therefore their prevention – lie in the life course. A number of policies that support the promotion of mental health in later life itself have been identified in this chapter; key themes in mental health-related policy will also be discussed.

In 2008 the Commission on the Social Determinants of Health report distinguished between two contrasting approaches to addressing health inequalities: action through the individual versus action on social determinants. The report stated that while it is important to recognise the significant gains individuals can make by changes to their lifestyle and timely access to medical treatments, '… unless action also takes account of the structural drivers … it will not tackle health inequalities' (p 30). Forde and Raine (2008) argue for an emphasis on both and make the point that individuals need to be actively engaged in promoting and protecting their own health *alongside* policy interventions to address social determinants, particularly childhood adversity. Seeking help early on in the development of a mental health problem is also relevant. The 2014 WHO report on the *Social Determinants of Mental Health* (WHO, 2014) made a strong case for the need to reduce the steepness of the social gradient in mental health by, 'Taking action to improve the conditions of daily life from before birth, during early childhood, at school age, during family building and working ages, and at older ages provides opportunities both to improve population mental health and to reduce the risk of those mental disorders that are associated with social inequalities' (p 8). An approach that targets the individual, 'at risk' groups *and* the social determinants of health across the life course may be the most effective.

Some commentators would argue that addressing health inequalities has a very good claim to be the central objective of any policy programme intending to prevent physical *and* mental ill health across the life course (Kuh et al, 2014; Marmot, 2015). Others have suggested that it represents the core of 'an agenda for action on healthy ageing' (Howse, 2005, p 3). Certainly, the existence of health inequalities in the chances of living a long and healthy life provides governments everywhere with a measure of the potential health gains to be made by addressing its key cause, the social determinants of health. It might even be argued that this is how the largest gains in population health, including among older people, can most readily be made (Navarro and Shi, 2001). It is instructive to remind ourselves that one of the primary drivers for the development of comprehensive welfare systems in Europe was the need to break the links between poor health and poverty (DH, 2009a). The positive effect of access to universal health care systems and welfare benefits for families with children and those who are ill or disabled have been remarkable. This positive trend is, however, being eroded in many European countries, including the UK, with the concomitant negative impact on health and health inequalities (Marmot, 2015). This is a policy lesson which we ignore at our peril.

Health inequalities are persistent and stubborn to shift; they will not reduce unless they are actively addressed (Marmot, 2015; Public Health England, 2015). While public agencies no longer have specific targets in relationship to reducing health inequalities, under the Health and Social Care Act 2012, the Secretary of State for Health, NHS England and Clinical Commissioning Groups must 'in the exercise of their functions have regard to the need to reduce inequalities' (NHS England, 2014a, p 5). This is conceptualised as primarily in relationship to access to care and outcomes of care rather than broader issues such as social determinants. Regarding the role of local authorities', one of their general duties in terms of public health is to 'reduce health inequalities across the lifecourse, including within hard to reach groups' in their area. A primary reason for the government returning responsibility for public health to local government (in 2013) is their 'ability to influence wider social determinants of health' and take 'strategic action to prevent inequalities across a number of functions, such as housing, environmental issues … education, children and young people's services' (DH, 2011a, p 2). It is noteworthy that (some) policy commitments to reducing health inequalities have been retained and are enshrined in law albeit in a relatively diffuse form; for example the *Prevention Concordat for Better Mental Health* (Public Health England, 2019 – see later in the chapter). There is a certain logic for public health policy to incorporate the health inequalities agenda and for local authorities to have lead responsibility for addressing them and their social determinants. Time will tell how effective both policy and agency will be but concerns regarding cuts to local authority budgets, increasing levels of poverty and the influence of the neo-liberal narrative make it difficult to see how Marmot's (2015) demand for an 'active focus' can be realised in any sustainable way. The case for public health to grasp the 'mental health baton' is discussed in the conclusion.

In terms of the nature and range of policy focused on promoting mental health in later life, it is useful to highlight three examples of relevant, but different, policies. One example is international, one European and one English. A broader review of policy that intersects with mental health in later life is already offered in Chapter 1.

The WHO *Mental Health Action Plan for 2013–2020* (WHO, 2013) is a global policy that requires all member states to sign up to a number of specific actions, including improving strategies for promotion of mental health and prevention of mental ill health. WHO (2013) places particular emphasis on human rights, civil society and the key role that communities and support services can play in helping people at risk of developing, or with existing, mental health problems. While the policy is not particular to older people it does include the older population in its purview, reminding us, importantly, of rights issues as they relate to later life.

Many countries across the European Union signed up to a policy commitment to promote 'mental health for all'. In 2008 the *European Pact for Mental Health and Wellbeing* was launched (European Commission, 2008). It included a specific commitment to older people and was organised around six themes: mental health promotion; mental disorder prevention; older people in vulnerable situations (for example at risk of abuse); health care and support services; family carers; and research. The policy was supported by a range of resources including sharing examples of good practice in policy development and services (European Commission, 2009). An example of how the *European Pact* has impacted on mental health policy in the UK is its support and engagement with the *No Health without Mental Health* initiative (discussed in other chapters, HM Government, 2011).

The Mental Health Taskforce (NHS England, 2016) that was set up to drive forward the development of NHS England's mental health work, was committed to embedding a prevention agenda in the *Five Year Forward View for Mental Health* (NHS England, 2016: noted in Chapter 1). The Taskforce devised a national *Prevention Concordat for Better Mental Health* (Public Health England, 2019) to ensure that the planning infrastructure of the NHS, for example Health and Well-Being Boards and Sustainability and Transformation Plans, take full account of ways to prevent mental ill health and promote mental health. *The Concordat* promotes an evidence-based focus on reducing health inequalities including action that impacts on the wider determinants of mental health and well-being (Public Health England, 2019). It is intended to facilitate a cross-sector focus on adopting public mental health approaches (see conclusion). These policy aims link with those noted earlier.

Conclusion

Mental health and well-being in later life are promoted and protected by a range of factors. While we know what a number of these factors are, we know far less about how they are mediated and experienced by individual older people. That the majority of the factors are a product of the life course is a second, significant, issue; that they are embedded in a life course *and* a life narrative is a third. Evidence about how older people manage the 'ageing experience' and protect their mental health and well-being despite the challenges they face is a small but growing element of both the research arena and wider discourse. Research capturing the voices and perspectives of older people brings these four dimensions together in a way that makes them visible and coherent; it also reinforces the importance of taking account of the lived experience and the life course, including the third and fourth ages, in understanding mental health in later life and its intersection with age-related challenges.

Three other points are important to make. There is, as might be expected, a positive interaction between the factors that protect mental health. They interrelate in ways that strengthen their power. Older people who have a decent income tend to live in a more affluent area with a larger number of community resources, more green spaces and opportunities for social participation (Bowling and Stafford, 2007). This amplifies the point made earlier about the tautological nature of some of the discourse on positive mental health. It also underscores a third point, that mental health is a dynamic, rather than static, construct made up of a number of intersecting dimensions located in a number of different spheres.

Lastly, it is important to note that the majority of older people do not develop a mental health problem such as depression, despite being exposed to, often a number of, adverse events (Netuveli et al, 2008). They will not all have positive mental health – these conceptual distinctions have been discussed in earlier chapters – but we do need to appreciate the ways that older people protect their mental health, adapt to change and successfully manage sometimes profound age-related challenges and transitions. We need to listen and learn from their stories of survival, strength, resilience and reflexivity.

Despite some policy emphasis on the social determinants of mental ill health funding reductions to local authority services, especially in England, and a significant shift in the locus of public care towards those in greatest need has inevitably narrowed the focus, and breadth, of the preventive lens. This has not only resulted in the loss of investment in upstream and/or primary preventive interventions to address the determinants of mental ill health such as poverty, but more worryingly, the loss of policy acknowledgement that a link between inequalities and poor mental health outcomes even exists (Marmot, 2005). Means (2007) notes that, 'despite the rhetoric concerning prevention .... the dominant concern of government policies is with long term healthcare conditions and the role of health services' (p 53).

Ill health, including mental ill health, is now almost wholly conceptualised as the result of poor 'lifestyle choices' not a life course issue with roots in disadvantage or inequality. Policy makers have increasingly transferred responsibility for health onto the individual and away from life course and age-related structural and social determinants (Karban, 2017; Marmot, 2018). The tentacles of this policy narrative extend into mental health prevention and promotion activities and services and influence the tone, nature and focus of investment. At a time of reduced funding for the NHS and local authorities, and a financial squeeze on 'non-essential services' such as public health, this is a trend which has serious consequences for older people's mental health (WHO, 2014). These points echo arguments made in earlier chapters.

Exploring ways forward is the focus of the Conclusion.

Conclusion

This book has adopted a lens on mental health in later life that marks it out as distinctive. It conceptualises mental health as an outcome of a life course, including later life itself, and foregrounds the role played by social and structural inequalities in shaping mental health and well-being (Wistow et al, 2015). It has required the synthesis of material from a large number of theoretical, conceptual, practice-related, research and policy sources. While there are many texts that focus on mental illness, there are far fewer that focus on mental health and fewer still that attempt to weave together evidence from critical gerontology, life course analysis, research on inequalities, and work on exploring the issues that undermine, and/or promote, mental health and well-being. The intersection of these axes is where my book is situated and discourse located.

The term later life has been deliberately used in place of old age or its sister terms throughout the book (most of the time). One of the most damaging consequences of constructing 'old age' as a separate life stage(s) is its disconnection from the rest of life. Age-related risks become the dominant paradigmatic lens through which mental health is viewed, and connections with what has gone before and the wider determinants of ill health become lost, or at best, marginalised. This lens engages with a chain of responses that turn away from social structures and socially determined risks and face towards individualised treatment and support. That services or commissioners tend not to take account of an older person's biography in developing responses to 'need' and practitioners rarely engage with life course issues is testament to this pattern. It is more comfortable too. Most people struggle to think about the depressogenic effects of long-term poverty on older women's mental health whereas being depressed as a response to being widowed is both understandable and treatable. It is sad but (perhaps) inevitable and not in any way linked to the woman's life course or socio-political issues relating to gender inequality, domestic abuse or inadequate welfare benefits.

The value of a life course approach is its capacity to inform and make links between life stages, experiences, inequalities and biography and to illuminate patterns. One of the key challenges – in a book focused on later life – is the need to accommodate the *whole* life course. While a number of childhood and midlife events, for example abuse, have been discussed these have been limited to the most relevant and evidence-based. Most attention has been paid to establishing links between exposure to social and structural inequalities, both earlier in life *and* in later life itself, and mental health in later life. It is noteworthy that existing work on inequalities and older people is limited, particularly in relationship to the life course. Many of the causative connections have been made by bringing hitherto unconnected pieces of evidence together and joining up arguments that exist in separate, but often parallel, spheres. Ensuring a focus on age-related risks in their own right has also been important, reflecting Grenier's (2012) observation that '... there is an ongoing tension between (conceptualising) late life as a part of an entire lifecourse, and age as a separate period characterised by distinct biological, psychological, social and cultural issues' (p 20). Incorporating the lived experiences and narratives of older people is key to the book's credibility; it also strengthens claims about connectivity and enlivens what can at times seem a rather dry debate.

It has been challenging to achieve a balance between identifying risks to mental health alongside celebrating the capacity of (many) older people to maintain good mental health and manage later life's challenges. We need to know more about how this is achieved and what the ingredients of an infrastructure that support these processes are. To regard it simply as a matter of individual 'resilience' is not only failing to acknowledge the complexity of managing the 'ageing experience' but denies the role played by wider issues and by the context in which the older person is situated (see research section later in the chapter).

Ways forward are now discussed, located in five cross-cutting domains: public mental health; policy and services for people living with dementia and their families; care services and care practice; research lenses, approaches and methods; and values and principles.

Public mental health

If, as I have argued, many of the factors that place an older person at risk of impaired mental health are life course and age-related inequalities, it is axiomatic that policy should aim to address these (Marmot, 2014). While initiatives to tackle pensioner poverty are useful, given its likely life course roots, tackling the structural issues that created it in the first place may seem an obvious way to reduce both its upstream causes and its downstream consequences. However, as has been pointed out in Chapter 3, because these links are probabilistic rather than definitive there is room for alternative, often politically expedient, explanations. As I state in Chapter 3, 'If the relationship is not a definitive one then the role of policy to address life course inequalities may be questioned allowing the locus of policy rubric to be realigned, from life course to lifestyle and from structure to individual choice.'

Even when action on the social determinants of health, and on reducing health inequalities, is 'accepted in theory, in practice policy makers often direct their attention to strategies to change individual behaviour' (Lloyd, 2012, p 79; Allen et al, 2018). This is the case even for mental health promotion activities which tend to take the form of a state endorsed call to 'help yourself' and 'take up new interests'. This conceptual lens has been amplified by the neo-liberal agenda which, in addition to reinforcing an individualised model, constructs late life health problems as unconnected to either the life course or to inequalities. Neo-liberal policies exacerbate both individual *and* area-based health inequalities (Oliver, 2018).

The link between inequalities and mental health is, however, accepted by some policy makers, notably in the public mental health field (Babones, 2009; see Box 11.1). The Royal College of Psychiatrists' (2010) report *No Health without Public Mental Health* draws together evidence about what can be done to prevent mental health problems and reduce the population burden of mental illness. It makes a strong case for upstream interventions to reduce risk (primary prevention) while simultaneously arguing that at all stages of the life course, and all stages of a mental health problem, there is preventive potential (secondary and tertiary). A subsequent report – *Better Mental Health for All: A Public Mental Health Approach to Mental Health Improvement* – written by the Faculty of Public Health and the Mental Health Foundation (2016) reinforces the preventive role of public mental health. It highlights the importance of adopting a life course approach and the important complementary role mental health promotion can play.

Box 11.1: Definition of public mental health

Public mental health is the art and science of improving mental health and wellbeing and preventing mental illness through the organised efforts of society, organisations, the public, communities and individuals. It is a term that has been coined to underline the need to emphasise the neglected element of mental health in public health policy and practice. It spans promotion, prevention, effective treatment, care and recovery.

Source: Adapted from Acheson, 1988 and Faculty of Public Health and Mental Health Foundation, 2016

Both reports endorse Marmot and colleagues' (2010) proportionate universalism approach in relationship to older people. *Better Mental Health for All* (Faculty of Public Health and the Mental Health Foundation, 2016) proposes a number of universal actions, for example a country-wide campaign to reduce pensioner poverty, community level initiatives, for example to enhance social participation, and more targeted interventions, for example support for older carers. As is characteristic of many public health interventions these reflect a combination of preventive and promotional goals. They also reflect cross agency commitment to planning, commissioning and delivering services, a feature widely regarded as essential to effectiveness and sustainability. It is increasingly recognised that public health, including public mental health, is the responsibility of a range of different agencies of which the National Health Service is one. Other relevant policy mechanisms include the *Public Health Outcomes Framework*, which explicitly refers to reducing inequalities in health (DH, 2015a).

There is a synergy between the aims and principles of public mental health policy and the dimensions of an agenda to promote mental health in later life and prevent mental ill health. It is also a 'good fit' for the conceptual lens I have advocated in this book. As a framework it is also helpful in terms of informing the infrastructure that is needed to deliver public mental health goals for older people, including people living with dementia.

Policy and services for people living with dementia and their families

A number of commentators, particularly Manthorpe and Iliffe (2016b), make a powerful plea for a radical refocusing of policy, services and practice in the dementia field. Their arguments dovetail with a number of those made in relationship to the mental health sphere more broadly and mirror those relating to engaging with a paradigmatic shift in our understanding of dementia as a condition.

In terms of social policy Manthorpe and Iliffe (2016b) suggest that currently, emphasis is placed on 'containment and cure', reflecting outcomes of the biomedical approach whereas what is needed is 'assimilation and accommodation', consistent with adoption of a social disability model of dementia. The medical model has wide appeal and the search for a 'cure' for a chronic and frightening condition is very seductive. Being seen to support the development of treatments, diagnosis and medical services, such as memory clinics, also suggests a vigorous and measurable response on the part of government to an increasingly demanding public and care-related challenge. It is perhaps also the case, Manthorpe and Iliffe (2016b) suggest, that the medical colonisation of dementia is partly about health professionals claiming ownership of a condition that is growing in size and political importance.

There is, however, limited evidence of the effectiveness of drug treatments or of memory clinics, despite the huge sums invested, and an emphasis on diagnosis may be misguided. As symptoms and individuals vary significantly, diagnosis may be inaccurate and if there are few services to support the person and their family post-diagnosis, it is difficult to defend its primacy as a core aim of policy (National Collaborating Centre for Mental Health, 2018). There are also concerns about the 'tentacles of the biomedical' reaching into the corners of ordinary life in ways that raise concerns about the encroachment of medical knowledge and power (Milne, 2010b). Being diagnosed may also be disempowering and stigmatising; the older person may feel they no longer have agency over their life or choices but are defined by their dementia. While there may be some psychosocial and therapeutic benefits to diagnosis, as a medical intervention both its effectiveness and cost-effectiveness are questionable.

Two tectonic shifts are required if we are to develop a care and support infrastructure that can respond effectively to people living with dementia and their families. One relates to policy and the other to services. Inevitably, they intersect.

Growing appreciation of alternative causal pathways for dementia has significant implications for policy (see Chapter 8). If one accepts that dementia is a tractable consequence of accumulated damage across the life course, policy needs to take a very different form from current policy, which is predicated on a pathological model of neuro-generative decline confined (largely) to later life (Mental Health Foundation, 2013). The fact that the Lancet Commission on dementia prevention, intervention and care identified that over a third of all dementia cases could be prevented if nine *modifiable* risk factors were fully eliminated, supports this argument (Livingstone et al, 2017; Pickett et al, 2018).

Manthorpe and Iliffe (2016a) make the case for a public health approach to dementia policy that would focus on: upstream determinants such as increasing access to education and reducing poverty; treating midlife health risks such as high blood pressure and risks of heart disease; and developing social and psychological interventions for people living with dementia and their families such as psycho-educational support groups for carers (Alzheimer's Disease International, 2014; International Longevity Centre, 2014; Milne et al, 2014). A public health approach to dementia would also have read across to broader public health goals such as addressing social isolation and developing community resources to enhance social participation.

In terms of services there is a profound need for less medicine and more social care. In Manthorpe and Iliffe's (2016a; 2016b) view, for people living with dementia and their families, there can be little doubt that social care services play a much greater role, and offer many more benefits, than medical interventions. This is particularly the case in the later stages of the condition. Investment in services is facing in the wrong direction. In the early and mid-2000s funding for memory clinics was being significantly increased; at the same time funding for social care services was being radically reduced. As noted in earlier chapters one of the groups most affected by the cuts are people with complex long-term needs, including dementia; the people on the lowest incomes have been the hardest hit (Forder and Fernández, 2010). The burden of care has been transferred onto families with a range of negative health, psychosocial and financial consequences for them (Manthorpe and Iliffe, 2016a; see Chapter 9). As services to carers have also been cut this represents a 'double whammy'.

There are also a number of issues relating to practice. As will be clear from earlier chapters a number of core skills are pivotal to the delivery of meaningful care. Relationships are key as is engagement, communication skills and the delivery of nuanced crafted care that fits around the person's routines and rhythms and is sensitive to the protection of their identity and selfhood (Tanner, 2013). Given the importance of services such as home care, day care and respite care to people living with dementia and services such as support groups to carers, there is an urgent need to invest in training, pay and conditions of work, and staff retention. If services are to take account of what matters to people living with dementia and their carers far more emphasis needs to be placed on the relational and skilled nature of social care and its embedded, often long-term, role in their lives.

In terms of interventions, Manthorpe and Iliffe argue for investment (2016a) in life course prevention rather than the 'elusive cure' and for much greater emphasis on the role and importance of 'ordinary' social care services whose reach is much greater than (often short-term) medical interventions. They suggest that a revised dementia strategy should include the following dimensions:

- prioritise care and support *and* prevention;
- reward and resource care and support for people living with dementia properly and in a way that recognises its complexity and skilled nature;
- recognise the role and importance of social care services in the promotion of well-being and enhancement of mental health and quality of life of both people living with dementia and their carers;
- rebalance the debate about dementia; challenge the public narrative about it as a catastrophic threat, encourage engagement with a more critical view of scientific knowledge, and engage with a life course perspective;
- frame dementia as a disability and prioritise ways forward that place emphasis on changes relating to the social model rather than the medical model;
- invest in support for family carers that recognises and respects their role but at the same time accepts that care is a shared responsibility with public services, particularly social care;

- refocus research investment to face towards what matters to people living with dementia and their family carers and to the role of social care services and staff.

Care services and care practice

A number of these themes are relevant to other groups of older people who use care and support services. As noted in Chapter 7, 'feeling' frail is very different from 'being' frail. Its biomedical construction ignores the way it is shaped by social and economic issues, community support and life course events, such as having been a carer for a frail parent in midlife (Grenier, 2007). Emotional needs tend to lie outside the optic of the care system. The 'management of functional deficit' and 'reduction of risk' tends to be disconnected from the person: from emotions, sense of self, identity, biography and relationships.

Grenier suggests that 'linking the social, cultural, psychological and personal processes that occur in relation to continuity and change' (2012, p 202), such as becoming frail, holds significant therapeutic potential. Interventions that are sensitive to the person's emotional journey not only reduce anxiety but normalise the psychological processes that (often) accompany adjustment to frailty. They also bolster older people's efforts to protect their own well-being and impact positively on mental health (Baars et al, 2014; Lloyd et al, 2014b). When services are offered 'within the context of a lifecourse and tailored to individual needs' it is possible to utilise a person-centred and inclusive approach that honours preferences, upholds dignity and fosters quality of life (Hodson and Keady, 2008, p 372). They may also support the goals of prevention, for example delay entry to a care home. Lloyd (2015) argues that there is a strong case to be made for building a bridge between the medical-functional approach taken by services and the emotional, meaning-making and identity maintenance approach taken by older people. These points echo those made in Chapter 7 in relationship to the ageing experience.

Manthorpe and Iliffe (2016a) discuss the particular challenges relating to assessment of need, a task most often undertaken by social workers (or care managers) working for local authorities. They emphasise the importance of: not undermining the person's agentic capacity; recognising the strengths and life skills the older person (still) has; acknowledging the power imbalance inherent in the encounter; promoting the person's engagement with decision-making and choice; and sensitively appreciating the influence of socio-structural issues such as poverty and societal stigma on their mental health and well-being (Boudiny, 2013). It can also be helpful to acknowledge that there is a tension between policy goals, such as those relating to personalisation, and the economic constraints that underpin assessment processes and service allocation.

I recognise that I am suggesting the development of an approach that is very different to the current model and that the shift required is considerable. If, however, claims of empowerment, co-production and engagement with service users' perspectives are to have any credibility at all then those issues that act to protect older people's well-being need to be embedded into the culture of care services. If we do not do this not only will services continue to develop in ways that are oppositional, and at times harmful, to older people's mental health, but what matters to older people will continue to be (partially) captured by research but rarely operationalised in services or practice (Kontos and Naglie, 2007; Oliver et al, 2014).

This argument extends beyond the individual into the community and links with the public health agenda discussed earlier. Whether in the community, in groups, or with individuals the goal of mental health policy, and of services, is to protect individual, social, socio-economic and environmental attributes that promote mental health and well-being, enhance resilience (see Figures 2.3 and 10.3) and support older citizens and older service users to manage late life adversity.

Research lenses

There are a number of ways in which research needs to improve if it is to engage effectively with mental health in later life.

(Re)conceptualising adversity and health problems

The first issue relates to the conceptualisation and assessment of life course adversity. While it is important to acknowledge the powerful influence of one or more individually experienced adverse events, such as childhood neglect on mental health, the impact of chronic disadvantage and psychosocial stress is equally, if not more, influential and much harder to capture. Its profound and opaque multi-dimensional influence is a challenge to evaluate and evidence, especially over the longer term.

Research on childhood adversity is taking two interesting directions. The first is that it combines individual experiences and experiences linked to exposure to social and structural inequality under the term 'adversity' (Hughes et al, 2017). By doing this, researchers are not only reflecting the experiences of children, that is, that adversity is more than a series of single atomised experiences, but they are also conceptualising adversity as taking a number of interleaving forms (Marmot, 2015). Their work additionally highlights the fact that adversity rarely travels alone. A second important issue is that their work increasingly identifies the long and permanently damaging reach of adversity in childhood across the whole life course. Researchers involved in this work make a strong case for preventive early interventions in the lives of disadvantaged children to alleviate exposure to harm in the present *and* the future (Kuh et al, 2014).

This is a model that could inform critical gerontological research. Adversity may have a different profile in later life and have (some) different dimensions but to explore the impact of harms, whatever their 'type', in a joined-up way could teach us much about what adversity 'looks like' through the late life lens. The current fragmented model, for example exploring the effects of elder abuse and of poverty separately, does not reflect the lived experiences of older people and nor does it capture the ways in which the different types of adversity combine to undermine mental health and well-being. 'Late life adversity' may be a useful concept to develop and employ in research and policy analysis.

Recognition that it is the interaction of a number of factors through time that influence health outcomes is also a growing focus of epidemiological research, including in the ageing field (Victor, 2010). Many epidemiologists consider medical care to be of limited value partly because once someone is ill the capacity to act preventively is limited. As Daniels and colleagues (2000) state, 'By the time a 60-year-old heart attack victim arrives at the emergency room, bodily insults have accumulated over a lifetime. For such a person, medical care, is figuratively speaking the 'ambulance waiting at the bottom of the cliff'' (quoted by Lloyd, 2012, p 77). Current health care models, including health-related research, are also predicated on the management of one 'risk factor' or 'one condition with one cause'. A disease-centred approach is ill-suited to addressing the many physiological, environmental, social and contextual dimensions of causes of mental ill health. It is especially ill-suited to taking account of their intersection and of life course influences. Cattan and colleagues (2005) in Lloyd (2012) makes a similar point in relationship to interventions to 'treat' the 'problem' of isolation and loneliness. They observe that a unidimensional approach appears ineffective perhaps because the causes of isolation and loneliness are rarely unidimensional!

Older people's perspectives

Older people's perspectives are an increasingly prominent part of research. This reflects, and is reflected by, a greater commitment to doing research that is meaningful for older people and their families. The engagement with older people as research participants is fundamental. While they may have been research 'subjects' for many years, their status has shifted towards that of 'active participant'. Older people, including (some) people living with dementia, are increasingly being treated as reliable witnesses to their own lives and health. How older people deal with age-related changes and challenges that accompany later life is one such example (for example Tanner, 2010). More nuanced appreciation of age-related constructs, such as frailty and dementia, is another. Their multi-dimensional and life course-related dimensions, and socio-political location, are made more visible by exploring their meaning and embedded nature with older people. The deficit accumulation model, which grew out of research with frail older people, suggests that frailty 'represents the accumulation of physical, psychological and social impairments, which places individuals at risk of adverse outcomes' (Tomkow, 2018, p 3). This is a direct challenge to its dominant definition as an age-related syndrome and adds to the arguments, made earlier, about frailty being linked to the life course and to issues beyond the corporeal. There are also obvious connections with the point made earlier in the book – and reinforced earlier in this chapter – in relationship to accumulated damage and dementia. In the health and care arena engagement is also about developing responses to need that is informed by research *with* older people, and where appropriate, their families.

There is also greater assimilation of older people's perspectives in research-related models and measures. Godfrey and Denby's (2004) socio-cultural model of successful ageing is one such example (see Chapters 2 and 10). The recently developed *Index of Wellbeing in Later Life* is another (Institute of Social and Economic Research, 2017). Age UK, using data from the *Understanding Society* longitudinal survey, has developed the *Index of Wellbeing* drawing heavily on consultations with older people. It has five domains: personal, social, health, resources and local, and incorporates 40 indicators. The *Index* reflects the important role played by 'social issues' including family and personal relationships and social participation as well as local services, income, wealth and home ownership, physical activities and health conditions. Health incorporates a measure of mental health. It highlights the need to view older people's well-being 'in the round'; also that the different dimensions are interdependent. For example, the *Index* makes visible links between poverty and ability to participate and between the availability of local exercise classes and physical and mental health.

Another dimension of participation is the much higher level of involvement of patients and service users in research panels and funding decisions. This is driven by three issues: a commitment by research councils and funders to engage more effectively with the end users of research, an emphasis on evidence-based practice, and the rights-infused service user movement. This has been particularly visible in the dementia field. Increasingly, older people and people living with dementia are involved in research panels and as reviewers of research bids. Examples of funders include the Alzheimer's Society and the National Institute for Health Research. Patients, service users and the public are also involved in oversight of research studies. They are often members of project steering groups and/or act as advisors, for example reviewing information leaflets, consent issues or co-producing project materials for dissemination (for example Dewar, 2005).

Less commonly, users are involved as partners or co-researchers in projects and are funded as members of the research team. It is particularly unusual in research with people living with dementia. Tanner and Littlechild (2016) employed people living with dementia as co-researchers as part of a project exploring older people's experiences of transitions between care services. They were involved in all stages of the research process, including interviewing other older people living with dementia. Research of this type not only reflects commitment to user involvement but also to the principles of social action and empowerment; the people living with dementia are regarded as a source of expert knowledge which can be of direct benefit to the project and to the implications of any findings for policy and practice (Tanner, 2012).

Despite this positive shift there are a number of groups of older people who remain on the margins of meaningful engagement in research. These include care home residents with advanced dementia, older people from black and minority communities and LGBTQ+ older people (Train et al, 2005; Milne, 2011). There are also particular groups whose experiences need to be explored much more if we are to understand their perspectives and import them into the development of appropriate responses. Capturing the perspectives of older victims of domestic abuse is one such example (O'Brien et al, 2011). Older people's experiences of transitions and of frailty are also underexplored arenas (Tanner et al, 2015).

Approaches and methods

In this section I will focus on three ways in which I consider that research on mental health and later life can be strengthened drawing on the approaches that have informed analysis in this book and the research methods to which they are aligned.

The research community needs to get much better at establishing links between, and collecting robust evidence about, the operation of life course factors as determinants of mental health in later life. This research requires a mix of methods informed by a life course perspective and those that can explore the role played by social and health inequalities (Wistow et al, 2015). Not only do such methods need to offer the potential to examine development over time for the same cohort but allow for 'an accounting of the bi-directional influence of individuals and contexts'

(Phillips et al, 2010, p 142). They also need to be able to capture evidence from multiple sources and connect factors such as socio-economic status to health outcomes (Lloyd, 2012). While this is a considerable challenge, it is pivotal to address in order to be able to make the case for reducing the impact of life course issues that create, or amplify, risks to mental health in later life and for investing in those issues that support the development and promotion of good mental health.

Life course analysis methods include: longitudinal studies, cohort sequential studies and the comparative study of cohorts' subgroups; these are time and resource rich and are also complex. Some longitudinal survey data exists in the public domain such as ELSA and *Understanding Society*, and routinely collected data on health inequalities such as those related to the *Public Health Outcomes Framework* (DH, 2015a) may also be useful. Methodological lessons can also be learned from the work of the Marmot Review Team, particularly in relationship to capturing links between social determinants, health inequalities and health outcomes (Marmot et al, 2010; Institute of Social and Economic Research, 2017). It is interesting to note that a similar call is being made by an expert panel in the mental health field. The 2017 *Framework for Mental Health Research* makes a strong case for the adoption of a life course approach in mental health research in order to enhance understanding of the causes of mental health problems. It specifically highlights a need for the adoption of methods that can address 'questions around social and structural inequality' so that opportunities to act preventively, and intervene early to reduce risks, can be taken (WHO, 2003; 2014; Department of Health, 2017). When prevention is understood at a population level, and longitudinally, the range of factors associated with mental health is considerable and the causal chains complex. This framework intersects with the goals of public mental health, including a focus on the upstream determinants of mental health and connectivity between the individual, their life course and the broader social and environmental context (Manthorpe and Iliffe, 2016a). Framing these aims as linked to policy and research strengthens both.

A number of the key issues that promote mental health in later life, including among older people living with dementia, are related to social participation, social capital, social networks and relationships. As older people spend more time in their own homes and communities than other age groups and tend to rely to a greater degree on local resources, investing in research that can enhance the capacity of the community to meet their mental health needs is invaluable (Friedli, 2009). This includes research that explores the roles of new models to enhance well-being, for example asset-based community development, and models that prevent mental health problems developing among those at risk, for example peer mentoring to reduce social isolation (see Box 10.1). A recent study explored enhancing the social networks and social capital of people with long-term mental health problems (Webber et al, 2015). It drew upon the practice wisdom of a sample of local community workers – who were helping to create opportunities for social engagement – and the lived experiences of a group of service users; the findings were used to enrich understanding of the processes involved and to inform future developments of social capital.

Community-based work takes research beyond academic and health care settings into everyday spaces and captures the experiences and support needs of people on their 'home turf'. This includes engaging with settings such as community centres and places of worship; with voluntary and community-led agencies, for example Age UK, local community leaders, and service providers, for example the local authority; also with the wider citizenry to encourage their participation with, and ownership of, plans and initiatives. It is important to ensure that engagement is not just with the groups that are most visible but with those who are less visible too, for example people living with dementia, care home residents, black and minority ethnic elders. This point links to the issue of incorporating older people's voices and the principles of empowerment, inclusion and social citizenship.

Community-related research offers an opportunity to employ a range of mixed approaches too, including participatory research methods, community mapping techniques, action research, case studies and ethnography (Lucero et al, 2018). These are methods drawn from the public mental health field and to an increasing degree the mental health and psychology fields for example, work on developing community resilience (Windle and Bennett, 2011; Department of Health, 2017). Research exploring the role of community-based interventions in strengthening the building blocks of social engagement and participation can contribute a great deal to informing investment in this essential dimension of older people's mental health (Foot, 2012).

A third focus of research relates to older people's lived experiences. Although we know quite a lot about the issues that promote, protect and undermine older people's mental health, there has been limited work exploring what older people themselves consider to be both life course and age-related influences. Also, their views about what can be done to address the first and bolster the second. It may be useful to conceptualise two tiers of risks and protective factors that dovetail with those identified by older people reviewed in Chapter 10: issues that are fundamental to creating vulnerability to mental ill health – causal factors – and issues that prompt a slide into it – trigger factors. The tiers, or levels, conceptualised in the Framework of risk and protective factors in securing mental health and well-being in later life (see Chapter 10, Box 10.2) may also be helpful.

Research methods drawn from critical gerontology such as biographical and narrative approaches would be well suited to this research; these methods contextualise the ageing process and facilitate engagement with individuals' life histories and life course. They also align with human rights and empowerment principles (Ray et al, 2009). Such research would not only deepen understanding of the issues but would inform the work of public mental health agencies and health and social care service providers. An example is greater primacy being placed on the role of relationships in the commissioning and delivery of care, an issue of pivotal importance to older people's mental health (noted earlier). There may also be opportunities to co-produce innovative forms of support that respond to critical points in older people's lives when their mental health is particularly threatened, for example when being discharged from hospital or becoming frail (Tanner, 2010; 2016).

Service evaluation

There is a separate research challenge relating to the evaluation of secondary and/or tertiary services whose aim is to promote the mental health of specific groups of older people. A number of these have been discussed in earlier chapters. Some work has been done on effectiveness, including evaluating cost-effectiveness, for example Knapp and colleagues' 2013 study (discussed in Chapter 10) which evaluated time banks, befriending and community navigators. However, there is considerable room to strengthen this evidence base. Greater use of mixed methods is likely to be useful achieving a balance between quantitative evidence of impact on mental health and/or quality of life as assessed by a research instrument, alongside qualitative evidence about the role and value of the service from the perspectives of older people. Capturing a sense of what the service does beyond the 'issue' being targeted would also be interesting. For example, in addition to reducing isolation does the befriending service help the older person make better use of community resources and/or facilitate engagement with social media? There is a need for the methodological bricolage referred to in Chapter 3 (Holstein and Minkler, 2007). I acknowledge that there is a tension between this broader approach and the need to provide evidence of relatively narrowly defined 'impact' which both service commissioners and research funders tend to want. Surely, we can do both.

One of the main reasons for investing in more, and more robust, research is that policy direction and service development is strongly influenced by evidence. There is a profound need to design and implement high-quality research that engages with the big questions around reducing threats to mental health and promoting mental health across the life course; addressing issues that undermine mental health in later life itself; and linking 'what matters' more coherently with 'what works'. It is also needed to acquire a 'comprehensive understanding of contemporary ageing' and mental health in later life (Estes et al, 2003).

Dementia-related research: the role of social citizenship

Although there have been recent challenges to the so-called 'hierarchy of evidence' randomised controlled trials (RCTs) – and related models – tend to be regarded as the gold standard in health-related research. While qualitative methods and lived experiences are becoming increasingly important in research with older people, 'traditional positivistic standards continue to prevail' (Bartlett and O'Connor, 2010, p 97). Bartlett and O'Connor (2010) make the case for a broader more inclusive lens informed by the principles of social citizenship. Although their focus is people living with dementia their arguments have wider resonance.

There is a tendency in ageing-related research to focus on illness, care and services. The mental health field, particularly dementia, is no exception. We know far less about ordinary citizens with dementia than we do about long-term care or the challenges of caring for a relative with advanced dementia (National Audit Office, 2009). There is a need to refocus the dementia research agenda onto 'lives and experiences' and away from 'illness and services'. This would not only engage with a richer discourse about how people living with dementia manage their daily lives but would disrupt the existing victim-sufferer-tragedy narrative and reframe dementia as a condition that, until quite late on, is experienced in the community and (often) adjusted to effectively by the person and their family.

This approach would not only open up the possibility of exploring how people living with dementia cope with the condition but also how they manage the accompanying social challenges: discrimination, oppression, exclusion and stigma. Making these wider societal issues more visible highlights the importance of tackling them and obliges a higher level of engagement with questions of how universal services, for example libraries, GP surgeries, and communities can better accommodate the needs of people living with dementia. It also shifts the lens of analysis towards recognition of people living with dementia as located in a broader socio-political context challenging their biomedical status as patients. Further, it would help to foreground the agency of people living with dementia and confirm their legitimacy as witnesses to their lives and experiences. A number of these points dovetail with the arguments made by Manthorpe and Iliffe (2016a) earlier.

It is well established that participatory research with people with more advanced dementia is challenging. In recent years a number of different methods have been developed with the aim of authentically capturing their perspectives; these have mainly been used in care home research. Dementia Care Mapping (DCM) is the best-known example (Brooker, 2005; see Chapter 8). Walking interviews, photo-video diaries, and a range of visual and arts methods are also used to actively engage with participants; they are especially helpful for those with limited verbal skills as they do not rely on the spoken word (Gubrium et al, 2016). They give expression to 'an experience that could not otherwise be captured and communicated' (Warren and Karner, 2005 in Bartlett and O'Connor, 2010, p 107). Approaches that explore the interplay between the subjective experience and cultural context, such as institutional ethnography, offer additional opportunities to explore how organisational practices and policies shape the lives and well-being of care home residents with, and without, dementia (Mikelyte and Milne, 2016).

In parallel, there is a need to challenge the 'incapacitated person with dementia' discourse. While ethical concerns are predicted on the basis of protecting vulnerable adults from harm, the requirements of gaining traditional ethical approval to conduct research is criticised by some commentators as undermining the principles of citizenship and participation (Dixon-Woods and Angell, 2009). Efforts are now being made to develop 'inclusionary ethical consent processes' (Dewing, 2007). These attempt to engage with people living with dementia in different ways, for example using pictures not words; they also revisit the issue of 'consent' regularly as a project progresses. Their aim is to achieve a balance between protection and citizenship rather than to exclude people with advanced dementia on the grounds of lack of capacity to consent.

The nature of the evidence base: some overarching issues

Overall, the nature of the evidence base relating to mental health and later life warrants comment: it is uneven, contested and has indeterminate edges.

While there is considerable consensus about the factors that contribute to and/or protect mental health in later life there are significant differences in emphasis and foci. Whereas traditional research tends to focus on specific threats to mental health, for example chronic illness, bereavement, evidence drawn from older people themselves is more likely to capture the day-to-day management of 'age-related challenges' in the round. That is not to suggest older people do not recognise ill health or loss as a threat but it is interwoven into the fabric of their lives rather than a single entity that can be separated off from the whole. This has implications for how we think about 'interventions'; most focus on resolving a single 'problem' or issue, for example bereavement counselling. This may reflect a model that suits younger adults and mirrors the atomised nature of the health and care system: a point made in earlier chapters.

There is also a distinction between perspectives that appreciate the life course relevance of issues such as physical health and the role played by exposure to disadvantage, and those that treat 'old age' as a life stage unconnected to earlier life stages. Older people themselves tend to recognise – sometimes indirectly and implicitly – the relevance of links, for example those relating to social networks or income. Researchers are less inclined to do so; they recognise the importance of alleviating isolation but not that it may be a product of a life course characterised by limited choices, poverty and living in a run-down neighbourhood. There are also stark distinctions in relationship to the weight of evidence. There is a lot of research exploring the role of social relationships in protecting mental health but far less about the role played by an adequate income or decent housing. A linked challenge relates to the nature of research. While there is limited evidence of the cost-effectiveness of preventive services, there is ample evidence of their impact on older people's mental health and quality of life (for example Knapp et al, 2013).

There is some conceptual confusion about where the boundary is situated between mental health and mental ill health, and where the promotion of the former, and prevention of the latter, intersect. The boundary between health and mental health is also a challenge. For older people – in the main – these are not important issues. Promotion, protection and prevention are overlapping – even shared – dimensions of the 'ageing experience' which includes mental health. For example, social relationships prevent isolation, protect well-being and promote engagement. A linked issue relates to what matters to older people. One of the starkest observations is the schism between older people's perspectives and those of policy makers. The high priority placed on relational issues by older people, particularly older women, finds limited promotional purchase inside commissioning models that prioritise cost. Older people's emphasis on the role played by 'ordinary' services, issues and relationships also positions mental health inside a universalist arena that disrupts a policy orientation facing towards privatisation and limited public investment in communities and public infrastructure.

These differences reflect a number of fundamental tensions that exist in the fields of ageing and mental health more broadly. Is mental health an issue we should all engage with or it is reserved for those who have 'problems'? Is ageing, by definition, one of the 'problems' or is it a sufficiently ordinary stage(s) of life to justify the attention of researchers, policy makers and those concerned with mental health promotion? Both personal and public ambivalence about ageing *and* about mental health is writ large in this complex terrain. A profound reluctance to, or perhaps disinterest in, considering the relevance of the life course and inequalities to mental health in later life amplifies the challenge. These tensions need to be acknowledged if we are to move forward in an intelligent, inclusive way.

Values and principles

The role played by values and principles in informing policy development and driving decision-making is profound. Research, policy and service development are located in a political context underpinned by an, often implicit or obscured, set of values. Making these visible, exploring the ways in which they operate and their direct and indirect links with mental health outcomes in later life is important, as it is by doing this that the role of political ideology is made apparent and rendered open to challenge.

I have identified a number of distinctive ways in which the neo-liberal political agenda infuses policy and public perspectives. One of its most powerful and seductive narratives is that relating to health as 'individual lifestyle choice' rather than, as I have argued, a product of a life course and linked to inequalities (Scharf et al, 2017). Lakoff (2004) suggests that the political right aligns itself with the values of 'the strict father' holding individuals responsible for their socio-economic and health status, constructing illness as a consequence of unhealthy choices, and the individual 'consumer' as having control of their health and care options. These are accessible principles that have wide appeal.

This narrative has a number of damaging consequences for older people's mental health and well-being. Many feel personally responsible for being poor, ill or lonely and are reluctant to ask for help. Although this reluctance is partly about stigma and not wishing to identify as 'unable to cope' it is aided and abetted by the reductionist nature of health and care-related policy and by radical and punitive cuts to publicly funded services (Humphries, 2015). Being obliged to meet restrictive eligibility criteria (for social care particularly) and accept labels of 'dependent' and 'at risk' is demeaning and amplifies the mental health risks associated with chronic ill health, the fourth age and dementia. As noted in Chapter 3, the erosion of the scaffolding of the welfare system highlights the mechanisms by which a wholly individualised model of blame reinforces adverse outcomes associated with life course-related disadvantage, poverty and inequality. The commodified nature of care services, and the economic considerations that underpin them, are also corrosive of well-being (see Chapter 6). It appears that even cuts to services can be turned to the benefit of neoliberalism, 'placing responsibility for inadequately resourced health and care services on the shoulders of sick older people' (Lloyd, 2012, p 135). This point echoes that made in Chapter 9 about family carers feeling 'blamed' for 'failing' to support their relative (Manthorpe and Iliffe, 2016b). The practices of public health can also be recruited, diverting attention from socio-economic determinants towards a 'moral enterprise' designed to encourage self-governance and self-regulation in health (Peterson and Lupton, 2000).

There are wider issues too. The rollback of the welfare state is accompanied – or even justified – by the abandonment of the intergenerational compact that has assured vulnerable and ill older people a secure old age since the 1940s (Townsend, 2007). This is a significant shift with a number of mental health consequences for older people, particularly those who have few resources; it has not only produced a much more unequal later life but one marked by uncertainty, insecurity and anxiety about the future (Whitehead, 2011).

A discourse aligned to the principles of human rights and social justice is the most widely accepted alternative to the individualised model of health and neo-liberal narrative (Labonté, 2008). 'To ensure social justice, health and sustainability are at the heart of all policies' is one of the main mechanisms by which Marmot and colleagues (2010) recommend governments act to reduce health inequalities. Recognition of the importance of social justice lies at the heart of the social citizenship model of dementia, and the promotion of human rights is an embedded aim of a number of recent dementia policies and standards (WHO, 2015). It has even been suggested that the 'public mental health equivalent of sewers and clean water are social justice and human rights' (Gostin, 2001).

Townsend (2007) argues that '… human rights are not only a moral and quasi legal salvation but offer a framework of thought and planning' (p 43) that is positive in tone, faces towards addressing the social determinants of health and accepts collective responsibility for health and care services for those people who need them. Lakoff (2004) recommends that the left should adopt a 'nurturant parent model' as an alternative to the 'strict father model' in political debate. The nurturant parent has the attributes of compassion, empathy and understanding and promotes the principles of dignity, respect, equality and public duty. This model 'translates' into a very different set of responses to health and care issues than the neo-liberal model including: recognition of the importance of reducing risks to mental health across the life course, supporting older people to deal with age-related challenges and viewing individual need inside its wider social and relational context (Shakespeare et al, 2017).

It is important to acknowledge the challenge of operationalising these principles and define their mental health benefits in an easily understood way. Social justice and human rights tend to be presented and understood as rather abstract concepts. This is in sharp contrast to the 'health as commodity' and private responsibility narrative which continues to gather political and economic momentum. Even if the human rights agenda is accepted as intrinsic to policy development and the promotion of mental health in later life, concerns about resources and costs will always eclipse it (Lloyd, 2012).

Limitations

The book has a number of limitations. As I said in the introduction, the needs and profile of a number of specific populations have not been explored. These include: older people with lifelong mental health problems, older people with learning disabilities and mental health problems, and issues relating to end of life care. These groups and issues justify dedicated attention in their own right. I have said less about cohorts than I'd have liked. I also recognise that there is more to say about diversity, intersectionality and ageing. For example, there are important ways in which intersectionality affects the well-being and mental health of older people from black and minority ethnic populations and older people from LGBTQ+ communities; space constraints have not permitted me to explore these in any depth. Decisions had to made about what was in and what was less in!

The majority of material reviewed in the book has been drawn from the UK, Europe or the US. Very little attention has been paid to developing countries or the global stage. There are significant issues relating to mental health in later life across the world. Many of the issues raised in my book are relevant to authors and older populations in most human societies and countries: I hope it is of value to those outside of the Western purview.

Although I have discussed the shape, size and nature of the material I have reviewed, it is useful to reiterate that this is, of itself, a constraint. There is a tendency in research to explore some areas a great deal and others not at all. One of the reasons I decided to write this book was to shine a light on some of the less explored areas, issues and questions.

It has been harder to present good news than it has bad news; it's easier to discuss the ways in which life course and age-related issues damage mental health than promote it. This reflects the evidence base as well as the fact that establishing links between a mental health problem, rather than the lack of one, and a factor(s) or experience is easier.

Towards a new paradigm

For us to move forward we need a fundamental rethink of how we conceptualise, understand, research and respond to mental health in later life issues.

A paradigmatic shift is required drawing on life course analysis, work on social and structural inequalities and critical gerontology; the lived experiences and perspectives of older people must lie at the core of this recalibration and it needs to be underpinned by the principles of social justice and human rights. Most importantly, the new paradigm must have the capacity to engage meaningfully with reducing risks, preventing harm, and promoting mental health and well-being in later life. It needs to achieve a balance between knowledge generation and policy advice; theory and practice; the individual and the social context; the life course and later life; the micro, meso and macro. It also needs to include the voices and profiles of people living with frailty and/or dementia. This is a big ask.

In this conclusion I have discussed a number of the key ingredients of the new paradigm and identified directions of travel. I am not proposing a single path and do not have a definitive route through the territory. What I have offered is some guidance – a map perhaps – to help navigate it and explore (some of) the multiplicity of issues that underpin and influence mental health in later life. It is important to recognise that we already know quite a lot. There is a great deal of high-quality material out there. There is also disquiet. There are some strong pleas *from* the field *for* the field to develop in a more coherent, creative and inclusive direction, to adopt a longer and broader lens and to engage with the needs and voices of older people. Further, there is growing recognition that mental health in later life is a political issue as well as an academic, policy and health-related concern.

It is in all of our interests to advance this agenda. Although it is a complex multi-dimensional issue there are many opportunities to think and do things differently, address the life course and age-related issues that undermine well-being and improve the chances of our own, and subsequent generations, achieving and protecting good mental health in later life.

Notes

Chapter 1

1 Older is defined as being aged 65 years and above.

2 Cardiovascular disease (CVD) is an umbrella term for all heart and circulatory diseases, including coronary heart disease (CHD) and stroke.

3 Blue Zones are regions of the world where people live much longer than average and have much lower levels of health problems.

4 Coronary heart disease refers to a narrowing of the coronary arteries, the blood vessels that supply oxygen and blood to the heart.

Chapter 2

1 The Health Survey for England provides an annual snapshot of the health of the nation and tracks change over time.

Chapter 3

1 The *1946 Birth Cohort* survey has followed up a sample of children born in one week in March 1946 to the present day to capture longitudinal data about their health and well-being.

2 Thalidomide was marketed in the United Kingdom by Distillers (Biochemicals) Ltd under the brand name Distaval from April 1958 until late 1961.

3 Metabolic syndrome is a combination of diabetes, high blood pressure and obesity: together they increase the risk of CVD.

4 Epigenetics is the study of changes in organisms caused by modification of gene expression rather than alteration of the genetic code itself. The standard definition of epigenetics requires these alterations to be heritable.

5 The Crime Survey for England and Wales excludes people aged 60 years or over; it may include them for part of the survey in the future.

Chapter 4

1 Defined as before, or at, 55 years of age.

2 Breast cancer screening is currently offered to women aged 50 to 70 in England; the NHS is trialling the inclusion of women aged 47 to 73 years of age.

3 The quality-adjusted life year (QALY) is a generic measure of disease burden. It is used in economic evaluation to assess the value for money of medical interventions. QALYs are used to inform health care decisions and evaluate programmes.

4 Improving Access to Psychological Therapies service was introduced in 2008/09 in primary care to treat patients with depression and anxiety.

5 Every person assessed as having eligible needs by their local authority will be given a personal budget.

6 A direct payment is a model whereby the service user manages their own personal budget from the local authority.

7 'Excess deaths' refer to deaths that could have been prevented and/or are in greater number than would be expected in similar circumstances.

Chapter 5

1 Poverty is defined as having an income of less than 60% of median income after housing costs; severe poverty is defined as incomes of less than 50% of median income; 'just above the poverty line' is defined as having an income of more than 60% of median income but less than 70%.

2 Attendance allowance is claimed from the age of 65 years onwards: Disability Living Allowance must be claimed before 65 years but can continue to be paid beyond that age. An older person can only claim one of these benefits.

3 Fuel poverty: where at least 10% of household income is spent on fuel.

4 Households with a member over 65 years old.

5 The 'excess winter death' rate is calculated by subtracting the number of deaths that occur between August to November and April to July of any given year from the number of deaths occurring between December and March.

Chapter 6

1 The term abuse will be used as a term to include mistreatment and neglect unless more specific 'types' of abuse are discussed.

2 Residential care homes, nursing care homes and NHS continuing care in hospitals.

3 Care home includes both nursing homes and residential homes.

4 A serious case review (SCR) takes place after a vulnerable adult dies or is seriously injured and abuse or neglect is thought to be involved. It looks at lessons that can help prevent similar incidents from happening in the future.

5 The Care Quality Commission was established in 2009 to regulate and inspect health and social care services in England.

6 The authors used freedom of information requests to police forces to access their data. Data were obtained from 45 forces relating to 655 cases of rape and sexual assault *by penetration* over a five-year period.

7 Ball and Fowler's (2008) study defined 'older' as starting at 55 years; it also focused on 'all sexual assaults' not just those involving penetration.

8 There is similar legislation in Scotland, Wales and Northern Ireland.

Chapter 8

1 Oophorectomy means the surgical removal of one or both ovaries.

2 The majority of residents had cognitive impairment in this study; those with an MMSE score of 15 or less were excluded.

3 The 'we' used in these statements encompasses people with dementia, their carers and families, and everyone else affected by dementia: www.dementiaaction.org.uk/nationaldementiadeclaration

Chapter 9

1 Article 19: Living independently and being included in the community: 'all parties to this Convention shall recognise the equal right of all persons with disabilities to live in the community, with choices equal to others, and shall take effective and appropriate measures to facilitate their full inclusion and participation in the community'.

Chapter 10

1 Updated and slightly amended to reflect more recent evidence by the author.

2 Cattan (2015) defined mental well-being as 'a complex subjective state with no one single agreed definition'. This term was preferred by the National Institute for Health and Care Excellence to 'mental health'.

3 Allostatic load refers to the biological 'cost' associated with maintaining stability during change.

4 Tanner employed a pseudonym in her case study.

References

Abrams, D. and Swift, H.J. (2012) 'Ageism doesn't work', *Public Policy and Aging Report*, 22(3): 3–8.

Acheson, D. (1988) *Public Health in England: The Report of the Committee of Inquiry into the Future Development of the Public Health Function*. London: HMSO.

Acierno, R., Hernandez, H., Amstadter, A.B., Resnick, H.S., Steve, K., Muzzy, W. and Kilpatrick D.G. (2010) 'Prevalence and correlates of emotional, physical, sexual, and financial abuse and potential neglect in the United States: the national elder abuse mistreatment study', *American Journal of Public Health*, 100(2): 292–7.

Action on Elder Abuse (2004) *Hidden Voices: Older People's Experience of Abuse*. London: Action on Elder Abuse and Help the Aged.

Adams, L., Koerbitz, C., Murphy, L. and Tweddle, M. (2013) *Older People and Human Rights in Home Care: Local Authority Responses to the 'Close to Home' Inquiry Report*, Manchester: Equality and Human Rights Commission.

Adda, J., Chandola, T. and Marmot, M. (2003) 'Socio-economic status and health: causality and pathways', *Journal of Econometrics*, 112(1): 57–63.

Adler, N.E. and Snibbe, A.C. (2003) 'The role of psychosocial processes in explaining the gradient between socioeconomic status and health', *Current Directions in Psychological Science*, 12(4): 119–23.

Adler, N.E., Cutler, D.M., Jonathan, J.E., Galea, S., Glymour, M., Koh, H.K. and Satcher, D. (2016) 'Addressing social determinants of health and health disparities', *Discussion Paper, Vital Directions for Health and Health Care Series*. Washington DC: National Academy of Medicine.

Age Concern and Mental Health Foundation (2006) *Promoting Mental Health and Well Being in Later Life*, London: Age Concern.

Age Concern and University of Kent (2005) *Age Discrimination*, London: Age Concern England.

Age Concern England (2003) *Adding Quality to Quantity: Older People's Views on Quality of Life and its Enhancement*, London: Age Concern England.

Age Concern England (2007) *Improving Services and Support for Older People with Mental Health Problems*, London: Age Concern.

Age International and Age UK (2015) *A UN Convention on the Rights of Older People: Time for the UK to Lead*, London: Age International.

Age NI (2018) *Act4Age: Tackling Pensioner Poverty*, Belfast: AgeNI.

Age UK (2011) *Spread the Warmth*, London: Age UK.

Age UK (2012) *Fit as a Fiddle Final Evaluation Report Yorkshire and Humber*, York: Age UK.

Age UK (2014a) *Agenda for Later Life*, London: Age UK.

Age UK (2014b) *£61 Billion – The Economic Contribution of People Aged 65 Plus*, London: Age UK, [online] www.ageuk.org.uk/latest-press/archive/61-billion-the-economic-contribution-of-people-aged-65-plus/ [Accessed 12 January 2019].

Age UK (2015) *Improving Later Life: Vulnerability and Resilience in Older People*, London: Age UK.

Age UK (2016a) *Later Life in the United Kingdom: Factsheet*, London: Age UK.

Age UK (2016b) *Hidden in Plain Sight: The Unmet Mental Health Needs of Older People*, London: Age UK.

Age UK (2016c) *Briefing: Health and Care of Older People in England 2017*, London: Age UK.

Age UK (2016d) *Later Life in a Digital World*, London: Age UK.

Age UK (2017) *Briefing: Human Rights and Older People and Their Comprehensive Care*, London: Age UK.

Age UK (2018) *Exercise and Physical Activity*, London: Age UK, [online] www.ageuk.org.uk/services/in-your-area/exercise/ [Accessed 12 January 2019].

Albert, S.M., Del Castillo-Castaneda, C., Sano, M., Jacobs, D.M., Marder, K., Bell, K., Bylsma, F., Lafleche, G., Brandt, J., Albert, M. and Stern, Y. (1996) 'Quality of life in patients with Alzheimer's disease as reported by patient proxies', *Journal of the American Geriatrics Society*, 44(11): 1342–7.

Albrecht, G.L. and Devlieger, P.J. (1999) 'The disability paradox: high quality of life against all odds', *Social Science and Medicine*, 48(8): 977–88.

Alcock, P. (2008) 'Poverty and Social Exclusion', in T. Ridge and S. Wright (eds) *Understanding Inequality, Poverty and Wealth: Policies and Prospects*, Bristol: Policy Press, pp 37–75.

All Party Parliamentary Group on Dementia (2016) *Dementia Rarely Travels Alone: Living with Dementia and Other Conditions*, London: Alzheimer's Society.

Allan, K. (2001) *Communication and Consultation: Exploring Ways for Staff to Involve People in Developing Services*, York: Joseph Rowntree Foundation.

Allen, J. (2008) *Older People and Wellbeing*, London: Institute for Public Policy Research.

Allen, J. and Daly, S. (2016) 'Briefing Paper (1): Older people and the social determinants of health, in British Medical Association', in *Growing Older in the UK: A Series of Expert-Authored Briefing Papers on Ageing and Health*, London: The British Medical Association.

Allen, J., Goldblatt, P., Daly, S., Jabbal, J. and Marmot, M. (2018) *Reducing Health Inequalities through New Models of Care: A Resource for New Care Models*, London: Institute of Health Equity.

Allen, K. and Glasby, J. (2013) 'The "billion-dollar question": embedding prevention in older people's services – ten "high-impact" changes', *Advance Discussion Paper*, Birmingham: Health Services Management Centre.

Alzheimer Scotland (2018) *The Scottish Dementia Working Group*, [online] www.alzscot.org/campaigning/scottish_dementia_working_group [Accessed 13 December 2018].

Alzheimer's Disease International (2014) *World Alzheimer Report: Dementia and Risk Reduction, An Analysis of Preventable and Modifiable Factors*, [online] www.alz.co.uk/research/world-report-2014 [Accessed 13 December 2018].

Alzheimer's Disease International (2015) *Women and Dementia: A Global Research Review*, [online] www.alz.co.uk/sites/default/files/pdfs/Women-and-Dementia-Summary-Sheet.pdf [Accessed 13 December 2018].

Alzheimer's Disease International (2016) *Dementia Friendly Communities: Key Principles*, London: Alzheimer's Disease International.

Alzheimer's Research UK (2015) *Women and Dementia: A Marginalised Majority*, Cambridge: Alzheimer's Research.

Alzheimer's Society (2007) *Dementia UK*, London: Alzheimer's Society.

Alzheimer's Society (2013) *Dementia 2013: The Hidden Voice of Loneliness*, London: Alzheimer's Society.

Alzheimer's Society (2015) *Alzheimer's Society's View on Equality, Discrimination, and Human Rights*, [online] www.alzheimers.org.uk/about-us/policy-and-influencing/what-we-think/equality-discrimination-human-rights [Accessed 13 December 2018].

Alzheimer's Society (2016) *Fix Dementia Care: NHS and Care Homes*, London: Alzheimer's Society.

Alzheimer's Society (2017) *Depression and Anxiety Factsheet*, London: Alzheimer's Society.

Alzheimer's Society (2018) *Dementia: The True Cost*, London: Alzheimer's Society.

Alzheimer's Society (2019a) *Hidden No More: Dementia and Disability*, London: Alzheimer's Society.

Alzheimer's Society (2019b) *How Dementia Progresses*, London: Alzheimer's Society, [online] www.alzheimers.org.uk/about-dementia/symptoms-and-diagnosis/how-dementia-progresses [Accessed 13 January 2019].

Amieva, H., Stoykova, R., Matharan, F., Helmer, C., Antonucci, T.C. and Dartigues, J-F. (2010) 'What aspects of social networks are protective for dementia? Not the quantity but the quality of social interactions is protective up to 15 years later', *Psychometric Medicine*, 72(9): 905–11.

Aminzadeh, F., Byszewski, A., Molnar, F.J. and Eisner, M. (2007) 'Emotional impact of dementia diagnosis: exploring persons with dementia and caregivers' perspectives', *Aging and Mental Health*, 11(3): 281–90.

Anderson, D. (2005) 'Preventing delirium in older people', *British Medical Bulletin*, 73(1): 25–34.

Antonovsky, A. (1979) *Health, Stress and Coping: New Perspectives on Mental and Physical Wellbeing*, San Fransisco, CA: Jossey-Bass.

Antonovsky, A. (1987) *Unravelling the Mystery of Health: How People Manage Stress and Stay Well*, San Fransisco, CA: Jossey-Bass.

Arber, S. and Ginn, J. (1991) 'The invisibility of age: gender and class in later life', *The Sociological Review*, 39(2): 260–91.

Arber, S. and Ginn, J. (1995a) 'Connecting gender and ageing: a sociological approach', *The British Journal of Social Work*, 26(3): 433–5.

Arber, S. and Ginn, J. (1995b) 'Gender differences in informal caring', *Health and Social Care in the Community*, 3(1): 19–31.

Archer, M. (2000) *Being Human: The Problem of Agency*, Cambridge: Cambridge University Press.

Archer, M.S. (2003) 'The private life of the social agent: what difference does it make?', in J. Cruickshank (ed) *Critical Realism: The Difference it Makes*, London: Routledge, pp 29–41.

Association for the Conservation of Energy (2013) *The Cold Man of Europe*, London: Association for the Conservation of Energy.

Association of Directors of Adult Social Services (2011) *Carers and Safeguarding Adults: Working Together to Improve Outcomes*, London: ADASS.

Association of Directors of Social Services/Local Government Association (2003) *All Our Tomorrows; Inverting the Triangle of Care*, London: ADSS/LGA.

Audickas, L. (2017). 'Sport participation in England', https://researchbriefings.parliament.uk/ResearchBriefing/Summary/CBP-8181#fullreport

Auge (1995) *Non-Places: Introduction to an Anthropology of Supermodernity*, New York: Verso.

Ayalon, L. (2008) 'Subjective socioeconomic status as a predictor of long-term care staff burnout and positive caregiving experiences', *International Psychogeriatrics*, 20(3): 521–37.

Azad, N.A., Al Bugami, M. and Loy-English, I. (2007) 'Gender differences in dementia risk factors', *Gender Medicine*, 4(2): 120–9.

Baars, J. (1991) 'The challenge of critical gerontology: the problem of social constitution', *Journal of Aging Studies*, 5(3): 219–43.

Baars, J., Dohmen, J., Grenier, A. and Phillipson, C. (eds) (2014) *Ageing, Meaning and Social Structure: Connecting Critical and Humanistic Gerontology*, Bristol: Policy Press.

Babones, S.J. (eds) (2009) *Social Inequality and Public Health*, Bristol: Policy Press.

Bagley, H., Cordingley, L., Burns, A., Mozley, C.G., Sutcliffe, C., Challis, D. and Huxley, P. (2000) 'Recognition of depression by staff in nursing and residential homes', *Journal of Clinical Nursing*, 9(3): 445–50.

Bailey, C., Clarke, C., Gibb, C., Haining, S., Wilkinson, H. and Tiplady, S. (2013) 'Risky and resilient life with dementia: review of and reflections on the literature', *Health, Risk and Society*, 15(5): 390–401.

Bailey, E.M., Stevens, A.B., LaRocca, M.A. and Scogin, F. (2017) 'A randomized controlled trial of a therapeutic intervention for nursing home residents with dementia and depressive symptoms', *Journal of Applied Gerontology*, 36(7): 895–908.

Baldwin, C. (2008) 'Narrative, citizenship and dementia: the personal and the political', *Journal of Aging Studies*, 22(3): 222–8.

Balfour, R. and Allen, J. (2014) *Fuel Poverty and Cold Home-Related Health Problems*, London: Public Health England.

Ball, H.N. and Fowler, D. (2008) 'Sexual offending against older female victims: an empirical study of the prevalence and characteristics of recorded offences in a semi-rural English county', *The Journal of Forensic Psychiatry and Psychology*, 19(1): 14–32.

Ball, J., Philippou, J., Pike, G. and Sethi, J. (2014) 'Survey of district and community nurses in 2013', *Report to the Royal College of Nursing*, London: Kings College London.

Ball, K., Berch, D.B., Helmers, K.F., Jobe, J.B., Leveck, M.D., Marsiske, M., Morris, J.N., Rebok, G.W., Smith, D.M., Tennstedt, S.L., Unverzagt, F.W. and Willis, S.L. (2002) 'Effects of cognitive training interventions with older adults: a randomized controlled trial', *Journal of the American Medical Association*, 288(18): 2271–81.

Ballard, C., Bannister, C., Solis, M., Oyebode, F. and Wilcock, G. (1996) 'The prevalence, associations and symptoms of depression amongst dementia sufferers', *Journal of Affective Disorders*, 36(3–4): 135–44.

Ballard, C., Neill, D., O'Brien, J., McKeith, I.G., Ince, P. and Perry, R. (2000) 'Anxiety, depression and psychosis in vascular dementia: prevalence and associations', *Journal of Affective Disorders*, 59(2): 97–106.

Ballard, C., Corbett, A., Orrell, M., Williams, G., Moniz-Cook, E., Romeo, R., Woods, B., Garrod, L., Testad, I., Woodward-Carlton, B., Wenborn, J., Knapp, M. and Fossey, J. (2018) 'Impact of person-centred care training and person-centred activities on quality of life, agitation, and antipsychotic use in people with dementia living in nursing homes: a cluster-randomised controlled trial', *PLoS Medicine*, 15(2), e1002500.

Baltes, M.M. (1998) 'The psychology of the oldest-old: the fourth age', *Current Opinion in Psychiatry*, 11(4): 411–15.

Baltes, M.M. and Carstensen, L.L. (1996) 'The process of successful ageing', *Ageing and Society*, 16(4): 397–422.

Baltes, P.B. and Baltes, M.M. (1990) 'Psychological perspectives on successful aging: the model of selective optimization with compensation', *Successful Aging: Perspectives from the Behavioral Sciences*, 1(1): 1–34.

Baltes, P.B. and Smith, J. (2003) 'New frontiers in the future of aging: from successful aging of the young old to the dilemmas of the fourth age', *Gerontology*, 49(2): 123–35.

Bambra, C. (2016) *Health Divides*, Bristol: Policy Press.

Bamford, S. (2011) *Women and Dementia – Not Forgotten*, London: ILC-UK.

Banerjee, S., Murray, J., Foley, B., Atkins, L., Schneider, J. and Mann, A. (2003) 'Predictors of institutionalisation in older people with dementia', *Journal of Neurology Neurosurgery and Psychiatry*, 74(9): 1315–16.

Banerjee, S., Smith, S.C., Lamping, D.L., Harwood, R.H., Foley, B., Smith, P., Murray, J., Prince, M., Levin, E., Mann, A. and Knapp, M. (2006) 'Quality of life in dementia: more than just cognition. An analysis of associations with quality of life in dementia', *Journal of Neurology, Neurosurgery and Psychiatry*, 77(2): 146–8.

Banks, J., Nazroo, J. and Steptoe, A. (eds) (2012) *The Dynamics of Ageing: Evidence from the English Longitudinal Study of Ageing 2002–10* (Wave 5), London: The Institute of Fiscal Studies.

Banks, J., Marmot, M., Oldfield, Z. and Smith, J.P. (2006) 'Disease and disadvantage in the United States and in England', *Journal of the American Medical Association*, 295(17): 2037–45.

Bann, D., Hardy, R., Cooper, R., Lashen, H., Keevil, B., Wu, F., Holly, J., Ong, K., Ben-Shlomo, Y. and Kuh, D. (2015) 'Socioeconomic conditions across life related to multiple measures of the endocrine system in older adults: Longitudinal findings from a British cohort study', *Social Science and Medicine*, 147, 190–9.

Baranski, J. (2016) *Mask and Shame of Ageing*, Łódź: Wydawnictwo Uniwersytetu Łódzkiego.

Barker, D.J. (1990) 'The fetal and infant origins of adult disease', *British Medical Journal*, 301(6761): 1111.

Barnard, H., Kumar, A., Wenham, A., Smith, E., Drake, B., Collingwood, A. and Leese, D. (2017) *UK Poverty 2017*, York: Joseph Rowntree Foundation.

Barnes, D.E. and Yaffe, K. (2011) 'The projected effect of risk factor reduction on Alzheimer's disease prevalence', *The Lancet Neurology*, 10(9): 819–28.

Barnes D.E., Yaffe, K., Byers, A.L., McCormick, M., Schaefer, C. and Whitmer R.A. (2012) 'Midlife vs late-life depressive symptoms and risk of dementia: Differential effects for Alzheimer disease and vascular dementia', *Archives of General Psychiatry*, 69(5): 493–8.

Barnes, M. (2012) *Care in Everyday Life: An Ethic of Care in Practice*, Bristol: Policy Press.

Barnes M., Brannelly, T., Ward, L. and Ward, N. (2015) *Ethics of Care: Critical Advances in International Perspective*, Bristol: Policy Press.

Barnes, M., Blom, A.G., Cox, K., Lessof, C. and Walker, A. (2006) *The Social Exclusion of Older People: Evidence from the First Wave of the English Longitudinal Study of Ageing (ELSA)*. Final report. London: Social Research in Transport (SORT) Clearinghouse.

Barrett, G. and McGoldrick, C. (2013) 'Narratives of (in) active ageing in poor deprived areas of Liverpool, UK', *International Journal of Sociology and Social Policy*, 33(5/6): 347–66.

Barrett, S. and Savage, G. (2012) *A Comparison of People Presenting with Symptoms of Dementia in Northern Ireland and the Republic of Ireland*, Dublin: Centre for Ageing Research and Development in Ireland.

Barth, J., Schumacher, M. and Herrmann-Lingen, C. (2004) 'Depression as a risk factor for mortality in patients with coronary heart disease: a meta-analysis', *Psychosomatic Medicine*, 66(6): 802–13.

Bartlam, B. and Machin, L. (2016) 'Living well with loss in later life', in C. Chew-Graham and M. Ray (eds) *Mental Health and Older People: A Guide for Primary Care Practitioners*, Silver Spring: Springer.

Bartlett, R. (2014a) 'Citizenship in action: the lived experiences of citizens with dementia who campaign for social change', *Disability and Society*, 29(8): 1291–304.

Bartlett, R. (2014b) 'The emergent modes of dementia activism', *Ageing and Society*, 34(4): 623–44.

Bartlett, R. and O'Connor, D. (2007) 'From personhood to citizenship: broadening the lens for dementia practice and research', *Journal of Aging Studies*, 21(2): 107–18.

Bartlett, R. and O'Connor, D. (2010) *Broadening the Dementia Debate*, Bristol: Policy Press.

Bartlett, R., Gjerens, T., Lotherington, A. and Obstfelder, A. (2018) 'Gender, citizenship and dementia care: a scoping review of studies to inform policy and future research', *Health and Social Care in the Community*, 26(1): 14–26.

Bartolini, S., Bilancini, E. and Pugno, M. (2013) 'Did the decline in social connections depress Americans' happiness?', *Social Indicators Research*, 110(3): 1033–59.

Bauer, M., Fetherstonhaugh, D., Haesler, E., Beattie, E., Hill, K.D. and Poulos, C.J. (2018) 'The impact of nurse and care staff education on the functional ability and quality of life of people living with dementia in aged care: a systematic review', *Nurse Education Today*, 67: 27–45.

Beard, R.L. (2004) 'In their voices: identity preservation and experiences of Alzheimer's disease', *Journal of Aging Studies*, 18(4): 415–28.

Beard, R.L. and Fox, P.J. (2008) 'Resisting social disenfranchisement: negotiating collective identities and everyday life with memory loss', *Social Science and Medicine*, 66(7): 1509–20.

Beattie, A. (2002) 'Knowledge and control in health promotion: a test case for social policy and social theory', in M. Bury, M. Calnan and J. Gabe (eds) *The Sociology of the Health Service*, London: Routledge, pp 172–212.

Beaulaurier, R.L., Seff, L.R. and Newman, F.L. (2008) 'Barriers to help-seeking for older women who experience intimate partner violence: a descriptive model', *Journal of Women and Aging*, 20(3–4): 231–48.

Beaumont, J. (2013) *Measuring National Well-being: Older People and Loneliness*, London: Office for National Statistics.

Becker, G. and Newsom, E. (2005) 'Resilience in the face of serious illness among chronically ill African Americans in later life', *The Journals of Gerontology Series B: Psychological Sciences and Social Sciences*, 60(4): S214–23.

Beecham, J., Knapp, M., Fernandez, L., Huxley, P., Mangalore, R., McCrone, P., Snell, T., Winter, B. and Wittenberg, R. (2008) *Age Discrimination in Mental Health Services* [online] www.lse.ac.uk/collections/PSSRU/staff/knappPublications2008.htm [Accessed 13 January 2019].

Beerens, H.C., Sutcliffe, C., Renom-Guiteras, A., Soto, M.E., Suhonen, R., Zabalegui, A., Bökberg, C., Saks, K. and Hamers, J.P.H. on behalf of the RightTimePlaceCare Consortium (2014) 'Quality of life and quality of care for people with dementia receiving long term institutional care or professional home care: the European RightTimePlaceCare study', *Journal of the American Medical Directors Association*, 15(1): 54–61.

Behuniak, S.M. (2010) 'Toward a political model of dementia: power as compassionate care', *Journal of Aging Studies*, 24(4): 231–40.

Bell, S.E. and Figert, A.E. (2012) 'Medicalization and pharmaceuticalization at the intersections: looking backward, sideways and forward', *Social Science and Medicine*, 75(5): 775–83.

Belza, B., Walwick, J., Schwartz, S., LoGerfo, J., Shiu-Thornton, S. and Taylor, M. (2004) 'Older adult perspectives on physical activity and exercise: voices from multiple cultures', *Preventing Chronic Disease*, 1(4): A09.

Benbow, S.M. and Jolley, D. (2012) 'Dementia: stigma and its effects', *Neurodegenerative Disease Management*, 2(2): 165–72.

Bengtson, V.L., Elder Jr, G.H. and Putney, N.M. (2012) 'The life course perspective on ageing: linked lives, timing, and history', *Adult Lives: A Life Course Perspective*: 493–509.

Bennett, D.A., Schneider, J.A., Tang, Y., Arnold, S.E. and Wilson, R.S. (2006) 'The effect of social networks on the relation between Alzheimer's disease pathology and level of cognitive function in old people: a longitudinal cohort study', *The Lancet Neurology*, 5(5): 406–12.

Bennett, J., Guangquan, L., Foreman, K., Best, N., Kontis, V., Pearson, C., Hambly, P. and Ezzati, M. (2015) 'The future of life expectancy and life expectancy inequalities in England and Wales: Bayesian spatiotemporal forecasting', *The Lancet*, 386 (9989): 163–70.

Bennett, K.M. (2005) 'Psychological wellbeing in later life: the longitudinal effects of marriage, widowhood and marital status change', *International Journal of Geriatric Psychiatry*, 20(3): 280–4.

Bennett, K.M. and Soulsby, L.K. (2014) 'Psychological wellbeing in later life', in T. Kirkwood and C. Cooper (eds) *Wellbeing in Later Life*, Oxford: Wiley Blackwell, pp 69–90.

Ben-Shlomo, Y. and Kuh, D. (2002) 'A life course approach to chronic disease epidemiology: conceptual models, empirical challenges and interdisciplinary perspectives', *International Journal of Epidemiology*, 31(2): 285–93.

Benyamini, Y., Gerber, Y., Goldbourt, U. and Drory, Y. (2010) 'Subjective recovery of self-rated health as a predictor of future health after first myocardial infarction: a 13-year follow-up', *Psychology and Health*, 25: 20–20.

Beresford, P., Fleming, J., Glyn, M., Bewley, C., Croft, S., Branfield, F. and Postle, K. (2011) *Supporting People: Towards a Person-Centred Approach*, Bristol: Policy Press.

Bergland, A. and Slettebo, A. (2015) 'Health capital in everyday life of the oldest old living in their own homes', *Ageing and Society*, 35 (10): 2156–75.

Bernard, M. (2000) *Promoting Health in Old Age*, Buckingham: Open University Press.

Biggs, S. and Haapala, I. (2013) 'Elder mistreatment, ageism and human rights', *International Psychogeriatrics*, 25(8): 1299–306.

Billings, J. and Hashem, F. (2009) *Literature Review: Salutogenesis and the Promotion of Positive Mental Health in Older People*, Brussels: European Communities.

Binstock, R. (2004) 'Anti-aging medicine and research', *Journal of Gerontology: Biological Sciences*, 59A(6): B523–33.

Bisschop, M.I., Kriegsman, D.M., Beekman, A.T. and Deeg, D.J. (2004) 'Chronic diseases and depression: the modifying role of psychosocial resources', *Social Science and Medicine*, 59(4): 721–33.

Bland, R. (1999) 'Independence, privacy and risk: two contrasting approaches to residential care for older people', *Ageing and Society*, 19(5): 539–60.

Blomgren J., Martikainen P., Grundy E. and Koskinen, S. (2010) 'Marital history 1971–91 and mortality 1991–2004 in England and Wales and Finland', *Journal of Epidemiology and Community Health*, 66(1): 30–6.

Blood, I. (2004) *Older Women and Domestic Violence*, London: Help the Aged and HACT.

Blood, I. (2013) *A Better Life: Valuing Our Later Years*, York: Joseph Rowntree Foundation.

Boeck, T. and Fleming, J. (2005) 'Social policy – a help or a hindrance to social capital?', *Social Policy and Society*, 4(3): 259–70.

Bolam, B., Murphy, S. and Gleeson, K. (2004) 'Individualisation and inequalities in health: a qualitative study of class identity and health', *Social Science and Medicine*, 59(7): 1355–65.

Bolton, M. (2012) *Loneliness: The State We're In*, Oxford: Age UK.

Bond, J. (1992) 'The medicalization of dementia', *Journal of Aging Studies*, 6(4): 397–403.

Bond, J. and Corner, L. (2004) *Quality of Life and Older People*, Maidenhead: Open University Press.

Bond, J., Stave, C., Sganga, A., Vincenzino, O., O'Connell, B. and Stanley, R.L. (2005) 'Inequalities in dementia care across Europe: key findings of the Facing Dementia Survey', *International Journal of Clinical Practice*, 59(146): 8–14.

Boneham, M.A. and Sixsmith, J.A. (2006) 'The voices of older women in a disadvantaged community: issues of health and social capital', *Social Science and Medicine*, 62(2): 269–79.

Bonnewyn, A., Shah, A., Bruffaerts, R., Schoevaerts, K., Rober, P., Van Parys, H. and Demyttenaere, K. (2014) 'Reflections of older adults on the process preceding their suicide attempt: a qualitative approach', *Death Studies*, 38(9): 612–18.

Boorsma, M., Joling, K.J., Frijters, D.H., Ribbe, M.E., Nijpels, G. and van Hout, H.P. (2012) 'The prevalence, incidence and risk factors for delirium in Dutch nursing homes and residential care homes', *International Journal of Geriatric Psychiatry*, 27(7): 709–15.

Borgonovi, F. (2010) 'A life-cycle approach to the analysis of the relationship between social capital and health in Britain', *Social Science and Medicine*, 71(11): 1927–34.

Borson, S. (2010) 'Post-traumatic stress disorder and dementia: a lifelong cost of war?', *Journal of the American Geriatrics Society*, 58(9): 1797–8.

Borza, T., Engedal, K., Bergh, S., Barca, M.L., Benth, J.Š. and Selbæk, G. (2015) 'The course of depressive symptoms as measured by the Cornell scale for depression in dementia over 74 months in 1158 nursing home residents', *Journal of Affective Disorders*, 175: 209–16.

Bosmans, J.E., Dozeman, E., van Marwijk, H.W., van Schaik, D.J., Stek, M.L., Beekman, A.T. and van der Horst, H.E. (2014) 'Cost-effectiveness of a stepped care programme to prevent depression and anxiety in residents in homes for the older people: a randomised controlled trial', *International Journal of Geriatric Psychiatry*, 29(2): 182–90.

Botsford, J. and Harrison-Dening, K. (eds) (2015) *Dementia, Culture and Ethnicity: Issues for All*, London: Jessica Kingsley Publishers.

Boudiny, K. (2013) '"Active ageing": from empty rhetoric to effective policy tool', *Ageing and Society*, 33(6): 1077–98.

Bourdieu, P. (1977) *Outline of a Theory of Practice*, Cambridge: Cambridge University Press.

Bourdieu, P. (1984) *Distinction: A Social Critique of the Judgement of Taste*, Cambridge: Harvard University Press.

Bourdieu, P. (1986) 'The forms of capital', in I. Szeman, and T. Kaposy (eds) *Cultural Theory: An Anthology*, Malden: Wiley-Blackwell, pp 81–93.

Bowers, H., Clark, A., Crosby, G., Easterbrook, L., Macadam, A., MacDonald, R., Macfarlane, A., Maclean, M., Patel, M., Runnicles, D., Oshinaike, T. and Smith, C. (2009) *Older People's Vision for Long Term Care*, York: Joseph Rowntree Foundation.

Bowling, A. (2004) *Measuring Health*, New York: McGraw-Hill Education.

Bowling, A. (2005) *Ageing Well: Quality of Life in Old Age*, Berkshire: Open University Press.

Bowling, A. (2008) 'Enhancing later life: how older people perceive active ageing?', *Aging and Mental Health*, 12(3): 293–301.

Bowling, A. (2009a) 'Perceptions of active ageing in Britain: divergences between minority ethnic and whole population samples', *Age and Ageing*, 38(6): 703–10.

Bowling, A. (2009b) 'The Psychometric Properties of the Older People's Quality of Life Questionnaire, Compared with the CASP-19 and the WHOQOL-OLD', *Current Gerontology and Geriatrics Research*: e298950.

Bowling, A. and Dieppe, P. (2005) 'What is successful ageing and who should define it?', *British Medical Journal*, 331(7531): 1548–51.

Bowling, A. and Gabriel, Z. (2007) 'Lay theories of quality of life in older age', *Ageing and Society*, 27(6): 827–48.

Bowling, A. and Stafford, M. (2007) 'How do objective and subjective assessments of neighbourhood influence social and physical functioning in older age? Findings from a British survey of ageing', *Social Science and Medicine*, 64(12): 2533–49.

Bowling, A. and Iliffe, S. (2011) 'Psychological approach to successful ageing predicts future quality of life in older adults', *Health and Quality of Life Outcomes*, 9(1): 13.

Bowling, A. and Stenner, P. (2011) 'Which measure of quality of life performs best in older age? A comparison of the OPQOL, CASP-19 and WHOQOL-OLD', *Journal of Epidemiology and Community Health*, 65(3), 273–280.

Bowling, A., Banister, D., Sutton, S., Evans, O. and Windsor, J. (2002) 'A multi-dimensional model of the quality of life in older age', *Aging and Mental Health*, 6(4): 355–71.

Bows, H. and Westmarland, N. (2015) 'Rape of older people in the United Kingdom: challenging the "real rape" stereotype', *British Journal of Criminology*, 57(1): 1–17.

Boyle, G. (2008) 'The Mental Capacity Act 2005: promoting the citizenship of people with dementia?', *Health and Social Care in the Community*, 16(5): 529–37.

Brannelly, T. (2011) 'Sustaining citizenship: people with dementia and the phenomenon of social death', *Nursing Ethics*, 18(5): 662–71.

Braun, M., Scholz, U., Bailey, B., Perren, S., Hornung, R. and Martin, M. (2009) 'Dementia caregiving in spousal relationships: a dyadic perspective', *Aging and Mental Health*, 13(3): 426–36.

Braunholtz, S., Davidson, S., Myant, K. and O'Connor, R. (2007) *Well? What do you think? The Third National Scottish Survey of Public Attitudes to Mental Health, Mental Wellbeing and Mental Health Problems*, Edinburgh: Scottish Executive.

Brayne, C., Gao, L., Dewey, M. and Matthews, F.E. (2006) 'Dementia before death in ageing societies – the promise of prevention and the reality', *PLoS Medicine*, 3(10): e397.

Brayne, C., Ince, P.G., Keage, H.A., McKeith, I.G., Matthews, F.E., Polvikoski, T. and Sulkava, R. (2010) 'Education, the brain and dementia: neuroprotection or compensation?' *Brain*, 133(8): 2210–16.

British Geriatrics Society (2014) *Fit for Frailty: Consensus Best Practice Guidance for the Care of Older People Living in Community and Outpatient Settings*, London: British Geriatrics Society.

British Medical Association (2011) *Social Determinants of Health: What Doctors Can Do*, London: British Medical Association.

British Medical Association (2017) *Breaking Down Barriers – The Challenge of Improving Mental Health Outcomes*, London: British Medical Association.

British Psychological Society (2014) *A Guide to Psychosocial Interventions in Early Stages of Dementia*, Leicester: British Psychological Society.

Brod, M., Stewart, A.L., Sands, L. and Walton, P. (1999) 'Conceptualization and measurement of quality of life in dementia: the dementia quality of life instrument (DQoL)', *The Gerontologist*, 39(1): 25–35.

Bronfenbrenner, U. (1994) 'Ecological models of human development', *International Encyclopedia of Education*, 3(2nd edn), Oxford: Elsevier.

Brooker, D. (2005) 'Dementia care mapping: a review of the research literature', *The Gerontologist*, 45(Special Issue): 11–18.

Brooker, D. (2011) 'Promoting health and well-being: good practice inside the care homes', in T. Dening and A. Milne (eds) *Mental Health and Care Homes*, Oxford: Oxford University Press, pp 279–96.

Brooker, D. and Latham, I. (2015) *Person-Centred Dementia Care: Making Services Better with the VIPS Framework*, London: Jessica Kingsley Publishers.

Brown, H. (2011) 'Abuse in care homes for older people: the case for safeguards', in T. Dening and A. Milne (eds) *Mental Health and Care Homes*, Oxford: Oxford University Press, pp 113–30.

Brown, J., Bowling, A. and Flynn, T. (2004) *Models of Quality of Life: A Taxonomy, Overview and Systematic Review of the Literature*, Sheffield: Department of Sociological Studies.

Bruens, M.T. (2013) 'Dementia: beyond structures of medicalisation and cultural neglect', in J. Baars, J. Dohmen, A. Grenier and C. Phillipson (eds) *Ageing, Meaning and Social Structure*, Bristol: Policy Press, pp 81–96.

Bruggencate, T.T., Luijkx, K.G. and Sturm, J. (2018) 'Social needs of older people: a systematic literature review', *Ageing and Society*, 38(9): 1745–70.

Bryant, C., Bei, B., Gilson, K., Komiti, A., Jackson, H. and Judd, F. (2012) 'The relationship between attitudes to aging and physical and mental health in older adults', *International Psychogeriatrics*, 24(10): 1674–83.

Bryant, L.L., Corbett, K.K. and Kutner, J.S. (2001) 'In their own words: a model of healthy aging', *Social Science and Medicine*, 53(7): 927–41.

Buchmann, C., DiPrete, T.A. and McDaniel, A. (2008) 'Gender inequalities in education', *Annual Review of Sociology*, 34: 319–37.

Buck, D. and Maguire, D. (2015) *Inequalities in Life Expectancy: Changes Over Time and Implications for Policy*, London: The King's Fund.

Buettner, D. (2015) *The Blue Zones Solution: Eating and Living Like the World's Healthiest People*, Washington DC: National Geographic Books.

Buffel, T., Phillipson, C. and Sharf, T. (2013) 'Experiences of neighbourhood exclusion and inclusion among older people living in deprived inner-city areas in Belgium and England', *Ageing and Society*, 33(1): 89–109.

Bun Cheung, Y. (2002) 'A confirmatory factor analysis of the 12-item General Health Questionnaire among older people', *International Journal of Geriatric Psychiatry*, 17(8): 739–44.

Burholt, V. (2011) 'Loneliness of older men and women in rural areas of the UK', in *Safeguarding the Convoy: A Call to Action from the Campaign to End Loneliness*, Abingdon: Age UK.

Burri, A., Maercker, A., Krammer, S. and Simmen-Janevska, K. (2013) 'Childhood trauma and PTSD symptoms increase the risk of cognitive impairment in a sample of former indentured child laborers in old age', *PloS One*, 8(2): e57826.

Bury, M. (1991) 'The sociology of chronic illness: a review of research and prospects', *Sociology of Health and Illness*, 13(4): 451–68.

Bury, M. (2005) *Health and Illness*, Cambridge: Polity Press.

Butler, J. (2009) *Frames of War: When is Life Grievable?* London: Verso.

Butler, R.N. (1969) 'Ageism: another form of bigotry', *Gerontologist*, 9(4): 243–6

Butler, R.N., Lewis, M.I. and Sunderland, T. (1998) *Aging and Mental Health: Positive Psychological and Biomedical Approaches*, (5th edn), Boston, MA: Allyn and Bacon.

Byrne, G. (2013) 'Anxiety disorders in older people' in T. Dening and A. Thomas (eds) *The Oxford Textbook of Old Age Psychiatry*, Oxford: Oxford University Press, pp 589–602.

Byrne-Davis, L.M.T., Bennett, P.D. and Wilcock, G.K. (2006) 'How are quality of life ratings made? Toward a model of quality of life in people with dementia', *Quality of Life Research*, 15(5): 855–65.

Bytheway, B. (1995) *Ageism*, Milton Keynes: Open University Press.

Bywaters, P. (2009) 'Tackling Inequalities in health: a global challenge for social work', *British Journal of Social Work*, 39(2), 353–67.

Bywaters, P., Bunting, L., Davidson, G., Hanratty, J., Mason, W., McCartan, C. and Steils, N. (2016) *The Relationship Between Poverty, Child Abuse and Neglect: An Evidence Review*, York: Joseph Rowntree Foundation.

Cahill, S. (2018) *Dementia and Human Rights*, Bristol: Policy Press.

Calasanti, T.M. and Slevin, K.F. (2001) *Gender, Social Inequalities, and Aging*, Maryland: AltaMira Press.

Campaign to End Loneliness (2011) *Safeguarding the Convoy*, Campaign to End Loneliness, [online] www.campaigntoendloneliness.org/ [Accessed 13 January 2019].

Campaign to End Loneliness (2013) *Alone in a Crowd: Loneliness and Diversity*, Campaign to End Loneliness, [online] www.campaigntoendloneliness.org/ [Accessed 13 January 2019].

Campion, J., Bhugra, D., Bailey, S. and Marmot, M. (2013) 'Inequality and mental disorders: opportunities for action', *The Lancet*, 382: 183–4.

Cantley, C. and Bowes, A. (2004) 'Dementia and social inclusion: the way forward', in A. Innes, C. Archibald and C. Murphy (eds) *Dementia and Social Inclusion: Marginalized Groups and Marginalized Areas of Dementia Research, Care and Practice*, London: Jessica Kingsley Publishers, pp. 255–71.

Care Quality Commission (2013) *Dignity and Nutrition Inspection Programme*, London: Care Quality Commission.

Care Quality Commission (2017) *The State of Adult Social Care Services 2014 to 2017: Findings from CQC's Initial Programme of Comprehensive Inspections in Adult Social Care*, Newcastle: Care Quality Commission.

Carers UK (2016) *The State of Caring 2016*, London: Carers UK.

Carpenter, B.D., Xiong, C., Porensky, E.K., Lee, M.M., Brown, P.J., Coats, M., Johnson, D. and Morris, J.C. (2008) 'Reaction to a dementia diagnosis in individuals with Alzheimer's disease and mild cognitive impairment', *Journal of the American Geriatrics Society*, 56(3): 405–12.

Caselli, G. and Luy, M. (2013) 'Determinants of unusual and differential longevity: an introduction', *Vienna Yearbook of Population Research*, 11, 1–13.

Cattan, M. (2009) *Mental Health and Well-Being in Later Life*, Maidenhead: Open University Press.

Cattan, M. (2015) *The Development of a Multi-Dimensional, Theoretical Model of the Foundations of Mental Wellbeing*, Newcastle-upon-Tyne: Northumbria University.

Cattan, M., White, M., Bond, J. and Learmouth, A. (2005) 'Preventing social isolation and loneliness among older people: a systematic review of health promotion interventions', *Ageing and Society*, 25(1): 41–67.

Centre for Ageing Better (2019) *The State of Ageing in 2019*, London: Centre for Ageing Better.

Centre for Policy on Ageing (2009a) *Achieving Age Equality in Health and Social Care: A Report to the Secretary of State for Health*, [online] www.cpa.org.uk/cpa/achieving_age_equality_in_health_and_social_care.pdf [Accessed 12 December 2018].

Centre for Policy on Ageing (2009b) *Ageism and Age Discrimination in Secondary Health Care in the United Kingdom*, London: Centre for Policy on Ageing.

Centre for Social Justice (2010) *The Forgotten Age: Understanding Poverty and Social Exclusion in Later Life*, London: Centre for Social Justice.

Centre for Workforce Intelligence (2012) *Workforce Risks and Opportunities*, [online] https://www.basw.co.uk/system/files/resources/basw_22629-2_0.pdf [Accessed 12 December 2018].

Chambers, P. (2005) 'Widowhood in later life', in M. Bernard, V. Harding Davies, L. Machin and J. Phillips (eds) *Women Ageing*, London: Routledge, pp 142–62.

Chaudhury, H. and Cooke, H. (2014) 'Design matters in dementia care: the role of the physical environment in dementia care settings', in M. Downs and B. Bowers (eds) *Excellence in Dementia Care*, London: Open University Press, pp 144–58.

Chen, L.P., Murad, M.H., Paras, M.L, Colbenson, K.M., Sattler, A.L., Goranson, E.N., Elamin, M.B., Seime, R.J., Shinozaki, G., Prokop, L.J. and Zirakzadeh, A. (2010) 'Sexual abuse and lifetime diagnosis of psychiatric disorders: systematic review and meta-analysis', *Mayo Clinic Proceedings*, 85(7): 618–29.

Choi, N.G. and Mayer, J. (2000) 'Elder abuse, neglect, and exploitation: risk factors and prevention strategies', *Journal of Gerontological Social Work*, 33(2): 5–26.

Chua, K.C., Brown, A., Little, R., Matthews, D., Morton, L., Loftus, V., Watchurst, C., Tait, R., Romeo, R. and Banerjee, S. (2016) 'Quality-of-life assessment in dementia: the use of DEMQOL and DEMQOL-Proxy total scores', *Quality of Life Research*, 25(12): 3107–18.

Chumbler, N.R., Rittman, M.R. and Wu, S.S. (2008) 'Associations in sense of coherence and depression in caregivers of stroke survivors across 2 years', *The Journal of Behavioral Health Services and Research*, 35(2): 226–34.

Chung, J.C. (2004) 'Activity participation and well-being of people with dementia in long-term—care settings', *Occupation, Participation and Health*, 24(1): 22–31.

Clare, L. (2003) 'Managing threats to self: awareness in early stage Alzheimer's disease', *Social Science and Medicine*, 57(6): 1017–29.

Clare, L., Marková, I., Verhey, F. and Kenny, G. (2005) 'Awareness in dementia: a review of assessment methods and measures', *Aging and Mental Health*, 9(5): 394–413.

Clare, L., Woods, R.T., Moniz Cook, E.D., Orrell, M. and Spector, A. (2003) *Cognitive Rehabilitation and Cognitive Training for Early-Stage Alzheimer's Disease and Vascular Dementia. The Cochrane Collaboration*, Hoboken, NJ: John Wiley and Sons.

Clare, L., Rowlands, J., Bruce, E., Surr, C. and Downs, M. (2008) 'The experience of living with dementia in residential care: an interpretative phenomenological analysis', *The Gerontologist*, 48(6): 711–20.

Clare, L., Woods, R.T., Nelis, S.M., Martyr, A., Markova, I.S., Roth, I., Whitaker, C.J. and Morris, R.G. (2014) 'Trajectories of quality of life in early-stage dementia: individual variations and predictors of change', *International Journal of Geriatric Psychiatry*, 29(6): 616–23.

Clare, L., Wu, Y-T., Jones, I.R., Victor, C.R., Nelis, S.M., Martyr, A., Quinn, C., Litherland, R., Pickett, J.A., Hindle, J.V., Jones, R.W., Knapp, M., Kopelman, M.D., Morris, R.G., Rusted, J.M., Thom, J.M., Lamont, R.A., Henderson, C., Rippon, I., Hillman, A., Matthews, F.E., On behalf of the IDEAL study team. (2019). 'A comprehensive model of factors associated with subjective perceptions of "living well" with dementia: findings from the IDEAL study', *Alzheimer Disease and Associated Disorders*, 33, 36–41.

Clark, C., Smuk, M., Lain, D., Stansfeld, S.A., Carr, E., Head, J. and Vickerstaff, S. (2017). 'Impact of childhood and adulthood psychological health on labour force participation and exit in later life', *Psychological Medicine*, 47(9): 1597–608.

Clark, D.O. (1999) 'Identifying psychological, physiological, and environmental barriers and facilitators to exercise among older low income adults', *Journal of Clinical Geropsychology*, 5(1): 51–62.

Clarke, A., Hanson, E.J. and Ross, H. (2003) 'Seeing the person behind the patient: enhancing the care of older people using a biographical approach', *Journal of Clinical Nursing*, 12(5): 697–706.

Clarke, C.L. and Heyman, B. (1998) 'Risk management for people with dementia', in B. Heyman (ed) *Risk, Health and Health Care: A Qualitative Approach*, London: Edward Arnold, pp 228–40.

Clarke, J., Newman, J. and Westmarland, L. (2007) 'Creating citizen-consumers? Public service reform and (un) willing selves', in S. Maasen and B. Sutter (eds) *On Willing Selves*, London: Palgrave Macmillan, pp 125–45.

Clarke, P., Ailshire, J., House, J., Morenoff, J., King, K., Melendez, R. and Langa, K. (2012) 'Cognitive function in the community setting: the neighbourhood as a source of "cognitive reserve"?', *Journal of Epidemiology and Community Health*, 66(8): 730–6.

Clegg, A., Young, J., Iliffe, S., Rikkert, M. and Rockwood, K. (2013) 'Frailty in elderly people', *The Lancet*, 381(9868): 752–62.

Clegg, A., Bates, C., Young, J., Ryan, R., Nichols, L., Teale, E., Mohammed, M.A., Parry, J. and Marshall, T. (2016) 'Development and validation of an electronic frailty index using routine primary care electronic health record data', *Age and Ageing*, 45(3): 353–60.

Cohen-Mansfield, J. and Taylor, J.W. (2004) 'Hearing aid use in nursing homes. Part 2: barriers to effective utilization of hearing aids', *Journal of the American Medical Directors Association*, 5(5): 289–96.

Cohen-Mansfield, J., Golander, H. and Arnheim, G. (2000) 'Self-identity in older persons suffering from dementia: preliminary results', *Social Science and Medicine*, 51(3): 381–94.

Cole, T.R. and Sierpina, M. (2007) 'Humanistic gerontology and the meaning(s) of aging', in J.M. Wilmot and K.F. Ferraro (eds) *Gerontology: Perspectives and Issues*, New York: Springer, pp 245–63.

Commission for Health Improvement (2004) *Lessons from Commission for Health Improvement Investigations 2000–2003*, London: The Stationery Office.

Commission on Dignity in Care for Older People (2012) *Delivering Dignity: Securing Dignity in Care for Older People in Hospitals and Care*, London: Local Government Association, NHS Confederation and Age UK.

Commission on the Future of Health and Social Care in England (2014) *A New Settlement for Health and Social Care*, London: The King's Fund.

Commission on Social Determinants of Health (2008) *Final Report. Closing the Gap in a Generation: Health Equity through Action on the Social Determinants of Health*, Geneva: World Health Organization.

Compton, S.A., Flanagan, P. and Gregg, W. (1997) 'Elder abuse in people with dementia in Northern Ireland: prevalence and predictors in cases referred to a psychiatry of old age service', *International Journal of Geriatric Psychiatry*, 12(6): 632–5.

Conwell, Y., Duberstein, P.R. and Caine, E.D. (2010) 'Health status and suicide in the second half of life', *International Journal of Geriatric Psychiatry*, 25(4): 371–9.

Cooper, C., Selwood, A. and Livingstone, G. (2008) 'The prevalence of elder abuse and neglect: a systematic review', *Age and Ageing*, 37(2): 151–60.

Cooper, C., Katona, C., Orrell, M. and Livingston, G. (2006) 'Coping strategies and anxiety in caregivers of people with Alzheimer's disease: The LASER-AD study', *Journal of Affective Disorders*, 90(1): 15–20.

Cooper, C., Blanchard, M., Selwood, A. and Livingstone, G. (2010) 'Antidementia drugs: prescription by level of cognitive impairment or by socio-economic group?', *Aging and Mental Health*, 14(1): 85–9.Cooper, C., Selwood, A., Blanchard, M., Walker, Z., Blizard, R. and Livingstone, G. (2009) 'Abuse of people with dementia by family carers: representative cross sectional survey', *British Medical Journal*, 338: b155.

Cooper, C., Lodwick, R., Walters, K., Raine, R., Manthorpe, J., Iliffe, S. and Petersen, I. (2016) 'Inequalities in receipt of mental and physical healthcare in people with dementia in the UK', *Age and Ageing*, 46(3): 393–400.

Cooper, C., Bebbington, P., King, M., Jenkins, R., Farrell, M., Brugha, T., McManus, R., Stewart, R. and Livingston, G. (2011) 'Happiness across age groups: results from the 2007 National Psychiatric Morbidity Survey', *International Journal of Geriatric Psychiatry*, 26(6): 608–14.

Cordner, Z., Blass, D.M., Rabins, P.V. and Black, B.S. (2010) 'Quality of life in nursing home residents with advanced dementia', *Journal of the American Geriatrics Society*, 58(12): 2394–400.

Cornwell, E.Y. and Waite, L.J. (2009) 'Social disconnectedness, perceived isolation, and health among older adults', *Journal of Health and Social Behavior*, 50(1): 31–48.

Cortes, B.P., Demoulin, S., Rodriguez, R.T., Rodriguez, A.P. and Leyens, J.P. (2005) 'Infrahumanization or familiarity? Attribution of uniquely human emotions to the self, the ingroup, and the outgroup', *Personality and Social Psychology Bulletin*, 31(2): 243–53.

Crampton, J., Dean, J. and Eley, R. (2012) *Creating a Dementia-Friendly York*, York: Joseph Rowntree Foundation.

Crane, M. and Warnes, A.M. (2010) 'Homelessness among older people and service responses', *Reviews in Clinical Gerontology*, 20(4): 354–63.

Creighton, A.S., Davison, T.E. and Kissane, D.W. (2017) 'The correlates of anxiety among older adults in nursing homes and other residential aged care facilities: a systematic review', *International Journal of Geriatric Psychiatry*, 32(2): 141–54.

Crepaz-Keay, D. (2016) 'Improving mental health in later life: the role of service user involvement', *Special Issue of Quality in Ageing, Mental Health and Later Life*, 17(3): 179–88.

Crespo, M., Hornillos, C. and Gómez, M.M. (2013) 'Assessing quality of life of nursing home residents with dementia: feasibility and limitations in patients with severe cognitive impairment', *International Psychogeriatrics*, 25(10): 1687–95.

Crome, I., Dar, K., Janikiewicz, S., Rao, T. and Tarbuck, A. (2011) '*Our Invisible Addicts. First report of the Older Persons' Substance Misuse Working Group of the Royal College of Psychiatrists. College Report CR165*, London: Royal College of Psychiatrists.

Crosland, A. and Wallace. A. (2011) 'Mental Health Promotion in Later Life', in J. Keady and S. Watts (eds) *Mental Health and Later Life: Developing a Holistic Model for Practice*, Oxon: Routledge, pp 35–54.

Cross-Party Group on Alzheimer's (2009) *Scottish Charter of Rights for People Living with Dementia and their Carers*, Edinburgh: Cross-Party Group on Alzheimer's.

Crystal, S. (2006) 'Dynamics of late-life inequality: Modeling the interplay of health disparities, economic resources, and public policies', in J. Bars, D. Dannefer, C. Phillipson and A. Walker (eds) *Aging, Globalization and Inequality: The New Critical Gerontology*, Oxon: Routledge, pp 205–13.

Crystal, S. and Shea, D. (2003) *Focus on Economic Outcomes in Later Life: Public Policy, Health, and Cumulative Advantage*, New York: Springer.

Cullum, S. (2013) 'Management of dementia', in T. Dening and A. Thomas (eds) *The Oxford Textbook of Old Age Psychiatry*, Oxford: Oxford University Press, pp 513–24.

Curtis, S. (2010) *Space, Place and Mental Health*, Farnham: Ashgate.

Da Silva, J., Goncalves-Pereira, M., Xavier, M. and Mukaetova-Ladinska, E.B. (2013) 'Affective disorders and risk of developing dementia: systematic review', *The British Journal of Psychiatry*, 202(3), 177–86.

Dahlgren G. and Whitehead M. (1991) *Policies and Strategies to Promote Social Equity in Health*, Stockholm: Institute for Futures Studies.

Dalby, D.M., Hirdes, J.P., Hogan, D.B., Patten, S.B., Beck, C.A., Rabinowitz, T. and Maxwell, C.J. (2008) 'Potentially inappropriate management of depressive symptoms among Ontario home care clients', *International Journal of Geriatric Psychiatry*, 23(6): 650–9.

Daniel, B. and Bowes, A. (2011) 'Re-Thinking harm and abuse: insights from a lifespan perspective', *British Journal of Social Work*, 41(5), 820–36.

Daniels, N., Kennedy, B. and Kawachi, I. (2000) *Is Inequality Bad for Our Health?*, Boston, MA: Beacon Press.

Dannefer, D. (1987) 'Aging as intracohort differentiation: accentuation, the Matthew effect, and the life course', *Sociological Forum*, 2(2): 211–36.

Dannefer, D. (2003) 'Cumulative advantage/disadvantage and the life course: cross-fertilizing age and social science theory', *The Journals of Gerontology Series B: Psychological Sciences and Social Sciences*, 58(6): S327–37.

Dannefer, D. (2011) 'Age, the life course, and the sociological imagination: prospects for theory', in R.H. Binstock and L.K. George (eds) *Handbook of Aging and the Social Sciences* (7th edn), London: Elsevier, pp 3–16.

Dannefer, D. and Settersten, R.A. (2010) 'The study of the life course: implications for social gerontology', in D. Dannefer and R.A. Settersten (eds) *The SAGE Handbook of Social Gerontology*, London: SAGE Publications, pp 3–19.

Darch, K. (2014) Gloucestershire Village and Community Agents: April 2013 to March 2014 Full Year Report, [online] www.cpa.org.uk/cpa-lga-evidence/Gloucestershire_Rural_Community_Council/VillageandCommunityAgentEndofYearReportFINAL.pdf [Accessed 13 January 2019]

Davis, D.H. (2004) 'Dementia: sociological and philosophical constructions', *Social Science and Medicine*, 58(2): 369–78.

Davis, N.J. (2005) 'Cycles of discrimination: older women, cumulative disadvantages, and retirement consequences', *Journal of Education Finance*, 31(1): 65–81.

Davison, T.E., Mccabe, M.P., Mellor, D., Ski, C., George, K. and Moore, K.A. (2007) 'The prevalence and recognition of major depression among low-level aged care residents with and without cognitive impairment', *Aging and Mental Health*, 11(1): 82–8.

De Botton, A. (2004) *Status Anxiety*, London: Hamish Hamilton.

De Donder, L., Lang, G., Luoma, M.L., Penhale, B., Alves, J.F., Tamutiene, I., Santos, A.J., Koivusilta, M., Enzenhofer, E., Perttu, S., Savola, T. and Verte, D. (2011) 'Perpetrators of abuse against older women: a multi-national study in Europe', *The Journal of Adult Protection*, 13(6): 302–14.

De Vogli, R., Brunner, E. and Marmot, M.G. (2007) 'Unfairness and the social gradient of metabolic syndrome in the Whitehall II Study', *Journal of Psychosomatic Research*, 63(4): 413–19.

De Vries, B. (2007) 'LGBT couples in later life: a study in diversity', *Generations*, 31(3): 18–23.

DeHart, D.D., Follingstad, D.R. and Fields, A.M. (2010) 'Does context matter in determining psychological abuse? Effects of pattern, harm, relationship, and norms', *Journal of Family Violence*, 25(5): 461–74.

Dementia Action Alliance (2010) *National Dementia Declaration for England*, London: Dementia Action Alliance.

Dementia Action Alliance (2017) *National Dementia Declaration for England*, London: Dementia Action Alliance.

Dementia Alliance International (2016) *The Human Rights of People Living with Dementia: from Rhetoric to Reality*, [online] www.dementiaallianceinternational.org/wp-content/uploads/2016/04/The-Human-Rights-of-People-Living-with-Dementia-from-Rhetoric-to-Reality.pdf [Accessed 13 January 2019].

Dementiavoices.org.uk (2018) *What is DEEP?*, [online] http://dementiavoices.org.uk/ [Accessed 13 January 2019].

Dening, T. and Milne, A. (eds) (2011) *Mental Health and Care Homes*, Oxford: Oxford University Press.

Dening, T. and Milne, A. (2013) 'Mental health in care homes for older people', in T. Dening and A. Thomas (eds) *The Oxford Textbook of Old Age Psychiatry*, Oxford: Oxford University Press, pp 343–58.

Dening, T. and Milne, A. (2020) 'Mental health in care homes for older people', in T. Dening, A. Thomas, R. Stewart and J-P. Taylor (eds) *Oxford Textbook of Old Age Psychiatry* (3rd edn), Oxford: Oxford University Press, pp 343–58. Dening, T. and Thomas, A. (eds) (2013) *Oxford Textbook of Old Age Psychiatry*, Oxford: Oxford University Press.

Department for Work and Pensions (2012) *Households below Average Income 2010/11*, London: Department for Work and Pensions.

Department for Work and Pensions (2014) *Fuller Working Lives: A Framework for Action*, London: Department for Work and Pensions.

Department for Work and Pensions (2017a) *Households below Average Income: An Analysis of the UK Income Distribution 1994/95 to 2015/16*, London: Department for Work and Pensions.

Department for Work and Pensions (2017b) *Income-Related Benefits: Estimates of Take-Up: Financial Year 2015/16, (Tables PC2, HB2)*, London: Department for Work and Pensions.

Department of Communities and Local Government (2013) *English Housing Survey Household Report 2011/12*, London: Department of Communities and Local Government.

Department of Communities and Local Government (2014) *Local Authority Revenue Expenditure and Financing: 2014–15 Budget, England (revised)*, [online] https://assets.publishing.service.gov.uk/government/uploads/system/uploads/attachment_data/file/365581/RA_Budget_2014-15_Statistical_Release.pdf [Accessed 5 December 2018].

Department of Health (2005) *Securing Better Mental Health in Older Adults*, London: Department of Health.

Department of Health (2009a) *Tackling Health Inequalities: 10 Years On*, London: Department of Health.

Department of Health (2009b) *New Horizons: Towards a Shared Vision for Mental Health*, London: Department of Health.

Department of Health (2009c) *Let's Get Moving: Commissioning Guidance*, London: Department of Health.

Department of Health (2009d) *Living Well with Dementia: A National Dementia Strategy*, London: Department of Health.

Department of Health (2010a) *A Vision for Adult Social Care: Capable Communities and Active Citizens*, London: Department of Health.

Department of Health (2010b) *Improving Care and Saving Money*, London: Department of Health.

Department of Health (2011a) *Public Health in Local Government: Factsheet*, London: Department of Health.

Department of Health (2011b) *Talking Therapies: A Four-Year Plan of Action*, London: Department of Health.

Department of Health (2012a) *Prime Minister's Dementia Challenge*, London: Department of Health.

Department of Health (2012b) Health and Social Care Act, London: Department of Health.

Department of Health (2013) *G8 Summit: Global Action Against Dementia*, London: Department of Health.

Department of Health (2014) *Wellbeing across the Lifecourse: Ageing Well*, London: Health Improvement Analytical Team, Department of Health.

Department of Health (2015a) *Government Response to the Consultation: Refreshing the Public Health Outcomes Framework*, London: Department of Health.

Department of Health (2015b) *Prime Minister's Challenge on Dementia 2020*, London: Department of Health.

Department of Health (2016) *Prime Minister's Challenge on Dementia 2020: Implementation Plan*, London: Department of Health.

Department of Health (2017) *A Framework for Mental Health Research*, London: Department of Health.

Department of Health, Social Services and Public Safety (2012) *Service Framework for Mental Health and Wellbeing*, Belfast: Department of Health, Social Services and Public Safety.

Depp, C.A and Jeste, D.V (2006) 'Definitions and predictors of successful aging: a comprehensive review of larger quantitative studies', *American Journal of Geriatric Psychiatry*, 14(1): 6–20.

Dewar, B.J. (2005) 'Beyond tokenistic involvement of older people in research – a framework for future development and understanding', *Journal of Clinical Nursing*, 14: 48–53.

Dewilde, C. (2012) 'Lifecourse determinants and incomes in retirement: Belgium and the United Kingdom compared', *Ageing and Society*, 32(4): 587–615.

Dewing, J. (2002) 'From ritual to relationship: a person-centred approach to consent in qualitative research with older people who have a dementia', *Dementia*, 1(2): 157–71.

Dewing, J. (2007) 'Participatory research: a method for process consent with persons who have dementia', *Dementia*, 6(1): 11–25.

Di Gessa, G., Corna, L.M., Platts, L.G., Worts, D., McDonough, P., Sacker, A., Price, D. and Glaser, K. (2017) 'Is being in paid work beyond state pension age beneficial for health? Evidence from England using a life-course approach', *Journal of Epidemiology and Community Health*, 71(5): 431–8.

Dickerson, S.S. and Kemeny, M.E. (2004) 'Acute stressors and cortisol responses: a theoretical integration and synthesis of laboratory research', *Psychological Bulletin*, 130(3): 355–91.

Diehl, M., Marsiske, M., Horgas, A.L., Rosenberg, A., Saczynski, J.S. and Willis, S.L. (2005) 'The revised observed tasks of daily living: a performance-based assessment of everyday problem solving in older adults', *Journal of Applied Gerontology*, 24(3): 211–30.

Diener, E., Suh, E.M., Lucas, R.E. and Smith, H.L. (1999) 'Subjective well-being: three decades of progress', *Psychological Bulletin*, 125(2): 276–302.

Diniz, B.S., Butters, M.A., Albert, S.M., Dew, M.A. and Reynolds, C.F. (2013) 'Late-life depression and risk of vascular dementia and Alzheimer's disease: systematic review and meta-analysis of community-based cohort studies', *The British Journal of Psychiatry*, 202(5): 329–35.

Dixon-Woods, M. and Angell, E.L. (2009) 'Research involving adults who lack capacity: how have research ethics committees interpreted the requirements?', *Journal of Medical Ethics*, 35(6): 377–81.

Djernes, J.K. (2006) 'Prevalence and predictors of depression in populations of elderly: a review', *Acta Psychiatrica Scandinavica*, 113(5): 372–87.

Dong, X., Chen, R., Chang, E.S. and Simon, M. (2013) 'Elder abuse and psychological well-being: a systematic review and implications for research and policy. A mini review', *Gerontology*, 59(2): 132–42.

Donovan, C. and Hester, M. (2010) 'I hate the word "victim": an exploration of recognition of domestic violence in same sex relationships', *Social Policy and Society*, 9(2): 279–89.

Dorling, D. (2011) *So You Think You Know About Britain?* London: Constable.

Dow, B. and Joosten, M. (2012) 'Understanding elder abuse: a social rights perspective', *International Psychogeriatrics*, 24(6): 853–55.

Dow, B. and Gaffy, E. (2015) 'Mental health and well-being in older people. Commentary paper', *Australasian Journal on Ageing*, 34(4): 220–3.

Downs, M. (2000) 'Dementia in a socio-cultural context: an idea whose time has come', *Ageing and Society*, 20(3): 369–75.

Doyle, P.J. and Rubinstein, R.L. (2013) 'Person-centered dementia care and the cultural matrix of othering', *The Gerontologist*, 54(6): 952–63.

Draper, H. and Fenton, S-J. (2014) *General Patterns of Health Inequality are Repeated in the Older Population*, Birmingham: University of Birmingham.

Duberstein, P.R., Conwell, Y., Conner, K.R., Eberly, S., Evinger, J.S. and Caine, E.D. (2004) 'Poor social integration and suicide: fact or artifact? A case-control study', *Psychological Medicine*, 34(7): 1331–7.

Durai, U.N.B., Chopra, M.P., Coakley, E., Llorente, M.D., Kirchner, J.E., Cook, J.M. and Levkoff, S.E. (2011) 'Exposure to trauma and posttraumatic stress disorder symptoms in older veterans attending primary care: comorbid conditions and self-rated health status', *Journal of the American Geriatrics Society*, 59(6): 1087–92.

Dyer, C.B., Pavlik, V.N., Murphy, K.P. and Hyman, D.J. (2000) 'The high prevalence of depression and dementia in elder abuse or neglect', *Journal of the American Geriatrics Society*, 48(2): 205–8.

Edmondson, R. (2013) 'The sociology of ageing', in T. Dening and A. Thomas (eds) *The Oxford Textbook of Old Age Psychiatry*, Oxford: Oxford University Press, pp 589–602.

Edmunds, D., Petterson, L. and Golder, I. (2013) *Let's Get Physical: The Impact of Physical Activity on Wellbeing*, London: Mental Health Foundation.

Edvardsson, D., Petersson, L., Sjogren, K., Lindkvist, M. and Sandman, P.O. (2014) 'Everyday activities for people with dementia in residential aged care: associations with person-centredness and quality of life', *International Journal of Older People Nursing*, 9(4): 269–76.

Ehrhardt, J.J., Saris, W.E. and Veenhoven, R. (2000) 'Stability of life-satisfaction over time', *Journal of Happiness Studies*, 1(2): 177–205.

Eikemo, T.A., Bambra, C., Judge, K. and Ringdal, K. (2008) 'Welfare state regimes and differences in self-perceived health in Europe: a multilevel analysis', *Social Science and Medicine*, 66(11): 2281–95.

Eley, S. (2003) 'Diversity among carers', in K. Stalker (ed) *Reconceptualising Work with 'Carers': New Directions for Policy and Practice*, London: Jessica Kingsley Publishers, pp 56–71.

Elming, W., Joyce, R. and Dias, M.C. (2016) *Gender Wage Gap Grows Year on Year After Childbirth as Mothers in Low-Hours Jobs See No Wage Progression*, London: Institute for Fiscal Studies, [online] http://josephrowntreefoundation.cmail19.com/t/y-l-duhijhd-jkwjitha-t/ [Accessed 13 January 2019].

Erevelles, N. (2002) 'Cognitive disability, race, and the politics of citizenship', *Disability, Culture, and Education*, 1(1): 5–25.

Erikson, E.H., Erikson, J.M. and Kivnick, H.Q. (1986) *Vital Involvement in Old Age: The Experience of Old Age in Our Time*, New York: Norton.

Eriksson, C. and Saveman, B.I. (2002) 'Nurses' experiences of abusive/non-abusive caring for demented patients in acute care settings', *Scandinavian Journal of Caring Sciences*, 16(1): 79–85.

Eritz, H., Hadjistavropoulos, T., Williams, J., Kroeker, K., Martin, R.R., Lix, L.M. and Hunter, P.V. (2016) 'A life history intervention for individuals with dementia: a randomised controlled trial examining nursing staff empathy, perceived patient personhood and aggressive behaviours', *Ageing and Society*, 36(10): 2061–89.

Erlangsen, A., Zarit, S.H. and Conwell, Y. (2008) 'Hospital-diagnosed dementia and suicide: a longitudinal study using prospective nationwide register data', *American Journal of Geriatric Psychiatry*, 16(3): 220–8.

Erol, R., Brooker, D. and Peel, E. (2015) *Women and Dementia: A Global Research Review*, London: Alzheimer's Disease International.

Eskelinen, K., Hartikainen, S. and Nykanen, I. (2016) 'Is Loneliness Associated with Malnutrition in Older People?', *International Journal of Gerontology*, 10: 43–5.

Estes, C., Biggs, S. and Phillipson, C. (2003) *Social Theory, Social Policy and Ageing: A Critical Introduction*, Buckingham, Open University Press.

Ettema, T.P., Dröes, R.M., de Lange, J., Mellenbergh, G.J. and Ribbe, M.W. (2007) 'QUALIDEM: Development and evaluation of a dementia specific quality of life instrument validation', *International Journal of Geriatric Psychiatry*, 22: 424–30.

Ettema, T.P., Dröes, R.M., de Lange, J., Ooms, M.E., Mellenbergh, G.J. and Ribbe, M.W. (2005) 'The concept of quality of life in dementia in the different stages of the disease', *International Psychogeriatrics*, 17(3): 353–70.

European Commission (2009) *Impact Assessment Guidelines*, [online] http://ec.europa.eu/smart-regulation/impact/commission_guidelines/docs/iag_2009_en.pdf [Accessed 13 January 2019].

Evandrou, M., Falkingham, J., Gomez Leon, M., Robards, J. and Vlachantoni, A. (2015) *Local Government and the Demography of Ageing*, Southampton: University of Southampton.

Evans, G.W., Wells, N.M. and Moch, A. (2003a) 'Housing and mental health: a review of the evidence and a methodological and conceptual critique', *Journal of Social Issues*, 59: 475–500.

Evans, O., Singleton, N., Meltzer, H., Stewart, R. and Prince, M. (2003b) *The Mental Health of Older People*, London: The Stationery Office.

Faculty of Public Health and Mental Health Foundation (2016) *Better Mental Health for All: A Public Health Approach to Mental Health Improvement*, London: Faculty of Public Health and Mental Health Foundation.

Fairley, L., Baker, M., Whiteway, J., Cross, W. and Forman, D. (2009) 'Trends in non-metastatic prostate cancer management in the Northern and Yorkshire region of England, 2000–2006', *British Journal of Cancer*, 101(11): 1839–45.

Fawcett, B. and Reynolds, J. (2010) 'Mental health and older women: the challenges for social perspectives and community capacity building', *British Journal of Social Work*, 40: 1488–1502.

Featherstone, K., Northcott, A., Bridges, J., Harrison Dening, K., Harden, J., Bale, S., Hopkinson, J., Tope, R., Hillman, A. and King, M. (2018) *Summary Results: An Evidence-Based Investigation Examining the Care People Living with Dementia Receive Following Acute Hospital Admission*, London: Stories of Dementia.

Fenton, W. (2015) *The Size and Structure of the Adult Social Care Sector and Workforce in England, 2015*, London: Skills for Care.

Ferguson, I. (2007) 'Increasing user choice or privatizing risk? The antinomies of personalization', *British Journal of Social Work*, 37(3): 387–403.

Fernandez, J.L., Snell T., Forder J. and Wittenberg, R. (2013) *Implications of Setting Eligibility Criteria for Adult Social Care Services in England at the Moderate Needs Level*. PSSRU Discussion Paper 2851. London: Personal Social Services Research Unit.

Ferraro, F.R., Muehlenkamp, J.J., Paintner, A., Wasson, K., Hager, T. and Hoverson, F. (2008) 'Aging, body image, and body shape', *The Journal of General Psychology*, 135(4): 379–92.

Ferraro, K.F., Shippee, T.P. and Schafer, M.H. (2009) 'Cumulative inequality theory for research on aging and the life course', in V.L. Bengtson, D. Gans, N.M. Pulney and M. Silverstein (eds) *Handbook of Theories of Aging*, New York: Springer, pp 413–33.

Ferri, C.P., Prince, M., Brayne, C., Brodaty, H., Fratiglioni, L., Ganguli, M., Hall, K., Hasegawa, K., Hendrie, H., Huang, Y., Jorm, A., Mathers, C., Menezes, P.R., Rimmer, E. and Acazufca, M. (2005) 'Global prevalence of dementia: a Delphi consensus study', *The Lancet*, 366(9503): 2112–17.

Fiori, K.L., Antonucci, T.C. and Cortina, K.S. (2006) 'Social network typologies and mental health among older adults', *The Journals of Gerontology Series B: Psychological Sciences and Social Sciences*, 61(1): 25–32.

Fisher, B.S. and Regan, S.L. (2006) 'The extent and frequency of abuse in the lives of older women and their relationship with health outcomes', *The Gerontologist*, 46(2): 200–9.

Fisher, M., Qureshi, H., Hardyman, W. and Homewood, J. (2006) *Using Qualitative Research in Systematic Reviews: Older People's Views of Hospital Discharge*, London: Social Care Institute for Excellence.

Fletcher, A., Smeeth, L. and Breeze, E. (2002) 'The end of age: But not for the worse off', *Age and Ageing*, 31(1): 11–12.

Floyd, M., Rice, J. and Black, S.R. (2002) 'Recurrence of posttraumatic stress disorder in late life: a cognitive aging perspective', *Journal of Clinical Geropsychology*, 8(4): 303–11.

Foot, J. (2012) *What Makes Us Healthy? The Asset Approach in Practice: Evidence, Action, Evaluation*, [online] http://silkandtweed.info/lovebespokepas/wp-content/uploads/2012/06/what_makes_us_healthy.pdf [Accessed 13 January 2019].

Forde, I. and Raine, R. (2008) 'Placing the individual within a social determinants approach to health inequity', *The Lancet*, 372(9650): 1694–6.

Forder, J. and Fernández, J-L. (2010) *The Impact of a Tightening Fiscal Situation on Social Care for Older People*, [online] www.pssru.ac.uk/pdf/dp2723.pdf [Accessed 28 August 2016].

Forder, J. and Caiels, J. (2011) 'Measuring the outcomes of long-term care', *Social Science and Medicine*, 73(12): 1766–74.

Forsey, A. (2018) *Hidden Hunger and Malnutrition in the Elderly*, London: All Party Parliamentary Group on Hunger.

Forsman, A.K., Herberts, C., Nyqvist, F., Wahlbeck, K. and Schierenbecks, I. (2013) 'Understanding the role of social capital for mental wellbeing among older adults', *Ageing and Society*, 33(5): 804–25.

Forssen, A.S. (2007) 'Humour, beauty, and culture as personal health resources: experiences of elderly Swedish women', *Scandinavian Journal of Public Health*, 35(3): 228–34.

Fossey, J., Ballard, C., Juszczak, E., James, I., Alder, N., Jacoby, R. and Howard, R. (2006) 'Effect of enhanced psychosocial care on antipsychotic use in nursing home residents with severe dementia: cluster randomised trial', *British Medical Journal*, 332(7544): 756–61.

Fox, K.R. (2003) 'The effects of exercise on self-perceptions and self-esteem', in S.J.H. Biddle, K. Fox and S. Boutcher (eds) *Physical Activity and Psychological Well-Being*, London: Routledge, pp 100–19.

Francis, R. (2013) *Report of the Mid Staffordshire NHS Foundation Trust Public Inquiry*, London: The Stationery Office.

Fratiglioni, L. and Qiu, C. (2013) 'Epidemiology of dementia', in T. Dening and A. Thomas (eds) *The Oxford Textbook of Old Age Psychiatry*, Oxford: Oxford University Press, pp 389–413.

Fratiglioni, L., Paillard-Borg, S. and Winblad, B. (2004) 'An active and socially integrated lifestyle in late life might protect against dementia', *The Lancet Neurology*, 3(6): 343–53.

Friedli, L. (2009) *Mental Health, Resilience and Inequalities*, Copenhagen: World Health Organization.

Fryers, T., Lezer, D., Jenkins, R. and Brugha, T. (2005) 'The distribution of the common mental disorders: social inequalities in Europe', *Journal of Public Mental Health*, 1(14): 1–12

Fuller-Iglesias, H.R., Webster, N.J. and Antonucci, T.C. (2015) 'The complex nature of family support across the life span: implications for psychological well-being', *Developmental Psychology*, 51(3): 277–88.

Gaboda, D., Lucas, J., Siegel, M., Kalay, E. and Crystal, S. (2011) 'No longer undertreated? Depression diagnosis and antidepressant therapy in elderly long-stay nursing home residents, 1999 to 2007', *Journal of the American Geriatrics Society*, 59(4): 673–80.

Gabriel, Z. and Bowling, A. (2004) 'Quality of Life in Old Age from the Perspectives of Older People', in A. Walker and C. Hennessy (eds) *Growing Older: Quality of Life in Old Age*, Maidenhead: Open University Press, pp 14–34.

Garner, J. and Evans, S. (2002) 'An ethical perspective on institutional abuse of older adults', *Psychiatric Bulletin*, 26(5): 164–6.

Garrett, H. and Burris, S. (2015) *Homes and Ageing in England*, Bracknell: IHS BRE Press.

Gatto, S.L. and Tak, S.H. (2008) 'Computer, internet, and e-mail use among older adults: benefits and barriers', *Educational Gerontology*, 34(9): 800–11.

Gauthier, S., Reisberg, B., Zaudig, M., Petersen, R.C., Ritchie, K., Broich, K. and Winblad, B. (2006) 'Mild cognitive impairment', *The Lancet*, 367(9518), 1262–70.

Geda, Y.E., Roberts, R.O., Knopman, D.S., Petersen, R.C., Christianson, T.J., Pankratz, V.S., Smith, G.E., Boeve, B.F., Ivnik, R.J., Tangalos, E.G. and Rocca, W.A. (2008) 'Prevalence of neuropsychiatric symptoms in mild cognitive impairment and normal cognitive aging: population-based study', *Archives of General Psychiatry*, 65(10): 1193–8.

Gerdtham, U.G., Johannesson, M., Lundberg, L. and Isacson, D. (1999) 'The demand for health: results from new measures of health capital', *European Journal of Political Economy*, 15(3): 501–21.

Ghosh, P. (2009) 'Improving access to psychological therapies for all adults', *Psychiatric Bulletin*, 33(5): 186–8.

Gibson, F. (2004) *The Past in the Present: Using Reminiscence in Health and Social Care*, London: Health Professions Press.

Giddens, A. (1999) *Modernity and Self-Identity: Self and Society in the Late Modern Age*, Cambridge: Polity Press.

Giebel, C., Sutcliffe, C., Verbeek, H., Zabalegui, A., Soto, M., Hallberg, I.R., Saks, K., Renom-Guiteras, A. and Challis, D. (2016) 'Depressive symptomatology and associated factors in dementia in Europe: home care versus long-term care', *International Psychogeriatrics*, 28(4): 621–30.

Gilleard, C. and Higgs, P. (2005) *Contexts of Ageing: Class, Cohort and Community*, Cambridge: Polity.

Gilleard, C. and Higgs, P. (2010a) 'Aging without agency: theorizing the fourth age', *Aging and Mental Health*, 14(2): 121–8.

Gilleard, C. and Higgs, P. (2010b) 'Frailty, disability and old age: a re-appraisal', *Health*, 15(5): 475–90.

Gilleard, C. and Higgs, P. (2011) 'Ageing, abjection and embodiment in the fourth age', *Journal of Aging Studies*, 25(2): 135–42.

Gilleard, C. and Higgs, P. (2017) 'Ageing, corporeality and social divisions in later life', *Ageing and Society*, 37(8): 1681–702.

Gilliard, J., Means, R., Beattie, A. and Daker-White, G. (2005) 'Dementia care in England and the social model of disability: lessons and issues', *Dementia*, 4(4): 571–86.

Gilsanz, P., Flatt, J., Quesenberry, C.P. and Whitmer, R.A. (2017) 'Midlife pulmonary function and risk of dementia later in life', *Alzheimer's and Dementia: The Journal of the Alzheimer's Association*, 13(7): 513.

Gladman, J.R.F., Jones, R.G., Radford, K., Walker, E. and Rothera, I. (2007) 'Person-centred dementia services are feasible, but can they be sustained?', *Age and Ageing*, 36(2): 171–6.

Glaser, K., Price, D., Willis, R., Stuchbury, R. and Nicholls, M. (2009) *Life Course Influences and Well-being in Later Life: A Review*, London: King's College London and Department for Work and Pensions.

Glymour, M.M., Weuve, J., Fay, M.E., Glass, T. and Berkman, L.F. (2008). 'Social ties and cognitive recovery after stroke: does social integration promote cognitive resilience?', *Neuroepidemiology*, 31(1): 10–20.

Godfrey, M. (2001) 'Prevention: developing a framework for conceptualizing and evaluating outcomes of preventive services for older people', *Health and Social Care in the Community*, 9(2): 89–99.

Godfrey, M. (2009) 'Depression and anxiety in later life: making the visible invisible', in T. Williamson (ed) *Older People's Mental Health Today: A Handbook*, Brighton: OLM-Pavilion and Mental Health Foundation 2009, pp. 79–95.

Godfrey, M. and Denby, T. (2004) *Depression and Older People*, Bristol: Policy Press and Help the Aged.

Godfrey, M., Townsend, J. and Denby, T. (2004) *Building a Good Life for Older People in Local Communities: Ageing in Time and Place*, York: Joseph Rowntree Foundation.

Godfrey, M., Townsend, J., Surr, C., Boyle, G. and Brooker, D. (2005) *Prevention and Service Provision: Mental Health Problems in Later Life*, Leeds: Institute of Health Sciences and Public Health Research University of Leeds and Division of Dementia Studies University of Bradford.

Goffman, E. (1961) *Asylums: Essays on the Social Situation of Mental Patients and Other Inmates*, Oxford: Doubleday.

Goffman, E. (1963) *Notes on the Management of Spoiled Identity*, New York: Simon and Schuster.

Goldie, I., Dowds, J. and O'Sullivan, C. (2013) *Mental Health and Inequalities, Starting Today*, Background Paper 3, London: Mental Health Foundation.

Goldie, I., Elliott, I., Regan, M., Bernal, L. and Makurah, L. (2016) *Mental Health and Prevention: Taking Local Action*, London: Mental Health Foundation.

Golub, S.A. and Langer, E.J. (2007) 'Challenging assumptions about adult development', in C.M. Aldwin, C.L. Park and A. Spiro, *Handbook of Health Psychology and Aging*, London: The Guilford Press, pp 9–29.

Gostin, O. (2001) 'Public health, ethics, and human rights: a tribute to the late Jonathan Mann Lawrence', *Journal of Medicine and Ethics*, 29(2): 121–30.

Government Office for Science (2008) *Mental Capital and Wellbeing: Making the Most of Ourselves in the 21st Century*, London: Government Office for Science.

Graham, H. (2004) 'Tackling inequalities in health in England: remedying health disadvantages, narrowing health gaps or reducing health gradients?', *Journal of Social Policy*, 33(1): 115–32.

Graham, H. and Power, C. (2004) *Childhood Disadvantage and Adult Health: A Lifecourse Framework*, London: Health Development Agency.

Grant, J. (2013) *Getting on with Life: Baby Boomers, Mental Health and Ageing Well – A Review*, London: Mental Health Foundation.

Gräske, J., Fischer, T., Kuhlmey, A. and Wolf-Ostermann, K. (2012) 'Quality of life in dementia care – differences in quality of life measurements performed by residents with dementia and by nursing staff', *Aging and Mental Health*, 16(7): 819–27.

Green, L. (2010) *Understanding the Life Course: Sociological and Psychological Perspectives*, Cambridge: Polity Press.

Gregg, E.W., Yaffe, K., Cauley, J.A., Rolka, D.B., Blackwell, T.L., Narayan, K.V. and Cummings, S.R. (2000) 'Is diabetes associated with cognitive impairment and cognitive decline among older women?', *Archives of Internal Medicine*, 160(2): 174–80.

Grenier, A. (2006) 'The distinction between being and feeling frail: exploring emotional experiences in health and social care', *Journal of Social Work Practice*, 20(3): 299–313.

Grenier, A. (2007) 'Crossing age and generational boundaries: exploring intergenerational research encounters', *Journal of Social Issues*, 63(4): 713–27.

Grenier, A. (2012) *Transitions and the Lifecourse: Challenging the Constructions of Growing Old*, Bristol: Policy Press.

Grenier, A. and Phillipson, C. (2013) 'Rethinking agency in late life: structural and interpretive approaches', in J. Baars, J. Dohmen, A. Grenier and C. Phillipson (eds) *Ageing, Meaning and Social Structure*, Bristol: Policy Press.

Grenier, A., Lloyd, L. and Phillipson, C. (2017) 'Precarity in late life: rethinking dementia as a "frailed" old age', *Sociology of Health and Illness*, 39(2): 318–30.

Griffin, J. (2010) *The Lonely Society*, London: Mental Health Foundation.

Grundy, E. and Sloggett, A. (2003) 'Health inequalities in the older population: the role of personal capital, social resources and socio-economic circumstances', *Social Science and Medicine*, 56(5): 935–47.

Grundy, E.M. and Tomassini, C. (2010) 'Marital history, health and mortality among older men and women in England and Wales', *BMC Public Health*, 10(1): 554.

Gubrium, A., Harper, K. and Otanez, M. (2016) *Participatory Visual and Digital Research in Action*, London: Routledge.

Gubrium, J. and Holstein, J. (1995) 'Individual agency, the ordinary, and postmodern life', *The Sociological Quarterly*, 36(3): 555–70.

Håkansson, K., Rovio, S., Helkala, E.L., Vilska, A.R., Winblad, B., Soininen, H., Nissinen, A., Mohammed, A.H. and Kivipelto, M. (2009) 'Association between mid-life marital status and cognitive function in later life: population based cohort study', *British Medical Journal*, 339: b2462.

Hall, P. and Taylor, R.C. (2009) 'Health, social relations and public policy', in P.A. Hall and M. Lamont (eds) *Successful Societies: How Institutions and Culture Affect Health*, Cambridge: Cambridge University Press, pp 82–103.

Hallgren, M.Å., Högberg, P. and Andréasson, S. (2010) 'Alcohol consumption and harm among elderly Europeans: falling between the cracks', *European Journal of Public Health*, 20(6): 616–17.

Hamer, M., Lavoie, K.L. and Bacon, S.L. (2014) 'Taking up physical activity in later life and healthy ageing: the English longitudinal study of ageing', *British Journal of Sports Medicine*, 48(3): 239–43.

Hamilton-West, K. (2011) *Psychobiological Processes in Health and Illness*, London: Sage Publications.

Hampson, C. and Morris, K. (2016) 'Dementia: sustaining self in the face of cognitive decline', *Geriatrics*, 1(4): 25.

Hancock, R., Morciano, M. and Pudney, S. (2016) *Disability and Poverty in Later Life*, York: Joseph Rowntree Foundation.

Hankin, C.S., Spiro III, A., Miller, D.R. and Kazis, L. (1999) 'Mental disorders and mental health treatment among US Department of Veterans Affairs outpatients: the Veterans Health Study', *American Journal of Psychiatry*, 156(12): 1924–30.

Hare, P. (2016) *Our Dementia, Our Rights: A Brief Guide Co-Produced by the Dementia Policy Think Tank (Member Group of DEEP) and Innovations in Dementia CIC*, [online] www.innovationsindementia.org.uk/wp-content/uploads/2018/01/Our-dementia-Our-rights-booklet.pdf [Accessed 12 January 2019].

Harris, A.H., Cronkite, R. and Moos, R. (2006). 'Physical activity, exercise coping, and depression in a 10-year cohort study of depressed patients', *Journal of Affective Disorders*, 93(1–3): 79–85.

Harris, T., Carey, I.M., Shah, S.M., DeWilde, S. and Cook, D.G. (2012) 'Antidepressant prescribing in older primary care patients in community and care home settings in England and Wales', *Journal of the American Medical Directors Association*, 13(1): 41–7.

Harrop A. and Jopling, K. (2008) *One Voice: Shaping Our Ageing Society*, London: Age Concern and Help the Aged.

Harwood, J., Hawton, K., Hope, T., Harriss, L. and Jacoby, R. (2006) 'Life problems and physical illness as risk factors for suicide in older people: a descriptive and case control study', *Psychological Medicine*, 36(9): 1265–74.

Haslam, N. and Loughnan, S. (2014) 'Dehumanization and infrahumanization', *Annual Review of Psychology*, 65, 399–423.

Hatton, C. and Walters, J. (2012*) Older People and Personal Budgets: A Re-Analysis of Data from the National Personal Budget Survey 2011*, CeDR Research Report, Lancaster: Lancaster University and in Control.

Hawkley, L.C. and Cacioppo, J.T. (2004) 'Stress and the aging immune system', *Brain, Behavior, and Immunity*, 18(2): 114–19.

Hayes, V. (2013) *Women's Equality in the UK – A Health Check*, Women's Resource Centre, [online] https://tbinternet.ohchr.org/Treaties/CEDAW/Shared%20Documents/GBR/INT_CEDAW_NGO_GBR_13333_E.pdf [Accessed 12 August 2016].

Hayward, M.D. and Gorman, B.K. (2004) 'The long arm of childhood: the influence of early-life social conditions on men's mortality', *Demography*, 41(1): 87–107.

Hayward, M.D., Miles, T.P., Crimmins, E.M. and Yang, Y. (2000) 'The significance of socioeconomic status in explaining the racial gap in chronic health conditions', *American Sociological Review*, 65(6): 910–30.

Health and Social Care Information Centre (2011) *Community Care Statistics 2010–11: Social Services Activity Report, England*, [online] https://files.digital.nhs.uk/publicationimport/pub05xxx/pub05264/comm-care-soci-serv-act-eng-10-11-fin-rep.pdf [Accessed 12 January 2019].

Health Scotland (2004) *Mental Health and Well Being in Later Life: Older People's Perceptions*, Edinburgh: Health Scotland.

Healthcare Commission (2009) *Equalities in Later Life: A National Study of Older People's Mental Health Services*, London: Social Care Institute for Excellence.

Healthy Working Lives and Chartered Institute of Personnel and Development (2012) *Managing a Healthy Ageing Workforce: A National Business Imperative*, [online] www.cipd.co.uk/binaries/managing-a-healthy-ageing-workforce-a-national-business-imperative_2012.pdf [Accessed 13 January 2019].

Heinz, W.R. (2003) 'From work trajectories to negotiated careers: the contingent work life course', in J.T. Mortimer and M.J. Shanahan (eds) *Handbook of the Life Course*, New York: Kluwer Academic Press, pp 185–204.

Hellström, I., Nolan, M. and Lundh, U. (2007) 'Sustaining couplehood: spouses' strategies for living positively with dementia', *Dementia*, 6(3): 383–409.

Help the Aged (2004) *Everyday Age Discrimination – What Older People Say*, London: Help the Aged.

HelpAge International (2015) *A New Convention on the Rights of Older People: A Concrete Proposal*, [online] www.helpage.org/download/5591235a62a92 [Accessed 13 January 2019].

Henwood, M., Larkin, M. and Milne, A. (2019) *The Wood for the Trees: Carer-Related Research and Knowledge*, London: National Institute for Health Research.

Hertzman, C., Frank, J. and Evans, R.G. (1994) 'Heterogeneities in health status and the determinants of population health' in R.G. Evans, M.L. Barer and T.R. Marmor (eds) *Why Are Some People Healthy and Others Not? The Determinants of Health Populations*, pp 67–92.

Hester, M. (2011) 'The three planet model: towards an understanding of contradictions in approaches to women and children's safety in contexts of domestic violence', *British Journal of Social Work*, 41(5): 837–53.

Hiam, L., Dorling, D., Harrison, D. and McKee, M. (2017) 'Why has mortality in England and Wales been increasing? An iterative demographic analysis', *Journal of the Royal Society of Medicine*, 110(4): 153–62.

Higgs, P. and Jones, I.R. (2009) *Medical Sociology and Old Age: Towards a Sociology of Health in Later Life*, Abingdon: Routledge.

Higgs, P. and Gilleard, C. (2016a) *Personhood, Identity and Care in Advanced Old Age*, Bristol: Policy Press.

Higgs, P. and Gilleard, C. (2016b) 'Interrogating personhood and dementia', *Aging and Mental Health*, 20(8): 773–80.

Hill, K., Sutton, L. and Cox, L. (2009) *Managing Resources in Later Life: Older People's Experience of Change and Continuity*, York: Joseph Rowntree Foundation.

Hirsch, R.D. and Vollhardt, B.R. (2008) 'Elder maltreatment', in R. Jacoby, C. Oppenheimer, T. Dening and A. Thomas (eds) *The Oxford Textbook of Old Age Psychiatry*, Oxford: Oxford University Press, pp 731–45.

Hirst, M. (2005) 'Carer distress: a prospective, population-based study', *Social Science and Medicine*, 61(3): 697–708.

Hirst, P. (2009) 'What do you expect at your age?', in T. Williamson (ed) *Older People's Mental Health Today: A Handbook*, Shoreham-by-Sea: Pavilion Publishing, pp 43–50.

Hitchcott, P.K., Fastame, M.C. and Penna, M.P. (2018) 'More to Blue Zones than long life: positive psychological characteristics', *Health, Risk and Society*, 20(3–4): 163–81.

HM Government (2010) *Healthy Lives, Healthy People: Our Strategy for Public Health*, London: The Stationery Office.

HM Government (2011) *No Health without Mental Health, A Cross-Government Mental Health Outcomes Strategy for People of All Ages*, London: Department of Health.

HM Government (2012) *Suicide Prevention Strategy for England*, London: Department of Health.

Hodge, G. (2016) 'Suicide in an ageing UK population: problems and prevention', *Quality in Ageing and Older Adults*, 17(4): 218–28.

Hodson, R. and Keady, J. (2008) 'Mild cognitive impairment: a review and nursing implications', *British Journal of Nursing*, 17(6): 368–73.

Hoe, J., Cooper, C. and Livingston, G. (2013) 'An overview of the LASER-AD study: a longitudinal epidemiological study of people with Alzheimer's disease', *International Review of Psychiatry*, 25(6): 659–72.

Hoe, J., Katona, C., Roch, B. and Livingston, G. (2005) 'Use of the QOL-AD for measuring quality of life in people with severe dementia—the LASER-AD study', *Age and Ageing*, 34(2): 130–5.

Hoe, J., Hancock, G., Livingston, G. and Orrell, M. (2006) 'Quality of life of people with dementia in residential care homes', *The British Journal of Psychiatry*, 188(5): 460–4.

Hoe, J., Hancock, G., Livingston, G., Woods, B., Challis, D. and Orrell, M. (2009) 'Changes in the quality of life of people with dementia living in care homes', *Alzheimer Disease and Associated Disorders*, 23(3): 285–90.

Hogg, J. (2013) 'Delirium', in T. Dening and A. Thomas (eds) *Oxford Textbook of Old Age Psychiatry* (2nd edn), Oxford: Oxford University Press, pp 529–41.

Holstein, M. and Minkler, M. (2007) 'Critical gerontology: reflections for the 21st Century', in M. Bernard and T. Scharf (eds) *Critical Perspectives on Ageing Societies*, Bristol: Policy Press, pp 13–26.

Holt-Lunstad, J., Smith, T.B. and Layton, J.B. (2010) 'Social relationships and mortality risk: a meta-analytic review', *PLoS Medicine*, 7(7): e1000316.

Hood, A. and Waters, T. (2017) *Living Standards, Poverty and Inequality in the UK*, London: Institute for Fiscal Studies.

House of Commons (2017) *The Care Home Market (England)*, Briefing Paper 07463, London: The Stationery Office.

House of Commons Health Select Committee (2013) *Inquiry on Public Health*, London: Parliament.

House of Lords Select Committee (2014) *Review on the Mental Capacity Act 2005*, London: House of Lords.

House of Lords Select Committee on the Equality Act 2010 and Disability (2016) *The Equality Act 2010: The Impact on Disabled People*. London: House of Lords.

Howden-Chapman, P.L., Chandola, T., Stafford, M. and Marmot, M. (2011) 'The effect of housing on the mental health of older people: the impact of lifetime housing history in Whitehall II', *BMC Public Health*, 11(1): 682.

Howse, K. (2005) 'Policies for healthy ageing', *Ageing Horizons*, 2: 3–14.

Hsiao, Y.H., Hung, H.C., Chen, S.H. and Gean, P.W. (2014) 'Social interaction rescues memory deficit in an animal model of Alzheimer's disease by increasing BDNF-dependent hippocampal neurogenesis', *Journal of Neuroscience*, 34(49): 16207–19.

Hu, Y., Leinonen, T., Myrskylä, M. and Martikainen, P. (2018) 'Changes in socioeconomic differences in hospital days with age: cumulative disadvantage, age-as-leveler, or both?', *The Journals of Gerontology, Series B, Psychological Sciences and Social Sciences*.

Huang, C.Q., Wang, Z.R., Li, Y.H., Xie, Y.Z. and Liu, Q.X. (2011) 'Cognitive function and risk for depression in old age: a meta-analysis of published literature', *International Psychogeriatrics*, 23(4): 516–25.

Huang, H.C., Chen, Y.T., Chen, P.Y., Hu, S.H.L., Liu, F., Kuo, Y.L. and Chiu, H.Y. (2015) 'Reminiscence therapy improves cognitive functions and reduces depressive symptoms in elderly people with dementia: a meta-analysis of randomized controlled trials', *Journal of the American Medical Directors Association*, 16(12): 1087–94.

Hubbard, R.E., Goodwin, V.A., Llewellyn, D.J., Warmoth, K. and Lang, I. (2014) 'Frailty, financial resources and subjective well-being in later life', *Archives of Gerontology and Geriatrics*, 58(3): 364–9.

Hughes, B. (1995) *Older People and Community Care: Critical Theory and Practice*, Columbus: McGraw-Hill.

Hughes, J.C. and Williamson, T. (2019) *The Dementia Manifesto: Putting Values-Based Practice to Work*, Cambridge: Cambridge University Press.

Hughes, K., Bellis, M.A., Hardcastle, K.A., Sethi, D., Butchart, A., Mikton, C., Jones, L. and Dunne, M.P. (2017) 'The effects of multiple adverse childhood experiences on health: a systematic review and meta analysis', *The Lancet Public Health*, 2(8): e356–66.

Hughes, M.E. and Waite, L.J. (2009) 'Marital biography and health at mid-life', *Journal of Health and Social Behavior*, 50(3): 344–58.

Hughes, T. (2014) *Stories of Professional Care: Narrative Analysis of Accounts from People with Dementia*, Doctoral dissertation, London: University of East London.

Huisman, M., Read, S., Towriss, C.A., Deeg, D.J.H. and Grundy, E. (2013) 'Socioeconomic inequalities in mortality rates in old age in the World Health Organization European Region', *Epidemiologic Reviews*, 35(1): 84–97.

Hulko, W. (2009) 'From "not a big deal" to "hellish": experiences of older people with dementia', *Journal of Aging Studies*, 23(3): 131–44.

Hulko, W. (2011) 'Intersectoinality in the Context of Later Life Experiences of Dementia', in O. Hankivsky (ed) *Health Inequities in Canada: Intersectional Frameworks and Practices*, Toronto: UBC Press, pp 198–219.

Humphrey, A., Lee, L. and Green, R. (2011) *Aspirations for Later Life*, London: Department for Work and Pensions.

Humphries, R. (2013) *Paying for Social Care: Beyond Dilnot*, London: The King's Fund.

Humphries, R. (2015) 'Health and social care for older people: progress, problems and priorities', *Quality in Ageing and Older Adults*, 16(1): 27–31.

Humphries R., Thorlby, R., Holder, H., Hall, P. and Charles, A. (2016) *Social Care for Older People: Home Truths*, London: The King's Fund.

Huppert, F.A. (2005) 'Positive mental health in individuals and populations', in F. Huppert., N. Bayliss and B. Keverne (eds) *The Science of WellBeing*, Oxford: Oxford University Press.

Huppert, F.A. (2009) 'Psychological well-being: evidence regarding its causes and consequences', *Health and Well-Being*, 1(2): 137–64.

Hurd-Clarke, L.H. and Korotchenko, A. (2016) 'I know it exists… but I haven't experienced it personally': older Canadian men's perceptions of ageism as a distant social problem', *Ageing and Society*, 36(8): 1757–73.

Hutchinson, S.L., Yarnal, C.M., Staffordson, J. and Kerstetter, D.L. (2008) 'Beyond fun and friendship: The Red Hat Society as a coping resource for older women', *Ageing and Society*, 28(7): 979–99.

Hyde, P., Burns, D., Killett, A., Kenkmann, A., Poland, F. and Gray, R. (2014) 'Organisational aspects of elder mistreatment in long-term care', *Quality in Ageing and Older Adults*, 15(4): 197–209.

Hyden, L.C. and Nilsson, E. (2015) 'Couples with dementia: positioning the "we"', *Dementia*, 14(6): 716–33.

Ichida, Y., Hirai, H., Kondo, K., Kawachi, I., Takeda, T. and Endo, H. (2013) 'Does social participation improve self-rated health in the older population? A quasi-experimental intervention study', *Social Science and Medicine*, 94: 83–90.

Iliffe, S. and Manthorpe, J. (2016) 'The dementias: risks to self and others', in C.A. Chew-Graham and M. Ray (eds) *Mental Health and Older People: A Guide for Primary Care Practitioner*, New York: Springer, pp 301–8.

Ingersoll-Dayton, B., Spencer, B., Kwak, M., Scherrer, K., Allen, R.S. and Campbell, R. (2013) 'The couples life story approach: a dyadic intervention for dementia', *Journal of Gerontological Social Work*, 56(3): 237–54.

Innes, A. and Manthorpe, J. (2013) 'Developing theoretical understandings of dementia and their application to dementia care policy in the UK', *Dementia*, 12(6): 682–96.

Institute for Public Policy Research (2018) *Better Health and Care for All*, London: Institute for Public Policy Research.

Institute of Social and Economic Research (2017) *How Well are Older People Doing? Case Study*, Colchester: University of Essex.

International Longevity Centre (2011) *Good Neighbours: Measuring Quality of Life in Older Age*, London: ILC-UK.

International Longevity Centre (2013) *Has the Sisterhood Forgotten Older Women?*, London: ILC-UK.

International Longevity Centre (2014) *Preventing Dementia: A Provocation*, London: ILC-UK.

Ipsos MORI (2015) *Later Life in 2015: An Analysis of the Views and Experiences of People Aged 60 and Over*, London: Centre for Ageing Better.

Isherwood, L.M., King, D.S. and Luszcz, M.A. (2017) 'Widowhood in the fourth age: support exchange, relationships and social participation', *Ageing and Society*, 37(1), 188–212.

Ismail, M., Hussein, S., Stevens, M., Woolham, J., Manthorpe, J., Aspinal, F., Baxter, K. and Samsi, K. (2017) 'Do personal budgets increase the risk of abuse? Evidence from English national data', *Journal of Social Policy*, 46(2): 291–311.

Jackson, J.S. and Knight, K.M. (2006) 'Race and self-regulatory health behaviors: the role of the stress response and the HPA axis in physical and mental health disparities', in K.W. Schaie and L.L. Carstensen (eds) *Societal Impact on Aging Series. Social Structures, Aging, and Self-Regulation in the Elderly*, New York: Springer, pp 189–239.

Jackson, S.E., Hackett, R.A. and Steptoe, A. (2019) 'Associations between age discrimination and health and wellbeing: cross-sectional and prospective analysis of the English Longitudinal Study of Ageing', *The Lancet Public Health*, 4(4): 200–8.

James, I.A. and Jackman, L. (2017) *Understanding Behaviour in Dementia that Challenges: A Guide to Assessment and Treatment*, London: Jessica Kingsley Publishers.

Jeary, K. (2005) 'Sexual abuse and sexual offending against elderly people: a focus on perpetrators and victims', *Journal of Forensic Psychiatry and Psychology*, 16(2): 328–43.

Jenkins, R., Bhugra, D., Bebbington, P., Brugha, T., Farrell, M., Coid, J., Fryers, T., Weich, S., Singleton, N. and Meltzer, H. (2008). 'Debt, income and mental disorder in the general population', *Psychological Medicine*, 38(10): 1485–93.

Jivraj, S., Nazroo, J., Vanhoutte, B. and Chandola, T. (2013) *Age, Ageing and Subjective Wellbeing in Later Life*, Manchester: Centre for Census and Survey Research.

Johansson, L., Guo, X., Waern, M., Östling, S., Gustafson, D., Bengtsson, C. and Skoog, I. (2010) 'Midlife psychological stress and risk of dementia: a 35-year longitudinal population study', *Brain*, 133(8): 2217–24.

Johnson, C.L. and Barer, B.M. (1997) *Life Beyond 85 Years: The Aura of Survivorship*, New York: Springer.

Johnstone, L. and Boyle, M. (2018) *The Power Threat Meaning Framework: Towards the Identification of Patterns in Emotional Distress, Unusual Experiences and Troubled or Troubling Behaviour, as an Alternative to Functional Psychiatric Diagnosis*, Leicester: British Psychological Society.

Jones, I.R. (2017) 'Social class, dementia and the fourth age', *Sociology of Health and Illness*, 39(2): 303–17.

Jones, I.R. and Higgs, P. (2015) 'Class and health inequalities in later life', in M. Formosa and P. Higgs (eds) *Social Class in Later Life*, Bristol: Policy Press.

Joseph Rowntree Foundation (2016) *UK Poverty: Causes, Costs and Solutions*, [online] https://www.jrf.org.uk/report/uk-poverty-causes-costs-and-solutions [Accessed 13 January 2019].

Kafonek, S., Ettinger, W.H., Roca, R., Kittner, S., Taylor, N. and German, P.S. (1989) 'Instruments for screening for depression and dementia in a long-term care facility', *Journal of the American Geriatrics Society*, 37(1): 29–34.

Kahn, R.L. and Antonucci, T.C. (1980) 'Convoys over the life course: attachment, roles, and social support', in P.B. Baltes and O.G. Grim (eds) *Life Span Development and Behavior*, New York: Academic Press, pp 253–86.

Kanabar, R. (2012) *Unretirement in England: An Empirical Perspective*, Discussion Papers in Economics No 12/31, York: University of York.

Kane, M. and Cook, L. (2013) *Dementia 2013: The Hidden Voice of Loneliness*, London: Alzheimer's Society.

Kanner, A.D., Coyne, J.C., Schaefer, C. and Lazarus, R.S. (1981) 'Comparison of two modes of stress measurement: daily hassles and uplifts versus major life events', *Journal of Behavioral Medicine*, 4(1): 1–39.

Karban, K. (2017) 'Developing a health inequalities approach for mental health social work', *British Journal of Social Work*, 47(3): 885–992.

Katsuno, T. (2005) 'Dementia from the inside: how people with early-stage dementia evaluate their quality of life', *Ageing and Society*, 25(2): 197–214.

Katz, J., Peace, S. and Spurr, S. (eds) (2011a) *Adult Lives: A Life Course Perspective*, Bristol: Policy Press.

Katz, J., Holland, C., Peace, S. and Taylor, E. (2011b) *A Better Life – What Older People with High Support Needs Value*, London: Joseph Rowntree Foundation.

Keady, J. and Jones, L. (2010) 'Investigating the causes of behaviours that challenge in people with dementia', *Nursing Older People*, 22(9): 25–9.

Keady, J. and Watts, S. (eds) (2011) *Mental Health and Later Life: Delivering a Holistic Model for Practice*, New York: Routledge.

Kelley-Moore, J.A., Schumacher, J.G., Kahana, E. and Kahana, B. (2006) 'When do older adults become "disabled"? Social and health antecedents of perceived disability in a panel study of the oldest old', *Journal of Health and Social Behavior*, 47(2): 126–41.

Kelly, F. (2010) 'Abusive interactions: research in locked wards for people with dementia', *Social Policy and Society*, 9(2): 267–77.

Kelly, F. and Innes, A. (2013) 'Human rights, citizenship and dementia care nursing', *International Journal of Older People Nursing*, 8(1): 61–70.

Kenney, K. and Diaz-Arrastia, R. (2018) 'Risk of dementia outcomes associated with traumatic brain injury during military service', *JAMA Neurology*, 75(9): 1043–4.

Keyes, C.L. (2002) 'The mental health continuum: from languishing to flourishing in life', *Journal of Health and Social Behavior*, 43(2): 207–22.

Keyes, C.L. (2004) 'The nexus of cardiovascular disease and depression revisited: the complete mental health perspective and the moderating role of age and gender', *Aging and Mental Health*, 8(3): 266–74.

Keyes, C.L. (2005) 'Mental illness and/or mental health? Investigating axioms of the complete state model of health', *Journal of Consulting and Clinical Psychology*, 73(3): 539–48.

Keyes, C.L. (2007) 'Promoting and protecting mental health as flourishing: a complementary strategy for improving national mental health', *American Psychologist*, 62(2): 95–108.

Killeen, D. (2008) *Is Poverty in the UK a Denial of People's Human Rights?*, York: Joseph Rowntree Foundation.

Killick, J. and Allan, K. (2001) *Communication and the Care of People with Dementia*, Buckingham: Open University Press.

Kim, J. and Kaplan, R. (2004) 'Physical and psychological factors in sense of community: new urbanist Kentlands and nearby Orchard Village', *Environmental and Behavior*, 36(3): 313–40.

Kim, M.M., Ford, J.D, Howard, D.L. and Bradford, D.W. (2010) 'Assessing trauma, substance abuse, and mental health in a sample of homeless men', *Health and Social Work*, 35(1): 39–48.

Kind, A.J., Bendlin, B.B., Kim, A.J., Koscik, R.L., Buckingham, W.R., Gleason, C.E., Blennow, K., Zetterberg, H., Carlsson, C.M. and Johnson, S.C. (2017) 'Neighborhood socioeconomic contextual disadvantage, baseline cognition and Alzheimer's disease biomarkers in the Wisconsin registry for Alzheimer's prevention (WRAP) study', *Alzheimer's & Dementia: The Journal of the Alzheimer's Association*, 13(7), 195–6.

Kittay, E. (1999) *Love's Labor: Essays in Women, Equality and Dependency*, New York: Routledge.

Kitwood, T. (1993a) 'Towards a theory of dementia care: the interpersonal process', *Ageing and Society*, 13(1): 51–67.

Kitwood, T. (1993b) 'Person and process in dementia', *International Journal of Geriatric Psychiatry*, 8(7): 541–5.

Kitwood, T. (1997) *Dementia Reconsidered: The Person Comes First*, Buckingham: Open University Press.

Kitwood, T. and Bredin, K. (1992) 'Towards a theory of dementia care: personhood and well-being', *Ageing and Society*, 12(3): 269–87.

Knapp, M., McDaid, D. and Parsonage, M. (2011) *Mental Health Promotion and Mental Illness Prevention: The Economic Case*, London: Department of Health.

Knapp, M., Bauer, A., Perkins, M. and Snell, T. (2013) 'Building community capital in social care: is there an economic case?' *Community Development Journal*, 48(2): 313–31.

Kneale, D (2012) *Is Social Exclusion Still Important for Older People?*, London: Age UK.

Knight, T., Davison, T.E., McCabe, M.P. and Mellor, D. (2011) 'Environmental mastery and depression in older adults in residential care', *Ageing and Society*, 31(5): 870–84.

Knipscheer, J.W., De Jong, E.E., Kleber, R.J. and Lamptey, E. (2000) 'Ghanaian migrants in the Netherlands: General health, acculturative stress and utilization of mental health care', *Journal of Community Psychology*, 28(4): 459–76.

Knowles, S., Combs, R., Kirk, S., Griffiths, M., Patel, N. and Sanders, C. (2016) 'Hidden caring, hidden carers? Exploring the experience of carers for people with long-term conditions', *Health and Social Care in the Community*, 24(2): 203–13.

Kohli, M. (1987) 'Retirement and the moral economy: an historical interpretation of the German case', *Journal of Aging Studies*, 1(2): 125–44.

Kohli, M. (2007) 'The institutionalization of the life course: looking back to look ahead', *Research in Human Development*, 4(3–4): 253–71.

Kontos, P.C. (2004) 'Ethnographic reflections on selfhood, embodiment and Alzheimer's disease', *Ageing and Society*, 24(6): 829–49.

Kontos, P.C. (2005) 'Embodied selfhood in Alzheimer's disease: rethinking person-centred care', *Dementia*, 4(4): 553–70.

Kontos, P.C. (2014) 'Selfhood and the body in dementia care', in M. Downs and B. Bowers (eds) *Excellence in Dementia Care: Research into Practice*, Maidenhead: Open University Press, pp 122–311.

Kontos, P.C. and Naglie, G. (2007) 'Bridging theory and practice: imagination, the body, and person-centred dementia care', *Dementia*, 6(4): 549–69.

Kontos, P.C. and Naglie, G. (2009) 'Tacit knowledge of caring and embodied selfhood', *Sociology of Health and Illness*, 31(5): 688–704.

Kontos, P.C. and Martin, W. (2013) 'Embodiment and dementia: exploring critical narratives of selfhood, surveillance, and dementia care', *Dementia*, 12(3): 288–302.

Kontos, P.C., Miller, K.L. and Kontos, A.P. (2017) 'Relational citizenship: supporting embodied selfhood and relationality in dementia care', *Sociology of Health and Illness*, 39(2): 182–98.

Krause, N. and Bastida, E. (2011) 'Church-based social relationships, belonging, and health among older Mexican Americans', *Journal for the Scientific Study of Religion*, 50(2): 397–409.

Krekula, C. (2009) 'Age coding on age-based practices of distinction', *International Journal of Ageing and Later Life*, 4(2): 7–31.

Krieger, N. (2011) *Epidemiology and the People's Health: Theory and Context*, Oxford: Oxford University Press.

Kuh, D. and Ben-Shlomo, Y.B. (eds) (2004) *A Life Course Approach to Chronic Disease Epidemiology*, Oxford: Oxford University Press.

Kuh, D., Hardy, R., Langenberg, C., Richards, M. and Wadsworth, M.E. (2002) 'Mortality in adults aged 26–54 years related to socioeconomic conditions in childhood and adulthood: post war birth cohort study,' *British Medical Journal*, 325(7372): 1076–80.

Kuh, D., Richards, M., Cooper, R., Hardy, R. and Ben-Shlomo, Y. (2014) 'Life course epidemiology, ageing research and maturing cohort studies: a dynamic combination for understanding healthy ageing', in D. Kuh, R. Cooper, R. Hardy, M. Richards and Y Ben-Sholmo (eds) *A Life Course Approach to Healthy Ageing*, Oxford: Oxford University Press, pp 3–15.

Kuh, D., Wong, A., Shah, I., Moore, A., Popham, M., Curran, P., Davis, D., Sharma, N., Richards, M., Stafford, M., Hardy, R. and Cooper, R. (2016) 'The MRC National Survey of Health and Development reaches age 70: maintaining participation at older ages in a birth cohort study', *European Journal of Epidemiology*, 31(11): 1135–47.

Kunzmann, U., Little, T.D. and Smith, J. (2000) 'Is age-related stability of subjective wellbeing a paradox? Cross-sectional and longitudinal evidence from the Berlin Aging Study', *Psychology and Aging*, 15(3): 511–26.

Kvæl, L.A.H., Bergland, A. and Telenius, E.W. (2017) 'Associations between physical function and depression in nursing home residents with mild and moderate dementia: a cross-sectional study', *BMJ Open*, 7(7): e016875.

La Fontaine, J. and Oyebode, J.R. (2014) 'Family relationships and dementia: a synthesis of qualitative research including the person with dementia', *Ageing and Society*, 34(7): 1243–72.

Labonté, R. (2008) 'Global health in public policy: finding the right frame?', *Critical Public Health*, 18(4): 467–82.

Lachs, M.S. and Pillemer, K. (2004) 'Elder abuse', *The Lancet*, 364(9441): 1263–72.

Lain, D. (2012) 'Comparing health and employment in England and the United States', in S. Vickerstaff, C. Phillipson and R. Wilkie (eds) *Work, Health and Well-Being: The Challenges of Managing Health at Work*, Bristol: Policy Press, pp 59–78.

LaingBuisson (2014) *Care of Older People, UK Market Survey 2013/14*, London: Laing and Buisson.

LaingBuisson (2016) *Care of Elderly People: Market Survey 2014–15*, London: Laing and Buisson.

LaingBuisson (2017) *Care Home Funding Shortfall Leaves Self-Funders Filling £1.3 Billion Gap*, [online] www.laingbuisson.com/laingbuisson-release/care-home-funding-shortfall-leaves-self-funders-filling-1-3-billion-gap/ [Accessed 13 January 2019].

Lakoff, G. (2004). *Don't Think of an Elephant: Know Your Values and Frame the Debate*, White River Junction, VT: Chelsea Green Publishing.

Lamont, R.A., Nelis, S.M., Quinn, C., Martyr, A., Rippon, I., Kopelman, M.D., Hindle, J.V., Jones, R.W., Litherland, R. and Clare, L. (2019) 'Psychological predictors of "living well" with dementia: findings from the IDEAL study', *Aging and Mental Health*, 1–9.

Lang, I.A., Hubbard, R.E., Andrew, M.K., Llewellyn, D.J., Melzer, D. and Rockwood, K. (2009) 'Neighbourhood deprivation, individual socioeconomic status, and frailty in older adults', *Journal of the American Geriatrics Society*, 57(10): 1776–80.

Langdon, S.A., Eagle, A. and Warner, J. (2007) 'Making sense of dementia in the social world: a qualitative study', *Social Science and Medicine*, 64(4): 989–1000.

Larkin, M. (2011) *Social Aspects of Health, Illness and Healthcare*, Maidenhead: McGraw-Hill Education.

Larkin, M. (2013) *Health and Well-Being across the Life Course*, London: Sage.

Larkin, M. and Milne, A. (2014) 'Carer Empowerment in the UK: a Critical Reflection', *Social Policy and Society*, 13(1): 25–38.

Larkin, M., Henwood, M. and Milne, A. (2019) 'Carer-related research and knowledge: findings from a scoping review', *Health and Social Care in the Community*, 27(1): 55–67.

Laslett, P. (1991) *A Fresh Map of Life*, Cambridge, MA: Harvard University Press.

Lawton, M.P. (1982) 'Competence, environmental press, and the adaptation of older people', in M.P. Lawton, P.G. Windley and T.O. Byerts (eds) *Aging and the Environment: Theoretical Approaches*, New York: Springer, pp 33–59.

Lawton, M.P. (1983) 'Environment and other determinants of well-being in older people', *The Gerontologist*, 23(4): 349–57.

Le Mesurier, N. and Northmore, S. (2003). 'So much more than just walking!', *Working with Older People*, 7(3): 11–14.

Leamy, M., Bird, V., Le Boutillier, C., Williams, J. and Slade, M. (2011) 'Conceptual framework for personal recovery in mental health: systematic review and narrative synthesis', *The British Journal of Psychiatry*, 199(6): 445–52.

Lee, H. and Adams, T. (eds) (2011) *Creative Approaches in Dementia Care*, Basingstoke: Palgrave Macmillan.

Lee, H. and Turney, K. (2012) 'Investigating the relationship between perceived discrimination, social status, and mental health', *Society and Mental Health*, 2(1): 1–20.

Leng, G. (2017) *The Impact of Homelessness on Health: Guide for Local Authorities*, London: Local Government Association.

Leontjevas, R., Gerritsen, D.L., Smalbrugge, M., Teerenstra, S., Vernooij-Dassen, M.J. and Koopmans, R.T. (2013) 'A structural multidisciplinary approach to depression management in nursing-home residents: a multicentre, stepped-wedge cluster-randomised trial', *The Lancet*, 381(9885): 2255–64.

Levy, B. (2016) 'Stereotype embodiment: a psychosocial approach to aging', *Current Directions in Psychological Science*, 18(6): 332–6.

Levy, B.R., Zonderman, A.B., Slade, M.D. and Ferrucci, L. (2011) 'Memory shaped by age stereotypes over time', *Journals of Gerontology Series B: Psychological Sciences and Social Sciences*, 67(4): 432–6.

Lewis, J. and West, A. (2014) 'Re-shaping social care services for older people in England: policy development and the problem of achieving "good care"', *Journal of Social Policy*, 43(1): 1–18.

Leyens, J.P., Paladino, M.P., Rodriguez, R.T., Vaes, J., Demoulin, S., Rodriguez, A.P. and Gaunt, R. (2000) 'The emotional side of prejudice: the attribution of secondary emotions to ingroups and outgroups', *Personality and Social Psychology Review*, 4(2): 186–97.

Leyens, J.P., Rodriguez-Perez, A., Rodriguez-Torres, R., Gaunt, R., Paladino, M.P., Vaes, J. and Demoulin, S. (2001) 'Psychological essentialism and the differential attribution of uniquely human emotions to ingroups and outgroups', *European Journal of Social Psychology*, 31(4): 395–411.

Leyland A.F., Scott J. and Dawson P. (2016) 'Involuntary relocation and safe transfer of care home residents: a model or risks and opportunities in residents' experiences', *Ageing and Society*, 36(2): 376–99.

Lievesley, N., Crosby, G. and Bowman, C. (2011) *The Changing Role of Care Homes*, London: BUPA and Centre for Policy on Ageing.

Link, B.G. and Phelan, J.C. (2001) 'Conceptualizing stigma', *Annual Review of Sociology*, 27(1): 363–85.

Litherland, R. (2015) *Developing a National User Movement of People with Dementia – Learning from the Dementia Engagement and Empowerment Project (DEEP)*, York: Joseph Rowntree Foundation.

Litwin, H. (2001) 'Social network type and morale in old age', *The Gerontologist*, 41(4): 516–24.

Litwin, H. and Stoeckel, K.J. (2014) 'Engagement and social capital as elements of active ageing: an analysis of older Europeans', *Sociologia e Politiche Sociali*, 23(3): 9–31.

Livingstone, G., Cooper, C., Woods, J., Milne, A. and Katona, C. (2008) 'Successful ageing in adversity – the LASER longitudinal study', *Journal of Neurology, Neurosurgery and Psychiatry*, 79(6): 641–5.

Livingstone, G., Sommerlad, A., Orgeta, V., Costafreda, S.G., Huntley, J., Ames, D.A., Ballard, C., Banerjee, S., Burns, A., Cohen-Mansfield, J., Cooper, C., Fox, N., Gitlin, L.N., Howard, R., Kales, H.C., Larson, E.B., Ritchie, K., Rockwood, K., Sampson, E.L., Samus, Q., Schneider, L.S., Selbaek, G., Teri, L. and Mukadam, N. (2017) 'Dementia prevention, intervention, and care', *The Lancet Commissions*, 390(10113): 2673–734.

Llewellyn-Jones, R.H., Deeks, J.J., Baikie, K.A., Smithers, H., Cohen, J., Snowdon, J. and Tennant, C.C. (1999) 'Multifaceted shared care intervention for late life depression in residential care: randomised controlled trial commentary: beyond the boundary for a randomised controlled trial?', *British Medical Journal*, 319(7211): 676–82.

Lloyd, B.T. and Stirling, C. (2011) 'Ambiguous gain: uncertain benefits of service use for dementia carers', *Sociology of Health and Illness*, 33(6): 899–913.

Lloyd, L. (2004) 'Mortality and morality: ageing and the ethics of care', *Ageing and Society*, 24(2): 235–56.

Lloyd, L. (2010) 'The individual in social care: the ethics of care and the "personalisation agenda" in services for older people in England', *Ethics and Social Welfare*, 4(2): 188–200.

Lloyd, L. (2012) *Health and Care in Ageing Societies: A New International Approach*, Bristol: Policy Press.

Lloyd, L. (2015) 'The fourth age', in J. Twigg and W. Martin (eds) *Routledge Handbook of Cultural Gerontology*, New York: Routledge, pp 261–8.

Lloyd, L., Calnan, M., Cameron, A., Seymour, J. and Smith, R. (2014a) 'Identity in the fourth age: perseverance, adaptation and maintaining dignity', *Ageing and Society*, 34(1): 1–19.

Lloyd, L., Tanner, D., Milne, A., Ray, M., Richards, S., Sullivan, M.P., Beech, C. and Phillips, J. (2014b) 'Look after yourself: active ageing, individual responsibility and the decline of social work with older people in the UK', *European Journal of Social Work*, 17(3): 322–35.

Local Government Association, Association of Directors of Adult Social Services Departments and the Social Care Institute for Excellence (2013) *Making Safeguarding Personal*, London: Local Government Association.

Logsdon, R.G., Gibbons, L.E., McCurry, S.M. and Teri, L. (1999) 'Quality of life in Alzheimer's disease: patient and caregiver reports', *Journal of Mental Health and Aging*, 5(1), 21–32.

Logsdon, R.G., Gibbons, L.E., McCurry, S.M. and Teri, L. (2002) 'Assessing quality of life in older adults with cognitive impairment', *Psychosomatic Medicine*, 64(3): 510–19.

Long, A., Godfrey, M., Randall, T., Grant, M. and Chapman, M. (2002) *Effectiveness and Outcomes of Preventive Services for Older People: Risk Factors, Coping Strategies and Outcomes for Interventions in Bereavement*, Leeds: Nuffield Institute for Health.

Longevity Science Advisory Panel (2011) *Life Expectancy: Past and Future Variations by Socioeconomic Group in England and Wales*, London: Longevity Science Advisory Panel.

Loopstra, R., McKee, M., Katikireddi, S.V., Taylor-Robinson, D., Barr, B. and Stuckler, D. (2016) 'Austerity and old-age mortality in England: a longitudinal cross-local area analysis, 2007–2013', *Journal of the Royal Society of Medicine*, 109(3): 109–16.

Loretto, W. and White, P. (2006) 'Employers' attitudes, practices and policies towards older workers', *Human Resources Management Journal*, 16(3): 313–30.

Lou, P., Zhu, Y., Chen, P., Zhang, P., Yu, J., Zhang, N., Chen, N., Zhang, L., Wu, H. and Zhao, J. (2012) 'Prevalence and correlations with depression, anxiety, and other features in outpatients with chronic obstructive pulmonary disease in China: a cross-sectional case control study', *BMC Pulmonary Medicine*, 12(1): 53.

Loughnan, S., Haslam, N., Sutton, R.M. and Spencer, B. (2014) 'Dehumanization and social class', *Social Psychology*, 45(1): 54–61.

Lucero, J., Wallerstein, N., Duran, B., Alegria, M., Greene-Moton, E., Israel, B., Kastelic, S., Magarati, M., Oetzel, J., Pearson, C., Schulz, A., Villegas, M. and White Hat, E.R. (2018) 'Development of a mixed methods investigation of process and outcomes of community-based participatory research', *Journal of Mixed Methods Research*, 12(1): 55–74.

Lum, T.Y. and Lightfoot, E. (2005) 'The effects of volunteering on the physical and mental health of older people', *Research on Aging*, 27(1): 31–55.

Lundman, B., Aléx, L., Jonsén, E., Norberg, A., Nygren, B., Fischer, R.S. and Strandberg, G. (2010) 'Inner strength: a theoretical analysis of salutogenic concepts', *International Journal of Nursing Studies*, 47(2): 251–60.

Luo, Y., Hawkley, L.C., Waite, L.J. and Cacioppo, J.T. (2012) 'Loneliness, health, and mortality in old age: a national longitudinal study', *Social Science and Medicine*, 74(6): 907–14.

Lupien, S.J., McEwen, B.S., Gunnar, M.R. and Heim, C. (2009) 'Effects of stress throughout the lifespan on the brain, behaviour and cognition', *Nature Reviews Neuroscience*, 10(6): 434–45.

Luthar, S.S. (2006) 'Resilience in development: a synthesis of research across five decades', in D. Cicchetti and D.J. Cohen (eds) *Developmental Psychopathology: Volume Three: Risk, Disorder, and Adaptation*, pp 739–95.

Lynch, J., Davey-Smith, G., Harper, S., Hillemeier, M., Ross, N., Kaplan, G. and Wolfson, M. (2004) 'Is income inequality a determinant of population health? Part 1: a systematic review', *Millbank Quarterly*, 82(1): 5–99.

Lynch, J.W., Kaplan, G.A. and Shema, S.J. (1997) 'Cumulative impact of sustained economic hardship on physical, cognitive, psychological, and social functioning', *New England Journal of Medicine*, 337(26): 1889–95.

Macdonald, A. (2001) 'Letters: maintaining older people's dignity and autonomy in healthcare settings', *British Medical Journal*, 323(7308): 340.

Mahoney, R., Regan, C., Katona, C. and Livingstone, G. (2005) 'Anxiety and depression in family caregivers of people with Alzheimer's disease', *American Journal of Geriatric Psychiatry*, 13(9): 795–801.

Majer, I.M., Nusselder, W.J., Mackenbach, J.P. and Kunst, A.E. (2011) 'Socioeconomic inequalities in life and health expectancies around official retirement age in 10 Western-European countries', *Journal of Epidemiology and Community Health*, 65(11): 972–9.

Maki, P.M. (2013) 'The critical window hypothesis of hormone therapy and cognition: a scientific update on clinical studies', *Menopause*, 20(6): 695–709.

Mani, A., Mullainathan, S., Shafir, E. and Zhao, J. (2013) 'Poverty impedes cognitive function', *Science*, 341(6149): 976–80.

Mann, A. (2000) 'Depression in the elderly: findings from a community survey', *Maturitas*, 38(1): 53–8.

Manthorpe, J. and Iliffe, S. (2005) *Depression in Later Life*, London: Jessica Kingsley Publishers.

Manthorpe, J. and Iliffe, S. (2011) 'Social work with older people – reducing suicide risk: a critical review of practice and prevention', *The British Journal of Social Work*, 41(1): 131–47.

Manthorpe, J. and Samsi, K. (2013) 'Inherently risky?': personal budgets for people with dementia and the risks of financial abuse: findings from an interview-based study with adult safeguarding coordinators', *The British Journal of Social Work*, 43(5): 889–903.

Manthorpe, J. and Samsi, K. (2016) 'Person-centered dementia care: current perspectives', *Clinical Interventions in Aging*, 11: 1733–40.

Manthorpe, J. and Iliffe, S. (2016a) 'What is dementia and how big a problem is it?', *Journal of Dementia Care*, 24(6): 16–17.

Manthorpe, J. and Iliffe, S. (2016b) *The Dialectics of Dementia*, London: Social Care Workforce Research Unit.

Manthorpe, J., Iliffe, S., Harris, J., Moriarty, J. and Stevens, M. (2018) 'Frailty and social care: over-or under-familiar terms?', *Social Policy and Society*, 17(1): 23–33.

Marmot, M. (2003) 'Understanding social inequalities in health', *Perspectives in Biology and Medicine*, 46(3): S9–23.

Marmot, M. (2005) 'Social determinants of health inequalities', *The Lancet*, 365(9464): 1099–104.

Marmot, M. (2006) *Status Syndrome*, London: Bloomsbury.

Marmot, M. (2014) 'Commentary: mental health and public health', *International Journal of Epidemiology*, 43(2): 293–6.

Marmot, M. (2015) *The Health Gap: The Challenge of an Unequal World*, London: Bloomsbury Publishing.

Marmot, M. (2018) 'Inclusion health: addressing the causes of the causes', *The Lancet*, 391(10117): 186–8.

Marmot, M. and Wilkinson, R. (eds) (2005) *Social Determinants of Health*, Oxford: Oxford University Press.

Marmot, M., Allen, J., Goldblatt, P., Boyce, T., McNeish, D., Grady, M. and Geddes, I. (2010) *Fair Society, Healthy Lives: Strategic Review of Health Inequalities in England Post-2010*, London: The Marmot Review.

Marshall, A., Nazroo, J., Tampubolon, G. and Vanhoutte, B. (2015) 'Cohort differences in the levels and trajectories of frailty among older people in England', *Journal of Epidemiology and Community Health*, 69(4): 316–21.

Marshall, A., Jivraj, S., Nazroo, J., Tampubolon, G. and Vanhoutte, B. (2014) 'Does the level of wealth inequality within an area influence the prevalence of depression amongst older people?', *Health and Place*, 27, 194–204.

Marshall, M. and Tibbs, M.A. (2006) *Social Work and People with Dementia: Partnerships, Practice and Persistence*, Bristol: Policy Press.

Marshall, T.H. (1950) 'Citizenship and social class', in C. Pierson and F.G. Castles (eds) *The Welfare State Reader*, Cambridge: Polity Press, pp 28–9.

Marshall V.W. and Clarke, P.J. (2010) 'Agency and social structure in aging and life course research', in D. Dannefer and C. Phillipson (eds) *The SAGE Handbook of Gerontology*, London: Sage, pp 294–305.

Martinez-Clavera, C., James, S., Bowditch, E. and Kuruvilla, T. (2017) 'Delayed-onset post-traumatic stress disorder symptoms in dementia', *Progress in Neurology and Psychiatry*, 21(3): 26–31.

Martyr, A., Nelis, S.M., Quinn, C., Wu, Y.-T., Lamont, R.A., Henderson, C., Clarke, R., Hindle, J.V., Thorn, J.M., Jones, I.R., Morris, R.G., Rusted, J.M., Victor, C.R. and Clare, L. (2018) 'Living well with dementia: a systematic review and correlational meta-analysis of factors associated with quality of life, well-being and life satisfaction in people with dementia', *Psychological Medicine*, 48(13): 2130–9.

Martz, E. and Livneh, H. (2016) 'Psychosocial adaptation to disability within the context of positive psychology: findings from the literature', *Journal of Occupational Rehabilitation*, 26(1): 4–12.

Maschi, T., Baer, J., Morrissey, M-B. and Moreno, C. (2013) 'The aftermath of childhood trauma on late life physical and mental health: a review of the literature', *Traumatology*, 19(1): 49–64.

Maslow, A.H. (1954) *Motivation and Personality*, New York: Harper and Row.

Mathur, R., Badrick, E., Boomla, K., Bremner, S., Hull, S. and Robson, J. (2011) 'Prescribing in general practice for people with coronary heart disease: equity by age, sex, ethnic group and deprivation', *Ethnicity and Health*, 16(2): 107–23.

Matthews, F.E., Stephan, B.C.M., Robinson, L., Jagger, C., Barnes, L. E., Arthur, A., Brayne, C. and Cognitive Function and Ageing Studies (CFAS) Collaboration (2016) 'A two-decade dementia incidence comparison from the Cognitive Function and Ageing Studies I and II', *Nature Communications*, 7: 11398.

Maughan, B. (2002) 'Depression and psychological distress: a life course perspective', in D. Kuh and R. Hardy (eds) *A Life Course Approach to Women's Health*, Oxford: Oxford University Press.

McAdams, D.P. (2008) 'Life Story' in *The Encyclopedia of Adulthood and Aging*, pp 241–61.

McAvinue, L.P., Golemme, M., Castorina, M., Tatti, E., Pigni, F.M., Salomone, S., Brennan, S. and Roberston, I.H. (2013) 'An evaluation of a working memory training scheme in older adults', *Frontiers in Aging Neuroscience*, 5: 20.

McCarthy, H. and Thomas, G. (2004) *Home Alone: Combating Isolation with Older Housebound People*, London: Demos.

McCartney, J.R. and Severson, K. (1997) 'Sexual violence, post-traumatic stress disorder and dementia', *Journal of the American Geriatrics Society*, 45(1): 76–8.

McCormick, J., Clifton, J., Sachrajda,A., Cherti, M. and McDowell I. (2009) *Getting On: Well-being in Later Life*, London: Institute for Public Policy Research.

McCrory, E.J., Gerin, M.I. and Viding, E. (2017) 'Annual research review: childhood maltreatment, latent vulnerability and the shift to preventive psychiatry – the contribution of functional brain imaging', *Journal of Child Psychology and Psychiatry*, 58(4): 338–57.

McCulloch, A. (2009) 'Old age and mental health in the context of the lifespan: what are the key issues in the 21st century', in T. Williamson (ed) *Older People's Mental Health Today: A Handbook*, London: Mental Health Foundation and Pavilion Publishing.

McGarry, J. and Simpson, C. (2011) 'Domestic abuse and older women: exploring the opportunities for service development and care delivery', *The Journal of Adult Protection*, 13(6): 294–301.

McGarry, J., Ali, P. and Hinchliff, S. (2016) 'Older women, intimate partner violence and mental health: a consideration of the particular issues for health and healthcare practice', *Journal of Clinical Nursing*, 26(15–16), 2177–91.

McGovern, P. and Nazroo, J. (2015) 'Patterns and causes of health inequalities in later life: a Bourdieusian approach', *Sociology of Health and Illness*, 37(1): 143–60.

McGuinness, F. (2018) *Poverty in the UK: Statistics*, House of Commons Library: London.

McKee, M. and Stuckler, D. (2013) 'Older people in the UK: under attack from all directions', *Age and Ageing*, 42(1): 11–13.

McKenzie, K. and Harpham, T. (2006) *Social Capital and Mental Health*, London: Jessica Kingsley Publishers.

McKeown, J., Clarke, A., Ingleton, C., Ryan, T. and Repper, J. (2010) 'The use of life story work with people with dementia to enhance person-centred care', *International Journal of Older People Nursing*, 5(2): 148–58.

McLaughlin, D.K. and Jensen, L. (2000) 'Work history and US elders' transitions into poverty', *The Gerontologist*, 40(4): 469–79.

McManus, S., Bebbington, P., Jenkins, R. and Brugha, T. (eds) (2016) *Mental Health and Wellbeing in England: Adult Psychiatric Morbidity Survey 2014*, Leeds: NHS Digital.

McManus, S., Meltzer, H., Brugha, T.S., Bebbington, P.E. and Jenkins, R. (2009) *Adult Psychiatric Morbidity in England, 2007: Results of a Household Survey*, London: The NHS Information Centre for Health and Social Care.

McNeil, C. and Hunter, J. (2014) *The Generation Strain, Collective Solutions to Care in an Ageing Society*, London: Institute of Public Policy Research.

McNeill, L.S. (2014) 'The place of debt in establishing identity and self-worth in transitional life phases: young home leavers and credit', *International Journal of Consumer Studies*, 38(1): 69–74.

McNicholas, J. (2014) 'The role of pets in the lives of older people: a review', *Working with Older People*, 18(3): 128–33.

Means, R. (2007) 'Safe as houses? Ageing in place and vulnerable older people in the UK', *Social Policy and Administration*, 41(1), 65–85.

Mein, G., Martikainen, P., Hemingway, H., Stansfeld, S. and Marmot, M. (2003) 'Is retirement good or bad for mental and physical health functioning? Whitehall II longitudinal study of civil servants', *Journal of Epidemiology and Community Health*, 57(1): 46–9.

Meltzer, H., Singleton, N., Lee, A., Bebbington, P., Brugha, T. and Jenkins, R. (2002) *The Social and Economic Circumstances of Adults with Mental Disorders*, London: Department of Health.

Meng, X. and D'Arcy, C. (2012) 'Education and dementia in the context of the cognitive reserve hypothesis: a systematic review with meta-analyses and qualitative analyses', *PloS One*, 7(6): e38268.

Menne, H.L., Judge, K.S. and Whitlatch, C.J. (2009) 'Predictors of quality of life for individuals with dementia: implications for intervention', *Dementia*, 8(4): 543–60.

Mental Health Foundation (2003) *Fact Sheet: What Is Mental Health?* London: Mental Health Foundation.

Mental Health Foundation (2006) *The Impact of Spirituality on Mental Health: A Review of the Literature*. [online] www.mentalhealth.org.uk/sites/default/files/impact-spirituality.pdf [Accessed 12 January 2019].

Mental Health Foundation (2009) *All Things Being Equal: Age Equality in Mental Health Care for Older People in England*, London: Mental Health Foundation.

Mental Health Foundation (2011a) *Brighter Futures*, London: Mental Health Foundation.

Mental Health Foundation (2011b) *Dementia Choices: Promoting Self-Directed Support for People Living with Dementia*, London: Mental Health Foundation.

Mental Health Foundation (2013) *Getting on … With Life: Baby Boomers, Mental Health and Ageing*, London: Mental Health Foundation.

Mental Health Foundation (2015) *Dementia, Rights, and the Social Model of Disability: A New Direction for Policy and Practice?* London: Mental Health Foundation.

Mental Health Foundation (2016a) *Fundamental Facts about Mental Health 2016*, London: Mental Health Foundation.

Mental Health Foundation (2016b) *The Interface Between Dementia and Mental Health: An Evidence Review*, London: Mental Health Foundation.

Mentality (2001) *Making It Happen: A Guide to Delivering Mental Health Promotion*, London: Department of Health.

Mentality (2004) *Literature and Policy Review on Mental Health Promotion in Later Life*, London: Age Concern and the Mental Health Foundation.

Mezuk, B., Eaton, W.W., Albrecht, S. and Golden, S.H. (2008) 'Depression and type 2 diabetes over the lifespan: a meta-analysis', *Diabetes Care*, 31(12): 2383–90.

Michalowsky, B., Thyrian, J.R., Eichler, T., Hertel, J., Wucherer, D., Flessa, S. and Hoffmann, W. (2016) 'Economic analysis of formal care, informal care, and productivity losses in primary care patients who screened positive for dementia in Germany', *Journal of Alzheimer's Disease*, 50(1): 47–59.

Midlöv, P., Andersson, M., Östgren, C.J. and Mölstad, S. (2014) 'Depression and use of antidepressants in Swedish nursing homes: a 12-month follow-up study', *International Psychogeriatrics*, 26(4): 669–75.

Mikelyte, R. and Milne, A. (2016) 'Exploring the influence of micro-cultures on the mental health and well being of older people living in long term care', *Quality in Ageing, Mental Health and Later Life*, 17(3): 198–214.

Milligan, C. (2009). *There's No Place Like Home: Place and Care in an Ageing Society*, London and New York: Routledge.

Milligan, C. and Wiles, J. (2010) 'Landscapes of care', *Progress in Human Geography*, 34(6), 736–54.

Milligan, C. and Liu, Y. (2015) 'Place and informal care in an ageing society: reviewing the state of the art in geographical gerontology', *Progress in Geography*, 34(12), 1558–76.

Milligan, C. and Thomas, C. (2016) 'Dementia and the social model of disability: does responsibility to adjust lie with society rather than people with dementia?', *Signpost*, 21(3), 5–16.

Milne, A. (2009a) 'Addressing the challenges to mental health and well being in later life', in T. Williamson (ed) *Older People's Mental Health Today: A Handbook*, London: Mental Health Foundation and Pavilion Publishing, pp 31–42.

Milne, A. (2009b) 'Mental health and well being in later life, definitions and determinants', in T. Williamson (ed) *Older People's Mental Health Today: A Handbook*, London: Mental Health Foundation and Pavilion Publishing, pp 19–30.

Milne, A (2010a) 'The "D" word: reflections on the relationship between stigma and dementia', *Journal of Mental Health*, 19(3): 227–33.

Milne, A. (2010b) 'Dementia screening and early diagnosis: the case for and against', *Health, Risk and Society*, 12(1): 65–76.

Milne, A. (2011) 'Living with dementia in a care home: capturing the experiences of residents', *Quality in Ageing and Older Adults*, 12(2): 76–85.

Milne, A. (2016) 'Depression in care homes', in C. Chew-Graham and M. Ray (eds) *Mental Health and Older People: a Guide for Primary Care Practitioners*, Silver Spring: Springer, pp 145–61.

Milne, A. and Williams, J. (2000) 'Meeting the mental health needs of older women: taking social inequality into account', *Ageing and Society*, 20(6): 699–723.

Milne, A. and Peet, J. (2008) *Challenges and Resolutions to Psycho-Social Well-Being for People in Receipt of a Diagnosis of Dementia: A Literature Review*, London: Alzheimer's Society.

Milne, A. and Larkin, M. (2015) 'Knowledge generation about care-giving in the UK: a critical review of research paradigms', *Health and Social Care in the Community*, 23(1): 4–13.

Milne, A. and Williamson, T. (2016) Editorial, *Special Issue of Quality in Ageing, Mental Health and Later Life*, 17(3), 153–156.

Milne, A., Hatzidimitriadou, E. and Wiseman, J. (2007) 'Health and quality of life among older people in rural England: exploring the impact and efficacy of policy', *Journal of Social Policy*, 36(3): 477–95.

Milne, A., Guss, R. and Russ, A. (2014) 'Psycho-educational support for relatives of people with mild to moderate dementia: evaluation of a "Course for Carers"', *Dementia*, 13(6): 768–87.

Milne, A., Cambridge, P., Beadle-Brown, J., Mansell, J. and Whelton, B. (2013) 'The characteristics and management of ender abuse: evidence and lessons from a UK case study', *European Journal of Social Work*, 16(4): 489–505.

Minkler, M. (1996) 'Critical perspectives on ageing: new challenges for gerontology', *Ageing and Society*, 16(4): 467–87.

Minkler, M. and Fadem, P. (2002) '"Successful Aging": a disability perspective', *Journal of Disability Policy Studies*, 12(4): 229–35.

Miron, A.M., McFadden, S.H., Nazario, A.S. and Buelow, J. (2017) 'Perspective taking, empathic concern, and perceived humanness of people with dementia', *Educational Gerontology*, 43(9): 468–79.

Mirza, S.S., Wolters, F.J., Swanson, S.A., Koudstaal, P.J., Hofman, A., Tiemeier, H. and Ikram, M.A. (2016) '10-year trajectories of depressive symptoms and risk of dementia: a population-based study', *The Lancet Psychiatry*, 3(7): 628–35.

Mishra, G., Ball, K., Dobson, A.J. and Byles, J.E. (2004) 'Do socioeconomic gradients in women's health widen over time and with age?', *Social Science and Medicine*, 58(9): 1585–95.

Missotten, P., Ylieff, M., Di Notte, D., Paquay, L., De Lepeleire, J., Buntinx, F. and Fontaine, O. (2007) 'Quality of life in dementia: a 2-year follow-up study', *International Journal of Geriatric Psychiatry*, 22(12): 1201–7.

Mitchell, A.J. and Shiri-Feshki, M. (2009) 'Rate of progression of mild cognitive impairment to dementia – meta-analysis of 41 robust inception cohort studies', *Acta Psychiatrica Scandinavica*, 119(4): 252–65.

Mittal, D., Torres, R., Abashidze, A. and Jimerson, N. (2001) 'Worsening of post-traumatic stress disorder symptoms with cognitive decline: case series', *Journal of Geriatric Psychiatry and Neurology*, 14(1): 17–20.

Moffatt, S. and Higgs, P. (2007) 'Charity or entitlement? Generational habitus and the welfare state among older people in north-East England', *Social Policy and Administration*, 41(5): 449–64.

Moffatt, S., Higgs, P., Rummery, K. and Rees-Jones, I. (2012) 'Choice, consumerism and devolution: growing old in welfare state(s) of Scotland, Wales and England', *Ageing and Society*, 32(5): 725–46.

Mölsä, M., Kuittinen, S., Tiilikainen, M., Honkasalo, M.L. and Punamäki, R.L. (2017) 'Mental health among older refugees: the role of trauma, discrimination, and religiousness', *Aging and Mental Health*, 21(8): 829–37.

Moniz-Cook, E., Stokes, G. and Agar, S. (2003) 'Difficult behaviour and dementia in nursing homes: five cases of psychosocial intervention', *Clinical Psychology and Psychotherapy*, 10(3): 197–208.

Moniz-Cook, E., Vernooij-Dassen, M., Woods, B., Orrell, M. and Network, I. (2011) 'Psychosocial interventions in dementia care research: the INTERDEM manifesto', *Aging and Mental Health*, 15(3): 283–90.

Moos, I. and Björn, A. (2006) 'Use of the life story in the institutional care of people with dementia: a review of intervention studies', *Ageing and Society*, 26(3): 431–54.

Moran, N., Arksey, H., Glendinning, C., Jones, K., Netten, A. and Rabiee, P. (2012) 'Personalisation and carers: Whose rights? Whose benefits?', *British Journal of Social Work*, 42(3): 461–79.

Moran, N., Glendinning, C., Wilberforce, M., Stevens, M., Netten, A., Jones, K., Manthorpe, J., Knapp, M., Fernandez, J., Challis, D. and Jacobs, S. (2013) 'Older people's experiences of cash-for-care schemes: evidence from the English Individual Budget pilot projects', *Ageing and Society*, 33(5): 826–51.

Moreton, R., Robinson, S., Howe, P., Corley, A., Welford, J. and Roberts, J. (2018) *Fulfilling Lives: Supporting People with Multiple Needs*, Annual report 2017, Leicester: CFE Research.

Moriarty, J. and Butt, J. (2004) 'Inequalities in quality of life among older people from different ethnic groups', *Ageing and Society*, 24(5): 729–53.

Morris, G. and Morris, J. (2010) *The Dementia Care Workbook*, Buckinghamshire: Open University Press.

Morrow, M. and Weisser, J. (2012) 'Towards a social justice framework of mental health recovery', *Studies in Social Justice*, 6(1): 27–43.

Moyle, W. and O'Dwyer, S. (2012) 'Quality of life in people living with dementia in nursing homes', *Current Opinion in Psychiatry*, 25(6): 480–4.

Moyle, W., Kellett, U., Ballantyne, A. and Gracia, N. (2011) 'Dementia and loneliness: an Australian perspective', *Journal of Clinical Nursing*, 20(9–10), 1445–53.

Murphy, C. (1994) *It Started with a Sea-Shell: Life Story Work and People with Dementia*, Stirling: Dementia Services Development Centre.

Murray, A. (2005) 'Recurrence of post-traumatic stress disorder', *Nursing Older People*, 17(6): 24–30.

Narayanasamy, A., Clissett, P., Parumal, L., Thompson, D., Annasamy, S. and Edge, R. (2004) 'Responses to the spiritual needs of older people', *Journal of Advanced Nursing*, 48(1): 6–16.

National Audit Office (2009) *Improving Dementia Services in England: An Interim Report*, London: National Audit Office.

National Audit Office (2014) *Adult Social Care in England: An Overview*, London: National Audit Office.

National Collaborating Centre for Mental Health (2018) *The Dementia Care Pathway*, London: National Collaborating Centre for Mental Health.

National Institute for Health and Care Excellence (2013) *Mental Wellbeing of Older People in Care Homes*, London: National Institute for Health and Care Excellence.

National Institute for Health and Care Excellence (2015a) *Older People in Care Homes, Local Government Briefing*, [online] www.nice.org.uk/guidance/lgb25 [Accessed on 13 January 2019].

National Institute for Health and Care Excellence (2015b) *Transition Between Inpatient Hospital Settings and Community or Care Home Settings for Adults with Social Care Needs*, NICE: London.

National Institute for Health and Care Excellence (2016) *Mental Wellbeing and Independence for Older People*, NICE: London.

National Institute for Health and Care Excellence and Social Care Institute for Excellence (2006) *The NICE – SCIE Guideline on Supporting People with Dementia and Their Carers in Health and Social Care*. Leicester: The British Psychological Society and Gaskell.

Navarro, V. and Shi, L. (2001) 'The political context of social inequalities and health', *Social Science and Medicine*, 52(3): 481–91.

Nazroo, J. and Matthews, K. (2012) *The Impact of Volunteering on Well-Being in Later Life*, Benfleet: Women Royal Voluntary Service.

Nazroo, J., Falaschetti, E., Pierce, M. and Primatesta, P. (2009) 'Ethnic inequalities in access to and outcomes of healthcare: analysis of the Health Survey for England', *Journal of Epidemiology and Community Health*, 63(12): 1022–7.

Neighbourhood Watch (2009) *Supporting Older Neighbours, Neighbourhood Watch: Coordinator Training Manual*, Leicester: Neighbourhood Watch.

Nelson, J.C. and Devanand, D.P. (2011) 'A systematic review and meta-analysis of placebo-controlled antidepressant studies in people with depression and dementia', *Journal of the American Geriatrics Society*, 59(4): 577–85.

Netten, A., Jones, K., Knapp, M., Fernandez, J., Chalis, D., Glendinning, C., Jacobs, S.M., Manthorpe, J., Moran, N., Stevens, M. and Wilberforce, M. (2012) 'Personalisation through Individual Budgets: does it work and for whom?', *British Journal of Social Work*, 42(8): 1556–73.

Netuveli, G., Wiggins, R.D., Montgomery, S.M., Hildon, Z. and Blane, D. (2008) 'Mental health and resilience at older ages: bouncing back after adversity in the British Household Panel Survey', *Journal of Epidemiology and Community Health*, 62(11): 987–91.

NHS Benchmarking Network (2016) *Older People's Care in Acute Settings: Benchmarking Report*, London: NHS Benchmarking Network.

NHS Digital (2017a) *Health Survey for England 2016 Well-Being and Mental Health*, London: The Health and Social Care Information Centre.

NHS Digital (2017b) *Adult Social Care Activity and Finance Report, England 2016–17*, [online] https://digital.nhs.uk/catalogue/PUB30121 [Accessed 13 January 2019].

NHS England (2014a) *Guidance for NHS Commissioners on Equality and Health Inequalities Legal Duties*, London: NHS England.

NHS England (2014b) *Safe, Compassionate Care for Frail Older People Using an Integrated Care Pathway*, London: NHS England.

NHS England (2016) *The Five Year Forward View For Mental Health: A Report From the Independent Mental Health Taskforce to the NHS in England*, London: NHS England.

NHS England (2017) *Toolkit for General Practice in Supporting Older People Living With Frailty*, London: NHS England.

NHS Health Scotland (2007) *Mind the Difference – Mental Health: Focus on Equality and Diversity*, Edinburgh: NHS Health Scotland.

NHS Health Scotland (2010) *What You Need to Know About Mental Health Inequalities*, Edinburgh: NHS Health Scotland.

NHS Health Scotland, University of Warwick and University of Edinburgh (2006) *The Warwick-Edinburgh Mental Wellbeing Scale*, [online] https://warwick.ac.uk/fac/sci/med/research/platform/wemwbs/about/ [Accessed 12 January 2019].

Ní Léime, A., Street, D., Vickerstaff, S., Krekula, C. and Loretto, W. (eds) (2017) *Gender, Ageing and Extended Working Life: Cross National Perspectives*, Bristol: Policy Press.

Nicholson, C., Gordon, A.L. and Tinker, A. (2016). 'Changing the way "we" view and talk about frailty…', *Age and Ageing*, 46(3), 349–51.

Nikmat, A.W., Hawthorne, G. and Al-Mashoor, S.H. (2015) 'The comparison of quality of life among people with mild dementia in nursing home and home care – a preliminary report', *Dementia*, 14(1): 114–25.

Nolan, M., Ryan, T., Enderby, P. and Reid, D. (2002) 'Towards a more inclusive vision of dementia care practice and research', *Dementia*, 1(2): 193–211.

Nolte, E. and McKee, M. (2008) *Caring for People with Chronic Conditions: a Health System Perspective*, Maidenhead: Open University Press.

Notterman, D.A. and Mitchell, C. (2015) 'Epigenetics and understanding the impact of social determinants of health', *Pediatric Clinics*, 62(5): 1227–40.

Nuffield Council on Bioethics (2009) *Dementia: Ethical Issues*, London: Nuffield Council on Bioethics.

Nutbeam, D. (2003) 'How does evidence influence public health policy? Tackling health inequalities in England', *Health Promotion Journal of Australia*, 14(3), 154–8.

Nygren, B. (2006) *Inner Strength among the Oldest Old: A Good Aging*, Doctoral dissertation, Umeå: Umeå University.

Nyqvist, F., Gustavsson, J. and Gustafsson, Y. (2006) 'Social capital and health in the oldest old: the Umeå 85+ study', *International Journal of Ageing and Later Life*, 1(1): 91–114.

O'Brien, J. and Grayson, L. (2013) 'Mild cognitive impairment and predementia syndromes', in T. Dening and A. Thomas (eds) *Oxford Textbook of Old Age Psychiatry*, Oxford: Oxford University Press, pp 415–30.

O'Brien, M., Begley, E., Anand, J.C., Killick, C. and Taylor, B.J. (2011) *A Total Indifference to Our Dignity: Older People's Understandings of Elder Abuse*, Dublin: Age Action Ireland and Centre for Ageing Research and Development in Ireland.

O'Connell, H., Chin, A-V., Cunningham, C. and Lawlor, B.A. (2004) 'Recent developments: suicide in older people', *British Medical Journal*, 329(7471): 895–9.

O'Connor, D. (1999) 'Living with a memory-impaired spouse: (re)cognizing the experience', *Canadian Journal on Aging*, 18(2): 211–35.

O'Connor, D. and Purves, B. (2009) *Decision-Making, Personhood and Dementia: Exploring the Interface*, London: Jessica Kingsley Publishers.

O'Connor, D., Phinney, A., Smith, A., Small, J., Purves, B., Perry, J., Drance, E., Donnelly, M., Chaudhury, H. and Beattie, L. (2007) 'Personhood in dementia care: developing a research agenda for broadening the vision', *Dementia*, 6(1): 121–42.

O'Keefe, M., Hills, A., Doyle, M., McCreadie, C., Scholes, S., Constantine, R., Tinker, A., Manthorpe, J., Biggs, S. and Erens, B. (2007) *UK Study of Abuse and Neglect of Older People, Prevalence Survey Report*, London: Department of Health and Comic Relief.

Office for National Statistics (2004) *Focus on Older People*, London: Office for National Statistics.

Office for National Statistics (2008) *Health Survey for England Adult Trend Tables 2006*, London: Office for National Statistics.

Office for National Statistics (2010) *Statistics on Obesity, Physical Activity and Diet*, London: Office for National Statistics.

Office for National Statistics (2011) *Labour Force Survey*, London: Office for National Statistics.

Office for National Statistics (2013) *Families and Households*, London: Office for National Statistics.

Office for National Statistics (2014) *Crime Survey for England and Wales, 2013–2014*, London: Office for National Statistics.

Office for National Statistics (2015a) *Life Expectancy at Birth and at Age 65 by Local Areas in England and Wales: 2012 to 2014*, London: Office for National Statistics.

Office for National Statistics (2015b) *National Life Tables: United Kingdom 2012–2014*, London: Office for National Statistics.

Office for National Statistics (2016a) *Leading Causes of Death in England and Wales*, London: Office for National Statistics.

Office for National Statistics (2016b) *Measuring National Well-being: At What Age is Personal Well-being the Highest?* London: Office for National Statistics.

Office for National Statistics (2017a) *National Population Projections: 2016-based statistical bulletin*, London: Office for National Statistics.

Office for National Statistics (2017b) *Deaths from Dehydration and Malnutrition, by Place of Death, England and Wales, 2014 to 2015*, London: Office for National Statistics.

Office for National Statistics (2017c) *Statistical Bulletin: Suicides in the UK: 2017*, London: Office for National Statistics.

Office for National Statistics (2017d) *Excess Winter Mortality in England and Wales: 2016 to 2017 (provisional) and 2015 to 2016 (final)*, London: Office for National Statistics.

Office for National Statistics (2018) *Health State Life Expectancies by National Deprivation Deciles, England and Wales: 2014 to 2016*, London: Office for National Statistics.

Office of the Deputy Prime Minister (2006) *The Social Exclusion of Older People: Evidence from the First Wave of the English Longitudinal Survey of Ageing*, London: Office for National Statistics.

Officer, A., Schneiders, M.L., Wu, D., Nash, P., Thiyagarajan, J.A. and Beard, J.R. (2016) *Valuing Older People: Time for a Global Campaign to Combat Ageism*, [online] https://www.who.int/bulletin/volumes/94/10/16-184960/en/ [Accessed 5 December 2017].

O'Leary, P. and Gould, N. (2008) 'Men who were sexually abused in childhood and subsequent suicidal ideation: community comparison, explanations and practice implications', *British Journal of Social Work*, 39(5): 950–68.

Oliver, D. (2018) 'England's social care models harm the poorest areas', *British Medical Journal*, 361: k2745.

Oliver, D., Foot, C. and Humphries, R. (2014) *Making Our Health and Care Systems Fit for an Ageing Population*, London: The King's Fund.

Oliver, M. (2013) 'The social model of disability: thirty years on', *Disability and Society*, 28(7): 1024–6.

Onega, L.L., Pierce, T.W. and Epperly, L. (2016) 'Effect of bright light exposure on depression and agitation in older adults with dementia', *Issues in Mental Health Nursing*, 37(9): 660–7.

Ong, A.D., Bergeman, C.S., Bisconti, T.L. and Wallace, K.A. (2006) 'Psychological resilience, positive emotions, and successful adaptation to stress in later life', *Journal of Personality and Social Psychology*, 91(4): 730–49.

O'Rand, A.M. (2001) 'Stratification and the life course: forms of life course capital and their interrelationships', in R.B. Binstock and L.K. George (eds) *Handbook of Aging and the Social Sciences* (5th edn), New York: Academic Press, pp 197–216.

Organisation for Economic Co-operation and Development (2015) *Addressing Dementia: The OECD Response*, Paris: OECD Publishing.

Österholm, J.H. and Hydén, L.C. (2018) 'Autobiographical occasions in assessment meetings involving persons with dementia', *Qualitative Social Work*, 17(1): 41–64.

Ostir, G.V., Markides, K.S., Peek, M.K. and Goodwin, J.S. (2001) 'The association between emotional well-being and the incidence of stroke in older adults', *Psychosomatic Medicine*, 63(2): 210–15.

Ottmann, G. and Maragoudaki, M. (2015) 'Fostering resilience later in life: a narrative approach involving people facing disabling circumstances, carers and members of minority groups', *Ageing and Society*, 35(10): 2071–99.

Oudman, E. and Veurink, B. (2007) 'Quality of life in nursing home residents with advanced dementia: a 2-year follow-up', *Psychogeriatrics*, 14(4): 235–40.

Owen, T., Meyer, J., Cornell, M., Dudman, P., Ferreira, Z., Hamilton, S., Moore, J. and Wallis, J. (2012) *My Home Life: Promoting Quality of Life in Care Homes*, York: Joseph Roundtree Foundation.

Ownby, R.L., Crocco, E., Acevedo, A., John, V. and Loewenstein, D. (2006) 'Depression and risk for Alzheimer disease: systematic review, meta-analysis, and metaregression analysis', *Archives of General Psychiatry*, 63(5): 530–8.

Oxley, H. (2009) *Policies for Health Ageing: An Overview*, Paris: Organisation for Economic Co-operation and Development.

Oyebode, J.R. and Parveen, S. (2016) 'Psychosocial interventions for people with dementia: an overview and commentary on recent developments', *Dementia*, 18(1): 8–35.

Pannell, J., Aldridge, H. and Kenway, P. (2012) *Older People's Housing: Choice, Quality of Life and Under-Occupation*, York: Joseph Rowntree Foundation.

Parker, J. (2001) 'Interrogating person-centred dementia care in social work and social care practice', *Journal of Social Work*, 1(3): 329–45.

Parliamentary and Health Service Ombudsman (2011) *Responsive and Accountable? The Ombudsman's Review of Complaint Handling by Government Departments and Public Bodies 2010–11*, London: The Stationery Office.

Patel, R. (2016) *The State of Social Capital in Britain: Policy Briefing*, Colchester: Understanding Society.

Peel, E. (2014) '"The living death of Alzheimer's" versus "Take a walk to keep dementia at bay": representations of dementia in print media and carer discourse', *Sociology of Health and Illness*, 36(6): 885–901.

Penhale, B. (1999) 'Bruises on the soul: older women, domestic violence, and elder abuse', *Journal of Elder Abuse and Neglect*, 11(1): 1–22.

Penninx, B.W., Guralnik, J.M., Ferrucci, L., Simonsick, E.M., Deeg, D.J. and Wallace, R.B. (1998) 'Depressive symptoms and physical decline in community-dwelling older persons', *Journal of the American Medical Association*, 279(21): 1720–6.

Peterson, A. and Lupton, D. (2000) *The New Public Health: Health and Self in the Age of Risk*, London: Sage.

Pettit, S., Qureshi, A., Lee, W., Stirzaker, A., Gibson, A., Henley, W. and Byng, R. (2017) 'Variation in referral and access to new psychological therapy services by age: an empirical quantitative study', *British Journal of General Practice*, 67(660): e453–9.

Phair, L. (2016) 'Living with dementia in a care home: the importance of well-being and quality of life on physical and mental health', in C. Chew-Graham and M. Ray (eds) *Mental Health and Older People: A Guide for Primary Care Practitioners*, Silver Spring: Springer.

Phillips, J.A. (2014) 'A changing epidemiology of suicide? The influence of birth cohorts on suicide rates in the United States', *Social Science and Medicine*, 114: 151–60.

Phillips, J.E., Ajrouch, K.J. and Hillcoat-Nallétamby, S. (2010) *Key Concepts in Social Gerontology*, London: Sage.

Phillips, L. (2000) 'Domestic abuse and aging women', *Geriatric Nursing*, 21(4): 188–95.

Phillipson, C. (2011) 'Towards a new sociology of ageing: from structured dependency to critical gerontology', in A. Walker, A. Sinfield and C. Walker (eds) *Fighting Poverty, Inequality and Injustice*, Bristol: Policy Press.

Phillipson, C. (2013) *Ageing*, Cambridge: Polity Press.

Phillipson, C. (2015) 'The political economy of longevity: developing new forms of solidarity for later life', *The Sociological Quarterly*, 56(1): 80–100.

Phillipson, C. and Walker, A. (1987) 'The case for a critical gerontology', in S. di Gregorio (ed) *Social Gerontology: New Directions*, London: Croom Helm, pp 1–15.

Phillipson, C. and Biggs, S. (1998) Modernity and identity: themes and perspectives in the study of older adults, *Journal of Aging and Identity*, 3(1): 11–23.

Phillipson, C., Vickerstaff, S. and Lain, D. (2016) 'Achieving fuller working lives: labour market and policy issues in the United Kingdom', *Australian Journal of Social Issues*, 51(2): 187–203.

Pickard, L., King, D. and Knapp, M. (2016) 'The "visibility" of unpaid care in England', *Journal of Social Work*, 16(3): 263–82.

Pickard, S. (2014) 'Frail bodies: geriatric medicine and the constitution of the fourth age,' *Sociology of Health and Illness*, 36(4): 549–63.

Pickett, J.A., Bird, C., Ballard, C., Banerjee, S., Brayne, C., Cowan, K., Clare, L., Comas-Herrera, A., Corner, L., Daley, S., Knapp, M., Lafortune, L., Livingston, G., Manthorpe, J., Marchant, N., Moriarty, J., Robinson, L., van Lynden, C., Windle, G., Woods, B., Gray, K. and Walton, C. (2018) 'A roadmap to advance dementia research in prevention, diagnosis, intervention, and care by 2025', *International Journal of Geriatric Psychiatry*, 33(7): 900–6.

Pickett, K.E., James, O.W. and Wilkinson, R.G. (2006) 'Income inequality and the prevalence of mental illness: a preliminary international analysis', *Journal of Epidemiology and Community Health*, 60(7): 646–7.

Pike, L. and Walsh, J. (2015) *Making Safeguarding Personal: 2014–15 Evaluation Report*, London: London Government Association.

Pilgrim, D. (2007) 'The survival of psychiatric diagnosis', *Social Science and Medicine*, 65(3): 536–47.

Pillemer, K. and Moore, D.W. (1989) 'Abuse of patients in nursing homes: findings from a survey of staff', *The Gerontologist*, 29(3): 314–20.

Pinquart, M. and Sörensen, S. (2000) 'Influences of socioeconomic status, social network, and competence on subjective well-being in later life: a meta-analysis', *Psychology and Aging*, 15(2): 187–224.

Plassman, B.L., Williams, J.W., Burke, J.R., Holsinger, T. and Benjamin, S. (2010) 'Systematic review: factors associated with risk for and possible prevention of cognitive decline in later life', *Annals of Internal Medicine*, 153(3): 182–93.

Ploubidis, G.B. and Grundy, E. (2009) 'Later-life mental health in Europe: a country-level comparison', *Journals of Gerontology Series B: Psychological Sciences and Social Sciences*, 64(5): 666–76.

Porter, V.R., Buxton, W.G., Fairbanks, L.A., Strickland, T., O'Connor, S.M., Rosenberg-Thompson, S. and Cummings, J.L. (2003) 'Frequency and characteristics of anxiety among patients with Alzheimer's disease and related dementias', *The Journal of Neuropsychiatry and Clinical Neurosciences*, 15(2): 180–6.

Pratschke, J., Haase, T. and McKeown, K. (2017) 'Direct and indirect influences of socioeconomic position on the wellbeing of older adults: a Structural Equation Model using data from the first wave of the Irish Longitudinal Study on Ageing', *Ageing and Society*, 37(9): 1770–97.

Price, D. (2006) 'The Poverty of People in the UK', *Journal of Social Work*, 20(3): 251–66.

Price, D., Glaser, K., Ginn, J. and Nicholls, M. (2016) 'How important are state transfers for reducing poverty rates in later life?', *Ageing and Society*, 36(9): 1794–825.

Priestley, M. (2004). 'Tragedy strikes again! Why community care still poses a problem for integrated living', in J. Swain, S. French, C. Barnes and C. Thomas (eds) *Disabling Barriers – Enabling Environments*, London: Sage, pp 258–63.

Prince, M.J., Harwood, R.H., Blizard, R.A., Thomas, A. and Mann, A.H. (1997) 'Social support deficits, loneliness and life events as risk factors for depression in old age. The Gospel Oak Project VI', *Psychological Medicine*, 27(2): 323–32.

Prince, M.J., Wimo, A., Guerchet, M.M., Ali, G.C., Wu, Y-T. and Prina, M. (2015) *World Alzheimer's Report 2015: The Global Impact of Dementia*, London: Alzheimer's Disease International.

Prince, M.J, Knapp, M., Guerchet, M., McCrone, P., Prina, M., Cormas-Herrera, A., Wittenberg, R., Adelaja, B., Hu, B., King, D., Rehill, A. and Salimkumar, D. (2014) *Dementia UK: Update*, London: Alzheimer's Society.

Prus, S. (2003) *A Life-Course Perspective on the Relationship Between Socioeconomic Status and Health: Testing the Divergence Hypothesis*, Hamilton, ON: McMaster University.

Public Health England (2013) *Obesity and Disability*, London: Public Health England.

Public Health England (2015) *Marmot Indicators 2015: Background Report*, London: UCL Institute of Health Equality.

Public Health England (2016) *Health Matters: Midlife Approaches to Reduce Dementia Risk*, London: Public Health England.

Public Health England (2019) *Prevention Concordat for Better Mental Health*, London: Public Health England.

Purdam, K., Garratt, E.A. and Esmail, A. (2016) 'Hungry? Food insecurity, social stigma and embarrassment in the UK', *Sociology*, 50(6): 1072–88.

Putnam, R.D. (2000). 'Bowling alone: America's declining social capital', in L. Crothers and C. Lockhart (eds) *Culture and Politics*, New York: Palgrave Macmillan, pp 223–34.

Qiu, C., Karp, A., von Strauss, E., Winblad, B., Fratiglioni, L. and Bellander, T. (2003) 'Lifetime principal occupation and risk of Alzheimer's disease in the Kungsholmen project', *American Journal of Industrial Medicine*, 43(2): 204–11.

Quince, C. (2013) *Low Expectations: Attitudes on Choice, Care and Community for People with Dementia in Care Homes*, London: Alzheimer's Society.

Qureshi, S.U., Long, M.E., Bradshaw, M.R., Pyne, J.M., Magruder, K.M., Kimbrell, T., Hudson, T.J., Jawaid, A., Schulz, P.E. and Kunik, M.E. (2011) 'Does PTSD impair cognition beyond the effect of trauma?', *The Journal of Neuropsychiatry and Clinical Neurosciences*, 23(1): 16–28.

Race Equality Foundation (2016) *Dementia Equity and Rights*, London: Race Equality Foundation.

Rand, S. and Malley, J. (2014) 'Carers' quality of life and experiences of adult social care support in England', *Health and Social Care in the Community*, 22(4): 375–85.

Rao, R.T., Buxey, R. and Jalloh, K. (2011) 'Alcohol and dual diagnosis in older people', in J. Keady and S. Watts (eds) *Mental Health and Later Life: Developing An Holistic Model for Practice*, Oxon: Routledge, pp 88–103.

Ratcliff, K.S. (2017) *The Social Determinants of Health: Looking Upstream*, Hoboken, NJ: Wiley.

Ray, K.D. and Mittelman, M.S. (2017) 'Music therapy: a nonpharmacological approach to the care of agitation and depressive symptoms for nursing home residents with dementia', *Dementia*, 16(6): 689–710.

Ray, M. (2016a) 'Policy context for mental health and older people', in C. Chew-Graham and M. Ray (eds) *Mental Health and Older People: A Guide for Primary Care Practitioners*, Silver Spring: Springer.

Ray, M. (2016b) 'Person centred care and dementia', in C. Chew-Graham and M. Ray (eds) *Mental Health and Older People: A Guide for Primary Care Practitioners*, Silver Spring: Springer.

Ray, M. and Phillips, J. (2012) *Social Work with Older People*, Basingstoke: Palgrave Macmillan.

Ray, M. and Sullivan, M.P. (2016) *Care Homes and Older People: Lessons from Research*, Lincoln: Community Care Inform.

Ray, M., Bernard, M. and Phillips, J. (2009) *Critical Issues in Social Work with Older People*, Basingstoke: Palgrave Macmillan.

Ray, M., Milne, A., Beech, C., Phillips, J., Richards, S., Sullivan, M.P., Tanner, D. and Lloyd, L. (2015) 'Gerontological social work: reflections on its role, purpose and value', *British Journal of Social Work*, 45(4): 1296–312.

Ray, R.E. (1996) 'A postmodern perspective on feminist gerontology', *The Gerontologist*, 36(5): 674–80.

Ready, R.E. and Ott, B.R. (2003) 'Quality of life measures for dementia', *Health and Quality of Life Outcomes*, 1(1): 11.

Rechel, B., Grundy, E., Robine, J.M., Cylus, J., Mackenbach, J.P., Knai, C. and McKee, M. (2013) 'Ageing in the European Union', *The Lancet*, 381(9874): 1312–22.

Rees, J. (2014) 'Public sector commissioning and the third sector: old wine in new bottles?', *Public Policy and Administration*, 29(1): 45–63.

Reeve, D. (2002) 'Negotiating psycho-emotional dimensions of disability and their influence on identity constructions', *Disability and Society*, 17(5): 493–508.

Regan, M. (2016) *The Interface Between Dementia and Mental Health: An Evidence Review*, London: Mental Health Foundation.

Rena, F., Moshe, S. and Abraham, O. (1996) 'Couples' adjustment to one partner's disability: the relationship between sense of coherence and adjustment', *Social Science and Medicine*, 43(2): 163–71.

Richards, S. (2000) 'Bridging the divide: elders and the assessment process', *British Journal of Social Work*, 30(1): 37–49.

Richards, S., Sullivan, M.P., Tanner, D., Beech, C., Milne, A., Ray, M., Phillips, J. and Lloyd, L. (2014) 'On the edge of a new frontier: is gerontological social work in the UK ready to meet 21st-century challenges?', *British Journal of Social Work*, 44(8): 2307–24.

Richardson, J.C. and Chew-Graham, C. (2016) 'Resilience and well-being', in C. Chew-Graham and M. Ray (eds) *Mental Health and Older People: A Guide for Primary Care*, Silver Spring: Springer.

Richardson, K., Fox, C., Maidment, I., Steel, N., Loke, Y.K., Arthur, A., Myint, P.K., Grossi, C.M., Mattishent, K., Nennett, K., Campbell, N.L., Boustani, M., Robinson, L., Brayne, C., Matthews, F.E. and Savva, G.M. (2018) 'Anticholinergic drugs and risk of dementia: case-control study', *British Medical Journal*, 361: k1315.

Richardson, S., Karunananthan, S. and Bergman, H. (2011) 'I may be frail but I ain't no failure', *Canadian Geriatrics Journal*, 14(1): 24–8.

Rippon, I., Kneale, D., de Oliveira, C., Demakakos, P. and Steptoe, A. (2014) 'Perceived age discrimination in older adults', *Age and Ageing*, 43(3): 379–86.

Robinson, L., Tang, E. and Taylor, J-P. (2015) 'Dementia: timely diagnosis and early intervention', *British Medical Journal*, 36(8013): 28–31.

Rocca, W.A., Bower, J.H., Maraganore, D.M., Ahlskog, J.E., Grossardt, B.R., De Andrade, M. and Melton, L. (2007) 'Increased risk of cognitive impairment or dementia in women who underwent oophorectomy before menopause', *Neurology*, 69(11): 1074–83.

Rockwood, K., Song, X., MacKnight, C., Bergman, H., Hogan, D.B., McDowell, I. and Mitnitski, A. (2005) 'A global clinical measure of fitness and frailty in elderly people', *Canadian Medical Association Journal*, 173(5): 489–95.

Rogalski, E., Gefen, T., Mao, Q., Connelly, M., Weintraub, S., Geula, C., Bigio, E.H. and Mesulam, M-M. (2018) 'Cognitive trajectories and spectrum of neuropathology in SuperAgers: the first 10 cases', *Hippocampus*, 29(5): 458–67.

Rogers, A. and Pilgrim, D. (2003) *Inequalities and Mental Health*, London: Palgrave Macmillan.

Rogers, A. and Pilgrim, D. (2014) *A Sociology of Mental Health and Illness*, Maidenhead: McGraw-Hill Education.

Rogers, N.T., Steptoe, A. and Cadar, D. (2018) 'Frailty is an independent predictor of incident dementia: evidence from the English Longitudinal Study of Ageing', *Scientific Reports*, 7(1): 15746.

Ropacki, S.A. and Jeste, D.V. (2005) 'Epidemiology of and risk factors for psychosis of Alzheimer's disease: a review of 55 studies published from 1990 to 2003', *American Journal of Psychiatry*, 162(11): 2022–30.

Ross, F., Donovan, S., Brearley, S., Victor, C., Cottee, M., Crowther, P. and Clark, E. (2005) 'Involving older people in research: methodological issues', *Health and Social Care in the Community*, 13(3): 268–75.

Rowlingson, K. (2011) *Does Income Inequality Cause Health and Social Problems?* London: Joseph Rowntree Foundation.

Royal College of Psychiatrists (2000) *Institutional Abuse of Older People*, London: Royal College of Psychiatrists.

Royal College of Psychiatrists (2010) *No Health without Public Mental Health: The Case for Action*, London: Royal College of Psychiatrists.

Royal College of Psychiatrists (2011) *Our Invisible Addicts. First Report of the Older Persons' Substance Misuse Working Group of the Royal College of Psychiatrists*, London: Royal College of Psychiatrists.

Royal College of Psychiatrists (2018) *Suffering in Silence: Age Inequality in Older People's Mental Health Care*, London: Royal College of Psychiatrists.

Royal College of Surgeons, Age UK and MHP Health Mandate (2015) *Access All Ages 2: Exploring Variations in Access to Surgery Among Older People*, London: The Royal College of Surgeons of England.

Russ, T.C., Stamatakis, E., Hamer, M., Starr, J.M., Kivimäki, M. and Batty, G.D. (2013) 'Socioeconomic status as a risk factor for dementia death: individual participant meta-analysis of 86,508 men and women from the UK', *The British Journal of Psychiatry*, 203(1): 10–17.

Rutherford, J. (2008) *Well-Being, Economic Growth and Social Recession*, London: Middlesex University.

Ryan, R.M. and Deci, E.L. (2001) 'On happiness and human potentials: a review of research on hedonic and eudaimonic well-being', *Annual Review of Psychology*, 52(1): 141–66.

Ryan, T., Nolan, M., Reid, D. and Enderby, P. (2008) 'Using the senses framework to achieve relationship-centred dementia care services: a case example', *Dementia*, 7(1): 71–93.

Ryff, C.D. (1989a) 'Beyond Ponce de Leon and life satisfaction: new directions in quest of successful ageing', *International Journal of Behavioral Development*, 12(1): 35–55.

Ryff, C.D. (1989b) 'Happiness is everything, or is it? Explorations on the meaning of psychological well-being', *Journal of Personality and Social Psychology*, 57(6): 1069–81.

Ryff, C.D. and Singer, B. (2002) 'From social structure to biology' in C.R. Snyder and S.J. Lopex (eds) *Handbook of Positive Psychology*, Oxford: Oxford University Press, pp 63–73.

Ryff, C.D., Singer, B. and Love, G.D. (2004) 'Positive health: connecting well-being with biology', *Philosophical Transactions of the Royal Society of Biological Sciences*, 359 (1449), 1383–94.

Ryff, C.D., Love, G.D., Urry, H.L., Muller, D., Rosenkranz, M.A., Friedman, E.M., Davidson, R.J. and Singer, B. (2006) 'Psychological well-being and ill-being: do they have distinct or mirrored biological correlates?', *Psychotherapy and Psychosomatics*, 75(2): 85–95.

Sabat, S.R. (1994) 'Excess disability and malignant social psychology: a case study of Alzheimer's disease', *Journal of Community and Applied Social Psychology*, 4(3): 157–66.

Sabat, S.R. (2002) 'Surviving manifestations of selfhood in Alzheimer's disease: a case study', *Dementia*, 1(1): 25–36.

Sabat, S.R. (2005) 'Capacity for decision-making in Alzheimer's disease: selfhood, positioning and semiotic people', *Australian and New Zealand Journal of Psychiatry*, 39(11–12): 1030–5.

Sabat, S.R. (2008) 'A bio-psycho-social approach to dementia', in M. Downs and B. Bowers (eds) *Excellence in Dementia Care: Research into Practice*, Maidenhead: McGraw-Hill Education, pp 70–84.

Sabat, S.R. (2014). 'The person with dementia as understood through Stern's critical personalism', in L-C. Hydén, H. Lindemann and J. Brockmeier (eds) *Beyond Loss: Dementia, Identity, Personhood*, Oxford: Oxford University Press, pp 24–38.

Sabat, S.R., Napolitano, L. and Fath, H. (2004) 'Barriers to the construction of a valued social identity: a case study of Alzheimer's disease', *American Journal of Alzheimer's Disease and Other Dementias*, 19(3): 177–85.

SafeLives (2016) *Safe Later Lives: Older People and Domestic Abuse*, [online] http://safelives.org.uk/sites/default/files/resources/Safe%20Later%20Lives%20-%20Older%20people%20and%20domestic%20abuse.pdf [Accessed 13 January 2019].

Samsi, K., Manthorpe, J. and Chandaria, K. (2014) 'Risks of financial abuse of older people with dementia: findings from a survey of UK voluntary sector dementia community services staff', *The Journal of Adult Protection*, 16(3): 180–92.

Samus, Q.M., Rosenblatt, A., Steele, C., Baker, A., Harper, M., Brandt, J., Mayer, L., Rabin, P.V. and Lyketsos, C.G. (2005) 'The association of neuropsychiatric symptoms and environment with quality of life in assisted living residents with dementia', *The Gerontologist*, 45(Special Issue 1): 19–26.

Sands, L.P., Ferreira, P., Stewart, A.L., Brod, M. and Yaffe, K. (2004) 'What explains differences between dementia patients' and their caregivers' ratings of patients' quality of life?', *The American Journal of Geriatric Psychiatry*, 12(3): 272–80.

Sargent-Cox, K. (2017) 'Ageism: we are our own worst enemy', *International Psychogeriatrics*, 29(1): 1–8.

Sarkisian, C.A., Lee-Henderson, M.H. and Mangione, C.M. (2003) 'Do depressed older adults who attribute depression to "old age" believe it is important to seek care?', *Journal of General Internal Medicine*, 18(12): 1001–5.

Savitch, N., Abbott, E. and Parker, G. (2011) *Dementia: Through the Eyes of Women*, York: Joseph Rowntree Foundation.

Scharf, T. and Keating, N. (2012) *From Exclusion to Inclusion in Old Age: A Global Challenge*, Bristol: Policy Press.

Scharf, T., Phillipson, C. and Smith, A. (2004) 'Poverty and social exclusion – growing older in deprived urban neighbourhoods', in A. Walker and C.H. Hennessy (eds) *Growing Older: Quality of Life in Old Age*, Maidenhead: McGraw-Hill, pp 81–106.

Scharf, T., Shaw, C., Bamford, S.M., Beach, B. and Hochlaf, D. (2017) *Inequalities in Later Life*, London: Centre for Ageing Better.

Schwarzbach, M., Luppa, M., Forstmeier, S., König, H.H. and Riedel-Heller, S.G. (2014) 'Social relations and depression in late life: a systematic review', *International Journal of Geriatric Psychiatry*, 29(1): 1–21.

Scott, K.M., Koenen, K.C., Aguilar-Gaxiola, S., Alonso, J., Angermeyer, M.C., Benjet, C., Bruffaerts, R., Caldas-de-Almeida, J.M., de Girolamo, G., Florescu, S., Iwata, N., Levinson, D., Lim, C.C.W., Murphy, S., Ormel, J., Posada-Villa, J. and Kessler, R.C. (2013) 'Associations between lifetime traumatic events and subsequent chronic physical conditions: a cross-national, cross-sectional study', *PloS One*, 8(11): e80573.

Scott, M., McKie, L., Morton, S., Seddon, E. and Wosoff, F. (2004) *Older Women and Domestic Violence in Scotland '… and for 39 Years I Got on with It'*, Edinburgh: NHS Health Scotland.

Scottish Government (2009) *Towards a Mentally Flourishing Scotland*, Edinburgh: Scottish Government.

Scottish Government (2010) *Scotland's National Dementia Strategy*, Edinburgh: Scottish Government.

Scottish Government (2012) *Mental Health Strategy for Scotland: 2012–2015*, Edinburgh: Scottish Government.

Scottish Government (2016) *The Scottish Health Survey 2015: Volume 1, Main Report*, Edinburgh: Scottish Government.

Secker, J., Hill, R., Villeneau, L. and Parkman, S. (2003) 'Promoting independence: but promoting what and how?', *Ageing and Society*, 23(3): 375–91.

Seeman, T.E., Crimmins, E., Huang, M.H., Singer, B., Bucur, A., Gruenewald, T., Berkman, L.F. and Reuden, D.B. (2004) 'Cumulative biological risk and socio-economic differences in mortality: McArthur studies of successful ageing', *Social Science and Medicine*, 58(10), 1985–97.

Segal, D.L., Qualls, S.H. and Smyer, M.A. (2017) *Aging and Mental Health*, Hoboken, NJ: John Wiley and Sons.

Seignourel, P.J., Kunik, M.E., Snow, L., Wilson, N. and Stanley, M. (2008) 'Anxiety in dementia: a critical review', *Clinical Psychology Review*, 28(7): 1071–82.

Selwood, A., Thorgrimsen, L. and Orrell, M. (2005) 'Quality of life in dementia – a one-year follow-up study', *International Journal of Geriatric Psychiatry*, 20(3): 232–7.

Sen, A. (1992) *Inequality Reexamined*, Wotton-under-Edge: Clarendon Press.

Sethi, D., Wood, S., Mitis, F., Bellis, M., Penhale, B., Marmolejo, I.I., Lowenstein, A., Manthorpe, J. and Ulvestad Kärki, F. (eds) (2011) *European Report on Preventing Elder Maltreatment*, Geneva: World Health Organization.

Settersten, R.A. (2003) 'Age structuring and the rhythm of the life course', in J.T. Mortimer and M.J. Shanahan (eds) *Handbook of the Life Course*, Boston, MA: Springer, pp 81–98.

Sevenhuijsen, S. (2004) 'Trace: a method for normative policy analysis from the ethic of care', in S. Svenhuijsen and A. Svab (eds) *The Heart of the Matter: The Contribution of the Ethic of Care to Social Policy in Some New EU Member States*, Ljubljana: The Peace Institute, pp 13–46.

Shakespeare, T. (2006) *Disability Rights and Wrongs*, London: Routledge.

Shakespeare, T. (2013) *Disability Rights and Wrongs Revsited*, London: Routledge.

Shakespeare, T., Zeilig, H. and Mittler, P. (2017) 'Rights in mind: thinking differently about dementia and disability', *Dementia*, 18(3): 1075–88.

Shankar, A., Hamer, M., McMunn, A. and Steptoe, A. (2013) 'Social isolation and loneliness: relationships with cognitive function during 4 years of follow-up in the English Longitudinal Study of Ageing', *Psychosomatic Medicine*, 75(2): 161–70.

Shaw, L.J., Lewis, J.F., Hlatky, M.A., Hsueh, W.A., Kelsey, S.F., Klein, R., Manolio, T.A. Richey Sharrett, A. and Tracy, R.P. (2004) 'Women's Ischemic Syndrome Evaluation: current status and future research directions: Report of the National Heart, Lung and Blood Institute workshop: October 2–4, 2002: Section 5: Gender-related risk factors for ischemic heart disease', *Circulation*, 109(6): e56–8.

Shonkoff, J.P., Boyce, W.T. and McEwen, B.S. (2009) 'Neuroscience, molecular biology, and the childhood roots of health disparities: building a new framework for health promotion and disease prevention', *Journal of the American Medical Association*, 301(21): 2252–9.

Shonkoff, J.P., Garner, A.S., Committee on Psychosocial Aspects of Child and Family Health and Committee on Early Childhood, Adoption, and Dependent Care (2011) 'The lifelong effects of early childhood adversity and toxic stress', *Pediatrics*, 129(1): e232–46.

Sidanius, J. and Pratto, F. (1999) *Social Dominance: An Intergroup Theory of Social Hierarchy and Oppression*, New York: Cambridge University Press.

Sixsmith, J., Sixsmith, A., Fänge, A.M., Naumann, D., Kucsera, S., Tomsone, S., Haak, M., Dahlin-Ivanhoff, S. and Woolrych, R. (2014) 'Healthy ageing and home: the perspectives of very old people in five European countries', *Social Science and Medicine*, 106: 1–9.

Skeggs, B. (2004) 'Context and background: Pierre Bourdieu's analysis of class, gender and sexuality', *The Sociological Review*, 52(2_suppl): 19–33.

Skidmore, P., Bound, K. and Lownsbrough, H. (2006) *Community Participation: Who Benefits?* York: Joseph Roundtree Foundation.

Skogen, J.C., Bergh, S., Stewart, R., Knudsen, A.K. and Bjerkeset, O. (2015) Midlife mental distress and risk for dementia up to 27 years later: the Nord-Trøndelag Health Study (HUNT) in linkage with a dementia registry in Norway', *BMC Geriatrics*, 15(1): 23.

Slasberg, C. and Beresford, P. (2016) 'The false narrative about personal budgets in England: smoke and mirrors? *Disability and Society*, 31(8): 1132–7.

Sloane, P.D., Brooker, D., Cohen, L., Douglass, C., Edelman, P., Fulton, B.R., Jarrott, S., Kasayka, R., Kuhn, D., Preisser, J.S., Williams, C. and Zimmerman, S. (2007) 'Dementia care mapping as a research tool', *International Journal of Geriatric Psychiatry*, 22(6): 580–9.

Smalbrugge, M., Pot, A., Jongenelis, K., Beekman, A.T. and Eefsting, J.A. (2005) 'Prevalence and correlates of anxiety among nursing home patients', *Journal of Affective Disorders*, 88(2): 145–53.

Smale, G., Tuson, G. and Statham, D. (2000) *Social Work and Social Problems: Working Towards Social Inclusion and Social Change*, Basingstoke: Macmillan Press.

Smith, G.D., Hart, C., Blane, D., Gillis, C. and Hawthorne, V. (1997) 'Lifetime socioeconomic position and mortality: prospective observational study', *British Medical Journal*, 314(7080): 547.

Smith, L. and Foxcroft, D. (2009) *Drinking in the UK: An Exploration of Trends*, York: Joseph Rowntree Foundation.

Smith, M., Gallagher, M., Wosu, H., Stewart, J., Cree, V.E., Hunter, S., Evans, S., Montgomery, C., Holiday, S. and Wilkinson, H. (2011) 'Engaging with involuntary service users in social work: findings from a knowledge exchange project', *British Journal of Social Work*, 42(8): 1460–77.

Smith, S.C., Lamping, D.L., Banerjee, S., Harwood, R., Foley, B., Smith, P., Cook, J.C., Murray, J., Prince, M., Levin, E., Mann, A. and Knapp, M. (2005) 'Measurement of health-related quality of life for people with dementia: development of a new instrument (DEMQOL) and an evaluation of current methodology', *Health Technology Assessment (Winchester, England)*, 9(10): 1–93.

Social Exclusion Unit (2006) *A Sure Start to Later Life, Ending Inequalities for Older People*, London: Office of the Deputy Prime Minister.

Sofi, F., Abbate, R., Gensini, G.F. and Casini, A. (2010) 'Accruing evidence on benefits of adherence to the Mediterranean diet on health: an updated systematic review and meta-analysis', *The American Journal of Clinical Nutrition*, 92(5): 1189–96.

Soulsby, L. and Bennett, K. (2015) 'How relationships help us to age well', *The Psychologist*, 28(2): 110–13.

Spencer, L. and Pahl, R. (2006). *Rethinking Friendship: Hidden Solidarities Today*, Princeton, NJ: Princeton University Press.

Sproston, K. and Mindell, J. (2006) *Health Survey for England 2004: The Health of Minority Ethnic Groups*, Leeds: NHS Information Centre.

Standing, G. (2010) *The Precariat: The New Dangerous Class*, London: Bloomsbury Press.

Starkstein, S.E., Jorge, R., Petracca, G., Robinson, R.G. (2007) 'The construct of generalized anxiety disorder in Alzheimer disease', *American Journal of Geriatric Psychiatry*, 15(1): 42–9.

Steel, N., Hardcastle, A.C., Bachmann, M.O., Richards, S.H., Mounce, L.T.A., Clark, A., Lang, I., Melzer, D. and Campbell, J. (2014) 'Economic inequalities in the burden of illness, diagnosis and treatment of five long-term conditions in England: panel study', *BMJ Open*, 4(10).

Steele, I.H., Thrower, N., Noroian, P. and Saleh, F.M. (2018) 'Understanding suicide across the lifespan: a United States perspective of suicide risk factors, assessment and management', *Journal of Forensic Sciences*, 63(1): 162–71.

Steeman, E., Godderis, J., Grypdonck, M., De Bal, N. and De Casterlé, B.D. (2007) 'Living with dementia from the perspective of older people: is it a positive story?', *Aging and Mental Health*, 11(2): 119–30.

Stenner, P., McFarquhar, T. and Bowling, A. (2011) 'Older people and "active ageing": subjective aspects of ageing actively', *Journal of Health Psychology*, 16(3): 467–77.

Steptoe, A. and Marmot, M. (2004) 'Socioeconomic status and coronary heart disease: a psychobiological perspective', *Population and Development Review*, 30, 133–50.

Steptoe, A., Wardle, J. and Marmot, M. (2005) 'Positive affect and health-related neuroendocrine, cardiovascular, and inflammatory processes', *Proceedings of the National Academy of Sciences of the United States of America*, 102(18): 6508–12.

Steptoe, A., Deaton, A. and Stone, A.A. (2015) 'Subjective wellbeing, health, and ageing', *The Lancet*, 385(9968): 640–8.

Steptoe, A., Shankar, A., Demakakos, P. and Wardle, J. (2013a) 'Social isolation, loneliness, and all-cause mortality in older men and women', *Proceedings of the National Academy of Sciences*, 110(15): 5797–801.

Steptoe, A., Breeze, E., Banks, J. and Nazroo, J. (2013b) 'Cohort profile: the English longitudinal study of ageing', *International Journal of Epidemiology*, 42(6): 1640–8.

Steptoe, A., Feldman, P., Kunz, S., Owen, N., Willemsen, G. and Marmot, M. (2002) 'Stress responsivity and socio-economic status: a mechanism for increased cardiovascular disease risk?', *European Heart Journal*, 23(22), 1757–63.

Stern, Y. (2012) 'Cognitive reserve in ageing and Alzheimer's disease', *The Lancet Neurology*, 11(11): 1006–12.

Subramaniam, P., Woods, B. and Whitaker, C. (2014) 'Life review and life story books for people with mild to moderate dementia: a randomised controlled trial', *Aging and Mental Health*, 18(3): 363–75.

Subramanian, S.V. and Kawachi, I. (2004) 'Income inequality and health: what have we learned so far?', *Epidemiologic Review*, 26: 78–91.

Sullivan, L.H. (1956) *The Autobiography of an Idea*, Mineola, NY: Dover Publications.

Surr, C.A. (2006) 'Preservation of self in people with dementia living in residential care: a socio-biographical approach', *Social Science and Medicine*, 62(7): 1720–30.

Swift H.J., Abrams D., Lamont R.A. and Drury L. (2017) 'The risks of ageism model: how ageism and negative attitudes toward age can be a barrier to active aging', *Social Issues and Policy Review*, 11: 195–231.

Syddall, H., Roberts, H.C., Evandrou, M., Cooper, C., Bergman, H. and Sayer, A.A. (2009) Prevalence and correlates of frailty among community-dwelling older men and women: findings from the Hertfordshire Cohort Study. *Age and Ageing*, 39(2), 197–203.

Takano, T., Nakamura, K. and Watanabe, M. (2002) 'Urban residential environments and senior citizens' longevity in megacity areas: the importance of walkable green spaces', *Journal of Epidemiology and Community Health*, 56(12): 913–18.

Tampubolon, G. (2015) 'Growing up in poverty, growing old in infirmity: the long arm of childhood conditions in Great Britain', *PloS ONE*, 10(12), e0144722.

Tanner, D. (2001) 'Sustaining the self in later life: supporting older people in the community', *Ageing and Society*, 21(3), 255–78.

Tanner, D. (2005) 'Promoting the well-being of older people: messages for social workers', *Practice: Social Work in Action*, 17(3): 191–205.

Tanner, D. (2007) 'Starting with lives: supporting older people's strategies and ways of coping', *Journal of Social Work*, 7(1): 7–30.

Tanner, D. (2010) *Managing the Ageing Experience: Learning From Older People*, Bristol: Policy Press.

Tanner, D. (2012) 'Co-research with older people with dementia: experience and reflections', *Journal of Mental Health*, 21(3): 296–306.

Tanner, D. (2013) 'Identity, selfhood and dementia: messages for social work', *European Journal of Social Work*, 16(2): 155–70.

Tanner, D. (2016) 'Sustaining the self in the 'fourth age': a case study', *Quality in Ageing and Older People*, 17(3): 157–67.

Tanner, D. and Littlechild, R. (2016) 'Enhancing older people's wellbeing through research: a case study', in C. Chew-Graham and M. Ray (eds) *Mental Health and Older People: A Guide for Primary Care Practitioners*, Silver Spring: Springer.

Tanner, D., Glasby, J. and McIver, S. (2015) 'Understanding and improving older people's experiences of service transitions: implications for social work', *British Journal of Social Work*, 45(7), 2056–71.

Tate, R.B., Lah, L. and Cuddy, T.E. (2003) 'Definition of successful aging by elderly Canadian males: the Manitoba follow-up study', *The Gerontologist*, 43(5): 735–44.

Taylor, C. and Donoghue, J. (2015) 'New ways to provide community aged care services', *Australasian Journal on Ageing*, 34(3): 199–200.

Teo, A.R., Choi., H., Andrea, S.B., Valenstein, M., Newsom, J.T., Dobscha, S.K. and Zivin, K. (2015) 'Does mode of contact with different types of social relationships predict depression in older adults? Evidence from a nationally representative survey', *Journal of the American Geriatrics Society*, 63(10): 2014–22.

Tew, J. (2011) *Social Approaches to Mental Distress*, London: Palgrave Macmillan.

The British Psychological Society (2014) *A Guide to Psychosocial Interventions in Early Stages of Dementia*, Leicester: The British Psychological Society.

The Dementia Policy Think Tank, the DEEP Network and Innovations in Dementia CIC (2017) *Our Lived Experience: Current Evidence on Dementia Rights in the UK. An Alternative Report to the UNCRPD Committee*, Exeter: DEEP.

The King's Fund (2018) *What Is Happening to Life Expectancy in the UK*, online www.kingsfund.org.uk/publications/whats-happening-life-expectancy-uk [Accessed 13 January 2019].

The Residents and Relatives Association (2010) *Together but Alone*, London: Relatives and Residents Association.

Theander, E. and Edberg, A.K. (2005) 'Preventive home visits to older people in Southern Sweden', *Scandinavian Journal of Public Health*, 33(5): 392–400.

Thomas, A. (2013) 'Psychiatric assessment of older people', in T. Dening and A. Thomas (eds) *Oxford Textbook of Old Age Psychiatry*, Oxford: Oxford University Press, pp 141–8.

Thomas, C. (1999) *Female Forms: Experiencing and Understanding Disability*, Buckingham: Open University Press.

Thomas, C. (2010) 'Medical sociology and disability theory', in G. Scrambler (ed) *New Directions in the Sociology of Chronic and Disabling Conditions: Assaults on the Lifeworld*, New York: Palgrave Macmillan.

Thomas, C. (2015) *Disability and Gender: Understanding Diversity and Promoting Equality*, NNDR conference, keynote paper, Bergen, Norway, 6–8 May, 2015.

Thomas, C. and Milligan, C. (2015) *How Can and Should UK Society Adapt to Dementia?*, York: Joseph Rowntree Foundation.

Thomas, C. and Milligan, C. (2018) 'Dementia, disability rights and disablism: understanding the social position of people living with dementia', *Disability and Society*, 33(1): 115–31.

Thompson, L. and Kingston, P. (2004) 'Measures to assess the quality of life for people with advanced dementia: issues in measurement and conceptualisation', *Quality in Ageing*, 5(4): 29–39.

Thompson, P., Itzin, C. and Abendstern, M. (1990) *I Don't Feel Old: The Experience of Later Life*, Oxford: Oxford University Press.

Thompson, S. (2005) *Age Discrimination*, Lyme Regis: Russell House Publishing.

Tilford, S. (2009) 'Theoretical perspectives on aging and health promotion', in M. Cattan (ed) *Mental Health and Well-Being in Later Life*, Maidenhead: Open University Press, pp 30–47.

Timonen, V. (2016) *Beyond Successful and Active Ageing: A Theory of Model Ageing*, Bristol: Policy Press.

Todd, S., Barr, S., Roberts, M. and Passmore, A.P. (2013) 'Survival in dementia and predictors of mortality: a review', *International Journal of Geriatric Psychiatry*, 28(11), 1109–24.

Tolhurst, E., Weicht, B. and Kingston, P. (2017) 'Narrative collisions, sociocultural pressures and dementia: the relational basis of personhood reconsidered', *Sociology of Health and Illness*, 39(2): 212–26.

Tomkow, L. (2018) 'The emergence and utilisation of frailty in the United Kingdom: a contemporary biopolitical practice', *Ageing and Society*, 1–18.

Tornstam, L. (1987) 'Gerotranscendence: the contemplative dimension of aging', *Journal of Aging Studies*, 11(2): 143–54.

Tornstam, L. (2005) *Gerotranscendence: A Developmental Theory of Positive Aging*, Silver Spring: Springer.

Torres, S. (2003) 'A preliminary empirical test of a culturally-relevant theoretical framework for the study of successful aging', *Journal of Cross-Cultural Gerontology*, 18(1): 79–100.

Townsend, P. (1962) *The Last Refuge*, London: Routledge and Kegan Paul.

Townsend, P. (2006) '25th volume celebration paper. Policies for the aged in the 21st century: more "structured dependency" or the realisation of human rights?', *Ageing and Society*, 26(2): 161–79.

Townsend, P. (2007) 'Using human rights to defeat ageism: dealing with policy-induced "structured dependency", in M. Bernard and T. Scharf (eds) *Critical Perspectives on Ageing Societies*, Boston, MA: Polity Press, pp 27–44.

Train, G., Nurock, S., Kitchen, G., Manela, M. and Livingston, G. (2005) 'A qualitative study of the views of residents with dementia, their relatives and staff about work practice in long-term care settings', *International Psychogeriatrics*, 17(2): 237–51.

Trevillion, K., Oram, S. and Howard, L.M. (2013) 'Domestic violence and mental health', in F. Howard, G. Agnew-Davies and R. London (eds) *Domestic Violence and Mental Health*, London: The Royal College of Psychiatrists, pp 18–28.

Trigg, R., Jones, R.W. and Skevington, S.M. (2007) 'Can people with mild to moderate dementia provide reliable answers about their quality of life?', *Age and Ageing*, 36(6): 663–9.

Tronto, J. (1993) *Moral Boundaries: A Political Argument for an Ethic of Care*, London: Routledge.

Tronto, J. (2010) 'Creating caring institutions: politics, plurality and purpose', *Ethics and Social Welfare*, 4(2): 158–71.

Truswell, D. (2018) 'Dementia, human rights and the BAME communities', *Journal of Dementia Care*, 26(1): 22.

Tsoh, J. and Chiu, H. (2013) 'Suicide and attempted suicide in older people', in T. Dening and A. Thomas (eds) *The Oxford Textbook of Old Age Psychiatry*, Oxford: Oxford University Press, pp 571–80.

Tucker-Seeley, R.D., Li, Y., Sorensen, G. and Subramanian, S.V. (2011) 'Lifecourse socioeconomic circumstances and multimorbidity among older adults', *BMC Public Health*, 11(1): 313.

Tuerk, R. and Sauer, J. (2015) 'Dementia in a Black and minority ethnic population: characteristics of presentation to an inner London memory service', *BJPsych Bulletin*, 39(4): 162–6.

Turner, B.S. (ed) (1993) *Citizenship and Social Theory*, London: Sage.

Turner, R.J. and Avison, W.R. (2003) 'Status variations in stress exposure: implications for the interpretation of research on race, socioeconomic status, and gender', *Journal of Health and Social Behavior*, 44(4): 488–505.

Twigg, J. (2006) *The Body in Health and Social Care*, London: Macmillan International Higher Education.

Tzouvara, V., Papadopoulos, C. and Randhawa, G. (2018) 'Self-stigma experiences among older adults with mental health problems residing in long-term care facilities: a qualitative study', *Issues in Mental Health Nursing*, 39(5): 403–10.

Umberson, D. and Karas Montez, J. (2010) 'Social relationships and health: a flashpoint for health policy', *Journal of Health and Social Behavior*, 51(Special Issue 1), S54–66.

Understanding Society and Economic and Social Research Council (2009) *A Summary of First Findings*, Swindon: Economic and Social Research Council.

United Nations (2006) Convention of the Rights of Persons with Disabilities, New York: United Nations.

United Nations (2010) Convention on the Elimination of All Forms of Discrimination Against Women, New York: United Nations.

United Nations (2016) *Inquiry Concerning the United Kingdom of Great Britain and Northern Ireland Carried Out by the Committee under Article 6 of the Optional Protocol to the Convention on the Rights of Persons with Disabilities*, New York: United Nations.

United Nations (2017a) *The United Nations Convention on the Rights of Persons with Disabilities: What Does it Mean for You?*, [online] www.equalityhumanrights.com/sites/default/files/the-united-nations-convention-on-the-rights-of-persons-with-disabilities-what-does-it-mean-for-you.pdf [Accessed 13 January 2019].

United Nations (2017b) *Being Disabled in Britain: A Journey Less Equal*, New York: United Nations.

University of Edinburgh and the Scottish Dementia Working Group (2014) *Core principles for involving people with dementia in research: the Scottish Dementia Working Group Research Sub-group*, Edinburgh: The University of Edinburgh and the Scottish Dementia Working Group.

Valtorta, N.K., Kanaan, M., Gilbody, S., Ronzi, S. and Hanratty, B. (2016) 'Loneliness and social isolation as risk factors for coronary heart disease and stroke: systematic review and meta-analysis of longitudinal observational studies', *Heart*, 102(13): 1009–16.

van Achterberg, M.E., Rohrbaugh, R.M. and Southwick, S.M. (2001) 'Emergence of PTSD in trauma survivors with dementia', *The Journal of Clinical Psychiatry*, 62(3), 206–7.

van Rijn, R.M., Robroek, S.J.W., Brouwer, S. and Burdorf, A. (2014) 'Influence of poor health on exit from paid employment: a systematic review', *Occupational and Environmental Medicine*, 71(4), 295–301.

Vassilev, I., Rogers, A., Blickem, C., Brooks, H., Kapadia, D., Kennedy, A., Sanders, C., Kirk, S. and Reeves, D. (2013) 'Social networks, the "work" and workforce of chronic illness self-management: a survey analysis of personal communities', *PloS ONE*, 8(4): e59723.

Vellone, E., Piras, G., Talucci, C. and Cohen, M.Z. (2008) 'Quality of life for caregivers of people with Alzheimer's disease', *Journal of Advanced Nursing*, 61(2): 222–31.

Venn, S. and Arber, S. (2011) 'Day-time sleep and active ageing in later life', *Ageing and Society*, 31(2): 197–216.

Vickerstaff, S. (2006) 'Entering the retirement zone: how much choice do individuals have?', *Social Policy and Society*, 5(4): 507–17.

Vickerstaff, S., Phillipson, C. and Wilkie, R. (2013) *Work, Health and Wellbeing*, Bristol: Policy Press.

Vickerstaff, S., Loretto, W., Billings, J., Brown, P., Mitton, L., Parkin, T. and White, P. (2008) *Encouraging Labour Market Activity Among 60–64-Year-Olds*, London: Department for Work and Pensions.

Victor, C. (2005) *The Social Context of Ageing: A Textbook of Gerontology*, Abingdon: Routledge.

Victor, C. (2010) *Ageing, Health and Care*, Bristol: Policy Press.

Victor, C., Scambler, S. and Bond, J. (2009) *The Social World of Older People: Understanding Loneliness and Social Isolation in Later Life*, New York: McGraw Hill.

Victor, C., Scambler, S., Bond, J. and Bowling, A. (2000) 'Being alone in later life: loneliness, social isolation and living alone', *Reviews in Clinical Gerontology*, 10(4): 407–17.

Victor, C.R. and Scharf, T. (2005) 'Social isolation and loneliness', in A. Walker (ed) *Understanding Quality of Life in Old Age*, Buckingham: Open University Press, pp 100–16.

Victor, C.R. and Bowling, A. (2012) 'A longitudinal analysis of loneliness among older people in Great Britain', *The Journal of Psychology*, 146(3): 313–31.

Vincent, J.A. (1995) *Inequality and Old Age*, London: University College Press.

Vincent, J.A. (2003) *Old Age*, London: Routledge.

Vincent, J.A. (2006) 'Ageing contested: anti-ageing science and the cultural construction of old age', *Sociology*, 40(4): 681–98.

Vink, D., Aartsen, M.J., Comijs, H.C., Heymans, M.W., Penninx, B.W., Stek, M.L., Deeg, D.J.H. and Beekman, AT.F. (2009) 'Onset of anxiety and depression in the aging population: comparison of risk factors in a 9-year prospective study', *The American Journal of Geriatric Psychiatry*, 17(8): 642–52.

Vitaliano, P.P., Young, H.M. and Russo, J. (1991) 'Burden: a review of measures used among caregivers of individuals with dementia', *The Gerontologist*, 31(1): 67–75.

Vlachantoni, A., Feng, Z., Evandrou, M. and Falkingham, J. (2017) 'Ethnic elders and pension protection in the United Kingdom', *Ageing and Society*, 37(5): 1025–49.

Wadd, S., Lapworth, K., Sullivan, M.P., Forrester, D. and Galvani, S. (2011) *Working with Older Drinkers*, Bedford: University of Bedfordshire.

Walker, A. (2009) 'Aging and social policy: theorizing the social', in V. Bengston and K.W. Schaie (eds) *Handbook of Theories of Aging*, New York: Springer, pp 361–78.

Walker, A., Sinfield, A. and Walker, C. (eds) (2011) *Fighting Poverty, Inequality and Injustice*, Bristol: Policy Press.

Walker, H., Grant, D., Meadows, M. and Cook, I. (2007) 'Women's experiences and perceptions of age discrimination in employment: implications for research and policy', *Social Policy and Society*, 6(1): 37–48.

Walsh, K. and O'Shea, E. (2008) 'Responding to rural social care needs: older people empowering themselves, others and their community', *Health and Place*, 14(4): 795–805.

Warburton, D.E., Nicol, C.W. and Bredin, S.S. (2006) 'Health benefits of physical activity: the evidence', *CMAJ*, 174(6): 801–9.

Ward, R., Vass, A.A., Aggarwal, N., Garfield, C. and Cybyk, B. (2008) 'A different story: exploring patterns of communication in residential dementia care', *Ageing and Society*, 28(5): 629–51.

Warmoth, K., Lang, I.A., Phoenix, C., Abraham, C., Andrew, M.K., Hubbard, R.E. and Tarrant, M. (2016) '"Thinking you're old and frail": a qualitative study of frailty in older adults', *Ageing and Society*, 36(7): 1483–500.

Warner, J., Milne, A. and Peet, J. (2010) *'My Name is Not Dementia': Literature Review*, London: Alzheimer's Society.

Warnes, A. and Crane, M. (2006) 'The causes of homelessness among older people in England', *Housing Studies*, 21(3): 401–21.

Warren, C. and Karner, T. (2005) *Discovering Qualitative Methods: Field Research, Interviews, and Analysis*, Los Angeles, CA: Roxbury Press.

Watkins, J., Wulaningsih, W., Da Zhou, C., Marshall, D.C., Sylianteng, G.D.C., Dela Rosa, P.G., Miguel, V.A., Raine, R., King, L.P. and Maruthappu, M. (2017) 'Effects of health and social care spending constraints on mortality in England: a time trend analysis', *British Medical Journal Open*, 7(11): e017722.

Wave Trust (2013) *Conception to Age 2 – The Age of Opportunity*, Croydon: Wave Trust.

Webber, M., Reidy, H., Ansari, D., Stevens, M. and Morris, D. (2015) 'Enhancing social networks: a qualitative study of health and social care practice in UK mental health services', *Health and Social Care in the Community*, 23(2): 180–9.

Weich, S., Brugha, T., King, M., McManus, S., Bebbington, P., Jenkins, R., Cooper, C., McBride, O. and Stewart-Brown, S. (2011) 'Mental well-being and mental illness: findings from the Adult Psychiatric Survey for England 2007', *The British Journal of Psychiatry*, 199(1): 23–8.

Weinfield, N.S., Sroufe, L.A. and Egeland, B. (2000) 'Attachment from infancy to early adulthood in a high-risk sample: continuity, discontinuity, and their correlates', *Child Development*, 71(3): 695–702.

Weinstein, J. (2014) *Mental Health: Critical and Radical Debates in Social Work*, Bristol: Policy Press.

Welch, S.S. (2001) 'A review of the literature on the epidemiology of parasuicide in the general population', *Psychiatric Services*, 52(3): 368–75.

Welsh Assembly Government (2012) *Better Together for Mental Health: A Strategy for Mental Health and Wellbeing in Wales*, Cardiff: Welsh Assembly Government.

Welsh Assembly Government and Alzheimer's Society (2011) *National Dementia Vision for Wales: Dementia Supportive Communities*, Cardiff: Welsh Assembly Government.

Welsh Assembly Health, Social Care and Sports Committee (2017) *Inquiry into Loneliness and Isolation*, Cardiff: Welsh Assembly Government.

Westendorp, R.G. and Kirkwood, T.B. (2007). 'The biology of ageing', in J. Bond, S. Peace, F. Dittmann-Kohli and G.J. Westerhof (eds) *Ageing in Society*, London: Sage Publications, 15–37.

Westerhof, G.J. and Keyes, C.L. (2010) 'Mental illness and mental health: the two continua model across the lifespan', *Journal of Adult Development*, 17(2): 110–19.

Westius, A., Kallenberg, K. and Norberg, A. (2010) 'Views of life and sense of identity in people with Alzheimer's disease', *Ageing and Society*, 30(7): 1257–78.

Westwood, S. (2016) 'Dementia, women and sexuality: how the intersection of ageing, gender and sexuality magnify dementia concerns among lesbian and bisexual women', *Dementia*, 15(6): 1494–514.

Wetzels, R.B., Zuidema, S.U., de Jonghe, J.F., Verhey, F.R.J. and Koopmans, R.T.C.M. (2010) 'Determinants of quality of life in nursing home residents with dementia', *Dementia and Geriatric Cognitive Disorders*, 29(3): 189–97.

Whalley, L.J., Dick, F.D. and McNeill, G. (2006) 'A life-course approach to the aetiology of late-onset dementias', *The Lancet Neurology*, 5(1): 87–96.

Whitehead, M. (2011) 'Addressing health inequalities: building on Peter Townsend's legacy', in A. Walker, A. Sinfield and C. Walker (eds) *Fighting Poverty, Inequality and Injustice*, Bristol: Policy Press, pp 175–92.

Whiteman, K., Ruggiano, N. and Thomlison, B. (2016) 'Transforming mental health services to address gender disparities in depression risk factors', *Journal of Women and Aging*, 28(6): 521–9.

Whitlatch, C.J., Feinberg, L.F. and Tucke, S. (2005) 'Accuracy and consistency of responses from persons with cognitive impairment', *Dementia*, 4(2): 171–83.

Wickham, S., Anwar, E., Barr, B., Law, C. and Taylor-Robinson, D. (2016) 'Poverty and child health in the UK: using evidence for action', *Archives of Disease in Childhood*, 101(8): 759–66.

Wilberforce, M., Challis, D., Davies, L., Kelly, M.P., Roberts, C. and Clarkson, P. (2017). 'Person-centredness in the community care of older people: a literature-based concept synthesis', *International Journal of Social Welfare*, 26(1): 86–98.

Wild, K., Wiles, J.L. and Allen, R.E.S (2013) 'Resilience: thoughts on the value of the concept for critical gerontology', *Ageing and Society*, 33(1): 137–58.

Wiles, J.L., Allen, R.E., Palmer, A.J., Hayman, K.J., Keeling, S. and Kerse, N. (2009) 'Older people and their social spaces: a study of well-being and attachment to place in Aotearoa New Zealand', *Social Science and Medicine*, 68(4): 664–71.

Wilhelmson, K., Andersson, C., Waern, M. and Allebeck, P. (2005) 'Elderly people's perspectives on quality of life', *Ageing and Society*, 25(4): 585–600.

Wilkinson, R. (2002) *Unhealthy Societies: The Afflictions of Inequality*, London: Routledge.

Wilkinson, R. and Pickett, K. (2006) 'Income inequality and population health: a review and explanation of the evidence', *Social Science and Medicine*, 62(7): 1768–84.

Wilkinson, R. and Pickett, K. (2007) 'The problems of relative deprivation: why some societies do better than others', *Social Science and Medicine*, 65(9): 1965–78.

Wilkinson, R. and Pickett, K. (2010) *The Spirit Level: Why Equality is Better for Everyone*, London: Penguin.

Williams, B.R., Blizard, T.I., Goode. P.S, Harada, C.N., Woodby. L.L., Burgio, K.L. and Sims, V. (2014) 'Exploring the affective dimension of the life review process: facilitators' interactional strategies for fostering personhood and social value among older adults with early dementia', *Dementia*, 13(4): 498–524.

Williams, C.L., Molinari, V., Bond, J., Smith, M., Hyer, K. and Malphurs, J. (2006) 'Development of a curriculum for long-term care nurses to improve recognition of depression in dementia', *Educational Gerontology*, 32(8): 647–67.

Williams, D.R., Neighbors, H.W. and Jackson, J.S. (2003) 'Racial/ethnic discrimination and health: findings from community studies', *American Journal of Public Health*, 93(2): 200–8.

Williams, D.R., Mohammed, S.A., Leavell, J. and Collins, C. (2010) 'Race, socioeconomic status, and health: complexities, ongoing challenges, and research opportunities', *Annals of the New York Academy of Sciences*, 1186(1): 69–101.

Williams, E., Tillin, T., Richards, M., Tuson, C., Chaturvedi, N., Hughes, A. and Stewart, R. (2015) 'Depressive symptoms are doubled in older British South Asian and Black Caribbean people compared with Europeans: associations with excess co-morbidity and socioeconomic disadvantage', *Psychological Medicine*, 45(9): 1861–71.

Williams, J. (2005) 'Women's mental health: taking inequality into account', in J. Tew (ed) *Social Perspectives in Mental Health*, London: Palgrave Macmillan, pp 151–67.

Williams, J. and Miller, J. (2008) 'Gender inequality and the mental health of women and men', in T. Stickley and T. Bassett (eds) *Learning about Mental Health Practice*, Chichester: John Wiley, pp 381–400.

Williams, J. and Watson, S. (2016) 'Surviving their lives: women's mental health in context', in D.J. Castle and K.M. Abel (eds) *Comprehensive Women's Mental Health*, Cambridge: Cambridge University Press, pp 1–13.

Williamson, T. (2008) 'From the 60s to their sixties: baby boomers – challenges and choices for public mental health', *Journal of Public Mental Health*, 7(1): 4–8.

Williamson, T. (2012a) *Ripple on the Pond*, London: Mental Health Foundation.

Williamson, T. (2012b) *A Stronger Collective Voice for People with Dementia*, York: Joseph Rowntree Foundation.

Wilson, R.S., Krueger, K.R., Arnold, S.E., Schneider, J.A., Kelly, J.F. and Barnes, L.L. (2007) 'Loneliness and risk of Alzheimer's disease', *Archives General Psychiatry*, 64(2): 234–40.

Windle, G. (2009) 'What is mental health and mental wellbeing?', in M. Cattan (ed) *Mental Health and Well-Being in Later Life*, Maidenhead: Open University Press, pp 9–29.

Windle, G. (2011) 'What is resilience? A review and concept analysis', *Reviews in Clinical Gerontology*, 21(2): 152–69.

Windle, G. (2012) 'The contribution of resilience to healthy ageing', *Perspectives in Public Health*, 132(4): 159–60.

Windle, G. and Woods, R.T. (2004) 'Variations in subjective wellbeing: the mediating role of a psychological resource', *Ageing and Society*, 24(4): 583–602.

Windle, G. and Bennett, K. (2011) 'Caring relationships: how to promote resilience in challenging times', in M. Ungar (ed) *Social Ecology of Resilience*, New York: Springer, pp 219–31.

Wistow, J., Blackburn, T., Byrne, D. and Wistow, G. (2015) *Studying Health Inequalities: An Applied Approach*, Bristol: Policy Press.

Women's Health and Equality Consortium and Age UK (2016) *Women and Dementia*. [online] www.researchgate.net/publication/308985807_Women_and_Dementia_Women's_Health_Equality_Consortium_October_2016 [Accessed 12 January 2019]

Women's Royal Voluntary Service (2012) *Loneliness amongst Older People and the Impact of Family Connections*, Cardiff: Women's Royal Voluntary Service.

Women's Royal Voluntary Service (2013) *Going Nowhere Fast: Impact of Inaccessible Public Transport on Wellbeing and Social Connectedness of Older People in Great Britain*, Cardiff: Women's Royal Voluntary Service.

Women's Aid (2013) *Statistics about Domestic Violence: Incidence and Prevalence of Domestic Violence*, London: Women's Aid.

Woods, B. (2012) 'Well-being and dementia – how can it be achieved?', *Quality in Ageing and Older Adults*, 13(3), pp 205–11.

Woods, B., Thorgrimsen, L., Spector, A., Royan, L. and Orrell, M. (2006) 'Improved quality of life and cognitive stimulation therapy in dementia', *Aging and Mental Health*, 10(3): 219–26.

Woodward, C.A., Abelson, J., Tedford, S. and Hutchison, B. (2004) 'What is important to continuity in home care? Perspectives of key stakeholders', *Social Science and Medicine*, 58(1): 177–92.

World Health Organization (1998) *Health Promotion Glossary*, Geneva: World Health Organization.

World Health Organization (2001) *Mental Health: New Understanding, New Hope*, Geneva: World Health Organization.

World Health Organization (2002a) *Active Ageing: A Public Policy Framework*, Geneva: World Health Organization.

World Health Organization (2002b) *Prevention and Promotion in Mental Health*, Geneva: World Health Organization.

World Health Organization (2002c) *Toronto Declaration on the Global Prevention of Elder Abuse*, Geneva: World Health Organization.

World Health Organization (2003) *Investing in Mental Health*, Geneva: World Health Organization.

World Health Organization (2011) *European Report on Preventing Elder Maltreatment*, Geneva: World Health Organization.

World Health Organization (2013) *Comprehensive Mental Health Action Plan 2013–2020*, Geneva: World Health Organization.

World Health Organization (2014) *Social Determinants of Mental Health*, Geneva: World Health Organization.

World Health Organization (2015) *Ensuring a Human-Rights Based Approach for People Living with Dementia*, Geneva: World Health Organization.

World Health Organization (2016) *Global Strategy and Action Plan on Ageing and Health*, Geneva: World Health Organization.

World Health Organization and the International Network for the Prevention of Elder Abuse (2002) *Missing Voices: Views of Older Persons on Elder Abuse*, Geneva: World Health Organization.

World Heart Federation (2011) *Diet, Overweight, and Obesity*. [online] https://www.world-heart-federation.org/resources/diet-overweight-obesity/ [Accessed 12 January 2019].

Wurm, S. and Benyamini, Y. (2014) 'Optimism buffers the detrimental effect of negative self-perceptions of ageing on physical and mental health', *Psychology and Health*, 29(7), 832–48.

Wurm, S., Warner, L.M., Ziegelmann, J.P., Wolff, J.K. and Schuz, B.E.C (2013) 'How do negative self-perceptions of aging become a self-fulfilling prophecy?', *Psychology and Aging*, 28(4), 1088–97.

Yaffe, K., Vittinghoff, E., Lindquist, K., Barnes, D., Covinsky, K.E., Neylan, T. and Marmar, C. (2010) 'Posttraumatic stress disorder and risk of dementia among US veterans', *Archives of General Psychiatry*, 67(6): 608–13.

Yang, K. and Victor, C. (2011) 'Age and loneliness in 25 European nations', *Ageing and Society*, 31(8): 1368–88.

Younger-Ross, S. (2008) *Devon LinkAge Plus Findings Paper Final Community Mentoring: Inclusion and Wellbeing*, Exeter: Devon County Council.

Yuan, A.S.V. (2007) 'Perceived age discrimination and mental health', *Social Forces*, 86(1): 291–311.

Yusuf, S.A. (2008) 'Social capital and household welfare in Kwara State, Nigeria', *Journal of Human Ecology*, 23(3): 219–29.

Zachary, I. (2005) 'Neuroprotective role of vascular endothelial growth factor: signalling mechanisms, biological function, and therapeutic potential', *Neurosignals*, 14(5): 207–21.

Zaidi, A., Makovec, M., Fuchs, M., Lipszyc, B., Lelkes, O., Rummel, M., Marin, B. and de Vos, K. (2006) *Poverty of Elderly People in EU25*, Vienna: European Centre for Social Welfare Policy and Research.

Zavaleta, D., Samuel, K. and Mills, C.T. (2017) 'Measures of Social Isolation', *Social Indicators Research*, 131(1): 367–91.

Zechmeister, I., Kilian, R. and McDaid, D. (2008) 'Is it worth investing in mental health promotion and prevention of mental illness? A systematic review of the evidence from economic evaluations', *BMC Public Health*, 8(1), 20.

Zeilig, H. (2013) 'Dementia as a cultural metaphor', *The Gerontologist*, 54(2): 258–67.

Zeller, A., Hahn, S., Needham, I., Kok, G., Dassen, T. and Halfens, R.J. (2009) 'Aggressive behavior of nursing home residents toward caregivers: a systematic literature review', *Geriatric Nursing*, 30(3): 174–87.

Zhong, G., Wang, Y., Zhang, Y., Guo, J.J. and Zhao, Y. (2015) 'Smoking is associated with an increased risk of dementia: a meta-analysis of prospective cohort studies with investigation of potential effect modifiers', *PloS One*, 10(3): e0118333.

Zimmerman, S., Sloane, P.D., Williams, C.S., Reed, P.S., Preisser, J.S., Eckert, J.K., Boustani, M. and Dobbs, D. (2005) 'Dementia care and quality of life in assisted living and nursing homes', *The Gerontologist*, 45(Special Issue 1): 133–46.

Index

D

E

P